Petersons.com/publishing

Check out our Web site at www.petersons.com/publishing to see if there is any new information regarding the test and any revisions or corrections to the content of this book. We've made sure the information in this book is accurate and up-to-date; however, the test format or content may have changed since the time of publication.

Prometric™

Prometric, the DSST program provider, has reviewed the contents of *Official Guide to Mastering DSST Exams* and found this study guide to be an excellent reflection of the content of the respective DSST tests. However, passing the sample tests provided in any study materials does not guarantee you will pass the actual tests.

Contents

Before You Begin

HOW THIS BOOK IS ORGANIZED

Peterson's *Official Guide to Mastering DSST Exams* provides diagnostic tests, post-tests, and subject matter reviews for eight different DSST tests. The following table provides a summary of the information covered in each chapter.

Chapter 1: Ethics in America	Development of ethical traditions from Greeks to modern philosophers; ethical analysis of various issues such as war, capital punishment, sexuality, and poverty
Chapter 2: Introduction to Computing	Hardware, operating systems, application software, networks, software development, and safety/security issues
Chapter 3: Principles of Supervision	Management functions, organizational environment, legal issues, managerial levels, and supervisory skills
Chapter 4: Substance Abuse	Various substances such as alcohol, inhalants, tobacco, stimulants, and opioids; societal costs; physical effects, psychological effects, and treatment options
Chapter 5: Business Math	Decimals, integers, fractions, ratios, averages, business graphs, interest, depreciation, corporate securities, and discounts/markups
Chapter 6: Principles of Public Speaking	Audience analysis, purpose, organization, supporting materials, style, delivery, criticism, and evaluation
Chapter 7: Fundamentals of College Algebra	Solving quadratic inequalities, operations of functions, rational functions, and exponential/logarithmic functions
Chapter 8: Technical Writing	Theory and practice of technical writing; purpose, content, and organizational patterns of various technical documents; elements found in common types of technical documents; technical editing

Each chapter of the book is organized in the same manner:

- Diagnostic Test—20 questions, followed by an answer key and explanations
- General subject overview and subject review
- Post-Test—60 questions, followed by an answer key and explanations

The purpose of the diagnostic test is to help you figure out what you know . . . or don't know. The 20 multiple-choice questions are similar to the ones found on the DSST, and they should provide you with a good idea of what to expect. Once you take the diagnostic test, check your answers to see how you did. Included with each correct answer is a brief explanation regarding why a specific answer is correct, and in many cases why other options are incorrect. Take note of the questions you miss, so that you can spend more time reviewing that information later. As with any exam, knowing your weak spots greatly improves your chances of success.

Following the diagnostic test in each chapter is a subject matter review. The review summarizes the various topics covered on the DSST exam. Key terms are defined, important concepts are explained, and, when appropriate, examples are provided. As you read the review, some of the information may seem familiar while other information may seem foreign. Again, take note of the unfamiliar because that will most likely cause you problems on the actual DSST. If you need more information about a topic than what the review provides, refer to one of the textbooks recommended for the test.

After studying the subject matter review, you should be ready for the post-test. The post-test for each chapter contains 60 multiple-choice items, and it will serve as a dry run for the real DSST. Take the time to answer all of the questions because they are similar to those found on the DSST exam for that particular subject matter. As with the diagnostic test, post-test answers and explanations are at the end of each chapter.

The DSST entitled *Principles of Public Speaking* differs from the other DSST exams. The DSST exam for *Principles of Public Speaking* is divided into two parts. The first part includes multiple-choice items. The second part requires candidates to record an impromptu speech that is approximately 4 minutes long—speeches less than 3 minutes or longer than 5 minutes automatically fail. Candidates are given a specific topic and have 10 minutes to prepare a speech. Test-takers then record the speech. The speech receives a score based on structure, delivery, content, effect, and style. Since speeches must be graded for the *Principles of Public Speaking* exam, candidates may not receive their scores for six to eight weeks. Chapter 6 of this book only provides the diagnostic test, post-test, and subject matter review for *Principles of Public Speaking*. Practice writing a few speeches before taking the DSST exam, so that you are comfortable with the process.

SPECIAL STUDY FEATURES

Peterson's *Official Guide to Mastering DSST Exams* is designed to be as user-friendly as it is complete. To this end, it includes two features to make your preparation more efficient.

Overview

Each chapter begins with a bulleted overview listing the topics covered in the chapter. This will allow you to quickly target the areas in which you are most interested and need to review.

Summing It Up

Each review chapter ends with a point-by-point summary that captures the most important information in the chapter. The summaries offer a convenient way to review key points.

YOU'RE WELL ON YOUR WAY TO SUCCESS

You've made the decision to take the DSST and earn college credit for your life experiences. Peterson's *Official Guide to Mastering DSST Exams* will help prepare you for the steps you'll need to achieve your goal—scoring high on the exam!

GIVE US YOUR FEEDBACK

Peterson's publishes a full line of resources to help guide you through the exam process. Peterson's publications can be found at college libraries and career centers and at your local bookstore or library.

We welcome any comments or suggestions you may have about this publication and invite you to complete our online survey at www.petersons.com/survey. Or you can fill out the survey at the back of this book, tear it out, and mail it to us at:

Publishing Department
Peterson's, a Nelnet company
2000 Lenox Drive
Lawrenceville, NJ 08648

Your feedback will help us make your educational dreams possible.

About the DSST

OVERVIEW

- What is the DSST?
- Why take the DSST?
- DSST test centers
- How to register for a DSST
- Preparing for the DSST
- Test day

WHAT IS THE DSST?

The DSST is a nationally accepted prior learning assessment program that enables individuals to earn college credit for knowledge they have acquired outside of the traditional university classroom. Experience gained through independent reading, work-related tasks, life experiences, or military training may provide you with the skills and qualifications needed to pass a DSST exam and receive college credit. The American Council of Education (ACE) suggests that colleges award 3 credit hours for passing scores on most DSST exams.

WHY TAKE THE DSST?

DSST exams, previously known as DANTES Subject Standardized Tests, offer a way for you to save both time and money in your quest for a college education. Why enroll in a college course in a subject you already understand? For over thirty years, the DSST program has offered the perfect solution for people who are knowledgeable in a specific subject and who want to save both time and money. A passing score on a DSST exam provides physical evidence to universities of proficiency in a specific subject. Nearly 2,000 accredited and respected colleges and universities across the nation award undergraduate credit for passing scores on DSST exams. With the DSST program, individuals can shave months off the time it takes to earn a degree.

The DSST program offers numerous advantages for people in all stages of their educational development:

- Adult learners
- College students
- Military personnel

Adult learners desiring college degrees face unique circumstances—demanding work schedules, family responsibilities, and tight budgets. Yet adult learners also have years of valuable work experience that can be applied toward a degree through the DSST program. For example, adult learners with on-the-job experience in business and management might be able to skip the Business 101 courses if they earn passing marks on DSST exams such as *Introduction to Business* and *Principles of Supervision*. Adult learners can put their prior learning into action and move forward with more advanced course work. Adults who have never enrolled in a college course may feel a little uncertain about their abilities. If this describes your situation, then sign up for a DSST exam and see how you do. A passing score may be the boost you need to realize your dream of earning a degree. With family and work commitments, adult learners often feel they lack the time to attend college. The DSST program enables adult learners the unique opportunity to work toward college degrees without the time constraints of semester-long course work. DSST exams take 2 hours or less to complete, so in one weekend, you could earn credit for multiple college courses.

The DSST exams also benefit students who are already enrolled in a college or university. With college tuition costs on the rise, most students face financial challenges. The fee for each DSST exam is $80 plus administration fees charged by some testing facilities—significantly less than the $300 average cost of a 3-hour college class. Maximize tuition assistance by taking DSST exams for introductory or mandatory course work. Once you earn a passing score on a DSST exam, you are free to move on to higher-level course work in that subject matter, take desired electives, or focus on courses in a chosen major.

Not only do students and adult learners profit from DSST exams, but military personnel reap the benefits as well. If you are a member of the armed services at home or abroad, you can initiate your post-military career by taking DSST exams in areas with which you have experience. Military personnel can gain credit anywhere in the world, thanks to the fact that almost all of the tests are available through the Internet at designated testing locations. DSST testing facilities are located at over 500 military installations, so service members on active duty can get a jump-start on a post-military career with the DSST program. As an additional incentive, DANTES provides funding for DSST test fees for eligible members of the military.

Thirty-seven subject matter tests are available in the fields of Business, Humanities, Natural Science, and Social Science.

Available DSST Exams

Business	Humanities
Business Law II	Art of the Western World
Business Mathematics	The Civil War and Reconstruction
Human Resources Management	Ethics in America
Introduction to Business	A History of the Vietnam War
Introduction to Computing	Human/Cultural Geography
Management Information Systems	An Introduction to the Modern Middle East
Money and Banking	Introduction to World Religions
Organizational Behavior	Principles of Public Speaking
Personal Finance	Rise and Fall of the Soviet Union
Principles of Finance	Technical Writing
Principles of Financial Accounting	Western Europe Since 1945
Principles of Supervision	
Social Science	**Natural Science**
Criminal Justice	Astronomy
Foundations of Education	Environment and Humanity: The Race to Save the Planet
Fundamentals of Counseling	Fundamentals of College Algebra
General Anthropology	Here's to Your Health
Introduction to Law Enforcement	Physical Geology
Lifespan Developmental Psychology	Principles of Physical Science I
Substance Abuse	Principles of Statistics

As you can see from the table, the DSST program covers a wide variety of subjects. However, it is important to ask two questions before registering for a DSST exam.

- Which universities or colleges award credit for passing DSST exams?
- Which DSST exams are the most relevant to my desired degree and my experience?

Knowing which universities offer DSST credit is important information to uncover. In all likelihood, a college in your area awards credit for DSST exams, but find out before taking an exam by contacting the university directly. Second, review the list of DSST exams to determine which ones are most relevant to the degree you are seeking and to your base of knowledge. Schedule an appointment with your college advisor to determine which exams best fit your degree program and which college courses the DSST exams can replace. Advisors should also be able to tell you the minimum score required on the DSST exam to receive university credit.

DSST TEST CENTERS

You can find DSST testing locations in community colleges and universities across the country. Contact your local college or university to find out if the school administers DSST exams, or check the DSST Web site (www.getcollegecredit.com) for a location near you. Keep in mind that some universities and colleges only administer DSST exams to enrolled students. DSST testing is available to men and women in the armed services at over 500 military installations around the world.

HOW TO REGISTER FOR A DSST

Once you have located a nearby DSST testing facility, you need to contact the testing center to find out the exam administration schedule. Many centers are set up to administer tests via the Internet, while others use printed materials. Almost all DSST exams are available as online tests, but the method used depends on the testing center. Each DSST exam costs $80, and many testing locations charge a fee to cover their costs for administering the tests. Credit cards are the only accepted payment method for taking online DSST exams. Credit card, certified check, and money order are acceptable payment methods for paper-and-pencil tests.

Test-takers are allotted two score reports—one mailed to them and another mailed to a designated college or university if requested. Online tests generate unofficial scores at the end of the test session, while individuals taking paper tests must wait four to six weeks for score reports.

PREPARING FOR THE DSST

Even though you are knowledgeable in a certain subject matter, you should still prepare for the test to ensure you achieve the highest score possible. The first step in studying for a DSST exam is to find out what will be on the specific test you have chosen. Information regarding test content is located on the DSST fact sheets, which can be downloaded at no cost from www.getcollegecredit.com. Each fact sheet outlines the topics covered on a subject matter test as well as the approximate percentage assigned to each topic. For example, questions on the *Principles of Supervision* exam break down in the following way: 20 percent on the roles and responsibilities of supervisors, 20 percent on the organizational environment, and 60 percent on management functions.

In addition to the breakdown of topics on a DSST exam, the fact sheet also lists recommended reference materials. If you do not own the recommended books, then check college bookstores. Avoid paying high prices for new textbooks by looking online for used textbooks. Don't panic if you are unable to locate a specific textbook listed on the fact sheet because the textbooks are merely recommendations. Instead, search for comparable books used in university courses on the specific subject. Current editions are ideal, and it is a good idea to use at least two references when studying for a DSST exam. Of course, the subject matter provided in this book will be a sufficient review for most test-takers. However, if you need additional information, then it is a good idea to have some of the reference materials at your disposal when preparing for the DSST.

Fact sheets include other useful information besides a list of reference materials and topics. On each fact sheet, you will find a few samples of questions found on the DSST exam in the specific subject matter. The sample questions provide an idea of the type of questions you can expect on the exam. Test questions are multiple choice with one correct answer and three incorrect choices. The fact sheet also includes information about the number of credit hours that ACE has recommended be awarded by colleges for a passing score on the DSST. However, you should keep in mind that not all universities and colleges adhere to the ACE recommendation for DSST credit hours. Some institutions require DSST exam scores higher than the minimum score recommended by ACE. Once you have acquired appropriate reference materials and you have the outline provided on the fact sheet, you are ready to start studying, which is where this book can help.

TEST DAY

After reviewing the material and taking practice tests, you are finally ready to take the DSST. As with any exam, preparation is the key to a successful test experience.

1. **Arrive on time.** Not only is it courteous to arrive on time to the DSST testing facility, but it also allows plenty of time for you to take care of check-in procedures and settle into your surroundings.

2. **Bring identification.** DSST test facilities require that candidates bring a valid government-issued identification card with a current photo and signature. Acceptable forms of identification include a current driver's license, passport, military identification card, or state-issued identification card. Individuals who fail to bring proper identification to the DSST testing facility will not be allowed to take an exam.

3. **Bring the right supplies.** You will need to bring several sharpened No. 2 pencils with erasers and a black pen if an essay section is included on the exam. You should also bring a watch since the tests are timed. However, do not bring a watch with a beeping alarm. Cell phones, books, and papers are not allowed inside the testing center. For some tests, candidates are allowed to use nonprogrammable calculators, slide rules, and scratch paper, but you should ask the test administrator when you arrive.

4. **Take the test.** During the exam, take the time to read each question and answer option carefully. Eliminate the choices you know are incorrect to narrow the number of potential answers. If a question completely stumps you, take an educated guess and move on—remember that the DSST is a timed test; you will have 2 hours to take the exam.

With the proper preparation, DSST exams will save you both time and money. So join the thousands of people who have already reaped the benefits of DSST exams and move closer than ever to your college degree.

Ethics in America

chapter

OVERVIEW

- Diagnostic test
- Answer key and explanations
- Ethical traditions
- Religious traditions
- Natural law theory
- Political theories
- Transcendental idealism
- Moral egoism
- Utilitarianism
- Feminist ethics
- Current ethical issues
- Post-test
- Answer key and explanations
- Summing it up

DIAGNOSTIC TEST

Directions: Carefully read each of the following 20 questions. Choose the best answer to each question and circle your answer choice. The Answer Key and Explanations can be found following this Diagnostic Test.

1. Which of the following thinkers developed the philosophy of utilitarianism?
   (A) Bentham
   (B) Nozick
   (C) Smith
   (D) Mill

2. For a Stoic, the ethical evaluation of a decision to commit suicide depends on whether it
   (A) adheres to basic liberties.
   (B) seems to be a reasonable act.
   (C) appears to be God's will.
   (D) increases overall happiness.

3. According to which of the following philosophers should people avoid helping others?
   (A) Locke, because receiving help is weak
   (B) Kant, because helping others is impractical
   (C) Gilligan, because being helpful is not a valuable trait
   (D) Rand, because helping oneself is the highest moral objective

4. Intentionally withholding treatment in order to allow a patient to die is
   (A) active euthanasia.
   (B) suicide.
   (C) passive euthanasia.
   (D) murder.

5. Which of the following said, "Man is the measure of all things"?
   (A) Protagoras
   (B) Socrates
   (C) Aristotle
   (D) Plato

6. According to Plato, which of the following would be rulers in an ideal state?
   (A) Philosophers
   (B) Trades people
   (C) Aristocrats
   (D) Soldiers

7. Which of the following best characterizes Thucydides?
   (A) Mathematician
   (B) Hedonist
   (C) Historian
   (D) Stoic

8. Which of the following is most often associated with Ancient Greece?
   (A) Pursuit of excellence
   (B) Search for civilizations
   (C) Quest for happiness
   (D) Commitment to God

9. Which of the following philosophies bases morality on the consequences of a behavior?
   (A) Determinism
   (B) Objectivism
   (C) Utilitarianism
   (D) Idealism

10. The concept of the golden mean is most often associated with which of the following thinkers?
    (A) Zeno
    (B) Epicurus
    (C) Socrates
    (D) Aristotle

11. Avoiding pain and increasing pleasure are characteristics of
    (A) Stoicism.
    (B) Marxism.
    (C) Empiricism.
    (D) Epicureanism.

12. Which of the following was encouraged by Epictetus?
    (A) Obey the golden rule
    (B) Protect your self-interests
    (C) Question everything
    (D) Live according to nature

13. Which of the following is NOT a monotheistic religion?
    (A) Islam
    (B) Judaism
    (C) Hinduism
    (D) Christianity

14. According to Just War theory, all of the following are important criteria for war EXCEPT
    (A) right intentions.
    (B) majority in favor.
    (C) possibility of success.
    (D) matches provocation.

15. The ideas of which of the following thinkers are evident in the U.S. Declaration of Independence?
    (A) John Locke
    (B) Adam Smith
    (C) Thomas Hobbes
    (D) John Stuart Mill

16. For a utilitarian, the ethical evaluation of the decision to have an abortion will NOT depend on whether the abortion will
    (A) cause emotional pain for the woman's family.
    (B) eliminate pain for the woman having the abortion.
    (C) cause suffering for the woman having the abortion.
    (D) instigate change for the woman and her family.

17. Which of the following best describes Sophists?
    (A) Politicians who disagreed with Protagoras
    (B) Students of Plato at the Athens Academy
    (C) Characters included in Aristotle's writings
    (D) Teachers who received fees for lectures

18. Which Hindu term refers to a person's actions determining what happens to them in the future?
    (A) Nirvana
    (B) Karma
    (C) Dharma
    (D) Ahisma

19. Which of the following thinkers frequently used dialogues in his writings to examine issues of justice?
    (A) Thucydides
    (B) Socrates
    (C) Aristotle
    (D) Plato

20. Aquinas was able to draw a connection between
    (A) mathematics and knowledge.
    (B) happiness and morality.
    (C) theology and science.
    (D) faith and virtue.

ANSWER KEY AND EXPLANATIONS

1. A	5. A	9. C	13. C	17. D
2. B	6. A	10. D	14. B	18. B
3. D	7. C	11. D	15. A	19. D
4. C	8. A	12. D	16. D	20. C

1. **The correct answer is (A).** Jeremy Bentham first developed the concept of British utilitarianism. Mill was a utilitarian inspired by Bentham, but he did not first develop the philosophy. Nozick and Smith were not utilitarian philosophers.

2. **The correct answer is (B).** For a Stoic, the ethical evaluation of a decision to commit suicide depends on whether it seems to be a reasonable act. In cases where a person has a debilitating disease for which there is no treatment, suicide would most likely be considered moral to a Stoic. A utilitarian bases decisions on whether overall happiness increases. Choices (A) and (C) are incorrect.

3. **The correct answer is (D).** Ayn Rand was a moral egoist who asserted that it is a sacrifice to personal happiness to help another person. The highest moral purpose is helping oneself, not others, unless helping others results in a material or psychological reward. Choices (A), (B), and (C) are incorrect.

4. **The correct answer is (C).** Passive euthanasia refers to the act of intentionally withholding treatment in order to allow a patient to die. Active euthanasia refers to intentionally killing a patient by lethal injection, smothering, or some other method. Choices (B) and (D) are incorrect.

5. **The correct answer is (A).** Protagoras, a Sophist, said, "Man is the measure of all things." The statement suggests that people rather than nature determine behavior. Choices (B), (C), and (D) are incorrect.

6. **The correct answer is (A).** Plato believed that in a utopia, there would be philosopher-kings who would be able to understand truth and justice better than anyone else. Soldiers and then trade people were part of the second and third tiers in Plato's ideal state.

7. **The correct answer is (C).** Thucydides was a Greek historian who reported on the Peloponnesian War between Athens and Sparta. He raised issues in *The History of the Peloponnesian War* about the ethics, justice, and power used during times of war. Thucydides was neither a Stoic nor a Hedonist, so choices (B) and (D) are incorrect.

8. **The correct answer is (A).** The pursuit of excellence is most often linked with Ancient Greece. The culture emphasized the development of virtue and character as indicated by the ideas of Socrates, Plato, and Aristotle. Choice (C) is linked to utilitarianism, while choice (D) is associated with the Judeo-Christian tradition of ethics.

9. **The correct answer is (C).** Utilitarianism, which is also known as consequentialism, is the philosophy that actions are morally acceptable if good consequences outweigh bad consequences. On the other hand, an action is immoral if bad consequences outweigh good consequences.

Determinism asserts that events occur because of natural laws, so choice (A) is incorrect. Choices (B) and (D) are not based on consequences.

10. **The correct answer is (D).** Aristotle believed in maintaining balance in life to achieve happiness, a concept known as the golden mean. Aristotle wrote that virtue could only be attained by balancing courage, honesty, moderation, and reason. Choices (A), (B), and (C) are incorrect.

11. **The correct answer is (D).** Followers of Epicureanism, or hedonism, attempt to avoid pain and increase pleasure. Epicurus believed that happiness was the purpose of life, so life should be enjoyed to the fullest. Stoics, choice (A), believe that life virtue calls for living and acting with reason and self-control. Marxism, choice (B), is an economic philosophy, and empiricism, choice (C), is the scientific view that observation leads to knowledge.

12. **The correct answer is (D).** Epictetus was a Stoic, and he encouraged his students to "live according to nature." According to Stoicism, human beings cannot change fate because absolute law rules the universe. "Do unto others as you would have them do unto you" is the golden rule in the Bible, but Epictetus was not likely a follower of God.

13. **The correct answer is (C).** There are many Hindu gods according to followers of Hinduism. Islam, Judaism, and Christianity are monotheisms, meaning that followers believe in the existence of one God and no other higher beings. Choices (A), (B), and (D) are incorrect.

14. **The correct answer is (B).** According to Just War theory, a war is justified if it is fought with the right intentions, if there is a reasonable chance for

success, and if the actions match the provocation. Therefore, choices (A), (C), and (D) are incorrect.

15. **The correct answer is (A).** The ideas of John Locke influenced Thomas Jefferson and the other Founding Fathers when writing the Declaration of Independence. Locke developed the idea of protecting individual rights to life, liberty, and property, which is similar to life, liberty, and the pursuit of happiness. Smith and Mill presented their ideas after the Declaration of Independence was written. Hobbes's work suggested submitting to a ruler as part of a social contract.

16. **The correct answer is (D).** A utilitarian views ethical decisions in terms of good and bad consequences. If the overall consequences are bad, then a decision is immoral. Choices (A), (B), and (C) affect the overall happiness or unhappiness of the people involved, so these are factors in the decision. Choice (D) is irrelevant, which means it is the correct answer.

17. **The correct answer is (D).** The Sophists were traveling teachers who lectured about various topics for fees. Protagoras was a Sophist, so choice (A) is incorrect. Plato and Socrates disdained the Sophists who were considered manipulative, so choice (B) is incorrect. Sophists were not characters in the writings of Aristotle, so choice (C) is incorrect.

18. **The correct answer is (B).** Karma is the Hindu and Buddhist principle that a person's actions determine what happens to them in the future and in future reincarnations. Nirvana, choice (A), refers to a state of bliss, so choice (A) is incorrect. Dharma, choice (C), is the duties that must be fulfilled based on a person's caste. Ahisma, choice

(D), is the way a person acts or feels about others.

19. **The correct answer is (D).** Plato frequently used dialogues in his writings. A dialogue is a format for writing that presents ideas in a conversation between characters. Most of Plato's dialogues involved Socrates as one of the speakers. Socrates never wrote anything himself, so most of what is known of him comes from Plato's writings. Thucydides and Aristotle were not frequent users of dialogue, so choices (A) and (C) are incorrect.

20. **The correct answer is (C).** St. Thomas Aquinas was a thirteenth-century Catholic priest who drew a connection between theology and science. Aquinas believed that learning about nature was a way to learn about God. Choices (A), (B), and (D) are incorrect.

ETHICAL TRADITIONS

Ethics refers to the academic discipline of analyzing morality. Reasoning, rules, and logic form the basis of ethical philosophy. The foundation of American ethics began thousands of years ago in Ancient Greece when philosophers such as Socrates, Plato, and Aristotle first began discussing virtue, justice, and politics.

Greek Views

Since at least 1200 BC, myths and stories provided explanations for virtually everything in Greek life from floods to war battles. Greek gods and goddesses resembled human beings, and mythology focused on the activities of Earth's residents. The Greek worldview considered people the center of everything, and the world was a playground for traveling, building societies, and engaging in warfare. Change occurred in the sixth century when pre-Socratic philosophers raised questions about the natural world. How was the world made? How does the world work? The theories of cosmology and cosmogony developed at this time. Cosmology is the study of the physical world, such as what it is made of and how it works. Cosmogony is the study of the origin of the universe, such as how it came into existence.

One of the most notable pre-Socratic philosophers was Pythagoras, who was also a mathematician and a cosmologist. Since Pythagoras wrote nothing, his exact philosophy is uncertain. However, evidence suggests that beliefs in the magic of numbers and reincarnation were aspects of his philosophy. The philosopher had a significant number of followers, perhaps because people believed he had miraculous powers.

The Sophists

The first philosophers in Greece studied nature, but philosophical focus shifted to man towards the second half of the fifth century BC. The democratic system in Athens was evolving, and it was the duty of every free adult male to participate in government. Because of the interest in society and politics among Athens citizens, a group of teachers known as the Sophists emerged. The Sophists traveled throughout Greece giving lectures about various popular topics, such as rhetoric, history, mathematics, and politics. Sophists received large sums of money in exchange for their presentations, unlike the wise men of Greece who freely shared their thoughts with the public.

The public viewed the first Sophists as teachers of virtue and excellence rather than as philosophers. Protagoras, one of the earliest and most respected Sophists, is best known for stating, "Man is the measure of all things." The statement suggests that people rather than nature determine behavior. Many experts consider the Sophists the first relativists. Ethical relativism proposes that every point of view is equally valid and that different people have different standards of behavior. Relativists often rely more heavily on persuasion than on truth. In addition, Protagoras questioned the existence of gods and thought that individuals should act according to their best interests without searching for wisdom from a higher power.

While many early Sophists were admired, others drew criticism for being untrustworthy. Some Sophists made boastful assertions that they could prove any position without knowledge of the subject matter. The term *sophistry,* which means to use purposely deceptive and invalid arguments, derives its meaning from actions of the Sophists. Despite the fact that the Sophists emphasized persuasive skills rather than the honest analysis of issues, they set the stage for intellectual discussion in Athens.

Thucydides

War broke out between Athens and Sparta in 431 BC. Thucydides, a Greek historian, wrote *The History of the Peloponnesian War* as a report of the battle that lasted until 404 BC. *The History of the Peloponnesian War* provides a graphic and exact account of military actions. Thucydides objectively presents the factual events of the war without any attribution to mythological beings. Thucydides adds drama to the document with the inclusion of fictional speeches that are factual in content. Considered one of the first and greatest historians, Thucydides raises questions in his publication about the ethics of war, especially with regard to justice and power.

Socrates

Socrates, one of the most influential thinkers of all times, lived in Athens during the fifth century BC. Socrates was an outspoken critic of the Sophists as well as Athenian politics and religious institutions. Socrates considered the teachings of the Sophists empty and manipulative, and he debated with them frequently. Socrates sought to uncover truth and spent much of his time discussing virtue, justice, and morality with the citizens of Athens. During the time of Socrates, most people equated virtue with beauty, and the philosopher hoped to change that notion. Socrates hoped to elevate the moral and intellectual nature of the city, and he sacrificed everything he had in this attempt.

Most information about Socrates' teachings stems from the writings of his most famous student, Plato, because Socrates never wrote any books. Socrates is renowned more for the way in which he taught than a specific philosophy. Socrates employed a questioning technique, later termed the Socratic Method or dialectic, to discuss philosophical issues with people. The method involves asking a series of questions and drawing out answers from students to develop understanding and insight about a particular issue. Socrates' series of questions eventually weakened the other person's argument by pointing out contradictions. Most of the time, Socrates claimed that he lacked any knowledge of the subject to illustrate that answers existed in the mind of the student.

For Socrates, virtue equaled knowledge. Socrates held that people never knowingly do wrong; wickedness results from ignorance. A person who is knowledgeable about morality will behave with morality. Socrates guided philosophy towards ethics by questioning the logic of Sophists, citizens, and politicians. Seen as a threat to society, Socrates was condemned for his teachings. When given the choice of renouncing his work or death, Socrates opted for a cup of poisoned hemlock.

Plato

Socrates' most famous student, Plato, was a philosopher and mathematician. After the death of Socrates, Plato continued with his teacher's work and established the Academy in 387 BC. The Academy, which is considered the first university, served as the most significant institution of higher learning in the Western world where discussion and research into mathematics, astronomy, politics, and natural history occurred. Plato's earliest writings, the Socratic dialogues, convey the ideas of his deceased teacher. A dialogue is a method of presenting ideas in the format of a fictional discussion with other people, which for Plato was usually Socrates.

Plato's most famous and influential work is *The Republic*. The text uses dialogues to examine whether it is always better to be just than unjust. Unhappy with the democracy and tyranny of Greek government, Plato believed that selfish individuals wielded too much power. Plato's discussion of an ideal republic, known as utopian thinking, leads to his conclusion that the ideal state is divided into three classes of citizens. The guardians of society are philosopher-kings. Philosopher-kings are capable of understanding truth and justice and are guided by wisdom rather than self-interest. Soldiers serve as the next level of Plato's ideal society because they are unselfish, moral, and courageous. The final societal level consists of workers or producers who are motivated by a certain level of greed, which Plato refers to as appetite. In Plato's ideal state, political justice replaces democracy and tyranny.

In *The Republic*, Plato employs an extended metaphor known as the Allegory of the Cave to compare untutored people to prisoners in a cave. The prisoners misinterpret shadows on a wall as reality. The parable and the rest of *The Republic* illustrate Plato's primary philosophical convictions:

- The world experienced through the senses is not the real world, which can only be understood intellectually.

- Some people are less virtuous than others, which is why government is necessary.

- Enlightened people have a responsibility to society.

As with other Greeks of the fourth and fifth century BC, Plato believed in pursuing personal excellence to achieve peace in a troubled world. Plato explains in *The Republic* that the world may not acknowledge or reward virtue, but ultimate happiness can only be achieved through virtue.

Aristotle

One of the most renowned students of Plato's Academy in Athens was the philosopher Aristotle. In addition to being a philosopher, Aristotle was an authority on nearly every subject, including ethics, physics, biology, and psychology. However, Aristotle's approach to philosophy differed significantly from his teacher's methods. Whereas Plato viewed the world in abstracts, Aristotle concentrated on observations and experiences, or empirical knowledge. Learning about so many subjects corresponds with two key beliefs of Aristotle:

- Everything has a purpose.
- Change is both necessary and natural.

Living virtuously is the purpose of human beings in the world according to Aristotle. In his book *Nicomachean Ethics*, Aristotle states that physical pleasures derived from money, work, and sex fail to bring ultimate happiness. Aristotle equates virtue to happiness, and he distinguishes between two types of virtues—moral excellence and intellectual excellence. Moral virtues, which indicate excellence of character, include self-control, bravery, self-respect, gentleness, truthfulness, and generosity. Intellectual virtues include scientific knowledge, intuitive reason, practical wisdom, skill, and wisdom. From Aristotle's perspective, maintaining balance and not going to the extreme in either direction is the key to happiness, a concept known as the golden mean.

Stoics and Hedonists

From the fourth through the first century BC, the philosophy of Plato and Aristotle spread to other countries along the Mediterranean Sea. During this period, multiple groups of thought emerged, including the Stoics and the Epicureans.

Founded around 300 BC by a philosopher named Zeno, Stoicism later influenced Christian thinkers and experienced a revival during the Renaissance. Stoicism is a philosophy based on the idea that absolute law rules the universe and that humans cannot change fate. According to Stoic ethics, virtue requires living and acting according to reason and self-control. Wise and happy people are content with whatever occurs in life because they realize everything is inevitable. Unhappiness occurs when a person feels disappointment or regret about a certain course of events. Epictetus, one of the most prominent Stoics of the second century AD, encouraged his students to "live according to nature." Epictetus, a Roman slave often tortured by his master, exemplified the Stoic philosophy by refusing to moan during beatings because he accepted his fate in life.

Also around 300 BC, the philosophy of hedonism or Epicureanism emerged under the guidance of Epicurus. The philosopher asserted that happiness was the purpose of life. According to hedonism, achieving happiness involves avoiding pain and increasing pleasure. Epicurus asserted that the universe was created by an accidental collision of atoms rather than by Greek gods. While Epicurus did not deny the existence of gods and goddesses, he suggested that they are indifferent to the activities of humans. Upon death, people's souls and bodies would dissolve back into atoms. As a result, hedonists felt free to enjoy life to the greatest extent without worrying about retribution from the gods.

RELIGIOUS TRADITIONS

The Bible has been the most popular tool for teaching morality in the Western world and serves as the center point for Judeo-Christian ethics. The Bible was first translated into Greek around 250 BC, and it offered a completely different approach to ethics than the Greek philosophers. For the Israelites, morality resided in one righteous God, and God's teachings were the basis of their laws.

Jews and Christians share the moral principles found in the Hebrew Bible, or Old Testament. The Ten Commandments are a list of rules indicating that it is immoral to murder, commit adultery, steal, and covet. Stories throughout the Old Testament indicate the importance of obeying God, taking responsibility, and exhibiting willpower. Whereas Judaism is based only on the Old Testament, Christianity also includes the teachings of Jesus Christ, found in the New Testament. The New Testament provides numerous ethical principles, most of which are focused on the concept of love. Christians are instructed to love God above all else and to love their neighbors, as indicated by the story of the Good Samaritan.

Although the Bible has been the most significant source of morality in America since the first colonists arrived, other religious traditions have had an effect on Western society as well. The following table provides a general overview of the major world religions.

Major World Religions

Christianity	Bible instructs that personal salvation occurs through faith and that God is merciful and all knowing.
Judaism	As the oldest monotheistic religion, Judaism places importance on history, laws, and religious community and is responsible for influencing both Islam and Christianity.
Islam	Koran believed to have been written by the prophet Mohammed under the direction of God. Muslims are instructed to be generous and obedient and to avoid being greedy or prideful.
Hinduism	Moral guidance based on a principle called ahimsa, which is the principle of nonviolence. Ahisma involves both behavior and feelings towards others, so hatred for another violates ahisma. Emphasis is on being detached from pain and desire and choosing actions that cause the least amount of harm.
Buddhism	Moral code does not have a divine origin. Dalai Lama asserts that morality helps people achieve happiness many times through reincarnation. Happiness to self and others derives from being loving, compassionate, patient, forgiving, and responsible.

The concepts of karma and dharma are connected with both Hinduism and Buddhism. Karma is the principle that a person's actions determine what happens to them in the future and in future reincarnations. Dharma refers to the righteous duties of a person toward people and gods. In contrast, the three monotheistic religions—Judaism, Christianity, and Islam—consider events in life as being the will of God. Monotheism means belief in only one god rather than multiple gods.

NATURAL LAW THEORY

Natural law theories are based on the idea that the moral standards guiding human behavior originate in human nature and the universe. Deviating from the norm is immoral, sinful, evil, and harmful. However, the disorder caused by deviation forces a reasoning individual to restore events back to normal. Such logic is based on the idea that the universe is morally neutral and that moral laws are part of nature. The attraction of natural law is its ability to provide meaning for life and behavior. Elements of natural law are evident in the beliefs of the Ancient Greeks and the Stoics.

Many medieval philosophers adopted natural law theories in an attempt to explain the relationship between God and humanity. Thirteenth-century Catholic priest St. Thomas Aquinas believed that faith and reason could exist together, and that theology and science were not contradictory. Well versed in the philosophy of Aristotle, Aquinas wrote that learning about nature is a way to learn about God. Aquinas's theory of natural law asserts that the laws discovered in nature stem from the eternal God. Human beings are naturally rational, so it is moral for humans to behave rationally.

POLITICAL THEORIES

In addition to questions about nature, numerous philosophers have raised questions about political authorities and the best way to manage societies. Social contract theory refers to the idea that the right to rule and the obligation to obey are based upon an agreement between an individual and society. The moral code put forth in a social contract creates a harmonious society in which all parties work together for mutual advantage. Thomas Hobbes, John Locke, and Jean-Jacques Rousseau wrote about social contract theory during the seventeenth and eighteenth centuries. As the most well-known social contract theorists, they attempted to explain how people join society for the purpose of security and societal order.

Thomas Hobbes

Thomas Hobbes, an English political philosopher, developed a theory suggesting that humans live fearfully in a natural world full of insecurity and violence. *Leviathan*, which Hobbes wrote during the English Civil War, describes the relationship between civil law and natural law. According to Hobbes, fear and insecurity force people into surrendering their natural rights to a sovereign ruler and forming a social contract. Failure to submit to a ruler, even a bad one, will result in conflict and savagery. Hobbes viewed virtues such as gratitude and modesty as traits that help people live harmoniously with the rest of society. He believed that it is in the self-interest of individuals to have such characteristics.

John Locke

Seventeenth-century British philosopher John Locke provided his thoughts about government in numerous writings, and he is often associated with the concept of empiricism. Empiricism refers to the notion that reliable knowledge is acquired by testing ideas against sensory evidence. Locke proposed that humans are not born with any ideas because the mind is a blank slate at birth. Understanding develops as people see, hear, and touch things.

Locke spent much of his efforts questioning the structure of British government. For centuries, people held that kings were direct descendants of Adam and thus had the divine right to rule. However, the bloodshed resulting from recent wars caused Locke to raise concerns about the monarchy. In *Two Treatises of Government,* Locke explains the function of political authority and proposes that individuals have certain natural rights:

- The right to live without being harmed by others
- The right to make their own choices
- The right to own property

According to Locke, the purpose of political authority is to protect individual rights to life, liberty, and property. Underlying Locke's theory is the idea that people have the right to resist unjust political authority. When a political power fails to uphold its half of a social contract, citizens should resist and revolt to protect their rights.

Locke's revolutionary ideas about government influenced many others, including Thomas Jefferson and the Founding Fathers in writing the U.S. Declaration of Independence.

> *We hold these truths to be self-evident, that all men are created equal, that they are endowed by their Creator with certain unalienable rights, that among these are life, liberty, and the pursuit of happiness.*

Jean-Jacques Rousseau

Locke also influenced Jean-Jacques Rousseau, the eighteenth-century French philosopher. Rousseau believed that human beings are innately good but that society, with its desires and greed, corrupts them. Rousseau developed the concept of general will in *Discourse on Political Economy* and *The Social Contract.* Under general will, citizens act as legislators to determine, as a collective body, the laws and legislation of society. According to the concept of general will, power rests with the citizens, and society becomes highly democratic. The French government banned Rousseau's controversial writings, and the philosopher fled to Switzerland.

John Rawls and Robert Nozick

Two American philosophers of the twentieth century are known for their ideas regarding political philosophy. John Rawls, author of *A Theory of Justice,* revived the social contract theory. Most of Rawls's writings raise questions about distributive justice, which refers to the way in which benefits and burdens are allocated within a society. Rawls attempts to refute the philosophy of utilitarianism based on the concept of "justice as fairness": First principle: *Each person is to have an equal right to the most extensive total system of equal basic liberties compatible with a similar system of liberty for all.*

Second principle: *Social and economic inequalities are to be arranged so that they are both: (a) to the greatest benefit of the least advantaged, and (b) attached to offices and positions open to all under conditions of fair equality of opportunity.*

According to Rawls, the first principle has priority over the second principle, which is known as the difference principle. So, basic liberties, like freedom of speech, should not be hindered to improve life for the least advantaged individuals in a society. Rawls sums up his philosophy when he states, "Injustice is simply inequalities that are not to the benefit of all."

One of Rawls's colleagues at Harvard, Robert Nozick, also addressed the concept of distributive justice. However, Nozick compared income tax to forced labor and stated that the redistribution of wealth is only justifiable when it is resolving a past injustice.

TRANSCENDENTAL IDEALISM

Eighteenth-century German philosopher Immanuel Kant is one of the greatest influences on Western philosophy. Much of Kant's work attempts to answer three primary questions:

- What can I know?
- What should I do?
- What can I hope for?

The concept of transcendental idealism plays a significant role in Kant's philosophy, as well as the philosophy of other German idealists. Transcendence means to be beyond the experience. Transcendental idealism is the concept that appearances should be viewed as only representations and not as things themselves. In other words, both the mind and understanding create reality. Kant used four categories of understanding—space, time, causality, and substance—to explain how the mind structures reality and enables people to make sense of experiences. Kant referred to these four concepts as *a priori* concepts to explain that the concepts occurred before a person's existence.

In addition, Kant developed two categories of moral thought—practical reason and pure reason. Practical reason is reasoning about how people should act, and pure reason is reasoning about what actually exists. Categorical imperatives are universal moral laws that act as the basis of practical reason and that help people behave morally. According to Kant, a behavior conforms to a categorical imperative if it is moral for all human beings.

MORAL EGOISM

Best known as the author of *The Wealth of Nations*, Adam Smith was more than a founder of capitalism. He was also an eighteenth-century moral philosopher. Smith proposed that the common good of society advances when individuals focus on benefiting themselves, a concept related to moral egoism. The theory of moral egoism asserts that it is always moral to act in a manner that benefits self-interest. According to Smith, individuals are able to achieve happiness in life when they focus on their own happiness rather than the happiness of others.

Ayn Rand, the twentieth-century Russian philosopher, also falls into the category of moral egoist. Rand asserted that pursuing self-interests and personal happiness are "the highest moral purpose" of life. According to Rand's philosophy of objectivism, doing anything for another person will sacrifice happiness unless there is a material or psychological reward involved. Rand's writings indicate her objection to the weak exploiting the strong and her admiration for individual accomplishment.

UTILITARIANISM

Utilitarianism, or Consequentialism, refers to the theory that actions are morally acceptable if good consequences outweigh bad consequences. Similarly, if bad consequences outweigh good consequences, an action is morally wrong. Therefore, morality is completely about the results of any behavior. A utilitarian does not seek answers to ethical dilemmas from the universe but from within. Behavior that brings pleasure is moral, while behavior that brings pain is immoral. Utilitarianism differs dramatically from another nineteenth-century philosophy—determinism. Thoughts, behaviors, and decisions have to happen because previous events and the laws of nature determine them. Determinism conflicts with philosophies based on concepts of individual freedom.

Jeremy Bentham (1748–1832) modified the philosophy of Epicurus, the first utilitarian, by arguing that service to society generates more pleasure than service to self. As the founder of British utilitarianism, Bentham asserted that behavior is wrong if it reduces overall happiness. For Bentham, behavior that produces long-term happiness to the community is preferred to short-term personal happiness. Bentham defines happiness as experiencing pleasure and avoiding pain. Bentham's ideas motivated the Philosophical Radicals, a group of social reformers in the early part of the nineteenth century. The Radicals advocated universal male suffrage and politics geared toward human happiness instead of natural rights.

Bentham's work inspired nineteenth-century British philosopher John Stuart Mill, whose father was a member of the Radicals. Mill conveyed his utilitarian ideas in numerous pieces, but his essay *On Liberty* is the most well known. In the essay, Mill asserts that the only time a government has the moral authority to limit a person's liberty is when harm may occur otherwise. In all other situations, people should be allowed the freedom to behave as desired. Continuing with utilitarian concepts, Mill wrote *The Subjugation of Women* as an argument in favor of women's equality. Mill asserts that the marital relationship improves when both partners have equal roles.

FEMINIST ETHICS

Feminism refers to the philosophical and political discourse geared toward exposing, analyzing, and addressing sexual inequality. Feminist philosophy emerged in the 1960s for a number of reasons. First, it was believed that the bulk of philosophical research omitted women from major studies. Second, it was believed that there was a masculine bias in philosophical research, so an accurate assessment of women's morals was either neglected or distorted.

Carol Gilligan is a psychologist best known for her research and writings about the moral development of women. Unlike feminists who assert that there are no differences between men and women, Gilligan indicates that women and men have different approaches to making moral decisions. Men, she believes, have an ethics of justice and focus on applying rules and minimizing emotions when making decisions. For example, Kant's categorical imperatives and utilitarianism are both masculine approaches to making decisions. In contrast, she contends that women have an ethics of care and consider responsibilities and relationships when making decisions. The moral decisions made by women often appeal to such emotions as sympathy, love, and concern. Gilligan argues that both types of ethics are valuable to society.

Philosopher Nel Noddings also studies the concept of ethics of care. Noddings has focused her research on the origins of care within the home, such as parent-child relationships. Noddings asserts that studying how people care for those around them leads to understanding how to care for people within society.

CURRENT ETHICAL ISSUES

The previous section of this review focused on the ethical concepts developed by different philosophers in history. This section provides a brief overview of some of the ethical issues facing American citizens today.

Morality and Sexuality

Morality regarding sexuality often centers on the idea of sex without marriage, and most of the attention garnered by this topic relates to teens having premarital sex. Many people consider sex outside of marriage morally wrong because God forbids it. However, there are also non-theological thoughts regarding morality and sexuality. According to utilitarianism, if the overall happiness of an unmarried couple increases by having sex, then it is morally acceptable. Yet, possible problems include guilt, sexually transmitted diseases, and unintentional pregnancy, which would all tip the happiness scale in the opposite direction. Both Aristotle and the Dalai Lama focus on long-term rather than temporal happiness, which might not be achieved through a sexual relationship outside of marriage.

Another related issue involves the morality of homosexuality, which raises strong opinions on both sides. While some people believe homosexuality disobeys the will of God, others condemn homosexuality because they consider it unnatural. The argument of natural versus unnatural raises questions about the definition of *natural*. If the meaning of *natural* is *abnormal,* then some might argue that abnormality does not equal immorality. For example, it is abnormal to jump 4 feet off the ground, but it is not immoral. Others argue that procreation is the purpose of sexual organs, and homosexual acts are an unnatural use of the body. Based on such a theory, is it immoral to use a foot for propping open a door? Some of the philosophers discussed in the previous section may not have written their views about sexuality, but an understanding of the different theories should provide the basis of an educated guess.

Abortion

Since the 1973 U.S. Supreme Court decision in *Roe v. Wade*, abortion has been a controversial issue in America. The justices determined that states could not prevent a woman from having an abortion during the first trimester of pregnancy. Right-to-life advocates assert that abortion is immoral because the fetus is a living human being from the moment of conception. In contrast, the most liberal view of abortion holds that a woman always has the right to decide what happens to her body at any point during a pregnancy. While these two opinions may represent extremes of the spectrum, many people grapple with whether and when abortion is moral. The following questions are often raised in the abortion debate:

- At what stage of development is abortion acceptable?

- What is the point of viability when a fetus can live outside of the womb?

- What are the reasons for seeking an abortion? Rape? Teen pregnancy? Career?

Recent advancements with infertility treatment raise ethical questions about destroying embryos. In addition, parents in some cultures desire male babies instead of female babies, so they abort girls. The public funding of abortions raises another concern. Opponents assert that the government should not fund an immoral activity, while advocates claim that a legal abortion should be available to everyone and not just the wealthy.

Suicide

Debate has raged for thousands of years about the morality or immorality of suicide. According to Plato, suicide is wrong unless the gods encourage it. In later writings, Plato indicates disapproval for suicide that occurs from "unmanly cowardice," but he seems to suggest that suicide is acceptable if a person faces hardship, disgrace, or extreme stress. Aristotle apparently agrees that suicide to "fly from evil" is acceptable, but suicide used to "escape from poverty or love" is not. Stoics believe suicide is acceptable when it seems like a reasonable and justifiable act, such as not having to live with a debilitating disease or avoiding being tortured into revealing information to a state enemy. Moreover, many Jews and Christians believe that God prohibits suicide based on the Commandment stating, "You shall not murder."

As indicated by both Plato and Aristotle, the reason for committing suicide often determines whether people view the act as moral or immoral. For example, if a person's quality of life has significantly diminished due to a terminal illness or a crippling disease, then suicide may be a reasonable alternative to living. In other cases, suicide is considered honorable, such as when Buddhist monks burned themselves to death in protest of the Vietnam War. A utilitarian would find suicide moral only if it increased the total happiness of everyone involved. However, Kant thought that suicide was always an immoral act.

Euthanasia

Euthanasia refers to killing or allowing the death of a sick or injured person for the sake of mercy. The act may involve killing someone, perhaps by giving a high dosage of drugs, or letting someone die without attempting to save them. While euthanasia is typically associated with the elderly, the issue relates to all stages of life:

- What should parents do when their infants are born with severe physical defects like an incomplete brain? Should they allow the child to die naturally or allow physicians to inject a lethal drug that will cause a peaceful death?

- What about a young adult with severe brain damage who is living in a persistent vegetative state? Do family members wait for an unlikely recovery or remove life support?

- What about a middle-aged man diagnosed with an untreatable and fatal form of cancer that is severely weakening his body? What if he wants to end the suffering and his family approves his decision?

Before deciding when or if euthanasia is morally acceptable, it is important to understand various relevant terms.

Euthanasia Terminology

Passive euthanasia	Intentionally withholding treatment to allow a patient to die
Active euthanasia	Intentionally killing a patient by lethal injection, smothering, or some other method
Extraordinary treatment	Surgery, medication, dialysis, oxygen, CPR, or any other treatment needed to help an unhealthy patient
Ordinary care	Food, water, and any other care people need regardless of their health
Voluntary euthanasia	A competent and completely informed patient freely requests or consents to euthanasia
Nonvoluntary euthanasia	An incompetent patient or one who has not given consent undergoes euthanasia
Involuntary euthanasia	Intentionally killing a patient against his or her will—considered murder

As indicated by the table, informed consent is required for voluntary euthanasia. Philosophers use the term *autonomy* when referring to the idea of informed consent. Actions are autonomous when they are intentional, understood, and chosen freely. Both Aristotle and Kant, for example, place great value in autonomy when making decisions.

Economic Inequality

The distribution of wealth and resources both within the United States and around the world raises ethical issues about economic inequality. John Rawls asserted that economic inequality is justified only when it benefits everyone, such as to encourage people to be more productive. Rousseau believed that an excessive degree of inequality destroys freedom if wealthy citizens act as tyrants in a society.

Opponents of economic equality claim that diversity within a society is highly valuable and that people should have the freedom to keep what they have earned. Economic redistribution, which refers to taking from those who have many resources and giving it to those who have few resources, violates the rights of the individuals who acquired the resources in the first place.

Affirmative Action

Affirmative action refers to policies and programs that consider race, gender, or ethnicity for a range of purposes. A moderate type of affirmative action program might attempt to increase the diversity of applicants for a school or a job. For example, a university includes pictures in its admissions brochures that show people of different races and ethnic backgrounds to convey the idea that the campus is diverse. Preferential treatment is a controversial method of implementing affirmative action. Preferential treatment involves basing decisions on race, gender, or ethnicity rather than qualifications. Opponents of preferential treatment assert that the practice is unfair to qualified applicants and lowers standards for everyone. However, advocates claim that preferential treatment for African Americans is justified because of historical examples of racial discrimination, such as slavery and school segregation.

Crime and Punishment

The majority of Americans view crime reduction as an important objective, but the best method of reducing crime remains debatable. Some people argue that the threat of punishment deters criminal activity, while others assert that focusing on societal problems like alcoholism, poverty, and drug abuse deters crime. However, giving attention to the causes of crime will most likely not eliminate all criminal activity. Moreover, most people believe that criminals should be punished. In general, punishment should match the crime, but such a concept raises many questions: How long should prison sentences be? What should the conditions in prison be like? How should youthful offenders be punished? What about criminals with mental disabilities?

Three general types of punishment are available within the American criminal justice system:

- *Disablement:* placing a convicted criminal in prison or executing a criminal
- *Deterrence:* potential criminals attempt to avoid being imprisoned or executed, so they do not commit crimes

- *Rehabilitation:* prisoners spend time earning an education or learning a trade that can be used once released from prison to avoid the lure of criminal activity

Capital punishment is a controversial topic in the United States, as exemplified by the fact that some states permit execution and others do not. Supporters of the death penalty assert that the threat of capital punishment is more effective than the threat of imprisonment for potential murderers. Advocates claim that capital punishment is morally acceptable because it protects society from the worst criminals. Additional reasons in favor of capital punishment include the idea that murderers deserve to die and that the death penalty provides closure for victims' families.

In contrast, opponents of capital punishment claim that life imprisonment satisfactorily removes a murderer from society. They also assert that imprisonment is just as effective in deterring crime as the death penalty. According to research studies, the likelihood of apprehension, conviction, and punishment are more significant than the severity of the punishment when people decide whether to commit crimes. Mistakes made in the criminal justice system, questions regarding discrimination, and the potential for prisoner reformation are issues continually raised in the death penalty debate as well.

War and Peace

Wars have been fought for thousands of years and continue in modern society. War occurs for a variety of reasons—defending from attack, protecting natural resources, acquiring territory, and settling disputes. The way in which militaries fight wars varies as well and may include bombings, assassinations, and biological weapons. There are two primary questions related to the morality of war that must be asked by government leaders, soldiers, and regular citizens:

- When is it morally acceptable to ensue in war?
- What are the moral limits, if any, during a war?

Peace refers to the absence of fighting, but such a non-warring condition varies. Peace occurred at the end of the U.S. Civil War when over 600,000 soldiers lay dead. Peace existed between the United States and the Soviet Union during the Cold War, although weapons on both sides were ready to go at any moment. Peace occurs at times between Israel and the Palestinians, but it is always tenuous.

While many people take the view that peace requires preparation for war, pacifists believe war is never morally acceptable or justified. Pacifists think that war is an immoral way to achieve any goal and that war is ineffective because violence leads to more violence. Pacifists often cite the Hebrew Bible and the New Testament in protest of war. Mohandas K. Gandhi, one of the most well-known pacifists, led a campaign against racist laws in South Africa through a method of nonviolent resistance.

Just War theory considers both the ethical and historical aspects of war. A war is justified under this theory if it meets certain criteria:

1. It is declared by a competent authority.
2. It is fought for a just cause.

3. It is fought with the right intentions.

4. It is appropriate for the provocation.

5. It is used as a last resort.

6. There is a reasonable chance for success.

The Just War tradition stems from the Roman Catholic Church, and St. Thomas Aquinas is linked to the first three justifications.

Environmental Ethics

Environmental ethics is a relatively new field of philosophy that focuses on human responsibility to nature. Protecting the natural environment is viewed as both practical and ethical for the future of humanity.

Much has been said in recent years about environmental threats such as global warming, air pollution, and energy consumption. The following list indicates the major environmental issues facing America and the rest of the world:

- Air pollution
- Deforestation
- Energy consumption
- Global warming
- Ozone depletion
- Population growth
- Water pollution
- Wilderness preservation

While everyone generally agrees on the causes of some environmental concerns, such as water pollution, other issues are highly debatable. For example, some scientists blame the burning of fossil fuels for global warming, while other experts attribute climate change to natural planetary and solar fluctuations. Energy consumption is another topic that triggers debate. Should the United States focus on developing alternative energy sources or should it drill for oil where it is known to exist? Not only do environmental concerns raise ethical questions, but they raise issues about government policies as well.

POST-TEST ANSWER SHEET

1. Ⓐ Ⓑ Ⓒ Ⓓ   13. Ⓐ Ⓑ Ⓒ Ⓓ   25. Ⓐ Ⓑ Ⓒ Ⓓ   37. Ⓐ Ⓑ Ⓒ Ⓓ   49. Ⓐ Ⓑ Ⓒ Ⓓ

2. Ⓐ Ⓑ Ⓒ Ⓓ   14. Ⓐ Ⓑ Ⓒ Ⓓ   26. Ⓐ Ⓑ Ⓒ Ⓓ   38. Ⓐ Ⓑ Ⓒ Ⓓ   50. Ⓐ Ⓑ Ⓒ Ⓓ

3. Ⓐ Ⓑ Ⓒ Ⓓ   15. Ⓐ Ⓑ Ⓒ Ⓓ   27. Ⓐ Ⓑ Ⓒ Ⓓ   39. Ⓐ Ⓑ Ⓒ Ⓓ   51. Ⓐ Ⓑ Ⓒ Ⓓ

4. Ⓐ Ⓑ Ⓒ Ⓓ   16. Ⓐ Ⓑ Ⓒ Ⓓ   28. Ⓐ Ⓑ Ⓒ Ⓓ   40. Ⓐ Ⓑ Ⓒ Ⓓ   52. Ⓐ Ⓑ Ⓒ Ⓓ

5. Ⓐ Ⓑ Ⓒ Ⓓ   17. Ⓐ Ⓑ Ⓒ Ⓓ   29. Ⓐ Ⓑ Ⓒ Ⓓ   41. Ⓐ Ⓑ Ⓒ Ⓓ   53. Ⓐ Ⓑ Ⓒ Ⓓ

6. Ⓐ Ⓑ Ⓒ Ⓓ   18. Ⓐ Ⓑ Ⓒ Ⓓ   30. Ⓐ Ⓑ Ⓒ Ⓓ   42. Ⓐ Ⓑ Ⓒ Ⓓ   54. Ⓐ Ⓑ Ⓒ Ⓓ

7. Ⓐ Ⓑ Ⓒ Ⓓ   19. Ⓐ Ⓑ Ⓒ Ⓓ   31. Ⓐ Ⓑ Ⓒ Ⓓ   43. Ⓐ Ⓑ Ⓒ Ⓓ   55. Ⓐ Ⓑ Ⓒ Ⓓ

8. Ⓐ Ⓑ Ⓒ Ⓓ   20. Ⓐ Ⓑ Ⓒ Ⓓ   32. Ⓐ Ⓑ Ⓒ Ⓓ   44. Ⓐ Ⓑ Ⓒ Ⓓ   56. Ⓐ Ⓑ Ⓒ Ⓓ

9. Ⓐ Ⓑ Ⓒ Ⓓ   21. Ⓐ Ⓑ Ⓒ Ⓓ   33. Ⓐ Ⓑ Ⓒ Ⓓ   45. Ⓐ Ⓑ Ⓒ Ⓓ   57. Ⓐ Ⓑ Ⓒ Ⓓ

10. Ⓐ Ⓑ Ⓒ Ⓓ   22. Ⓐ Ⓑ Ⓒ Ⓓ   34. Ⓐ Ⓑ Ⓒ Ⓓ   46. Ⓐ Ⓑ Ⓒ Ⓓ   58. Ⓐ Ⓑ Ⓒ Ⓓ

11. Ⓐ Ⓑ Ⓒ Ⓓ   23. Ⓐ Ⓑ Ⓒ Ⓓ   35. Ⓐ Ⓑ Ⓒ Ⓓ   47. Ⓐ Ⓑ Ⓒ Ⓓ   59. Ⓐ Ⓑ Ⓒ Ⓓ

12. Ⓐ Ⓑ Ⓒ Ⓓ   24. Ⓐ Ⓑ Ⓒ Ⓓ   36. Ⓐ Ⓑ Ⓒ Ⓓ   48. Ⓐ Ⓑ Ⓒ Ⓓ   60. Ⓐ Ⓑ Ⓒ Ⓓ

answer sheet

POST-TEST

Directions: Carefully read each of the following 60 questions. Choose the best answer to each question, and darken its letter on your answer sheet. The Answer Key and Explanations can be found following this post-test.

1. The philosophy of which of the following thinkers was based on numbers?
   (A) Thucydides
   (B) Aristotle
   (C) Pythagoras
   (D) Heraclitus

2. The philosophy of which of the following does NOT adhere to social contract theory?
   (A) Rawls
   (B) Kant
   (C) Rousseau
   (D) Hobbes

3. For a follower of Kant, the ethical evaluation of a decision to commit adultery depends on whether
   (A) the adulterer is a Christian.
   (B) adultery is a reasonable action.
   (C) the adulterer will be happy.
   (D) adultery is moral for everyone.

4. According to which of the following is it immoral to engage in war?
   (A) Smith, because war serves no self interests
   (B) Gandhi, because war is never justified
   (C) Rawls, because war destroys freedom
   (D) Mill, because war is irrational

5. Which of the following does Gilligan attribute to men?
   (A) Ethics of care
   (B) Ethics of society
   (C) Ethics of reason
   (D) Ethics of justice

6. The idea that all events occur because of previous actions and the laws of nature is
   (A) rationalism.
   (B) existentialism.
   (C) determinism.
   (D) scholasticism.

7. Which of the following is equivalent to murder in most cases?
   (A) Passive euthanasia
   (B) Involuntary euthanasia
   (C) Active euthanasia
   (D) Nonvoluntary euthanasia

8. According to Rawls, in which of the following situations is economic inequality ethical and justified?
   (A) When citizens are required to share resources
   (B) When the wealthy rule government offices
   (C) When citizens need to be more productive
   (D) When society has become too diverse

9. Plato uses the Allegory of the Cave to illustrate which of the following concepts?
   (A) The world can only be understood intellectually.
   (B) Happiness can be attained through physical experiences.
   (C) The world can only be understood through the senses.
   (D) Courage and morality are necessary in difficult situations.

10. The ethics of Judaism are based on the teachings of
    (A) the Old Testament.
    (B) Jesus Christ.
    (C) Mohammed.
    (D) the New Testament.

11. Which of the following refers to an Ancient Greek theory about the origin of the world?
    (A) Cosmology
    (B) Relativism
    (C) Cosmogony
    (D) Sophism

12. According to which of the following philosophies is premarital sex most likely immoral?
    (A) Moral egoism, because increasing knowledge is the most important goal
    (B) Hedonism, because the gods will disapprove
    (C) Transcendental idealism, because logical thinking equals happiness
    (D) Stoicism, because self-control is virtuous

13. Which of the following thinkers evaluates the morality of actions in terms of categorical imperatives?
    (A) Rawls
    (B) Kant
    (C) Smith
    (D) Rand

14. The statement "To each according to need" is an example of the principles of
    (A) retributive justice.
    (B) economic rationalism.
    (C) distributive justice.
    (D) social virtue.

15. According to which of the following philosophers is economic equality moral?
    (A) Smith, because the purpose of society is to share wealth
    (B) Rand, because helping others is the greatest moral purpose
    (C) Bentham, because individual happiness is the purpose of life
    (D) Rousseau, because excessive inequality undermines freedom

16. According to Hobbes, which of the following characteristics is most important for members of a society?
    (A) Fortitude
    (B) Modesty
    (C) Knowledge
    (D) Apprehension

17. The concept of transcendental idealism is most often associated with
    (A) twentieth-century American philosophers.
    (B) nineteenth-century French philosophers.
    (C) eighteenth-century German philosophers.
    (D) seventeenth-century British philosophers.

18. Which of the following argued in *The Subjugation of Women* that women's equality benefits marital relationships?
    (A) Nozick
    (B) Noddings
    (C) Gilligan
    (D) Mill

19. According to Smith, which of the following is the best way to find happiness in life?
    (A) Share resources with others.
    (B) Accept life the way it is.
    (C) Refrain from showing emotion.
    (D) Focus on personal interests.

20. According to Locke, what should citizens do when ruled by an unjust political authority?
    (A) Resist and revolt.
    (B) Search for answers.
    (C) Submit to authority.
    (D) Accept the fate of nature.

21. Which of the following concepts is central to making ethical decisions for both Kant and Aristotle?
    (A) Authenticity
    (B) Transcendence
    (C) Consequences
    (D) Autonomy

22. Which of the following is associated with the Just War tradition?
    (A) Bentham
    (B) Aquinas
    (C) Gandhi
    (D) Socrates

23. Sophism most likely arose in Ancient Greece because of the
    (A) condemnation of Socrates.
    (B) war between Athens and Sparta.
    (C) opening of the Athens Academy.
    (D) growing democratic system.

24. For an Epicurean, the ethical evaluation of a decision to perform euthanasia will depend on whether the action will
    (A) adhere to the natural laws of the world.
    (B) avoid pain and increase happiness.
    (C) maximize utility for everyone.
    (D) lead to retribution from the gods.

25. Which of the following is the oldest monotheistic religion?
    (A) Islam
    (B) Judaism
    (C) Christianity
    (D) Buddhism

26. The idea that the universe is morally neutral is a concept related to
    (A) feminist ethics.
    (B) Indian philosophy.
    (C) natural law theories.
    (D) social contract theories.

27. Socrates was critical of all of the following EXCEPT
    (A) Sophists.
    (B) Athenian politics.
    (C) Athenian religious institutions.
    (D) Plato's Academy.

28. Which of the following writings develops the concept of the general will in society?

    (A) *Discourse on Political Economy* by Rousseau

    (B) *A Theory of Justice* by Rawls

    (C) *The Wealth of Nations* by Smith

    (D) *On Liberty* by Mill

29. According to Kant, all of the following are *a priori* concepts EXCEPT

    (A) substance.

    (B) causality.

    (C) morality.

    (D) space.

30. Which of the following was documented by Thucydides?

    (A) Peloponnesian War

    (B) Spartan War

    (C) Trojan War

    (D) Persian War

31. Which philosopher inspired the Philosophical Radicals?

    (A) Bentham

    (B) Hobbes

    (C) Locke

    (D) Kant

32. Which of the following would most likely disagree with the concept of redistributing wealth?

    (A) Hobbes, because it is an irrational concept

    (B) Rand, because of the personal sacrifices required

    (C) Rawls, because of the burden placed on some citizens

    (D) Kant, because of an individual's right to property

33. For a Kantian, the ethical evaluation of capital punishment mostly depends on

    (A) natural and civil laws.

    (B) assessing consequences.

    (C) long-term societal benefits.

    (D) developing a universal law.

34. Which of the following statements best explains ethical relativism?

    (A) Knowledge is derived from observations.

    (B) Every point of view is equally valid.

    (C) Reality consists of one substance.

    (D) Nothing in life actually matters.

35. A method used by Socrates to discuss philosophical issues by asking a series of questions is known as

    (A) deconstruction.

    (B) deduction.

    (C) dialectic.

    (D) dogma.

36. All of the following are assertions made by Locke in *Two Treatises of Government* EXCEPT

    (A) people have the right to own property.

    (B) people have the right to form militias.

    (C) people have the right to make their own choices.

    (D) people have the right to live without being harmed by others.

37. According to Rousseau, which of the following best explains why people commit crimes?

    (A) Society has corrupted them.

    (B) People are innately selfish.

    (C) People lack moral knowledge.

    (D) Natural laws encourage immorality.

38. Which of the following concepts are most closely associated with Hinduism and Buddhism?

    (A) Love and salvation

    (B) Laws and responsibilities

    (C) Obedience and remorse

    (D) Actions and duties

39. According to Mill, when does government have the moral authority to limit a person's freedom?

    (A) When pursuing national interests

    (B) All the time

    (C) When preventing harm to others

    (D) Never

40. According to Socrates, a man who robs a store at gunpoint is most likely

    (A) acting out of personal freedom.

    (B) immoral because he wants to be.

    (C) behaving in the way nature intended.

    (D) immoral because he lacks knowledge.

41. Which of the following best describes how Aquinas viewed nature?

    (A) As a way to understand humanity

    (B) As the ultimate source of life

    (C) As an accidental collection of atoms

    (D) As a way to draw close to God

42. Which of the following is the primary intention of social contract theory?

    (A) Rectifying historical wrongs

    (B) Creating harmony in society

    (C) Balancing natural and civil laws

    (D) Establishing racial equality

43. According to which of the following philosophers is it immoral to tax people's income?

    (A) Rawls, because income taxes burden the wealthy

    (B) Smith, because income taxes discourage productivity

    (C) Nozick, because income tax is equivalent to forced labor

    (D) Noddings, because income tax does not create equity

44. According to Gilligan, when a woman faces a moral decision she is most likely to

    (A) consider relationships.

    (B) minimize emotions.

    (C) apply standard rules.

    (D) assess ethical principles.

45. Which of the following believed that suicide was wrong unless the gods encouraged it?

    (A) Zeno

    (B) Plato

    (C) Socrates

    (D) Aristotle

46. All of the following philosophers advocated focusing on self-interests in life EXCEPT

    (A) Protagoras.

    (B) Pythagoras.

    (C) Smith.

    (D) Rand.

47. In *The Republic,* which of the following describes the character of kings?

    (A) Manipulative

    (B) Selfish

    (C) Loving

    (D) Wise

48. Which of the following statements is a core belief of Aristotle?
    (A) Change is a manmade process.
    (B) Virtue is a transcendent quality.
    (C) Everything in life has a purpose.
    (D) Wisdom brings contentment.

49. Which of the following thinkers believed that humans cannot change fate because absolute law rules the universe?
    (A) Aquinas
    (B) Epictetus
    (C) Gandhi
    (D) Epicurus

50. A concept in which citizens act as legislators to determine collectively the laws of a society is known as
    (A) distributive justice.
    (B) social constructivism.
    (C) social contract theory.
    (D) general will.

51. Which of the following questions would most likely be asked by a utilitarian when making an ethical decision about an affirmative action policy?
    (A) Will an affirmative action policy benefit more people than it will harm?
    (B) How does an affirmative action policy correspond with natural laws?
    (C) Will an affirmative action policy allocate resources fairly and equally?
    (D) What do the majority of people think about an affirmative action policy?

52. Which of the following is a similarity between Kant's categorical imperatives and utilitarianism?
    (A) Both are methods for addressing societal immorality.
    (B) Both are ways to conceptualize people and decisions.
    (C) Both are preventive techniques for avoiding immorality.
    (D) Both are masculine approaches to ethical decision making.

53. Which of the following was the main criticism against the Sophists?
    (A) Their disbelief in the existence of the gods
    (B) Their support of the ideas presented by Socrates
    (C) Their domination in the Athenian government
    (D) Their reliance on persuasion instead of truth

54. Which of the following best describes Plato's ideal state in *The Republic*?
    (A) A society ruled by a political tyrant
    (B) A society based upon political justice
    (C) A society ruled by the general will
    (D) A society based upon a social contract

55. Which of the following is a type of moral excellence according to Aristotle?
    (A) Gentleness
    (B) Wisdom
    (C) Reason
    (D) Skill

56. The Judeo-Christian view of how the universe was created contrasts most sharply with the view of which philosopher?

    (A) Aquinas

    (B) Rousseau

    (C) Locke

    (D) Epicurus

57. For a Hindu, the ethical evaluation of a decision to drill for oil in the Alaska wilderness depends on whether drilling

    (A) serves the self-interests of the citizens of Alaska.

    (B) causes minimal harm to citizens and the environment.

    (C) follows the desires of the majority of people in America.

    (D) reduces American dependency on foreign oil.

58. Which of the following is better known for his manner of teaching than his philosophy?

    (A) Plato

    (B) Aristotle

    (C) Socrates

    (D) Pythagoras

59. Which of the following thinkers provides the most pessimistic view of society?

    (A) Hobbes, because he views society as a violent and insecure place

    (B) Mill, because he views citizens as weak against the government

    (C) Rousseau, because he views the monarchy as untrustworthy

    (D) Locke, because he views citizens as immoral and irrational

60. Which of the following concepts is suggested in the works of Plato?

    (A) Creating and appreciating beauty leads to contentment.

    (B) Enlightened people receive their abilities from nature.

    (C) Courage and morality lead societies out of darkness.

    (D) Pursuing excellence helps attain peace in the world.

ANSWER KEY AND EXPLANATIONS

1. C	13. B	25. B	37. A	49. B
2. B	14. C	26. C	38. D	50. D
3. D	15. D	27. D	39. C	51. A
4. B	16. B	28. A	40. D	52. D
5. D	17. C	29. C	41. D	53. D
6. C	18. D	30. A	42. B	54. B
7. B	19. D	31. A	43. C	55. A
8. C	20. A	32. B	44. A	56. D
9. A	21. D	33. D	45. B	57. B
10. A	22. B	34. B	46. A	58. C
11. C	23. D	35. C	47. D	59. A
12. D	24. B	36. B	48. C	60. D

1. **The correct answer is (C).** Pythagoras was a pre-Socratic philosopher and mathematician who believed that numbers had a magical power in the world. Thucydides, choice (A), was a historian who wrote about the Peloponnesian War. Aristotle, choice (B), believed in maintaining balance in life to achieve happiness, a concept known as the golden mean, and wrote that virtue could only be attained by balancing courage, honesty, moderation, and reason. Heraclitus, choice (D), was a pre-Socratic philosopher who thought the world was made of fire.

2. **The correct answer is (B).** Rousseau and Hobbes are the most well-known Social Contract theorists, but Rawls revived the concept in the twentieth century. Social contract theory refers to the idea that the right to rule and the obligation to obey are based on an agreement between an individual and society. Therefore, choices (A), (C), and (D) are incorrect.

3. **The correct answer is (D).** The basis of morality for followers of Kant is whether the behavior is moral or immoral for all human beings according to universal moral laws. God, reason, and happiness are not important factors in ethical decisions based on Kant's philosophy, so choices (A), (B), and (C) are incorrect.

4. **The correct answer is (B).** Gandhi was a pacifist, and pacifists believe that war is never moral or justified. According to pacifists, war is an immoral method to attain a goal in all situations. In many cases, war brings freedom and is a rational choice, so choices (C) and (D) are incorrect. Wars can be self-serving if they are the only way to acquire land or other resources, so choice (A) is incorrect.

5. **The correct answer is (D).** Carol Gilligan's research showed that men have an ethics of justice in that they focus on applying rules and minimizing emotions in various situations. In contrast, women have an ethics of care, which means they consider relationships and responsibilities during the decision-making process.

6. **The correct answer is (C).** The concept that all events occur because of previous actions and the laws of

nature is determinism. Rationalism, choice (A), is the idea that knowledge can be gained without having experiences. Existentialism, choice (B), is the idea that people have to determine what life means. The philosophy of scholasticism, choice (D), combines logic with a belief in God.

7. **The correct answer is (B).** Involuntary euthanasia involves killing a patient against his or her will, which is considered murder in most cases. Passive euthanasia involves withholding treatment to allow a patient to die, while active euthanasia involves actively killing a patient, perhaps by lethal injection. Nonvoluntary euthanasia occurs when an incompetent patient undergoes euthanasia. Choices (A), (C), and (D) do not involve going against the will of the patient.

8. **The correct answer is (C).** Rawls asserted that economic inequality is justified only when it benefits everyone, such as to encourage people to be more productive. Sharing resources would bring about equality, so choice (A) is incorrect. Rawls might argue that choice (B) is a reason for equality. The lack of diversity is an argument used against equality, so choice (D) is incorrect.

9. **The correct answer is (A).** The Allegory of the Cave illustrates the idea that the world experienced through the senses is not the real world. The world can only truly be understood on an intellectual level. Plato believed that happiness could only be attained through virtue, so choice (B) is incorrect.

10. **The correct answer is (A).** The Old Testament, which is also known as the Hebrew Bible, is the ethical source for Judaism. Christians find ethical principles in both the Old Testament and the New Testament, which contains the teachings of Jesus Christ. Muslims turn to the words of the prophet Mohammed, so choice (C) is incorrect.

11. **The correct answer is (C).** Cosmogony is an Ancient Greek theory about the origin of the world. Cosmology refers to the study of the physical world, so choice (A) is incorrect. Sophists were teachers in Ancient Greece, and they are considered by some to be the first relativists.

12. **The correct answer is (D).** Stoicism finds self-control and reasoning the greatest virtues, and premarital sex most likely shows a lack of self-control. Stoics also advocated experiencing a passionless life. Moral egoism, choice (A), focuses on self-interests, which may or may not be gained through premarital sex. Hedonists approved of anything pleasurable, so choice (B) is incorrect. Choice (C) is incorrect.

13. **The correct answer is (B).** Kant evaluates the morality of actions in terms of categorical imperatives. Categorical imperatives are universal moral laws that act as the basis of practical reason. According to Kant, behavior conforms to a categorical imperative if it is moral for all human beings. Choices (A), (C), and (D) are incorrect.

14. **The correct answer is (C).** The statement "To each according to need" is an example of the principles of distributive justice. Distributive justice refers to the appropriate way of allocating benefits and obligations in a society. Retributive justice refers to what type of punishment is appropriate for a crime. Choices (B) and (D) are incorrect.

15. **The correct answer is (D).** Rousseau believed that an excessive degree of inequality destroys freedom if wealthy citizens act as tyrants in a society. Smith and Rand advocated moral egoism and the protection of personal rather than societal interests. Bentham believed people should improve happiness within society rather than increase personal happiness.

16. **The correct answer is (B).** According to Hobbes, traits like gratitude and modesty enable people to live harmoniously together in society. Hobbes viewed the world as insecure and violent, so most people felt apprehensive. Hobbes suggested submitting to a ruler and forming a social contract. Knowledge and fortitude are less important characteristics for getting along in the world envisioned by Hobbes.

17. **The correct answer is (C).** The concept of transcendental idealism is most often associated with eighteenth-century German philosophers, such as Kant. Kant and other German idealists of the time began viewing the world in terms of transcendence, or beyond the experience. Choices (A), (B), and (D) are incorrect.

18. **The correct answer is (D).** John Stuart Mill, the nineteenth-century British philosopher, wrote *The Subjugation of Women*. He used a utilitarian approach to argue in favor of women's equality, stating that an equal partnership benefits the institution of marriage. Gilligan, choice (C), and Noddings, choice (B), are feminist philosophers, and Nozick, choice (A), focused on distributive justice and individual rights.

19. **The correct answer is (D).** Focusing on personal interests is the way to find happiness in life according to Smith. As a moral egoist, Smith asserted that the happiness of oneself is more important than the happiness of others. Choices (B) and (C) describe Stoics.

20. **The correct answer is (A).** Locke asserted that people have the right to reject and resist any unjust political authority. Hobbes stated that failure to submit to an unjust ruler results in conflict. Stoics live their lives accepting what happens as fate.

21. **The correct answer is (D).** Both Kant and Aristotle placed significant value in autonomy during the decision-making process. Autonomy refers to the idea of informed consent or the freedom to make choices. Choice (B) is associated with Kant but not Aristotle. Consequences influence decisions made by utilitarians, so choice (C) is incorrect.

22. **The correct answer is (B).** St. Thomas Aquinas and the Roman Catholic Church are linked to the Just War tradition—that a war is just if it is declared by a competent authority, fought for a just cause, and fought with the right intentions. In addition, a war should match the provocation, be used as a last resort, and involve a reasonable chance of success. Choices (A), (C), and (D) are incorrect.

23. **The correct answer is (D).** The burgeoning democratic system in Ancient Greece most likely led to Sophism. The Sophists traveled around discussing politics and justice with the citizens of Athens, many of whom were required to participate in government. Choices (A) and (C) occurred after Sophism developed. The Peloponnesian War was less influential on Sophism than democracy.

24. **The correct answer is (B).** For an Epicurean, the ethical evaluation of a decision to perform euthanasia will depend on whether the action will avoid pain and increase happiness. Epicureans do not worry about retribution from the gods or nature, so choices (A) and (D) are incorrect. A utilitarian, not an Epicurean, would be concerned about maximizing utility for everyone.

25. **The correct answer is (B).** Judaism is the oldest monotheistic religion. Islam, choice (A), and Christianity, choice (C), are also monotheistic, but they are not as old as Judaism. Buddhism is not a monotheistic religion, so choice (D) is incorrect.

26. **The correct answer is (C).** The idea that the universe is morally neutral is a concept related to natural law theories. Natural law theories also assume that moral laws are part of nature. Social contract theories, feminist ethics, and Indian philosophies are not based on assumptions regarding a morally neutral universe.

27. **The correct answer is (D).** Plato's Academy was not established until after the death of Socrates. Socrates criticized the Sophists because he believed they were manipulative. Socrates also criticized Athenian politics and religious institutions, which was why he was eventually condemned. Therefore, choices (A), (B), and (C) are incorrect.

28. **The correct answer is (A).** Rousseau develops the idea of the general will in society in *Discourse on Political Economy*. Under general will, citizens act as legislators to determine as a collective body the laws and legislation of society. Choices (B), (C), and (D) are incorrect.

29. **The correct answer is (C).** Substance, causality, space, and time are the four categories of understanding that Kant refers to as *a priori* concepts. *A priori* means that the concepts occurred before a person existed. Therefore, choices (A), (B), and (D) are incorrect.

30. **The correct answer is (A).** Thucydides wrote *The History of the Peloponnesian War* as a report of the battle between Athens and Sparta that took place between 431 BC and 404 BC. Thucydides provided a graphic and exact account of military actions, which was a unique approach at the time. He was considered one of the first historians.

31. **The correct answer is (A).** Bentham, the utilitarian, inspired the Philosophical Radicals. The Radicals were a group of social reformers who advocated politics geared toward human happiness and universal male suffrage. Hobbes, Locke, and Kant were not utilitarians.

32. **The correct answer is (B).** Rand would most likely disagree with the concept of redistributing wealth because she believed that doing anything for another person sacrificed personal happiness. In addition, she objected to what she viewed as the weak exploiting the strong. Rawls, choice (C), was an advocate of distributive justice, so he would support wealth redistribution. Choices (A) and (D) are incorrect.

33. **The correct answer is (D).** A follower of Kant makes an ethical evaluation of capital punishment based on the development of a universal law. In other words, capital punishment is moral if it is moral for all human beings. A Kantian would focus less on

natural laws, civil laws, consequences, and long-term societal benefits.

34. **The correct answer is (B).** According to ethical relativism, every point of view is equally valid, and different people have different behavior standards. Choice (A) refers to empiricism, and choice (C) refers to monism, a theory held by pre-Socratic philosophers. Choice (D) describes stoicism.

35. **The correct answer is (C).** Socrates used a questioning method that later became known as the Socratic Method or dialectic. The method involves asking questions to draw out the truth from students to help them form their own insight about a topic. Choices (A), (B), and (D) are incorrect.

36. **The correct answer is (B).** In *Two Treatises of Government*, Locke asserts that people have three primary rights—life, liberty, and property. A modified version of these rights was included in the U.S. Declaration of Independence. The right to form militias is the Second Amendment to the U.S. Constitution, but it was not one of Locke's propositions.

37. **The correct answer is (A).** Rousseau asserted that people are born innately good but that the greed and corruption in society corrupts them, which rules out choice (B). The Greek philosophers believed that knowledge led to virtue, so choice (C) is incorrect. Rousseau did not blame natural laws for immorality, so choice (D) is incorrect.

38. **The correct answer is (D).** Hinduism and Buddhism are most closely linked to actions and duties, or karma and dharma. Karma is the idea that a person's actions determine the future. Dharma refers to the righteous duties a person has toward people and gods. Choices (A), (B), and (C) are less associated with Buddhism and Hinduism.

39. **The correct answer is (C).** As Mill wrote in the essay *On Liberty*, the government has the moral authority to limit a person's freedom only when harm may occur otherwise. In all other situations, people should be free to act as they choose. Choices (A), (B), and (D) are incorrect.

40. **The correct answer is (D).** According to Socrates, a man who robs a store at gunpoint is most likely immoral because he lacks knowledge. Socrates believed that virtue equaled knowledge, and wickedness resulted from ignorance. Choice (B) is incorrect because Socrates thought that people did not knowingly act with immorality. Nature and personal freedom were less significant factors in morality than knowledge.

41. **The correct answer is (D).** Aquinas viewed nature as a way to understand and draw close to God. Aquinas states that the laws discovered in nature stem from God. Aquinas attempted to understand the relationship between God and humanity, but he viewed nature as a way to understand God, not humans. Epicurus believed the universe was created by an accidental collision of atoms, so choice (C) is incorrect.

42. **The correct answer is (B).** Creating harmony in society is the primary intention of the social contract theory, which is the idea that the right to rule and the obligation to obey are based on an agreement between an individual and society. The moral code put forth in social contracts creates harmony because all parties work together for mutual advantage. Choices (A), (C), and (D) are not the main intentions of social contract theory.

43. **The correct answer is (C).** Nozick compared income taxes to forced labor.

Rawls advocated distributive justice, so he would probably think taxes are moral. Smith wrote about capitalism in *The Wealth of Nations,* but he does not indicate that taxes discourage productivity. Noddings has focused her work on the ethics of care.

44. **The correct answer is (A).** Gilligan found that women are more likely than men to consider responsibilities and relationships when making decisions. Men are more likely to minimize emotions and apply standard rules and principles when reaching a moral decision. Therefore, choices (B), (C), and (D) are incorrect.

45. **The correct answer is (B).** Plato stated that suicide is wrong unless the gods encourage it. He also indicated that if a person is facing disgrace or extreme hardship, suicide is not immoral. Aristotle, choice (D), stated that suicide is only acceptable if it is to avoid extreme hardship, but he did not write about the influence of the gods. Since Socrates, choice (C), did not write, it is unknown what he thought of suicide. Choice (A) is incorrect.

46. **The correct answer is (A).** Protagoras, the Sophist, thought that people should act in their own best interests without looking for wisdom from higher powers. Pythagoras, choice (B), was a mathematician and philosopher, and there is no indication that he advocated the promotion of his self-interests. Smith, choice (C), and Rand, choice (D), were both moral egoists who focused on improving their self-interests.

47. **The correct answer is (D).** In Plato's ideal republic, philosopher-kings rule society. Philosopher-kings are capable of understanding truth and justice and are guided by wisdom rather than self-interest. Manipulative, selfish, and loving are not characteristics of the philosopher-kings, so choices (A), (B), and (C) are incorrect.

48. **The correct answer is (C).** The idea that everything in life has a purpose was one of Aristotle's core beliefs. The other one is that change is both necessary and natural, so choice (A) is incorrect. Aristotle was extremely wise and learned, yet he continued to gain more knowledge, which means choice (D) is incorrect. Aristotle believed that virtue could be achieved through balance in life, so choice (B) is incorrect.

49. **The correct answer is (B).** Stoics, such as Epictetus, believe that human beings cannot change fate because absolute law rules the universe. Epicurus was a hedonist who believed the universe was created by atoms colliding accidentally, so choice (D) is incorrect. Aquinas, choice (A), was a Catholic priest who believed in God rather than fate. Hindus believe in many gods and karma rather than absolute law.

50. **The correct answer is (D).** According to Rousseau's concept of general will, citizens act as legislators to determine as a collective body the laws and legislation of society. Rousseau is a social contract theorist, but the definition is of general will rather than social contract theory.

51. **The correct answer is (A).** A utilitarian views issues in terms of consequences and results. A utilitarian will most likely ask choice (A) because the question addresses the benefits of the policy. Utilitarians are not concerned with natural laws, so choice (B) is incorrect. Choice (C) relates to a policy of distributive justice rather than utilitarianism. The opinion of the majority is insignificant to utilitarians, so choice (D) is incorrect.

52. **The correct answer is (D).** Both Kant's categorical imperative's and utilitarianism are masculine approaches to ethical decision making. Carol Gilligan researched how men and women make moral decisions, and men typically focus on rules, as with Kant's method and utilitarianism. Choices (A), (B), and (C) are not similarities between the two philosophies.

53. **The correct answer is (D).** Most of the criticism against the Sophists regarded their reliance on persuasion and manipulation instead of truth. The Sophists questioned the existence of the gods, but that was not a primary criticism against them. Socrates was the most vocal critic of the Sophists, so choice (B) is incorrect. The Sophists did not dominate the government, although they were influential.

54. **The correct answer is (B).** In *The Republic,* society is based on political justice. Democracy, which is similar to Rousseau's general will, and tyranny are replaced, so choices (A) and (C) are incorrect. The idea of a social contract was not developed until the seventeenth century, so choice (D) is incorrect.

55. **The correct answer is (A).** Gentleness is one of the moral virtues proposed by Aristotle in his book *Nicomachean Ethics.* Self-respect, bravery, truthfulness, and generosity are other moral virtues. Wisdom, reason, and skill are examples of intellectual virtues, so choices (B), (C), and (D) are incorrect.

56. **The correct answer is (D).** The Judeo-Christian view of how the universe was created contrasts most sharply with the view of Epicurus. Epicurus believed that the universe was created by an accidental collision of atoms. The Judeo-Christian belief is that God created the universe. Aquinas was a Catholic priest, so choice (A) is incorrect. Both Locke and Rousseau were Christians, so choices (B) and (C) are incorrect.

57. **The correct answer is (B).** A Hindu would base a decision to drill for oil in the Alaska wilderness on the amount of harm it would cause. Hinduism advocates choosing actions that cause the least amount of harm, which in this case involves people and the environment. The opinion of the majority and self-interests would not be relevant factors in the decision-making process.

58. **The correct answer is (C).** Socrates is better known for his method of teaching than for a specific philosophy. Socrates employed what is now known as the Socratic Method, which involves asking a student a series of questions in order to draw out the truth. Plato and Aristotle are both highly regarded for their philosophies, so choices (A) and (B) are incorrect. Pythagoras was better known as a mathematician, so choice (D) is incorrect.

59. **The correct answer is (A).** Hobbes holds the most pessimistic view of society, which he considers savage and full of conflict. He developed the social contract theory because he felt it was better for people to surrender some of their rights for the protection offered by a society. Rousseau, choice (C), and Locke, choice (D), were also social contract theorists, but they did not view the world as such a violent place like their peer. Mill, choice (B), was a utilitarian who believed that the government had very limited moral authority over people.

60. The correct answer is (D). Plato believed in pursuing personal excellence to achieve peace in a troubled world. During Plato's time, many people believed beauty equaled virtue, but Plato believed enlightenment gained from knowledge was the key to virtue. Although the soldiers in Plato's republic are courageous and moral, the wise philosopher is the ruler, which means choice (C) is incorrect.

SUMMING IT UP

- Ethics refers to the academic discipline of analyzing morality. Reasoning, rules, and logic form the basis of ethical philosophy.

- Since at least 1200 BC, myths provided explanations for virtually everything in Greek life. Change occurred in the sixth century when philosophers questioned the natural world, and theories of cosmology and cosmogony developed. Cosmology is the study of the physical world—what it is made of and how it works. Cosmogony is the study of the origin of the universe—how it came into existence.

- Pythagoras, one of the most notable pre-Socratic philosophers, was also a mathematician and a cosmologist. No writings of his exist, but evidence shows his philosophy was based on beliefs in the magic of numbers and reincarnation.

- The Sophists were traveling teachers who lectured about various topics for fees. Protagoras, a well-respected Sophist, is best known for stating, "Man is the measure of all things," suggesting that people rather than nature determine behavior.

- Thucydides, a Greek historian, wrote *The History of the Peloponnesian War* as a report of the battle between Athens and Sparta (431–404 BC). He objectively presented factual events and questioned the ethics of war.

- Socrates lived in Athens during the fifth century BC. An outspoken critic of the Sophists, and Athenian politics and religious institutions, he believed that virtue equaled knowledge and that a person who is knowledgeable about morality will behave with morality.

- Socrates' most famous student, Plato, was a philosopher and mathematician. After Socrates' death, Plato established the Academy in 387 BC. His most influential work, *The Republic,* examines whether it is always better to be just than unjust.

- Aristotle, a renowned student of Plato's Academy, was a philosopher and an authority on nearly every subject. Aristotle believed everything had a purpose and change is both necessary and natural.

- Stoicism is a philosophy based on the idea that absolute law rules the universe and that humans cannot change fate. Epictetus was one of the most prominent Stoics of the second century AD.

- Around 300 BC, hedonism or Epicureanism emerged under the guidance of Epicurus who asserted that happiness was the purpose of life and that the universe was created by an accidental collision of atoms rather than by Greek gods.

- The Bible has been the most popular tool for teaching morality in the Western world and serves as the center point for Judeo-Christian ethics.

- The major world religions include Christianity, Judaism, Islam, Hinduism, and Buddhism. Judaism, Christianity, and Islam are monotheistic religions—believing in only one god rather than multiple gods.

- Hinduism and Buddhism share the concepts of karma and dharma. Karma is the principle that a person's actions determine what happens to them in the future and in future reincarnations. Dharma refers to the righteous duties of a person toward people and gods.

- Natural law theories are based on the idea that the moral standards guiding human behavior originate in human nature and the universe and deviating from the norm is immoral, sinful, evil, and harmful. Many medieval philosophers adopted natural law theories to explain the relationship between God and man, including St. Thomas Aquinas, who believed that faith and reason could exist together.

- Social contract theory refers to the idea that the right to rule and the obligation to obey are based upon an agreement, a moral code, between an individual and society. Thomas Hobbes, John Locke, and Jean-Jacques Rousseau wrote about social contract theory during the seventeenth and eighteenth centuries.

- John Rawls and Robert Nozick, twentieth-century American philosophers, were known for their ideas regarding political philosophy.

- Transcendental idealism, a concept most often associated with eighteenth-century German philosophers, such as Immanuel Kant, contends that appearances should be viewed as only representations and not as things themselves—that both the mind and understanding create reality.

- Adam Smith, a founder of capitalism, proposed that the common good of society advances when individuals focus on benefiting themselves, a concept related to the theory of moral egoism.

- Ayn Rand, twentieth-century Russian philosopher and moral egoist, asserted that pursuing self-interests and personal happiness are "the highest moral purpose" of life.

- Utilitarianism (Consequentialism): The theory that actions are morally acceptable if good consequences outweigh bad consequences. Utilitarian philosophers include Jeremy Bentham and John Stuart Mill. Determinism asserts that thoughts, behaviors, and decisions happen because previous events and the laws of nature determine them.

- Feminism: The philosophical and political discourse aimed at exposing, analyzing, and addressing sexual inequality. Feminist philosophy emerged in the 1960s.

- Psychologist Carol Gilligan asserts that women and men have different approaches to making moral decisions—men focus on applying rules and minimizing emotions, and women appeal to emotions such as sympathy, love, and concern.

- Philosopher Nel Noddings studies the concept of ethics of care, focusing on the origins of care within the home, such as parent-child relationships.

- Current ethical issues include morality and sexuality, abortion, suicide, euthanasia, economic inequality, affirmative action, crime and punishment, war and peace, and environmental ethics.

Introduction to Computing

OVERVIEW

- **Diagnostic test**
- **Answer key and explanations**
- **Computers: history and the basics**
- **Software: system and application**
- **Software copyrights and licenses**
- **Software development**
- **Networks, communication, and security**
- **Computers and everyday life**
- **Post-test**
- **Answer key and explanations**
- **Summing it up**

DIAGNOSTIC TEST

Directions: Carefully read each of the following 20 questions. Choose the best answer to each question and circle your answer choice. The Answer Key and Explanations can be found following this Diagnostic Test.

1. What term describes application software that is free to use on a trial basis?
   - **(A)** Commercial
   - **(B)** System
   - **(C)** Open source
   - **(D)** Shareware

2. Which of the following networks is typically limited to a single office building?
   - **(A)** WAN
   - **(B)** PAN
   - **(C)** MAN
   - **(D)** LAN

3. Which of the following involved the use of the first digital computer?
   - **(A)** World War I
   - **(B)** World War II
   - **(C)** Korean War
   - **(D)** Vietnam War

4. What is the term for a utility program that is used to block certain Web sites from children?
   - **(A)** Defragmenter
   - **(B)** Antivirus
   - **(C)** Filtering
   - **(D)** Backup

5. What is the term for sending fraudulent e-mails intending to fool users into revealing personal information?
   (A) Phishing
   (B) Encrypting
   (C) Streaming
   (D) Hacking

6. Which stage of the software life cycle usually involves testing the software?
   (A) Investigation
   (B) Analysis
   (C) Development
   (D) Design

7. What is the term for a tiny piece of silicon containing electronic circuits that serves as the CPU of personal computers?
   (A) Server
   (B) Hard disk
   (C) Peripheral
   (D) Microprocessor

8. What is the term for software that allows multiple users to collaborate on a project and share data?
   (A) Groupware
   (B) Freeware
   (C) Shareware
   (D) Demoware

9. Which of the following is a malicious program that repeatedly copies itself into a computer's memory?
   (A) Worm
   (B) Spam
   (C) Firewall
   (D) Key logger

10. ARPANET was developed in
    (A) 1959.
    (B) 1969.
    (C) 1979.
    (D) 1989.

11. Which of the following computers is built into devices such as digital cameras and MP3 players?
    (A) Supercomputer
    (B) Microcontroller
    (C) Microcomputer
    (D) Mainframe

12. Which of the following security tools requires a person's fingerprint before allowing computer access?
    (A) Biometrics
    (B) Encryption
    (C) Firewall
    (D) Password

13. Which of the following is a program that enables peripherals to communicate with a computer system?
    (A) Utility software
    (B) Operating system
    (C) Device driver
    (D) User interface

14. Which of the following licensing agreements is displayed on the screen during software installation?
    (A) Shrink-wrap
    (B) End-user
    (C) Multiple-user
    (D) Single-user

15. What is the term for a full-duplex device that connects computers to a network?
    (A) Hub
    (B) Node
    (C) Switch
    (D) Gateway

16. Which programming language is the oldest one used for business- and finance-related systems?

    (A) COBOL

    (B) BASIC

    (C) NOMAD

    (D) FORTRAN

17. Which of the following is a textual portrayal of a writer's mood or intention often used in e-mails?

    (A) Handshaking

    (B) Netiquette

    (C) Emoticon

    (D) Blog

18. What is the term for the process of loading an operating system into the main memory of the computer?

    (A) Booting

    (B) Queuing

    (C) Spooling

    (D) Multitasking

19. What is the term for the temporary holding location for data and the operating system while the computer is on?

    (A) ROM

    (B) BMP

    (C) RAM

    (D) JPEG

20. What is the term for the address of a Web site?

    (A) URL

    (B) WWW

    (C) UNIX

    (D) HTML

diagnostic test

ANSWER KEY AND EXPLANATIONS

1. D	5. A	9. A	13. C	17. C
2. D	6. C	10. B	14. B	18. A
3. B	7. D	11. B	15. C	19. C
4. C	8. A	12. A	16. A	20. A

1. **The correct answer is (D).** Shareware is software available at no cost on a trial basis. Users must pay to continue using shareware at the end of the trial. Commercial software costs money. System software manages the computer system and is not application software. Open source software may be free or sold, but it is not typically used on a trial basis.

2. **The correct answer is (D).** Local area networks (LAN) serve limited geographical areas, such as single office buildings. Wide area networks (WAN) cover entire countries, so choice (A) is incorrect. Personal area networks (PAN) are very short range, so choice (B) is incorrect. Metropolitan area networks (MAN) typically cover 50-mile areas, so they would be able to serve more than one building.

3. **The correct answer is (B).** The first digital computers were designed for World War II. The military used the computers to calculate missile trajectories and to break enemy codes. Digital computers were not used during WWI, and they were already in full use by the time of the Korean and Vietnam Wars.

4. **The correct answer is (C).** Filtering software is a utility used to prevent children from viewing inappropriate Web sites. Defragmenter utilities find and reorganize the scattered files on a hard drive to speed up operation. Antivirus utilities block viruses, spam, and pop-ups. Backup utilities make copies of a system's hard drive.

5. **The correct answer is (A).** Phishing refers to sending fraudulent e-mails intending to fool users into revealing personal information. Encrypting is a method of protecting a computer or network. Streaming is a method for moving data so that it can be processed as a steady and continuous stream, as in streaming audio and video. Hackers often break into computers and networks for the challenge, but they are not necessarily associated with fraudulent e-mails. Crackers are the individuals who break into systems for malicious reasons.

6. **The correct answer is (C).** The development stage of the software life cycle usually involves testing. Investigation relates to conducting a cost/benefit analysis of developing the software. Analysis calls for gathering and analyzing data. In the design stage, software engineers build a prototype.

7. **The correct answer is (D).** A microprocessor chip is a small piece of silicon that contains millions of tiny electronic circuits. The microprocessor acts as the central processing unit (CPU) of personal computers. A server is a computer that processes requests from other computers, so choice (A) is incorrect. Choices (B) and (C) are incorrect.

8. **The correct answer is (A).** Groupware allows multiple users to collaborate on a project and share data. Freeware is free software, so choice (B) is incorrect. Demoware and shareware

are both available either for a limited basis or with limited features.

9. **The correct answer is (A).** Worms are malicious programs that repeatedly copy themselves into a system's memory, causing crashes. Choices (B) and (C) are both security problems for computer users, but neither makes numerous copies. A firewall is a security measure that attempts to protect systems from worms and viruses.

10. **The correct answer is (B).** The U.S. Department of Defense developed ARPANET in 1969, and the small network was the starting point for today's Internet. ARPANET consisted of four linked computers at different university campuses and defense contractor offices. Choices (A), (C), and (D) are incorrect.

11. **The correct answer is (B).** Microcontrollers, or embedded computers, are tiny microprocessors built into the devices that they control, such as digital cameras, cars, and MP3 players. A microcomputer is the same as a personal computer, so choice (C) is incorrect. Choices (A) and (D) are large and expensive.

12. **The correct answer is (A).** Biometrics uses physical attributes like fingerprints, voices, faces, or eyes to confirm an individual's identity. Encryption involves scrambling data to prevent unauthorized access. Firewalls shield computers from intruders by filtering incoming and outgoing packets. Passwords are unique codes that restrict access.

13. **The correct answer is (C).** A device driver is a software program that enables peripheral devices, such as printers and sound cards, to communicate with a computer system. Utility software enables users to monitor and configure the settings of hardware, application software, and the operating system. The operating system manages files, tasks, and security, while user interfaces enable users and computers to communicate.

14. **The correct answer is (B).** The end-user license agreement (EULA) is displayed on the screen during installation of the software. Choice (A) appears on the package. Choices (C) and (D) are types of licensing agreements, but they are not specifically displayed on the screen during installation.

15. **The correct answer is (C).** A switch is a full-duplex device that connects computers to a network. Full-duplex devices transmit data back and forth at the same time. Hubs are half-duplex devices that transmit data one direction at a time. Nodes are the devices that attach to networks, like PCs and printers. A gateway is an interface that allows different types of networks to communicate.

16. **The correct answer is (A).** COBOL, one of the oldest programming languages, is used in business systems. BASIC serves as a teaching tool, so choice (B) is incorrect. FORTRAN is an old language used for science and engineering applications. NOMAD is a problem-oriented language not commonly used for business systems.

17. **The correct answer is (C).** Emoticons, such as smiley faces, are textual portrayals of a writer's mood or intention used in e-mails. Emoticons are an example of netiquette, or Internet etiquette, so choice (B) is incorrect. Handshaking is a process that enables two network devices to communicate.

18. **The correct answer is (A).** Booting refers to the sequence of events that

loads an operating system into the main memory of the computer. Choices (B) and (C) are terms used for CPU task management. Multitasking occurs when two or more programs run at nearly the same time on one computer.

19. **The correct answer is (C).** Random access memory (RAM) is the temporary holding location for data, software instructions, and the operating system while the computer is on. ROM (read-only memory) contains a computer's fixed startup instructions.

Choices (B) and (D) are both format terms for bitmap files.

20. **The correct answer is (A).** The URL (Uniform Resource Locator) is the unique address of a Web page. WWW is the World Wide Web, so choice (B) is incorrect. UNIX is a server operating system, so choice (C) is incorrect. HTML (Hypertext Markup Language) is the format used to specify the layout of Web pages.

COMPUTERS: HISTORY AND THE BASICS

During World War II, engineers designed the first digital computers to help calculate missile flights and break enemy codes. By the next decade, computers were assisting large businesses with managing payroll and inventory. However, the computers of the 1940s and 1950s filled up entire rooms and were too costly for individuals or small businesses. Over the years, engineers developed smaller computer components. Transistors and then integrated circuits replaced the vacuum tubes installed in the early computers. By the mid-1970s, Apple was selling personal computers, but a lack of software made most consumers leery of spending $2400 for the Apple II. Eventually software caught up to hardware, and computers replaced typewriters and mechanical calculators in many businesses and homes. Since the early 1980s, the number of U.S. households that own computers has increased from 10 percent to over 60 percent today. In addition, more than 70 percent of adults in the United States regularly use the Internet. Computers continue to become smaller and more powerful every year, and their uses are nearly endless. Understanding computer hardware, software, and networks is essential to success in the twenty-first century.

Computer Terminology

Computers serve numerous purposes—accepting input, processing data, storing data, and producing output. Being familiar with basic terminology helps one understand how computers function, make purchasing decisions, and troubleshoot problems.

Basic Computer Terms

CPU	Central processing unit that manipulates data
File	Collection of data given a specific name; may be stored on a hard disk, CD, DVD, or flash drive
Hardware	Equipment and machinery in a computer, such as the keyboard, screen, and the CPU
Input	Information placed into a computer through a device like a keyboard, thermostat, mouse, camera, or microphone
Microprocessor chip	Small piece of silicon that holds millions of tiny electronic circuits; serves as CPU of most computers; can be programmed to perform certain tasks
Motherboard	Main circuit board of a computer; also known as the system board; includes ports or connections to which the keyboard, mouse, and printer are attached; processor and memory chips are also attached to the motherboard; includes expansion slots for adding additional circuit boards, such as for video or sound
Network	Communication system
Output	Results generated by a computer, such as reports, graphs, and pictures that are provided by an output device like a screen or a printer

Peripheral device	Components or equipment that expand or enhance the input, output, and storage functions of a computer; includes printers, disk drives, scanners, joysticks, speakers, and digital cameras
RAM	Random access memory; temporary or working storage that holds data, software instructions, and the operating system for quick access; also known as primary storage or memory
Software	Programs that instruct computers how to perform specific tasks
Storage	Area where data is left permanently in files when not needed for processing; a hard disk drive inside a PC serves as the main storage device; also known as secondary storage

Computers require processing and memory components in order to function. The case or system unit holds the motherboard, microprocessor chip, memory, power supply, storage devices, and a fan to prevent overheating.

Data Representation

The symbols a computer uses to represent facts and ideas, such as names, numbers, or colors, are data. Computers convert data into signals, marks, or binary digits that electronic circuitry is able to understand. The format in which data is stored, processed, and transmitted is known as data representation.

The electronic circuitry of computers requires the use of certain units of measurement. Computers use the binary number system, or base-2 number system. In the binary number system there are only two digits—0 and 1. Such a system enables computers to represent nearly any number with 0s and 1s. A group of 8 binary digits is a byte, which is abbreviated with a capital B. A kilobyte (KB) equals 1,024 bytes and refers to small computer files. A megabyte (MB) is approximately 1 million bytes, and a gigabyte (GB) is approximately 1 billion bytes. Megabytes are typically used to describe the size of medium to large computer files. Gigabytes are most often used when referring to a computer's storage capacity.

Types of Computers

Engineers build computers in a variety of sizes and shapes, and each type serves a particular function. While most people are familiar with personal computers because they use them at home or at work, it is important to have a general understanding of the other types of computers that serve useful purposes in the world.

Types of Computers

Supercomputer	High-capacity machine with thousands of microprocessors; fastest and most expensive type; able to process trillions of calculations every second; used for weather forecasting, physical simulations, and image processing
Mainframe computer	Large, fast, and expensive computer typically used by large organizations, such as banks, airlines, universities, and government agencies; used to process, store, and manage large quantities of data; accessed from a computer terminal
Workstation	Expensive and powerful personal computer (PC) designed for specific, complex tasks like medical imaging or computer-aided design (CAD); term also used to refer to a PC connected to a network
Microcomputer	Computing device with a microprocessor intended to meet needs of individuals; also known as personal computers or PCs; capable of handling e-mail, word processing, photo editing, and other applications; available as laptops, desktops, or handheld computers; may be connected to a computer network
Microcontroller	Tiny, specialized microprocessor built into the device it controls; also known as an embedded computer; used in automobiles, MP3 players, digital cameras, and electronic appliances

Another type of computer with a specific purpose is the network server. A server is a central computer that serves the computers on a client/server network by supplying data and storage. Servers process requests from other computers when database access is needed. The clients are the PCs, workstations, or other digital devices that request data from the server. Small organizations use servers to store files and transmit e-mail, while large organizations store sizeable quantities of financial and product information on their servers. Servers allow multiple users to share equipment, data, and software. Any supercomputer, mainframe, workstation, or PC can be modified into a network server because servers do not require particular hardware.

Memory

Random access memory (RAM) is a temporary holding location for data, software instructions, and the operating system while the computer is running. When a person opens a word processing document, a copy of that file moves from the hard disk to RAM. As the person makes changes to the document, changes are made to the RAM copy rather than the version in the hard drive. As soon as the document is saved, the changed version moves from RAM back to the hard drive. Saving should occur frequently because RAM is volatile, which means RAM needs electrical power to hold data. Data in RAM is immediately and permanently lost when a computer's power is shut off.

Personal computers are installed with different amounts of RAM, which is measured in megabytes or gigabytes. The amount of RAM needed for a personal computer depends on the software. A number of RAM chips are included in most personal computers:

- DRAM: Dynamic RAM; dynamic means that it needs to be refreshed constantly by the CPU, or its contents are lost
- SDRAM: Synchronous dynamic RAM; synchronized by the system clock and faster than DRAM
- SRAM: Static RAM; faster than DRAM and holds on to its contents without needing to be refreshed by the CPU
- DDR-SDRAM: Double-data rate synchronous dynamic RAM; the newest and most popular RAM chip

Besides RAM, there are three other primary types of memory chips in computers. Read-only memory (ROM) chips contain a computer's fixed startup instructions loaded at the factory. The instructions in ROM cannot be erased, and ROM chips are not volatile like RAM chips. CMOS (complementary metal-oxide semiconductor) chips are battery powered, so they do not lose their contents when power is interrupted. CMOS chips hold flexible startup instructions kept up to date when the computer is not on, such as time and date. Flash memory chips store flexible programs in computers, cell phones, digital cameras, and MP3 players. Flash memory chips, which are nonvolatile, can be erased and reprogrammed.

SOFTWARE: SYSTEM AND APPLICATION

Software provides electronic instructions to computers regarding the way to perform a specific task. Two types of software exist—system software and application software.

System Software

System software serves as the link between the user, the application software, and the computer hardware. Operating systems, user interfaces, device drivers, and utility programs are four primary elements related to system software.

Operating Systems

The operating system controls activities occurring within the computer system and affects how a person is able to use a computer. Microsoft Windows and Mac OS are the operating systems most frequently installed into personal computers, while Linux is a popular system for servers. Numerous operating systems exist including UNICOS, Unix, and BeOS, and each one is intended for use with specific computers. A computer's hardware is designed to accept only one kind of operating system.

The operating system of a computer interfaces with software, peripheral devices, and hardware, and it manages all of the hardware resources of the computer. A computer resource is any component that handles tasks, including the microprocessor, memory, storage, and peripheral devices like scanners and printers. The operating system works at specific tasks that typically go unnoticed but are critical to the performance of a computer:

- Booting
- CPU management
- File management
- Task management
- Security management

A computer's operating system first gets to work when the computer is turned on and the system is booted. Booting refers to the sequence of events that occur to load an operating system into the main memory of the computer. Operating systems are very large, so they are stored in the hard disk. The center module of the operating system is the kernel, and it manages memory, processes, tasks, and storage devices while the computer is on. The rest of the operating system stays in ROM until needed for specific tasks. The boot process involves six steps to obtain the operating system from the hard disk and load it into the computer's RAM:

1. Distribute power to the computer circuitry
2. Start bootstrap program stored in ROM that is used to load the operating system
3. Activate diagnostic tests of various components
4. Identify peripheral devices connected to the computer
5. Load operating system onto RAM from hard drive
6. Check configurations and execute any specialized startup routine

In addition to booting the computer, the operating system manages the central processing unit (CPU). The operating system monitors the main memory for the locations of programs and data. Only the essential data and programs stay in the main memory; the rest move to secondary storage until needed. Data and programs wait in queues, or lines, before processing occurs. Buffers are disk areas where programs or documents wait. For example, a print job is spooled, or placed, into a buffer where it waits in a queue for its turn with the printer.

Operating systems also manage files, tasks, and security. The operating system records the location of data files and program files, and it enables users to copy, rename, move, and delete files as needed. Organizing files into directories, subdirectories, and paths can also be accomplished through the operating system. Task management refers to the ability of the operating system to perform different tasks, such as storing, printing, and calculating. Most operating systems enable users to use more than one program at a time, such as typing information into a spreadsheet and listening to a music CD. This ability of an operating system to execute two or more programs by one user on one processor nearly at the same time is termed multitasking. An operating system also enables users to control security of their computers by requiring user names and passwords.

User Interfaces

A user interface is the hardware and software that enables users and computers to interact. A computer's user interface includes hardware, such as the monitor, mouse, and keyboard, and software mechanisms, such as icons, menus, and toolbars. In the past, computers used command-line interface to link users and computers. A command-line interface requires users to type commands in order to run programs. Today, computers have graphical user interfaces (GUI). GUI allows users to choose icons or commands from menus with a mouse or a keyboard.

Device Drivers

A device driver is a specialized software program that enables peripheral devices to communicate with a computer system. Device drivers are utilized by numerous peripherals—printers, monitors, graphics cards, sound cards, modems, mice, and scanners. After it has been installed, a device driver starts automatically when needed and runs in the background without opening a window.

Utility Programs

Utility programs help users monitor and configure the settings for computer hardware, application software, and the operating system. Diagnostic and maintenance tools, setup wizards, and security software are types of utility programs. Computers typically come with pre-installed utility programs, but utility programs may also be purchased separately. Most utility software programs focus on one specific task:

- Antivirus software, such as McAfee Virus Scan, is a popular method of dealing with viruses, pop-up ads, and spam.

- Filtering software, such as Net Nanny, is a type of utility used by parents to prevent children from accessing inappropriate Web sites.

- Backup utilities make duplicate copies of a system's hard disk in case of hard drive failure.

- Data recovery utilities restore damaged or corrupted data caused by viruses or hardware failures.

- Data compression utilities, such as ZipIt and WinZip, eliminate unneeded data and gaps in a computer's storage space, so that less space is required.

- Defragmenter utilities find and reorganize the scattered files on a hard drive to speed up operation.

Application Software

Application software is any computer program that enables a user to perform a certain task, such as word processing or desktop publishing. Since people use computers for a multitude of purposes, there are many different kinds of applications software available, including entertainment software, education software, and specialty software such as drawing, publishing, and computer-aided design. Productivity software refers to any application software that improves the work efficiency of users. Examples of productivity software include word processing, spreadsheets, desktop publishing, and database managers. At times, productivity software is bundled together into a single package, such as Microsoft Office. In other cases, software companies sell productivity software as groupware, which is software that allows multiple users to work together on a project and share data and other resources.

Word Processing Software

Word processing software enables users to create, edit, format, print, and store documents such as reports, letters, memos, and manuscripts. As the most commonly used software application, word processors easily replaced typewriters decades ago. Although numerous word processing programs are available, Microsoft Word stands out as the one most commonly utilized.

The act of creating a word processing document involves entering text into the computer via the keyboard or through the diction function, if speech-recognition software is in use. The cursor, scrolling, and word wrap help users easily create documents with word processing software. The movable symbol on the display screen is the cursor. The cursor, which usually blinks, indicates the insertion point where text may be entered. Moving quickly up and down through text is known as scrolling. Word wrap is an automatic function that wraps text around to the next line when the user reaches the right margin.

Editing documents is simple with the numerous features offered by word processing software:

- Insert/Delete: Adding or inserting text can be done with the *Insert* key or by moving the cursor to a specific location. Deleting or removing text can be accomplished with the *Delete* or *Backspace* key.

- Find/Replace: Locate a word, phrase, or number with the *Find* or *Search* function. The *Replace* command enables users to replace a word, phrase, or number automatically with something else.

- Cut/Copy and Paste: Move text with *Copy* or *Cut* to the clipboard, a holding area in memory, and then use *Paste* to relocate the text somewhere else.

- Spelling Checker: This tests for incorrectly spelled words, which are indicated by a wavy line in Word.

- Grammar Checker: Grammar mistakes are highlighted but not automatically corrected.

- Thesaurus: On-screen thesaurus lists synonyms.

- Readability Formula: This analyzes the reading level of a document based on sentence length and vocabulary.

Word processing applications are also useful in modifying the appearance of text, a function known as formatting. Templates and wizards are the two primary formatting tools in word processing software. Templates serve as preformatted style guides for structuring a document. Wizards are interactive utilities programs that lead users through steps to format a certain type of document, such as a memo or a résumé. Additional formatting tools include font size and style, spacing, margins, headers, footers, page numbers, and tables. Most word processing applications have default settings automatically implemented unless the user overrides them.

The features available in most word processing programs are virtually endless. For example, the mail merge function automates the process of making customized documents by combining mailing list information with a form letter. The software is capable of numbering and positioning footnotes and generating indexes and tables of contents. Desktop publishing software is an advanced version of word processing that offers sophisticated graphic and design features. Software applications such as Print Shop and Adobe InDesign enable users to create professional-grade newsletters and brochures.

Spreadsheet Software

Spreadsheet software, such as Microsoft Excel, enables users to enter numerical data and formulas into rows and columns. The software then performs calculations based on the provided information to create tables. While spreadsheet software was originally popular among accountants and financial managers, it has since developed a following among other professions. The software is useful for creating budgets, balancing checkbooks, estimating costs, and maintaining a grade book. An especially helpful tool in spreadsheets is the what-if analysis. Users employ the recalculation function to see how changing one or more variables affects the outcome of the equation. For example, a user might wonder what a monthly car payment would be with different interest rates. By making changes to the interest rate and then recalculating, the user can see the effect on the monthly payment. With more than 16 million cells on every worksheet, electronic spreadsheets are extremely useful tools, and it is important to understand their specific terminology.

Spreadsheet Terms

Cell	Location where a row and a column intersect
Cell address	Cell's position as designated by the column letter and row number
Formula	Instructions for calculations
Function	Built-in formula provided by software
Label	Text used to describe data
Range	Groups of cells next to each other
Values	Numbers or dates entered into a cell

In addition, spreadsheet software typically offers analytical graphics capabilities. Analytical graphics, or business graphics, are graphical forms, such as bar charts, line graphs, and pie charts that present data visually and enhance data comprehension.

Database Software

A database is a collection of data stored on any type of computer. A wide range of information may be included in a database, such as inventory, addresses, and customer names. Databases organize interrelated files by common elements to simplify the process of retrieving data. Database software, such as Microsoft Access and FileMaker Pro, allow users to enter, locate, organize, and update information. Database software enhances data accuracy, reduces data repetition, and increases security.

Relational databases organize data into related tables with rows and columns. The columns are fields that contain one item of data. The rows are records that hold data for a single unit, which may be a person, place, thing, or event. A record is a complete set of fields. For example, a retail store's database contains a record of the contact information for each customer. Within each record are the separate fields—last name, first name, and address.

The ability to locate records efficiently is the chief benefit of database software. In order to find one record out of the thousands in a database, a user enters a query, which is a set of key words and commands describing the needed information. Database software provides at least one of the following methods for making queries:

- Structured query language (SQL): set of command words to instruct the computer to locate, sort, or modify data

- Natural language query: query constructed in human instead of machine language

- Query by example: provide examples of the data being sought

Four other types of databases exist in addition to relational databases—hierarchical, network, object-oriented, and multidimensional. The oldest database format is the hierarchical database in which fields and records are arranged in related groups similar to a family tree with lower-level (child) records subordinate to higher-level (parent) records. Network databases resemble hierarchical databases except each lower-level record can have more than one higher-level record. Object-oriented databases are used most often in manufacturing or scientific settings. Two types of object-oriented databases include hypertext databases with text links to other documents and hyper-media databases with links to graphics, audio, and video. Multidimensional databases are useful in analyzing large amounts of data that can be grouped in more than two dimensions. For example, data regarding country, year, and product could be placed into a three-dimensional data cube.

Specialty Software

A number of specialty software programs are available on the market, including graphics software and presentation software. Graphics software helps users create, manipulate, and print graphics such as drawings, photographs, and images that appear on a computer screen. Image editing software, or paint software, provides users with electronic pens, brushes, and paints to create images on a computer screen. The size, brightness, and quality of photographs can be adjusted with photo-editing software like Adobe Photoshop. Drawing software like Adobe Illustrator offers lines, shapes, and colors that can be manipulated to create diagrams, logos, and other images. Computer-aided design (CAD) software is a type of 3-D graphics software used by architects and engineers to create product specifications and design blueprints.

A particularly useful tool in the workplace is presentation software, which uses graphics, sound, data, and animation for visual presentations. Microsoft PowerPoint is a presentation graphics software frequently used during sales presentations and lectures. Each page of a presentation is a slide, so live sessions are slide shows. However, the software offers the capability of printing the slides on paper, placing the presentation on the Web, or transferring the presentation as an electronic file.

SOFTWARE COPYRIGHTS AND LICENSES

Certain legal restrictions apply to both purchased and free computer software. A copyright gives the software's creator the exclusive right to copy, distribute, sell, and modify the software. A software license is a legal contract defining the way in which a program may be used. There are various types of software licenses:

- Single-user license: limits use of the software to one person at a time
- Site license: may be used on all computers at a specific location and is purchased for a flat fee
- Multiple-user license: price based on the number of users; specified number of users may use the software at any given time
- Concurrent-use license: priced per copy; specific number of copies may be used at the same time
- Shrink-wrap license: agreement printed on package that becomes effective when package is opened
- End-user license (EULA): displayed on screen during first installation

In general, there are two software categories—public domain and proprietary. Public domain software is available to the public without any restrictions. Proprietary software, which may be commercially sold or free, has restrictions on its use. Proprietary software is typically distributed as commercial software, demoware, shareware, freeware, and open source software.

Types of Proprietary Software

Commercial	Sold in stores and on Web sites
Shareware	Available for free on a trial basis; must pay to continue using it at end of trial period
Freeware	Available for free
Demoware	Commercial software available in a trial version that has limited features; often pre-installed on new computers
Open source	Includes source codes, so programmers can make modifications and improvements

An additional type of software available illegally is pirated software. Individuals obtain pirated software from the Internet, friends, and foreign stores. Not only is using pirated software unethical, it may include a virus or may not function properly.

SOFTWARE DEVELOPMENT

Obviously, software does not just magically appear on store shelves. Someone creates the idea and then designs, develops, and tests the software before selling it to consumers. The following section will review the way in which software is developed.

Software Life Cycle

The system's development life cycle refers to the steps taken by organizations when analyzing and designing a system. A system is any group of components that work together to accomplish a task. Numerous models exist for developing software and other systems, and some organizations create their own models. In general, all software life cycle models follow a pattern similar to the six-stage process shown in the following table:

1	Preliminary investigation	Conduct an initial analysis, propose alternative solutions, indicate costs/benefits, submit preliminary plan in a written report to executives.
2	System analysis	Gather data from surveys and observations, analyze data using modeling tools to create graphic representations of the software system, and write a report for management.
3	System design	Create a preliminary design or a prototype of the software system, and then create a detail design that defines input/output requirements, storage/processing requirements, and system controls and backup. Write a report summarizing the preliminary and detail designs.
4	System development	Programmers develop the software. Software is tested in two stages—unit testing of individual parts and then system testing with actual data. System testing may involve using incorrect data or large quantities of data to force the system into failing or crashing.
5	System implementation	Convert hardware, software, and files of old system to new system with direct, parallel, phased, or pilot implementation. Direct implementation means user stops using old system and starts using new one. Parallel implementation means both old and new systems are used at the same time until the new one seems reliable. Phased implementation means parts of the new system are phased in gradually. Pilot implementation means a few users test the entire system before everyone else uses it. Users are then trained on the new system.
6	System maintenance	Modify and improve the system with audits and evaluations.

Programming

The fourth step of the life cycle involves developing the software program, which is a list of instructions written in programming language understood by the computer. Programming, or software engineering, involves following a five-step process to create instructions for a computer:

1. Clarify programming needs regarding input, output, and processing requirements
2. Design a solution with modeling tools
3. Write, or code, the program with the appropriate programming language
4. Test the program to remove errors or bugs
5. Write program documentation about what the program does and how to use it, and maintain the program with modifications, repairs, and tests

The second step of the programming process refers to designing a solution with modeling tools. When designing a solution, a programmer needs to create an algorithm, which is a formula for solving a specific problem. Algorithms, which are similar to cooking recipes, can be written in a number of ways. There are two steps involved in program design.

Program Design

Step 1: Determine program logic	a. Modularization—develop and test each sub-program or subroutine separately
	b. Top-down program design—use hierarchy chart to illustrate general purpose of program all the way down to specific purposes of each module
Step 2: Design details	Use pseudocode to generate a summary or outline of the program and/or flowcharts to graphically explain the logical flow of the program

Programming Languages

Programming languages have changed significantly over the years. In the 1940s, engineers used machine language, which is the basic language of any computer as represented by binary digits. By the 1950s, programmers were using assembly language to write programs with abbreviations instead of numbers. Third-generation languages of the late 1950s and early 1960s such as FORTRAN, COBOL, BASIC, Pascal, and C were high-level or procedural languages. Such languages enabled programmers to write in human language rather than abbreviations and numbers. Many modern languages, such as C++ and Java, are third-generation languages. The early 1970s brought very high-level, or problem-oriented, languages, such as SQL and NOMAD that allowed users to write programs with fewer commands. Fifth-generation languages of the 1980s are natural languages that allow programmers to phrase questions and commands in conversational ways. Prolog and Mercury are examples of fifth-generation languages.

Natural languages are associated with artificial intelligence, which is the technology geared toward humanizing machines.

In addition to traditional programming languages, object-oriented programming (OOP) and visual programming are options for software engineers. OOP is a method in which data and processing instructions are combined into objects, modules of programming code that can be used in other programs. A visual programming language, such as Visual BASIC, allows users to develop programs by drawing, pointing, or clicking on icons that represent certain programming routines.

Each programming language serves a different purpose, and the following list indicates some of the most commonly used languages for modern programs:

- C++—One of the most popular and commonly used languages; combines traditional C programming with object-oriented functions; used in writing systems software, application software, device drivers, and video game software
- Java—Object-oriented language used for writing compact programs to be downloaded over the Internet and immediately executed; similar to C++ but simpler to use
- JavaScript—Object-oriented scripting language supported in Web browsers that adds interactive functions to HTML pages
- Perl (Practical Extraction and Report Language)—General-purpose language used for Web development, network programming, system administration, and GUI development
- COBOL (Common Business-Oriented Language)—Oldest programming language but still used in business, finance, and administrative systems

NETWORKS, COMMUNICATION, AND SECURITY

In 1969, the U.S. Department of Defense developed ARPANET, the starting point for today's Internet. ARPANET consisted of four linked computers at different university campuses and defense contractor offices. By 1987, ARPANET linked the computers of 28,000 researchers and academics and provided text-based information. Since then, the World Wide Web has replaced ARPANET, and over 1 billion people use the Internet each day.

Networks

Before people can locate information on the Internet or send e-mails to friends, they need network access. A network is a group of interconnected computers, phones, and other communications devices that are able to communicate with each other and share resources. Networks are differentiated by geographic range, size, and purpose as indicated by the following table.

Types of Networks

LAN	Local area network serves a very limited geographical area, such as one building
MAN	Metropolitan area network serves a 50-mile area; local Internet service providers and cable TV companies are often MANs
NAN	Neighborhood area network connect a limited geographical area, often several buildings
PAN	Personal area network uses short-range (30 feet) wireless technology for connecting personal digital devices
WAN	Wide area network covers a large geographical area, such as a country or the world, and typically consists of several smaller networks; the Internet is the world's largest WAN
HAN	Home area network connects the digital devices inside a home

Networks are structured as either client/server or peer-to-peer. In a client/server network, processing is divided between the clients, which are the workstations, and the server that manages shared devices such as printers and scanners. In client/server mode, the server acts as the most important resource. In a peer-to-peer (P2P) network, all workstations on the network communicate with each other without depending on a server. A P2P network is less costly than a client/server approach, but users sacrifice speed when more than twenty-five computers are connected.

Within a network, data moves from one device to another through cables or through the air via wireless technologies. The following table consists of the various components found in most networks.

Network Components

Host	Mainframe or midsize central computer that controls a client/server network
Node	Any device attached to a network, such as a PC, storage device, or scanner
Packet	Unit of data transmitted over a network; communications, such as e-mails, are divided into packets when sent and reassembled upon arrival
Protocol	Set of rules that govern the exchange of data between hardware and software components; each device in a network has a unique Internet protocol (IP) address so that data is routed properly
Hub	Common connection point for devices in a network where data arrives and is forwarded out; hubs are half-duplex devices that transmit data in both directions but only one direction at a time
Switch	Device that connects computers to a network; switches are full-duplex devices that transmit data back and forth at the same time
Bridge	Interface that connects the same types of networks like two LANs joined to create a larger network

Gateway	Interface allowing communication between different types of networks, such as between a LAN and a WAN
Router	Special computer that joins multiple networks together and directs communicating messages, such as e-mails and HTML files
Backbone	Main highway that connects an organization's computer networks
Network interface card	Circuitry that transmits and receives data on a LAN; often inserted into an expansion slot
Network operating system	System software that manages network activity, such as data flow and security

Since network connections need to move data quickly, bandwidth, which is the data transmission capacity of a communications channel, is an important factor. The broadband available from high-bandwidth communications systems like cable TV and DSL transmits high-speed data and high-quality audio and video. Systems with less capacity, such as dial-up Internet access, are narrowband or voiceband.

Ethernet is a popular network architecture where nodes are connected by wire or cable. With small LANs, Ethernet prevents messages from colliding along the transmission line. When two workstations attempt to send data at the same time, Ethernet requires that the data be resent.

Networks use either wired or wireless connection systems. Wired networks with cables that connect devices offer high bandwidth, speed, security, and simplicity, but they lack the mobility of wireless networks. Wireless networks use a number of methods to connect devices.

- Infrared transmission: transports data with infrared-light waves that are just below the visible light spectrum

- Microwave radio: transmits voice and data with super high-frequency radio waves; can be aimed in one direction; more carrying capacity than broadcast radio waves; Bluetooth, an example, involves short-range microwave transmissions

- Broadcast radio: sends data long distances between states and countries; requires transmitters and receivers

- Communications satellites: microwave relay stations orbiting around the Earth; serve as basis for Global Positioning System (GPS)

Wireless fidelity—Wi-Fi—refers to an Ethernet-compatible wireless network that transmits data as radio waves. With Wi-Fi, people are able to use their Wi-Fi equipped laptops to work online wirelessly in areas with public access to Wi-Fi networks such as airports.

World Wide Web vs. the Internet

While many people believe the World Wide Web and the Internet are the same, the two are distinctly different yet related. The Internet is a worldwide communication infrastructure that connects computer networks. The Web is a collection of multimedia files linked and accessed through the Internet. Browsers, such as Microsoft Internet Explorer and Mozilla Firefox, enable people to access areas of the Web known as Web sites. Each Web site has a unique address or URL (Uniform Resource Locator) and is composed of one or more Web pages, or multimedia documents. Browsers find Web pages through the URL, which consists of four elements. The following Web address for Big Bend National Park will be used to explain the different parts of URLs: *http://www.nps.gov/bibe/index.htm.*

URL Terminology

Web protocol	http://	Hypertext Transfer Protocol (HTTP) refers to the communications rules enabling browsers to connect to Web servers
Domain name	*www.nps.gov*	Location on the Internet; last three letters describe the domain type—.gov (government), .com (commercial), .net (network), .org (nonprofit), .edu (educational), .mil (military), or .int (international organization)
Directory name	*bibe*	Name on the server for the directory from which the browser needs to retrieve a file
File name and extension	*index.htm*	File name is the specific page—*index.htm*; *.htm* is an extension of the file name that tells the browser that it is an HTML (Hypertext Markup Language) file; HTML is a standardized format that specifies the layout for Web pages

Web Searches

With the extensive amount of information on the Web, it is helpful to search effectively and efficiently. Search engines, such as Google and Bing, help users locate information on the Web. There are at least three search tools available to people who use search engines.

- Keyword index—Search for information with one or more keywords, and the search engine displays a list of Web pages containing the keywords.

- Subject directory—Search for information by choosing lists of categories or topics, such as "Sports" or "Arts and Humanities." Yahoo and Galaxy include subject directories.

- Metasearch engine—Search more than one search engine at the same time. Metacrawler and Dogpile are metasearch engines.

Personal Communication

An amazing 60 billion e-mails cross through the Internet every day. People's ability to communicate with others so efficiently may be one of the primary reasons for the Internet explosion. Electronic mail can be transmitted through an e-mail program, such as Microsoft's Outlook Express, or a Web-based e-mail program, such as Hotmail.

While e-mail is probably the most popular form of communication, other electronic methods exist for interacting with people. Instant messaging (IM) allows for real-time communication through transmitted text messages. Newsgroups are electronic bulletin boards where users participate in written discussions about various subjects. Social networking sites, such as Facebook and MySpace, enable users to post pictures and messages about personal activities and interests for the viewing pleasure of friends and family members.

As with other types of communication, e-mail writers should consider both the audience and the message when composing messages. Netiquette, or Internet etiquette, refers to various guidelines to ensure civil and effective communication when participating in online discussion groups or exchanging e-mails. For example, consult the FAQ (frequently asked questions) section of discussion groups to determine the behavior expectations. Avoid using obscene or inappropriate language, which is known as flaming. Instead, insert occasional emoticons, or smiley faces, to convey intention if the e-mail is not work-related. Using all capital letters is equivalent to shouting at the recipient. In addition, avoid sending large attachments that may slow down a recipient's computer system, or at least request permission before doing so.

Security Issues

Along with the vast amount of information available on the Internet come annoyances, such as spam. In particular, malware poses serious problems to computer users. Malware, or malicious software, is any program designed to secretly infiltrate a computer and disrupt normal operations. Spyware is similar to malware because it also secretly enters a computer system, but the purpose is usually to gather a user's personal information for advertising purposes. The following table describes various intrusive elements of the Internet, some of which pose serious security risks.

Security Problems

Browser hijacker	Spyware that secretly changes browser settings
Denial-of-service attack (DoS)	Repeated fraudulent requests of a computer system or network that result in a system overload
Key logger	Spyware that records characters being typed and relays the information to other Internet users, making it possible for strangers to know passwords and other private information
Pharming	Redirecting users to fake Web sites
Phishing	Sending forged e-mail with the intention of fooling users into revealing private information

Pop-up generator	Also known as adware; type of spyware that tracks Web surfing and online purchases so marketers can send unsolicited pop-up ads targeted to the user's interests
Search hijacker	Spyware that intercepts actual search requests and re-routes the user to other sites
Spam	Unsolicited e-mail typically in the form of advertising or chain letters
Spoofing	Forging the name of an e-mail sender
Trojan horse	Program that appears to be useful but actually carries a virus or destructive instructions; typically offered for free in the form of a game or a screen saver; may invite backdoor programs that enable illegitimate users to gain control of a computer secretly
Virus	Deviant program that copies itself and infects computers; attaches to hard disks and destroys and corrupts data
Worm	Program that repeatedly copies itself into a computer's memory; excessive copies cause computers to crash

Computer experts known as hackers and crackers are often the ones responsible for the spread of viruses and worms. The term *hacker* has multiple meanings. On the positive side, hackers are enthusiastic computer programmers who like to expand their knowledge of programming languages and computer systems. Other types of hackers appreciate the challenge of circumventing computer and network security systems. In general, hackers break into computers for fun, such as thrill-seeker hackers, or for work purposes, such as white-hat hackers hired to expose computer system weaknesses. In contrast, *crackers* break into systems for malicious purposes. Crackers may gather information for monetary gain, steal credit information, destroy data, or attempt to bring extensive harm to multitudes of people, such as cyber terrorists. However, protecting the safety of a computer system can be easily accomplished with a number of security tools:

- Antivirus software: programs that scan a computer's hard disk and memory to identify and destroy viruses
- Firewalls: system of hardware and/or software that shields a computer or network from intruders by analyzing, controlling, and filtering incoming and outgoing packets
- Passwords: unique set of symbols, words, or codes used for restricting access to a computer or network
- Biometrics: use of physical attributes like fingerprints, voices, faces, or eyes to confirm an individual's identity
- Encryption: process of scrambling or hiding data into an unreadable form to prevent unauthorized access

Not only is computer security important for individuals but also for businesses and government agencies. With so many organizations going paperless, the security of electronic databases is vital.

COMPUTERS AND EVERYDAY LIFE

Social Issues

Increased productivity, globalization, and efficient communication methods are only some of the societal benefits of computer technology. However, the technological revolution raises some social concerns as well. One environmental issue is e-waste, which refers to the millions of PCs, cell phones, printers, and other electronic equipment that are discarded when they break or become obsolete. Many technology firms, including Dell and Hewlett-Packard, are responding to environmental concerns by offering to recycle or refurbish unwanted computer devices.

Although technology enables people to connect with others around the world, it is also linked to mental health issues. With computer technology, people are able to work, shop, and play games without speaking or seeing another person, which may lead to isolation, loneliness, and depression. Online gambling is another mental health concern, since technology makes gambling so accessible. It is illegal to gamble by wire in the United States, but the global nature of the Internet simplifies the process of making bets in the Caribbean and other offshore locations.

Children and teenagers with computer access face security threats. Daily news reports indicate that sexual predators solicit children online, especially young girls. With the anonymity of cyberspace, predators easily portray themselves as caring peers to unsuspecting children and teenagers. Although parents are becoming increasingly aware of online threats, teenage girls remain the target of many online predators.

Computers and Careers

Nearly every job or career requires a certain level of computer knowledge and skills. In some jobs, computers are tools for accomplishing tasks effectively and efficiently. For example, police officers often have laptops installed in their cruisers, which enables them to quickly find data about stolen cars, arrest warrants, and criminal records. In other jobs, working with computers is the focal point of the position—database developer, games programmer, robotics engineer, technical writer, graphic designer, and Web developer. Advancements in computer technology have not only transformed jobs but also created new professions.

POST-TEST ANSWER SHEET

1. Ⓐ Ⓑ Ⓒ Ⓓ   13. Ⓐ Ⓑ Ⓒ Ⓓ   25. Ⓐ Ⓑ Ⓒ Ⓓ   37. Ⓐ Ⓑ Ⓒ Ⓓ   49. Ⓐ Ⓑ Ⓒ Ⓓ

2. Ⓐ Ⓑ Ⓒ Ⓓ   14. Ⓐ Ⓑ Ⓒ Ⓓ   26. Ⓐ Ⓑ Ⓒ Ⓓ   38. Ⓐ Ⓑ Ⓒ Ⓓ   50. Ⓐ Ⓑ Ⓒ Ⓓ

3. Ⓐ Ⓑ Ⓒ Ⓓ   15. Ⓐ Ⓑ Ⓒ Ⓓ   27. Ⓐ Ⓑ Ⓒ Ⓓ   39. Ⓐ Ⓑ Ⓒ Ⓓ   51. Ⓐ Ⓑ Ⓒ Ⓓ

4. Ⓐ Ⓑ Ⓒ Ⓓ   16. Ⓐ Ⓑ Ⓒ Ⓓ   28. Ⓐ Ⓑ Ⓒ Ⓓ   40. Ⓐ Ⓑ Ⓒ Ⓓ   52. Ⓐ Ⓑ Ⓒ Ⓓ

5. Ⓐ Ⓑ Ⓒ Ⓓ   17. Ⓐ Ⓑ Ⓒ Ⓓ   29. Ⓐ Ⓑ Ⓒ Ⓓ   41. Ⓐ Ⓑ Ⓒ Ⓓ   53. Ⓐ Ⓑ Ⓒ Ⓓ

6. Ⓐ Ⓑ Ⓒ Ⓓ   18. Ⓐ Ⓑ Ⓒ Ⓓ   30. Ⓐ Ⓑ Ⓒ Ⓓ   42. Ⓐ Ⓑ Ⓒ Ⓓ   54. Ⓐ Ⓑ Ⓒ Ⓓ

7. Ⓐ Ⓑ Ⓒ Ⓓ   19. Ⓐ Ⓑ Ⓒ Ⓓ   31. Ⓐ Ⓑ Ⓒ Ⓓ   43. Ⓐ Ⓑ Ⓒ Ⓓ   55. Ⓐ Ⓑ Ⓒ Ⓓ

8. Ⓐ Ⓑ Ⓒ Ⓓ   20. Ⓐ Ⓑ Ⓒ Ⓓ   32. Ⓐ Ⓑ Ⓒ Ⓓ   44. Ⓐ Ⓑ Ⓒ Ⓓ   56. Ⓐ Ⓑ Ⓒ Ⓓ

9. Ⓐ Ⓑ Ⓒ Ⓓ   21. Ⓐ Ⓑ Ⓒ Ⓓ   33. Ⓐ Ⓑ Ⓒ Ⓓ   45. Ⓐ Ⓑ Ⓒ Ⓓ   57. Ⓐ Ⓑ Ⓒ Ⓓ

10. Ⓐ Ⓑ Ⓒ Ⓓ   22. Ⓐ Ⓑ Ⓒ Ⓓ   34. Ⓐ Ⓑ Ⓒ Ⓓ   46. Ⓐ Ⓑ Ⓒ Ⓓ   58. Ⓐ Ⓑ Ⓒ Ⓓ

11. Ⓐ Ⓑ Ⓒ Ⓓ   23. Ⓐ Ⓑ Ⓒ Ⓓ   35. Ⓐ Ⓑ Ⓒ Ⓓ   47. Ⓐ Ⓑ Ⓒ Ⓓ   59. Ⓐ Ⓑ Ⓒ Ⓓ

12. Ⓐ Ⓑ Ⓒ Ⓓ   24. Ⓐ Ⓑ Ⓒ Ⓓ   36. Ⓐ Ⓑ Ⓒ Ⓓ   48. Ⓐ Ⓑ Ⓒ Ⓓ   60. Ⓐ Ⓑ Ⓒ Ⓓ

answer sheet

POST-TEST

Directions: Carefully read each of the following 60 questions. Choose the best answer to each question, and darken its letter on your answer sheet. The Answer Key and Explanations can be found following this post-test.

1. Which of the following has the shortest range?
   (A) WAN
   (B) PAN
   (C) NAN
   (D) LAN

2. What term is used for any preformatted style guide in word processing software?
   (A) Kernel
   (B) Label
   (C) Template
   (D) Cell

3. What term refers to the software that controls how a computer uses its hardware resources?
   (A) Application software
   (B) Operating system
   (C) Device driver
   (D) Utility program

4. Which of the following refers to a unit of data that is transmitted over a network?
   (A) Mail
   (B) Node
   (C) Packet
   (D) Attachment

5. What is the term for the main circuit board of a computer where chips and peripherals are connected?
   (A) Workstation
   (B) Motherboard
   (C) Mainframe
   (D) CPU

6. Which of the following network architectures prevents messages from colliding along transmission lines?
   (A) Internet
   (B) Ethernet
   (C) Intranet
   (D) Extranet

7. The structure of which type of database resembles a family tree?
   (A) Multidimensional
   (B) Relational
   (C) Object-oriented
   (D) Hierarchical

8. What is the term for software that eliminates unnecessary data in a computer's storage space?
   (A) Data compression utility
   (B) Antivirus utility
   (C) Filtering utility
   (D) Backup utility

9. What is the term for the data transmission capacity of a communications channel?
   (A) Bitmap
   (B) Fidelity
   (C) Bandwidth
   (D) Frequency

10. Which of the following is the newest and most popular RAM chip?
    (A) DRAM
    (B) SRAM
    (C) SDRAM
    (D) DDR-SDRAM

11. Which of the following is an example of a domain name?
    (A) .org
    (B) http://
    (C) home.htm
    (D) www.google.com

12. What term is used for a search specification that leads a computer to search for a record in a database?
    (A) Field
    (B) Query
    (C) Phish
    (D) Queue

13. Which of the following wireless network methods transmits is used for GPS?
    (A) Infrared transmission
    (B) Broadcast radio
    (C) Microwave radio
    (D) Communications satellites

14. Which of the following implementation methods requires all users to stop using an old system completely before beginning to use a new one?
    (A) Direct
    (B) Parallel
    (C) Phased
    (D) Pilot

15. Which of the following is most often used by airlines and banks to process and store large amounts of data?
    (A) Compiler
    (B) Graphics terminal
    (C) Mainframe computer
    (D) Supercomputer

16. What is a mechanism that scrambles data into an unreadable form to prevent security breaches?
    (A) Biometrics
    (B) Encryption
    (C) Executable
    (D) Antivirus software

17. What is the term for the core module of an operating system?
    (A) Menu
    (B) Buffer
    (C) Bootstrap
    (D) Kernel

18. Which of the following records characters typed by a computer user and enables strangers to learn passwords?
    (A) Key logger
    (B) Browser hijacker
    (C) Pop-up generator
    (D) Search hijacker

19. Which of the following is a holding area in memory used with the *Copy* command in word processing programs?
    (A) Template
    (B) Default
    (C) Desktop
    (D) Clipboard

20. What is the term for a component that expands the input, output, or storage functions of a computer?
    (A) Peripheral
    (B) Hard drive
    (C) Modem
    (D) Software

21. Which of the following is the first step of the programming process?
    (A) Writing documentation
    (B) Designing a solution
    (C) Clarifying needs
    (D) Writing code

22. Which of the following helps users locate information on the Web?
    (A) Search engine
    (B) Data warehouse
    (C) Network router
    (D) Local area network

23. Which of the following RAM chips retains its contents without needing to be refreshed by the CPU?
    (A) SRAM
    (B) DRAM
    (C) SDRAM
    (D) DDR-SDRAM

24. Which of the following software applications offers sophisticated graphic and design features?
    (A) Spreadsheet
    (B) Network database
    (C) Word processing
    (D) Desktop publishing

25. The format in which data is stored, processed, and transmitted by electronic circuitry in a computer is known as data
    (A) convergence.
    (B) representation.
    (C) transfer.
    (D) language.

26. What is the term for high-bandwidth communications systems like DSL?
    (A) Narrowband
    (B) Voiceband
    (C) Broadband
    (D) Crossband

27. Which of the following refers to a set of steps for solving a specific problem?
    (A) Documentation
    (B) Coding
    (C) Compiler
    (D) Algorithm

28. What is the final step of the boot process?
    (A) Power distributed to circuitry
    (B) CPU checks configurations
    (C) Diagnostic tests activated
    (D) Peripheral devices identified

29. Which of the following is a programming method of combining processing instructions with objects?
    (A) OOP
    (B) DOS
    (C) COBOL
    (D) FORTRAN

30. Which of the following describes a kilobyte?
    (A) 8 binary digits
    (B) 1,024 bytes
    (C) 1,048,576 bytes
    (D) 1,073,741,824 bytes

31. Which of the following databases may include links to audio and video?
    (A) Network database
    (B) Relational database
    (C) Object-oriented database
    (D) Multidimensional database

32. Which programming generation involved using assembly language to write programs with abbreviations?
    (A) First generation
    (B) Second generation
    (C) Third generation
    (D) Fourth generation

33. What is the term for developing and testing each subprogram or subroutine separately?
    (A) Prototyping
    (B) Interpretation
    (C) Implementation
    (D) Modularization

post-test

34. Which of the following adds interactive functions to HTML pages?
    (A) JavaScript
    (B) C++
    (C) Perl
    (D) C

35. Which of the following is a central computer that supplies a network with data and storage?
    (A) Central processing unit
    (B) Supercomputer
    (C) Ethernet
    (D) Server

36. Which of the following refers to the unique numbers assigned to each computer on a network?
    (A) Path
    (B) Domain
    (C) IP address
    (D) Query processor

37. What is the term for disk areas where programs or documents wait?
    (A) Directories
    (B) Spools
    (C) Buffers
    (D) Paths

38. What is the term for programs designed to secretly penetrate a computer and disrupt operations?
    (A) Freeware
    (B) Shareware
    (C) Demoware
    (D) Malware

39. What type of application software is most often used by architects and engineers?
    (A) Computer-aided design
    (B) Image editing
    (C) Multimedia
    (D) Drawing

40. What is the term used to describe data that can only exist with a constant power supply?
    (A) Zipped
    (B) Portable
    (C) Volatile
    (D) Unformatted

41. Which of the following is a software program that attaches to hard disks and corrupts data?
    (A) Spam
    (B) Pop-up
    (C) Virus
    (D) Cracker

42. Which programming tool results in an outline or summary of a program?
    (A) Flowchart
    (B) Pseudocode
    (C) JavaScript
    (D) Hypertext

43. Which of the following refers to the software and hardware that enables people to communicate with computers?
    (A) Operating systems
    (B) Utility programs
    (C) Architectures
    (D) User interfaces

44. Which of the following were used in the first digital computers?
    (A) Vacuum tube
    (B) Silicon chip
    (C) Integrated circuit
    (D) Transistor

45. Which of the following chips holds flexible startup instructions, such as time and date?
    (A) RAM
    (B) ROM
    (C) CMOS
    (D) DRAM

46. Which of the following is the unit of measurement used by computer circuitry?
    (A) Base-1 number system
    (B) Base-2 number system
    (C) Base-5 number system
    (D) Base-10 number system

47. Which of the following is a fourth-generation problem-oriented language?
    (A) NOMAD
    (B) COBOL
    (C) OOP
    (D) XML

48. Which of the following utilities rearranges files on a disk to speed up operation?
    (A) Data recovery
    (B) Backup
    (C) Defragmenter
    (D) Compression

49. Which of the following is a fifth-generation language?
    (A) Prolog
    (B) Pascal
    (C) Java
    (D) C++

50. Which of the following stores flexible programs in MP3 players and cell phones?
    (A) CMOS chips
    (B) Flash memory
    (C) Application software
    (D) Shareware

51. Which of the following is unrestricted software?
    (A) Open source
    (B) Public domain
    (C) Commercial
    (D) Proprietary

52. Which of the following units of measurement is most often used when referring to a computer system's storage capacity?
    (A) B
    (B) GB
    (C) KB
    (D) MB

53. What is the term for a personal computer connected to a network?
    (A) Supercomputer
    (B) Microcontroller
    (C) Workstation
    (D) Mainframe

54. Any hardware or software component available for use by a computer processor is a
    (A) resource.
    (B) device.
    (C) packet.
    (D) server.

55. What is the term for the area where data remains permanently in files?
    (A) Primary storage
    (B) Memory
    (C) Secondary storage
    (D) CPU

56. Which of the following mechanisms enables people to organize files into directories and subdirectories?
    (A) Device driver
    (B) Application software
    (C) Operating system
    (D) Utility software

post-test

57. What is the term for the most commonly used interface that allows people to choose icons from menus with a mouse?

(A) Natural-language interface

(B) Command-line interface

(C) Motion tracking interface

(D) Graphical user interface

58. What is the term for a word processing feature that automates the process of creating personalized form letters?

(A) Track changes

(B) Mail merge

(C) Hyperlink

(D) Wizard

59. What is the term for the location where a row and a column intersect in an electronic spreadsheet?

(A) Cell

(B) Label

(C) Range

(D) Value

60. What is the term for a computer that requests information from another computer or a server?

(A) Router

(B) Client

(C) Modem

(D) Bridge

ANSWER KEY AND EXPLANATIONS

1. B	13. D	25. B	37. C	49. A
2. C	14. A	26. C	38. D	50. B
3. B	15. C	27. D	39. A	51. B
4. C	16. B	28. B	40. C	52. B
5. B	17. D	29. A	41. C	53. C
6. B	18. A	30. B	42. B	54. A
7. D	19. D	31. C	43. D	55. C
8. A	20. A	32. B	44. A	56. C
9. C	21. C	33. D	45. C	57. D
10. D	22. A	34. A	46. B	58. B
11. D	23. A	35. D	47. A	59. A
12. B	24. D	36. C	48. C	60. B

1. **The correct answer is (B).** A personal area network only has a range of about 30 feet. A WAN covers large areas, such as entire countries, and NANs cover neighborhoods. A LAN serves a limited geographical area, such as a building, but it is still larger than a PAN.

2. **The correct answer is (C).** A template is any preformatted style guide in word processing software. Templates are often used for organizing memos and formal letters. Choices (B) and (D) are terms related to spreadsheets. A kernel, choice (A), is the core module of an operating system.

3. **The correct answer is (B).** Operating system software controls how a computer uses its hardware resources, such as memory and storage. Application software handles specific tasks, such as compiling spreadsheets. Device drivers enable peripheral devices to interact with the computer system. Utility programs have specialized tasks such as file management and security.

4. **The correct answer is (C).** A packet is a unit of data that is transmitted over a network. E-mails and attachments are broken into packets when sent, so choices (A) and (D) are close but incorrect. A node, choice (B), is a device that attaches a device to a network.

5. **The correct answer is (B).** The motherboard is the system board or main circuit board of a computer. Everything in the computer is attached to the motherboard—keyboard, mouse, printer, processor chip, and memory chips. Choices (A) and (C) are types of computers. The CPU is the processor chip, so choice (D) is incorrect.

6. **The correct answer is (B).** Ethernets are network architectures that prevent messages from colliding along transmission lines. Ethernet nodes are connected by coaxial cable or twisted-pair wire. Choices (A), (C), and (D) are incorrect.

7. **The correct answer is (D).** Hierarchical databases group data in a way that is similar to a family tree with lower-level records subordinate to higher-level records. Choice (A) structures data in more than one

dimension. Choice (B) organizes data into rows and columns. Choice (C) includes graphics, audio, and video.

8. **The correct answer is (A).** Data compression utilities eliminate unnecessary data in a computer's storage space to create additional space. Choice (B) handles viruses and pop-up ads, and choice (C) blocks Web sites from children. Backup utilities make duplicates of a system's hard drive.

9. **The correct answer is (C).** Bandwidth is the data transmission capacity of a communications channel. Cable TV and DSL provide high-bandwidth communications abilities, while dial-up offers less. Frequency refers to how often an event occurs in a period, so choice (D) is incorrect. Choices (A) and (B) are incorrect.

10. **The correct answer is (D).** Double-data rate synchronous dynamic RAM (DDR-SDRAM) is the newest and most popular RAM chip found in most PCs today. Both SDRAM and SRAM are faster than DRAM, which needs to be refreshed constantly by the CPU. Choices (A), (B), and (C) are incorrect.

11. **The correct answer is (D).** The domain name is the location of a Web site on the Internet, such as *www. google.com*. Choice (A) is the domain type, which is a nonprofit organization in this case. Choice (B) is the Web protocol. Choice (C) is the file name and extension.

12. **The correct answer is (B).** A query is a search specification that leads a computer to search for a record in a database. Information in a database is sorted into records and fields, so choice (A) is incorrect. Phishing refers to an e-mail scam, so choice (C) is incorrect. Queue, choice (D), refers to the line in which data and programs wait.

13. **The correct answer is (D).** Communications satellites transmit data wirelessly for Global Positioning Systems. Microwave radio is used for Bluetooth, so choice (C) is incorrect. Broadcast radio requires transmitters and receivers. Infrared transports data just below the visible light spectrum.

14. **The correct answer is (A).** The direct implementation method requires that all users stop using an old system before they begin using a new one. Parallel implementation means both old and new systems are used at the same time. Phased implementation means parts of the new system are phased in gradually. Pilot implementation means a few users test the entire system before everyone else uses it.

15. **The correct answer is (C).** Mainframe computers are large, fast computers capable of processing, storing, and managing great amounts of data. Large organizations, such as banks, airlines, and universities often use mainframes. Supercomputers are used for weather forecasting and other processes requiring extensive calculations. A compiler is a type of software used for translating computer language.

16. **The correct answer is (B).** Encryption is the process of scrambling data into an unreadable form to prevent security breaches. Only individuals with the necessary key can unscramble the information. Choices (A) and (D) are security tools but not ones that mix up data. Choice (C) is a file type that contains instructions for a computer.

17. **The correct answer is (D).** The kernel is the core module of an operating system, and it manages memory, processes, tasks, and storage devices

while the computer is on. The bootstrap program initiates the loading of the operating system. Buffer is the disk area where programs wait, so choice (B) is incorrect.

18. **The correct answer is (A).** A key logger records characters that are typed by a computer user and enables strangers to learn passwords and other private information. Choices (B) and (D) are types of spyware that interfere with browser settings and search requests. Choice (C) is a type of adware that monitors online surfing and spending.

19. **The correct answer is (D).** The clipboard is the holding area in memory used with the *Copy* command of word processing programs. Templates are preformatted style guides, so choice (A) is incorrect. Choices (B) and (C) are incorrect.

20. **The correct answer is (A).** Peripheral devices are components that expand the input, output, and storage capabilities of a computer. Printers, scanners, and speakers are types of peripheral devices. A hard drive is a type of peripheral that expands storage functions, so choice (B) is incorrect. Choices (C) and (D) are also incorrect.

21. **The correct answer is (C).** Clarifying the needs of the program in regards to input, output, and processing requirements is the first stage of the programming process. The second step involves designing a solution, followed by writing code. Writing documentation is the last stage of the process.

22. **The correct answer is (A).** Search engines, such as Google and Bing, help users locate information on the Web. People find information through keyword indexes, subject directories, and metasearch engines. Choices (C) and (D) are components of a network, but they do not provide help with locating information.

23. **The correct answer is (A).** Static RAM (SRAM) holds on to its contents without needing to be refreshed by the CPU. DRAM, SDRAM, and DDR-SDRAM are all dynamic RAM chips. Dynamic means that the chip needs to be refreshed constantly by the CPU or their contents will be lost. Therefore, choices (B), (C), and (D) are incorrect.

24. **The correct answer is (D).** Desktop publishing programs offer sophisticated graphic and design features. Word processing programs include only limited graphic options, so choice (C) is incorrect. Choices (A) and (B) are not equipped with significant graphic tools.

25. **The correct answer is (B).** Data representation refers to the format in which data is stored, processed, and transmitted. Computers convert characters, numerals, or audio/visual data into marks, or binary digits, that electronic circuitry is able to manage. Choices (A), (C), and (D) are incorrect.

26. **The correct answer is (C).** Broadband refers to high-bandwidth communications systems like DSL and cable TV. Narrowband, also known as voiceband, has less capacity than broadband and is associated with dial-up Internet access. Choice (D) is incorrect.

27. **The correct answer is (D).** An algorithm is a set of steps or a formula for solving a specific problem. Documentation refers to the written description of a program, so choice (A) is incorrect. Coding, choice (B), is the process of writing the software program. A compiler translates high-level language

into machine language, so choice (C) is incorrect.

28. **The correct answer is (B).** The final step of the boot process is when the microprocessor checks configurations. Choice (A) is the first step, and choice (C) is the third step. Peripheral devices are identified in the fourth step of the sequence.

29. **The correct answer is (A).** Object-oriented programming is a method in which data and processing instructions are combined into objects, which are modules of programming code that can be used in other programs. Choice (B) is an operating system. Choices (C) and (D) are programming languages.

30. **The correct answer is (B).** A kilobyte (KB) equals 1,024 bytes. One byte is a group of 8 binary digits, so choice (A) is incorrect. A megabyte is 1,048,576 bytes, so choice (C) is incorrect. A gigabyte is 1,073,741,824 bytes, so choice (D) is incorrect.

31. **The correct answer is (C).** A hypermedia database that includes links to audio, video, and graphics is a type of object-oriented database. Choices (A) and (B) include no links. Multidimensional databases organize data into two or more dimensions, but they do not include links to text, graphics, video, or audio.

32. **The correct answer is (B).** The second-generation languages developed in the 1950s involved using assembly language to write programs with abbreviations instead of numbers, which was characteristic of first-generation languages. Third- and fourth-generation languages do not require abbreviations, so choices (C) and (D) are incorrect.

33. **The correct answer is (D).** Modularization refers to developing and testing each subprogram or subroutine separately. Modularization is one of the steps of program design, followed by top-down program design. Choice (A) involves the construction of working models for testing purposes. Choices (B) and (C) are incorrect.

34. **The correct answer is (A).** Java Script adds interactive functions to HTML pages and is supported in Web browsers. JavaScript is an object-oriented language. Choices (B), (C), and (D) are incorrect.

35. **The correct answer is (D).** A server is a central computer that serves the computers on a client/server network by supplying data and storage. A central processing unit (CPU) is the microprocessor inside individual computers, so choice (A) is incorrect. Supercomputers can act as servers if they have been configured as such, but they are not defined as servers. Ethernet is a type of network, so choice (C) is incorrect.

36. **The correct answer is (C).** An IP (Internet Protocol) address consists of the unique numbers assigned to each computer on a network. The IP address enables data to be routed to the correct destination. Path, choice (A), is a file's storage location. Domain, choice (B), is a Web site's location on the Internet. A query processor, choice (D), is a search engine component.

37. **The correct answer is (C).** Buffers are the disk areas where programs or documents wait. *Spooled* refers to being placed in a buffer but not the waiting area itself. Paths and directories refer to where files are located for organizational purposes, so choices (A) and (D) are incorrect.

38. **The correct answer is (D).** Malware, or malicious software, is designed to secretly penetrate a computer and

disrupt operations. Viruses and worms are types of malware. Choices (A), (B), and (C) are proprietary software.

39. **The correct answer is (A).** Architects and engineers use computer-aided design (CAD) software to create blueprints and product specifications. Image editing and drawing software are used for illustrations and graphics, but they do not provide the accuracy of CAD software that is needed in architecture and engineering.

40. **The correct answer is (C).** Volatile refers to data that can only exist with a constant power supply. RAM is volatile because it requires electrical power to hold data, unlike ROM, which cannot be changed. Choices (A), (B), and (D) are incorrect.

41. **The correct answer is (C).** A virus is a software program that attaches to hard disks and corrupts data. Spam and pop-up ads are types of advertising found in e-mails and on Web sites. Crackers are often responsible for spreading viruses, so choice (D) is incorrect.

42. **The correct answer is (B).** Pseudocode enables software engineers to design a program in narrative form, and it results in an outline or a summary of the program. Flowcharts graphically explain the logical flow of a program. Choices (C) and (D) are scripting and markup languages.

43. **The correct answer is (D).** A user interface is the hardware and software that enables users and computers to interact. A computer's user interface includes hardware, such as the monitor, mouse, and keyboard, and software mechanisms, such as icons, menus, and toolbars. Operating systems and utility programs help a computer run, but they do not allow users to interact with computers.

Architecture refers to the computer's design.

44. **The correct answer is (A).** Vacuum tubes were used in the first digital computers developed in the 1940s. Vacuum tubes were replaced with transistors. Transistors were replaced with integrated circuits, which are also known as silicon chips.

45. **The correct answer is (C).** CMOS chips hold flexible startup instructions that must be kept up to date when the computer is not on, such as time and date. ROM contains fixed startup instructions, so choice (B) is incorrect. Choices (A) and (D) are memory chips that temporarily hold data.

46. **The correct answer is (B).** The base-2 number system is the unit of measurement used by computer circuitry. In the binary number system, there are only two digits—0 and 1. Such a system enables computers to represent nearly any number with 0s and 1s. Choices (A), (C), and (D) are incorrect.

47. **The correct answer is (A).** NOMAD is a problem-oriented language developed along with other fourth-generation languages during the 1970s. COBOL is a third-generation language, so choice (B) is incorrect. Choices (C) and (D) are not fourth-generation languages.

48. **The correct answer is (C).** Defragmenter utilities rearrange scattered files on a hard drive to speed up operation. Data recovery utilities restore damaged data, so choice (A) is incorrect. Backup utilities make duplicate copies of a hard disk, so choice (B) is incorrect. Data compression utilities help make more storage space available.

49. **The correct answer is (A).** Prolog is a fifth-generation programming language associated with artificial intelligence. Choices (A), (B), and (D) are third-generation languages that enable programmers to write in human language rather than abbreviations and numbers.

50. **The correct answer is (B).** Flash memory chips store flexible programs in computers, cell phones, digital cameras, and MP3 players. CMOS chips hold flexible startup instructions like time and date. Choices (C) and (D) are two types of software that do not store information.

51. **The correct answer is (B).** Public domain software is available to the public without restrictions or copyrights. Proprietary software has restrictions on the way it may be used. Choices (A) and (C) are both copyright protected.

52. **The correct answer is (B).** A gigabyte (GB) is approximately 1 billion bytes, and gigabytes are most often used when referring to a computer's storage capacity. Choices (A) and (C) are too small for the storage needs of a computer system. Megabytes are usually used for describing medium to large files.

53. **The correct answer is (C).** A personal computer connected to a network is a workstation. Supercomputers, choice (A), are high-capacity, costly machines used for complicated calculations. Microcontrollers, choice (B), are embedded in cars and MP3 players. Mainframes are accessed by workstations, so choice (D) is incorrect.

54. **The correct answer is (A).** Any hardware or software component available for use by a computer processor is a resource. Memory, storage, servers, and peripheral devices are resources, so choices (B) and (D) are close but incorrect. Packets are units of data transmitted through a network, so choice (C) is incorrect.

55. **The correct answer is (C).** Secondary storage, or storage, is where files remain permanently when they are not needed for processing. Primary storage, which is known as RAM or memory, is where data is temporarily stored, so choices (A) and (B) are incorrect. The CPU is the microprocessor of a computer, so choice (D) is incorrect.

56. **The correct answer is (C).** Through the operating system, users are able to organize files into directories and subdirectories. The operating system software controls the computer's use of memory and disk storage space. Choices (A), (B), and (D) are not involved with file organization.

57. **The correct answer is (D).** Graphical user interface (GUI) allows users to choose icons or commands from menus with a mouse or a keyboard, and it is used in most modern computers. Command-line interface was the original type of interface that required users to type commands for programs to run. Choices (A) and (C) are not common interfaces.

58. **The correct answer is (B).** Mail merge automates the process of creating personalized form letters by combining information in a mailing list with a form letter. Tracking changes, choice (A), is a useful tool when editing documents. A hyperlink, choice (C), is a reference within a document to another piece of information. Wizards, choice (D), are interactive utilities programs that lead users through steps in creating documents.

59. **The correct answer is (A).** The cell is the location where a row and a column

intersect in an electronic spreadsheet. The label, choice (B), is the text used to describe data in a spreadsheet. A group of cells adjacent to each other is a range, choice (C). The numbers entered into a cell are the values, choice (D).

60. The correct answer is (B). A client is any computer that requests information from another computer or a server. Clients may include PCs, workstations, or other digital devices. Routers, modems, and bridges are various components of a network, so choices (A), (C), and (D) are incorrect.

SUMMING IT UP

- The first digital computers were used in World War II to help calculate missile flights and break enemy codes. In the 1940s and 1950s, large businesses used computers for payroll and inventory, but they were too big and expensive for small businesses. Smaller computer components, such as transistors and then integrated circuits, replaced the early computers' vacuum tubes.

- Computer purposes: accepting input, processing data, storing data, and producing output. Basic computer terms: CPU, file, hardware, input, microprocessor chip, motherboard, output, peripheral device, RAM, software, and storage.

- Computers convert data into signals, marks, or binary digits that electronic circuitry can understand. Data representation is the format in which data is stored, processed, and transmitted.

- In the binary number system there are only two digits—0 and 1. A group of 8 binary digits is a byte, or B. A kilobyte (KB) equals 1,024 bytes and refers to small computer files. A megabyte (MB) is approximately 1 million bytes (size of medium to large computer files), and a gigabyte (GB) is approximately 1 billion bytes (generally refers to a computer's storage capacity).

- Random access memory (RAM) is a temporary holding location for data, software instructions, and the operating system while the computer is running. RAM chips included in most personal computers are *DRAM:* Dynamic RAM; *SDRAM:* Synchronous dynamic RAM; *SRAM:* Static RAM; and *DDR-SDRAM:* Double-data rate synchronous dynamic RAM. Three other primary types of memory chips in computers are ROM, CMOS, and Flash memory chips.

- The operating system controls activities occurring within the computer system and interfaces with software, peripheral devices, and hardware. The operating system controls booting and CPU, file, task, and security management.

- A system's development life cycle refers to the steps taken by organizations when analyzing and designing a system. Software life cycle includes preliminary investigation, system analysis, system design, system development, system implementation, and system maintenance.

- Programming, or software engineering, involves a five-step process to create instructions for a computer: (1) clarify programming needs regarding input, output, and processing requirements; (2) design a solution with modeling tools; (3) write, or code, the program with the appropriate programming language; (4) test the program to remove errors or bugs; and (5) write program documentation and maintain the program with modifications, repairs, and tests.

- The programming languages FORTRAN, COBOL, BASIC, Pascal, and C were used in the late 1950s and early 1960s. In the early 1970s, languages such as SQL and NOMAD allowed users to write programs with fewer commands. Prolog and Mercury, fifth-generation or natural languages, allow programmers to phrase questions and commands in conversational ways. Some of the most commonly used languages for today's programs are C++, Java, JavaScript, Perl, and COBOL.

- Certain legal restrictions apply to both purchased and free computer software. A copyright gives the software's creator the exclusive right to copy, distribute, sell, and modify the software. A software license is a legal contract that defines the way(s) that a program may be used. Software licenses include single-user, site, multiple-user, concurrent-user, shrink-wrap, and end-user licenses. The two software categories are public domain and proprietary.

- Proprietary software includes commercial, shareware, freeware, demoware, and open source. Pirated software is illegally obtained.

- In 1969, the U.S. Department of Defense developed ARPANET, the starting point for today's Internet. Since then, the World Wide Web has replaced ARPANET, and over 1 billion people use the Internet each day.

- A network is a group of interconnected computers, phones, and other communications devices that are able to communicate with each other and share resources. Types of networks include LAN (local area network), MAN (metropolitan area network), NAN (neighborhood area network), PAN (personal area network), WAN (wide area network), and HAN (home area network).

- Network components include the host, node, packet, protocol, hub, switch, bridge, gateway, router, backbone, network interface card, and network operating system. Networks use either wired or wireless connection systems. Wireless network methods include infrared transmission, microwave radio, broadcast radio, and communication satellites. Wireless fidelity, or Wi-Fi, transmits data as radio waves.

- The Web and the Internet are not the same. The Internet is a worldwide communication infrastructure that connects computer networks. The Web is a collection of multimedia files linked and accessed through the Internet. Browsers enable people to access Web areas or Web sites. Each Web site has a unique address or URL (Uniform Resource Locator).

- Malware, or malicious software, is any program designed to secretly infiltrate a computer and disrupt normal operations. Spyware also secretly enters a computer system, but it gathers personal information for advertising purposes. Security problems include browser hijacker, denial-of-service attack (DoS), key logger, pharming, phishing, pop-up generator, search hijacker, spam, spoofing, Trojan horse, virus, and worm.

- In general, *hackers* break into computers for fun or for work purposes. *Crackers* break into systems for malicious purposes. Computer security systems include antivirus software, firewalls, passwords, biometrics, and encryption.

Principles of Supervision

OVERVIEW

- Diagnostic test
- Answer key and explanations
- Management levels
- Skill requirements
- Managerial roles
- Business ethics
- Corporate social responsibility
- Organizational environment
- Management functions
- Post-test
- Answer key and explanations
- Summing it up

DIAGNOSTIC TEST

Directions: Carefully read each of the following 20 questions. Choose the best answer to each question and circle your answer choice. The Answer Key and Explanations can be found following this Diagnostic Test.

1. Differentiation in an organization occurs through
   (A) career development.
   (B) diversity training.
   (C) external recruiting.
   (D) task specialization.

2. Which of the following is in daily contact with blue-collar workers in an organization?
   (A) Middle-level manager
   (B) Tactical manager

   (C) Operational manager
   (D) Strategic manager

3. Which of the following is on the highest level of Maslow's hierarchy of needs?
   (A) Shelter
   (B) Achievement
   (C) Security
   (D) Friendship

4. The management process used to compare actual performance to organizational goals is known as
   (A) produce.
   (B) inspect.
   (C) control.
   (D) plan.

5. Which of the following terms is commonly used to refer to the system of behavior and rituals that distinguishes one company from another one in the same industry?
   (A) Organization
   (B) Environment
   (C) Society
   (D) Culture

6. Which of the following focuses on short-term goals of an organization?
   (A) Strategic planning
   (B) Control planning
   (C) Operational planning
   (D) Tactical planning

7. The process used in the first stage of planning to gather, evaluate, and summarize relevant information is a
   (A) situational analysis.
   (B) strategic control.
   (C) performance appraisal.
   (D) force-field analysis.

8. The ability of a manager to diagnose and solve problems is a function of
   (A) people skills.
   (B) computer skills.
   (C) analytical skills.
   (D) conceptual skills.

9. Which of the following terms is commonly used to refer to the process of assigning tasks to subordinates?
   (A) Delegation
   (B) Accountability
   (C) Authority
   (D) Responsibility

10. All of the following exert a direct and immediate influence upon the daily activities of a business EXCEPT
    (A) competitor pricing.
    (B) customer spending.
    (C) raw material quality.
    (D) population shifts.

11. Setting goals for employees and closely supervising quality and accuracy are behaviors that describe
    (A) transformational leadership.
    (B) charismatic leadership.
    (C) group maintenance leadership.
    (D) task performance leadership.

12. The ten roles of managers were first identified by
    (A) Carly Fiorina.
    (B) Henry Mintzberg.
    (C) Rensis Likert.
    (D) Abraham Maslow.

13. Directing and monitoring ongoing activities during production at a factory are typical of
    (A) clan control.
    (B) feedback control.
    (C) concurrent control.
    (D) feedforward control.

14. A person who buys four pairs of shoes at an outlet mall is best described as a(n)
    (A) intermediate consumer.
    (B) wholesale consumer.
    (C) mass consumer.
    (D) final consumer.

15. Which of the following methods of departmentalization is most likely to trigger confusion regarding authority?
    (A) Product organization
    (B) Matrix organization
    (C) Customer organization
    (D) Functional organization

16. The Sarbanes-Oxley Act was enacted in response to
    (A) corporate accounting scandals.
    (B) age discrimination lawsuits.
    (C) sexual harassment complaints.
    (D) hazardous waste disposal.

17. Which of the following serves as a benchmark for performance assessment?
    (A) Reward
    (B) Standard
    (C) Vision
    (D) Expectancy

18. General influences on a business, such as regulatory agencies and global markets, are known as the
    (A) competitive environment.
    (B) macroenvironment.
    (C) internal environment.
    (D) microenvironment.

19. Which of the following is NOT one of the four established functions of management?
    (A) Evaluating
    (B) Leading
    (C) Planning
    (D) Controlling

20. A leader who has a personality that employees find admirable is most likely using
    (A) expert power.
    (B) coercive power.
    (C) referent power.
    (D) legitimate power.

diagnostic test

ANSWER KEY AND EXPLANATIONS

1. D	5. D	9. A	13. C	17. B
2. C	6. C	10. D	14. D	18. B
3. B	7. A	11. D	15. B	19. A
4. C	8. C	12. B	16. A	20. C

1. **The correct answer is (D).** Differentiation occurs through a division of labor and task specialization. Differentiation refers to how an organization is made up of different units working on different tasks. Career development, diversity training, and external recruiting are not aspects of differentiation.

2. **The correct answer is (C).** Frontline or operational managers are in daily contact with the workers in an organization. Choices (A) and (B) are synonymous, and they are the link between top-level managers and frontline managers. Strategic managers, or top-level managers, are responsible for long-term planning rather than daily operations.

3. **The correct answer is (B).** Achievement falls in the category of ego, which is near the top of Maslow's hierarchy of needs. Shelter is a physiological need at the bottom, followed by security. Friendship is an element of social needs, which are beneath ego and self-actualization.

4. **The correct answer is (C).** The control process is a management function used to compare actual performance with organizational goals and standards. Controlling and planning are two closely connected management functions. Choices (A) and (B) are incorrect.

5. **The correct answer is (D).** Organizational culture is the term used to refer to the system of behavior and rituals that distinguish one company from another. Managers define the culture of a business through employee training, motivational methods, and behavioral expectations. Choices (A), (B), and (C) are not terms for describing the goals and practices shared by employees of a company.

6. **The correct answer is (C).** Operational planning focuses on the short-term plans of an organization, which are typically less than two years. Strategic planning relates to long-term goals, and tactical planning involves intermediate-term goals.

7. **The correct answer is (A).** A situational analysis is used in the first stage of the planning process and involves gathering, analyzing, and summarizing relevant information. Strategic control occurs in the final stage of strategic planning. Performance appraisals are used to assess employee performance. A force-field analysis relates to the forces that prevent and encourage change.

8. **The correct answer is (C).** Analytical skills refer to a manager's ability to diagnose and solve problems. A manager with good people skills works well with others, so choice (A) is incorrect. Computer skills refer to a manager's ability to use business software to maximize job performance, so choice (B) is incorrect. Conceptual skills involve seeing the big picture and developing long-range plans.

9. **The correct answer is (A).** Delegation involves assigning tasks or responsibilities to subordinates. Accountability is the expectation that a worker will complete a task or face consequences. Authority is the power to make a decision.

10. **The correct answer is (D).** A population shift is an indirect force on a business that has long-term effects. Competitors, customers, and suppliers are direct forces on an organization that have immediate and daily effects. The price of a competitor's product influences consumer spending, and the quality of raw materials provided by a supplier affects the quality of a product made by a business.

11. **The correct answer is (D).** Goal setting and close supervision characterize task performance leadership. Transformational leaders motivate others to focus on the good of the group. Charismatic leaders arouse excitement in followers. Group maintenance leaders focus on group stability and harmony.

12. **The correct answer is (B).** Henry Mintzberg is an academic who conducted research about management roles of which he identified ten. Carly Fiorina was the CEO of Hewlett-Packard who was fired in 2005. Rensis Likert researched management styles and developed the linking pin model. Abraham Maslow developed the theory of a hierarchy of needs.

13. **The correct answer is (C).** Concurrent control focuses on directing, monitoring, and modifying ongoing activities related to any type of business operation. Clan control is not typically used to manage specific tasks like manufacturing. Feedback control takes place before activities begin. Feedforward evaluates results.

14. **The correct answer is (D).** Final consumers purchase products or services in their completed form. Intermediate consumers buy raw materials from wholesalers to make products to sell to final consumers, so choice (A) is incorrect. Choices (B) and (C) are distracters.

15. **The correct answer is (B).** The Matrix organization is most likely to cause employees confusion regarding who is in charge because of its dual line of command. Matrix organization is a blending of functional and product organization. Choices (A), (C), and (D) are incorrect.

16. **The correct answer is (A).** The Sarbanes-Oxley Act was enacted in 2002 in response to corporate accounting scandals at Enron and WorldCom. The law established strict accounting rules that make top-level managers more responsible for violations. The Sarbanes-Oxley Act does not address choices (B), (C), and (D).

17. **The correct answer is (B).** Standards serve as benchmarks for performance assessments and clarify desired performance levels. In the control function, the first step involves setting performance standards based on quantity, quality, time, and cost. Choices (A), (C), and (D) are incorrect.

18. **The correct answer is (B).** Macroenvironment refers to general influences on a business, which are also known as indirect forces. Indirect forces include laws, economies, technological advancements, and global markets. Choice (A) refers to direct forces, such as suppliers and customers. The internal environment of an organization is employees, management style, and organizational culture.

19. **The correct answer is (A).** The four functions of management as developed

by Henri Fayol are planning, orga- nizing, leading, and controlling. Evaluating is not one of the specified functions, although evaluation occurs in the organizing stage. Choices (B), (C), and (D) are incorrect.

20. **The correct answer is (C).** A leader with a personality that employees find admirable is using referent power. Expert power refers to a leader's experience. A leader with coercive power controls punish- ments that employees want to avoid. Legitimate power is the authority to tell subordinates what to do.

MANAGEMENT LEVELS

Effective managers facilitate the activities within organizations through planning, organizing, leading, and controlling. Managers use the principles of supervision to guide the work of others and to help an organization accomplish its short-term needs and long-term goals.

Most large organizations have three different levels of management—frontline (also referred to as first-level or first-line), middle-level, and top-level. A frontline manager is a lower-level manager within an organization. Depending on the organization, a frontline manager may be referred to as a supervisor, office manager, foreman, or operational manager. Whatever the title, a frontline manager oversees daily operational activities and serves as the connection between management and employees. Frontline managers supervise the work of various units within an organization, such as sales, marketing, accounting, production, and information technology.

Middle-level managers oversee frontline managers and report to top-level managers. Tactical manager, department manager, plant manager, and director of operations are other titles for middle-level managers. Middle-level managers translate the ideas and objectives developed by top-level executives into specific goals and activities for frontline managers. A middle-level manager interprets corporate objectives into plans for the different units within an organization. Corporate reorganizations in the last decade have eliminated many middle-level management positions, a trend that is likely to continue.

Top-level managers, or strategic managers, are the smallest and highest tier of management. The senior executives in an organization, such as the chief executive officer, chief operating officer, president, and vice president, constitute top-level management. Responsible for the performance and effectiveness of an organization, a top-level manager reports to the board of directors, owners, and stockholders of a corporation. Top-level managers concentrate on the long-term issues and growth strategies that middle-level managers broadcast to frontline managers for implementation. The purpose, norms, and values of an organization trickle down from top-level managers.

SKILL REQUIREMENTS

The global and technical nature of modern organizations calls for managers with a range of skills:

- Technical
- Analytical
- Decision-making
- Conceptual
- Computer
- Communication
- Interpersonal

Technical skills refer to the ability to perform a specific task that requires knowledge of certain techniques, processes, and resources. Engineering directors, sales managers, and construction supervisors must have technical skills in their field to manage workers and to solve problems. For example, a director of an accounting department needs to understand accounting practices, while a nursing director needs the skills to perform medical procedures. Frontline managers require more technical skills than middle- and top-level managers do because frontline managers deal with daily operations and problems.

Analytical skills refer to a manager's ability to identify problems and develop solutions. Reasoning capabilities are necessary to understand a complex issue, but computer software is available to assist in analyzing data. Supervisors use software to monitor inventory, oversee budgets, and manage staff assignments. Such analytical tools assist managers in diagnosing, evaluating, and solving problems in the workplace.

Managers at every level of an organization use decision-making skills on a daily basis. Effective managers separate themselves from ineffective managers by the quality of their decisions. Analytical skills influence decision-making skills, and inadequate reasoning leads to poor decisions. In some instances, supervisors seek advice from a group before making a choice that involves several options, but some problems require quick decisions.

In conjunction with analyzing situations and making decisions is the capacity to understand the big picture. Conceptual skills refer to a supervisor's ability to perceive the objectives and strategies of an organization, to realize the interconnections within an organization, and to comprehend the role of the firm in the outside world. Top-level managers utilize their conceptual skills frequently as they make decisions regarding a firm's long-term strategy. For example, the CEO of a corporation attempts to forecast the future when considering mergers, acquisitions, and investments.

Computer skills are necessary for the success of today's managers. Managers do not necessarily need to know how to write programs, but they do need to know how to use business software. Supervisors must be proficient with software in order to generate spreadsheets, create presentations, schedule meetings, and manipulate data. Web-based businesses require supervisors who have the computer skills to monitor digital sales, to manage international supply chains, and to oversee Web site development. Quickly changing technology calls for supervisors who have both the technical knowledge and the desire to advance their computer skills.

Communication and interpersonal skills are closely connected concepts in management. The ability to convey ideas clearly is essential for success because managers communicate with employees and executives constantly. Communication skills refer to the ability to explain ideas orally or in writing to others. Effective managers encourage questions from employees to make certain everyone is on the same page. Managers who need results from their employees must clearly communicate what is required or everyone fails.

In addition, supervisors need interpersonal skills, or people skills, to develop strong relationships with other members of the organization. Managers spend the bulk of their days interacting with people, so the ability to lead, motivate, understand, and work with others is critical to success. Often supervisors fail due to a lack of people skills rather than a lack of technical or analytical skills. Showing appreciation, listening actively, resolving conflicts, expressing empathy, and creating a positive work environment are skills not often taught in school, but they are the characteristics of excellent supervisors.

Managers at every level actively work to acquire and develop the skills needed for efficient supervision in the workplace. Frontline, middle-level, and top-level managers need computer skills, interpersonal skills, decision-making, and communication skills. Frontline managers use technical skills often because they are close to employees who are performing specific technical tasks. Middle management and top management positions call for analytical skills, while top executives in an organization require conceptual skills.

MANAGERIAL ROLES

A role is a job-related behavioral expectation. Henry Mintzberg, a Canadian academic, has conducted research and written books about management. Mintzberg's most often cited study involved observing and interviewing 5 CEOs from different industries over a two-week period. Upon reviewing the information he collected, Mintzberg identified ten roles of managers:

1. Figurehead
2. Leader
3. Liaison
4. Monitor
5. Disseminator
6. Spokesperson
7. Entrepreneur
8. Disturbance Handler
9. Resource Allocator
10. Negotiator

Since many of the roles are closely related, Mintzberg sorted them into three general categories: interpersonal, informational, and decisional. The interpersonal roles—figurehead, leader, and liaison—stem from the formal authority of a supervisor and the interpersonal skills used in the position. Most managers are required to serve as figureheads when they perform ceremonial duties or receive visitors. Examples include a high school principal handing out diplomas to graduates and a manufacturing manager giving a tour of a new facility to stockholders. In the leadership role, a manager directs and coordinates the duties of subordinates. As a leader, a manager hires and fires personnel and ensures that tasks are progressing properly. The liaison role requires managers to maintain communication with individuals inside and outside of an organization. In general, the interpersonal roles of a manager relate to providing information to others and developing interpersonal relationships.

As a monitor, disseminator, and spokesperson, a manager processes information. In the informational role, a manager receives and sends information. As a monitor, a manager assesses the successes, problems, and opportunities that may affect a unit, such as trends or sales. Managers act as disseminators by relaying confidential information to subordinates, such as when a CEO learns about quality concerns from a large customer and instructs a vice president to handle the problem personally. The role of disseminator often requires a manager to filter information and to delegate responsibilities. A manager represents a unit or a group of people when acting as a spokesperson internally or externally. For example, a sales manager may attempt to persuade executives to pay bonuses to the sales team when acting as an internal spokesperson. When serving as an external spokesperson, a manager serves in a public relations capacity by representing the views of the organization to outsiders, such as civic organizations or the media.

Entrepreneur, disturbance handler, resource allocator, and negotiator are elements of the decisional role. Many people consider the decisional role more important than a manager's interpersonal or informational roles. Making improvements to the unit is the objective of the entrepreneurial role. For example, a restaurant manager is constantly planning changes to the menu and the service to meet customer needs. Taking quick measures to control immediate problems and to create stability is an aspect of the disturbance handler role. A frontline manager who responds to broken equipment or striking workers is acting as a disturbance handler attempting to return the work environment back to normal. The resource allocator determines how to distribute limited resources, such as money, people, time, and equipment. Decisions regarding how many workers to assign to a project and how much money to allocate for upgrading office equipment are related to a manager's role as resource allocator. As negotiators, managers bargain with others to acquire benefits for their unit. Executives negotiate salaries and benefits with labor union representatives, and office managers negotiate work schedules with employees.

The ten roles of a manager illustrate three general ideas:

1. The roles explain what management entails and illustrate how the roles are connected.

2. Neglecting one or more of the roles prevents subordinates from working effectively.

3. The significance of each role illustrates the need for supervisors to manage their time well.

According to Mintzberg, managers need to be both specialists and generalists for success in any organization. A specialist is an expert at a specific discipline, such as marketing, accounting, or sales. A generalist has a broad understanding of a variety of business elements that provides managerial perspective. The numerous roles expected of managers call for varied skills to handle complex situations.

BUSINESS ETHICS

Ethics is a system of rules that distinguishes between right and wrong. Business ethics refers to the moral principles that dictate behavior in the business realm. In most cases, customers, society, competitors, and special interest groups judge whether a business acts ethically. However, attempts have been made to institute universal business ethics. Swiss executives initiated the Caux Principles in conjunction with business leaders from Europe, Japan, and the United States. The two main concepts of the Caux Principles include showing concern for human dignity and working for the common good, a concept known as *kyosei.*

Although universal ethical principles are useful, laws are often required to ensure ethical business practices. In response to corporate scandals, such as those at Enron and WorldCom, the U.S. Congress enacted the Sarbanes-Oxley Act in 2002. The law sets strict accounting and reporting rules that make top-level managers more accountable in an attempt to promote ethical behavior within public companies. In addition to laws, business ethics are influenced by ethical standards established within organizations. A company's code of ethics typically addresses employee conduct, shareholders, customers, and suppliers.

Some organizations develop corporate ethics programs. In addition to an ethics code, an ethics program establishes committees to investigate ethics violations, communication systems to help employees report violations, and disciplinary procedures for employees found guilty of unethical activities. Ethics programs are either compliance-based, integrity-based, or somewhere in between.

- Compliance-based ethics programs are designed by an organization's lawyers to prevent, expose, and discipline violations; these programs involve establishing legal procedures and having top-level managers monitor compliance.

- Integrity-based ethics programs are designed to instill personal and ethical responsibility among employees; organizations and workers self-govern based on established guidelines with which they concur.

CORPORATE SOCIAL RESPONSIBILITY

Corporate social responsibility refers to the obligations that a business has toward society. A socially responsible company attempts to increase the positive impact it has on society and decrease its negative impact. Social responsibilities are divided into four major categories:

- *Economic responsibility:* produce goods and services that society desires and that are profitable

- *Legal responsibility:* obey local, state, federal, and international laws

- *Ethical responsibility:* meet society's moral expectations

- *Philanthropic responsibility:* participate in desirable behaviors and activities, such as contributing to charities

In recent years, many businesses have combined the concepts of social responsibility and capitalism—socio-capitalism. Once considered divergent philosophies, profit and social responsibility have been blended in many for-profit businesses, such as those that provide services to the poor or the physically impaired.

ORGANIZATIONAL ENVIRONMENT

Internal and external environmental factors affect how an organization functions. The internal environment refers to factors within an organization such as employees, office layout, management style, and bonus systems. These elements affect how work and business goals are accomplished. An organization's culture is an internal factor as well. Culture refers to the shared system of behavior, rituals, and practices of an organization's members. The culture of one corporation differs from that of another, and it gives employees behavioral expectations to follow. For example, the culture at Walt Disney Company promotes dedication to customer satisfaction, while the culture at Southwest Airlines encourages customer fun.

Culture is built through the organizational socialization process, which occurs when managers and co-workers help newcomers develop the skills needed for acceptance into the corporate team. A strong organizational culture benefits a business by encouraging employee loyalty and cooperation. However, if the dominant culture prevents change and growth, then it is problematic. For many decades, IBM exerted a strong organizational culture, which later became counterproductive. The IBM culture resisted change and hindered the company's ability to compete against new computer firms like Apple and Compaq, who eventually grabbed a significant portion of IBM's market.

External Environment

In addition to the internal culture of an organization, managers face decisions regarding the external environment. Factors outside of an organization that have direct and indirect effects on daily operations are defined as the external environment.

Direct and Indirect Forces

Direct forces	Immediate and daily influences on a business; also known as the competitive environment; includes suppliers, competitors, and customers.
Indirect forces	General influences on a business; also known as the macroenvironment; includes legal, political, economic, technological, social-cultural, and global.

Direct Forces

Each day, managers face the direct forces on an organization—competitors, suppliers, and customers. A competitor is any rival firm competing for the same group of customers. Colgate and Crest are rivals in the toothpaste market, while Mercedes and Lexus are rivals for luxury car buyers. Businesses attempt to distinguish themselves in the marketplace and to stay ahead of rival firms. Because of this, managers must monitor the competition to determine if rivals are making significant product adjustments or launching sales promotions.

Suppliers provide businesses with capital, office supplies, information, parts, and raw materials, so they directly affect product quality. A motorcycle is composed of parts and materials from suppliers, so low-quality parts will result in a low-quality motorcycle. In addition to quality issues, the price of supplies affects the price of a product or service, which is why some businesses rely on multiple suppliers rather than only one. Supply chain management has become increasingly important to businesses wanting to stay competitive and profitable. Supply chain management refers to managing an extensive network of facilities and people involved in the process of acquiring raw materials, creating products, and distributing products to customers.

In some industries, such as auto, steel, and transportation, labor unions act as suppliers of workers. Although only about 10 percent of the U.S. labor force belongs to a union, unions still wield significant power. Labor unions represent the interests of their members in issues related to hiring, salaries, working conditions, and job security. In the past, labor unions and managers have been on opposite sides, but the relationship has improved over the years. Managers and labor unions realize the need to work collaboratively to increase productivity and to stay competitive in the marketplace. Labor-management committees are one method of bringing labor and management together to negotiate contracts. Representatives from both sides meet to discuss solutions to problems, which often leads to mutual benefits and trust.

Customers make or break a business, so they are the most critical direct environmental force. There are two types of consumers—final and intermediate. Final consumers purchase products in their completed form, such as a Wendy's hamburger or a pair of Nike running shoes. An intermediate consumer buys raw materials or wholesale products and then sells the product to final consumers. For example, Macy's department store is an intermediate consumer that buys clothing from manufacturers and wholesalers. Similar to suppliers, consumers affect the price of products and services by demanding higher quality, better service, and lower prices. The Internet has forced businesses to be more competitive because savvy consumers easily search for low prices.

Indirect Forces

Laws and politics are indirect forces that affect business organizations through government rules and regulations. Regulators are government agencies with the power to investigate businesses. Regulatory agencies monitor businesses to ensure compliance with laws regarding workplace, product, and environmental safety, and they fine organizations guilty of illegal business practices. The Occupational Safety and Health Administration (OSHA), the Federal Aviation Administration (FAA), and the Environmental Protection Agency (EPA) are examples of regulatory agencies. In addition, the Securities and Exchange Commission (SEC) monitors U.S. financial markets, and the Food and Drug Administration (FDA) oversees medical devices, pharmaceuticals, cosmetics, and food. Antitrust laws, trade regulations, and investment tax credits are legal forces that have an impact on businesses.

The economy shapes management decisions and consumer demand. Management expands production when the economy is strong, but during difficult economic times, businesses reduce production and cut jobs. Managers adjust staffing, operations, and prices based on inflation rates, interest rates, productivity, and unemployment rates. High interest and inflation rates affect the costs associated with borrowing money to expand a business and reduce consumer demand for products and services. Unemployment rates influence labor availability and wages. Energy sources and costs also have an impact on business by increasing or decreasing the expenses associated with running a business.

Another indirect environmental force on the economy is technology, which businesses use to meet consumer needs. Technological innovations in communication devices, television, software, medical devices, energy, robotics, and transportation change the way in which people live. Advancements in technology create new businesses and increase competition. Effective managers utilize technology to lower costs, increase production, and improve services and products.

Social and cultural issues influence an organization's human resources. For example, as large numbers of older, experienced people retire, managers must find new employees to replace them. Improved education and skill levels overseas have led many managers to outsource telemarketing and manufacturing jobs to India and other countries with low labor costs. Increasing numbers of immigrants and women in the workforce create more diversity in businesses. With a varied labor force, managers are increasingly aware of the need to provide equal opportunities and compensation and to tackle diversity issues in business plans. Many businesses are also implementing programs to address employee concerns such as mental stress, substance abuse, health care, career planning, and skills training.

Managers face the challenge of competing with global firms in addition to local ones. As technology increases, it is becoming increasingly common for businesses to compete on an international level. In the past, the size of an organization and its level of experience were the most important qualities to consumers. Today, speed and efficiency are qualities that count. International trade agreements, exchange rates, and cultural environments are global factors that influence business management in the twenty-first century.

MANAGEMENT FUNCTIONS

In the early 1900s, Henri Fayol, a French business owner, developed the first general theory of management. Fayol wrote a book about his management experiences in the mining industry. He expressed the idea that professional management involves five primary functions: planning, organizing, leading, coordinating, and controlling. Despite the numerous books that have been written in the last century about management,

Fayolism remains the most influential theory. However, Fayol's original five functions have been reduced to four, which are discussed in the next sections:

1. Plan
2. Organize
3. Lead
4. Control

Function 1: Plan

Planning is the first function of management and directs the way in which managers organize, lead, and control. Planning requires managers to create proactive plans to accomplish the goals and objectives of an organization. Managers consider a number of factors when developing plans:

- *Resources:* organizational, human, financial, and physical
- *Opportunities and risks:* innovations, competition, and demand

Although planning is difficult due to the fluctuating nature of direct and indirect forces, effective and efficient managers develop plans to handle future changes in the business environment.

Planning is a process of making decisions. The following table outlines the six basic steps involved in the basic planning process.

Step 1: Situational analysis	Process used by planners to gather, analyze, and summarize relevant data; process reviews past events, identifies current conditions, anticipates future trends, and considers internal and external forces; results in identification of decisions that need to be made and helps managers decide whether to move to next step in process
Step 2: Alternative goals and plans	Generate alternate goals (desired targets) and plans (actions to achieve goals); stress creativity and open minds of managers and employees
Step 3: Goal and plan evaluation	Evaluate pros, cons, and possible outcomes of each alternative goal and plan; prioritize and eliminate goals and plans
Step 4: Goal and plan selection	Select plan and goal that is most practical and possible; requires experienced judgment
Step 5: Implementation	Implement the chosen plan once managers and employees understand the plan and the necessary resources become available
Step 6: Monitor and control	Monitor subordinates regarding implementation of the plan; create control systems to measure performance and take corrective actions when necessary

It should be noted that in Step 2, there are three different types of plans that may be developed. Single-use plans are intended to accomplish a set of goals one time only. An example of a single-use plan is a grand opening celebration for the opening of a new hospital wing. Standing plans are established for ongoing activities that accomplish constant goals, such as a corporation's plan to recruit minorities. Standing plans often develop into corporate policies. Contingency plans are established when an initial plan fails or events call for immediate changes. Many organizations have contingency plans for dealing with major disasters to make sure that both data and employees stay safe.

Levels of Planning

Just as there are three levels of management—frontline, middle-level, and top-level—there are three levels of planning that vary in scope and activities.

- *Strategic planning* focuses on an organization's long-term (more than five years) goals and strategies in general terms. Strategic plans clarify the company's mission and goals for the future, and they are developed by top-level managers. For example, a firm's strategic plan may involve penetrating a new market.

- *Tactical planning* involves developing specific and intermediate-term (two to five years) goals and plans for implementing elements of the strategic plan. For example, tactical plans, which are implemented by middle management, may include designing and testing equipment needed for a new product.

- *Operational planning* involves translating tactical plans into specific steps in the short-term (less than two years). Frontline managers implement operational plans, which may require scheduling production runs and staffing.

Strategic Planning

In the past, strategic plans filtered downward from the top of an organization, but in recent years, tactical and operational managers have participated in the strategic planning process. Top executives have learned through experience that middle-level and frontline managers offer valuable input and ideas. Strategic management is the term used to describe the process of multi-level managers working together to develop and implement a firm's goals and strategies. The strategic management process is composed of six steps:

1. Establish mission, vision, and goals
2. Analyze external opportunities and threats
3. Analyze internal strengths and weaknesses
4. Perform SWOT analysis and formulate strategy
5. Implement strategy
6. Implement strategic control system

In the first step of the strategic management process, managers develop a mission statement that conveys the purpose of the organization. Effective mission statements focus on the customer, and they are attainable, inspirational, and specific. A strategic vision is the desired future direction of an organization, while strategic goals are the primary targets.

The mission, vision, and goals of an organization drive the second step of the process, which is analyzing the external environment. Managers study industry growth rates, market segments, and consumer purchasing power. Managers also analyze competitors, political activity related to the industry, social issues, labor issues, macroeconomic conditions, and technological factors.

During the third step, managers conduct an analysis of the strengths and weaknesses of significant internal components, such as finances, human resources, marketing activities, and manufacturing capabilities. Management also assesses the resources of the organization to determine its core competencies. Core competencies refer to the special skills or knowledge held by organizations that are especially valuable and rare. The core competence of a company is what it does better than the competition. For example, the core competence of Intel is complex chip design, while the core competence of Honda is small engine manufacturing.

After managers have gathered the information regarding the external and internal environment, they perform a SWOT analysis. A SWOT analysis is a comparison of the strengths, weaknesses, opportunities, and threats, and it provides managers with a helpful way to summarize the relevant information gathered in the environmental analysis. Managers then formulate three levels of strategy based on the SWOT analysis.

Levels of Strategy

Corporate-level strategy	Focuses on the big picture and how to accomplish the organization's goal; may involve concentration on a single business, diversification, or vertical integration
Business-level strategy	Focuses on the way in which a business competes in a specific industry or market for competitive advantage; may implement a low-cost strategy to make basic, inexpensive products or a differentiation strategy to make unique, high-quality products
Functional-level strategy	Implemented by functional units in an organization, such as production, human resources, marketing, finance, and distribution; creates value for the consumer

In the fifth step of strategic planning, managers monitor whether strategies are being implemented appropriately. Strategy implementation requires middle-level and frontline managers to define strategic tasks, evaluate the organization's ability to complete the tasks, create an agenda for implementation, and develop an implementation plan. Implementation is followed by strategic control, which is a system that helps managers evaluate the organization's progress and correct problems when necessary.

Function 2: Organize

Structuring a company's human and physical resources in a way that achieves organizational objectives is the process of organizing. Tasks, people, and departments all require organization to accomplish a company's goals. One of the initial steps in organizing is determining the organizational structure, which is the configuration of tasks and departments in a business. Organization charts visually clarify the reporting structure and levels of management. Differentiation and integration form the basis of organizational structure.

- *Differentiation:* an organization consists of different units that work on different tasks with different work methods and skills. Differentiation occurs through the division of labor and task specialization.

- *Integration:* the extent that different units in an organization coordinate their efforts to create a product or service.

Organizations with numerous specialized tasks and units are highly differentiated. In such businesses, there is a greater need for integration to ensure that all areas of an organization are working toward accomplishing the same goal.

Authority in Organizations

Authority in an organization refers to the sanctioned right to make a decision or tell others what to do. For example, the vice president of sales has the authority to give an order to a sales representative. Hierarchy establishes authority in an organization. In private businesses, the owners hold the greatest authority, but in publicly owned businesses, stockholders are the owners. Since stockholders lack the most current information needed to make wise decisions, a board of directors oversees an organization. A board of directors serves four primary duties:

1. Choosing, evaluating, rewarding, and, when necessary, replacing the CEO
2. Assessing an organization's financial performance
3. Deciding an organization's strategic direction
4. Monitoring an organization's ethical, legal, and socially responsible activities

A board of directors is also responsible for reporting to stockholders, protecting the rights of stockholders, and advising management. As the senior member of top-level management, a CEO reports to the board of directors and is responsible for a firm's performance.

An important aspect of an organization's structure is its span of control, which is the number of subordinates who report to one manager. Wide spans form flat organizations with many workers reporting to one manager. A narrow span creates a tall organization with numerous reporting levels and fewer workers reporting to one manager. The ideal span of control depends on a number of variables:

- Competence of manager and workers
- Similarity or dissimilarity of tasks

- Amount of interaction required
- Degree to which tasks are standardized

Authority in an organization is dispersed over management levels and spans of control, so delegation is important. Delegation refers to assigning responsibilities to subordinates, and it occurs at every level of an organization as a method of accomplishing tasks through other people. Delegating authority forms a chain of command that defines the line of authority from the top of an organization to the bottom. A chain of command specifies a reporting relationship for communicating both upward and downward in an organization.

Managers who delegate assignments must consider the ideas of responsibility, authority, and accountability. Responsibility refers to an employee's obligation to carry out an assigned task. Managers must ensure that a subordinate who has a specific responsibility has the necessary authority. Does the worker have the power to make decisions and give orders? Is the worker able to use necessary resources to fulfill the responsibility? In many cases, subordinates are given responsibilities for which they have no authority. The effective use of delegation saves managers time, and it raises the quality of subordinates.

The delegation of authority in an organization is either centralized or decentralized. In centralized businesses, high-level managers make major decisions. Authority is distributed throughout a decentralized organization. Decentralization benefits an organization by helping managers at all levels develop decision-making skills. Moreover, the managers who are the most knowledgeable about a problem are the most qualified to make a decision.

In conjunction with responsibility and the delegation of authority is the concept of accountability. Accountability refers to the expectation that a worker will perform a job and that failure to do so will result in corrective measures. One method of accountability involves requiring status reports from subordinates regarding assigned tasks.

Horizontal Structure

The concepts of authority, span of control, and decentralization relate to the vertical nature of an organization, but the horizontal structure is equally important. Departmentalization refers to the process of subdividing a business into smaller units or departments. One of the primary methods of subdividing work is by distinguishing line departments from staff departments. Line departments are responsible for the primary activities of the organization, which may be making things, selling things, or providing customer service. At Ford Motor Company, line departments include product design, assembly, and distribution. Staff departments support line departments with people who have specialized or professional skills. Types of line departments at Ford include accounting, legal, public relations, and human resources.

Organizations vary in the way they departmentalize as indicated by the following table.

Methods of Departmentalization

Functional organization	Units grouped according to specific activities like production, marketing, finance, and human resources; common in large and small businesses but best in stable environments; efficient use of resources; discourages communication across departments
Product organization	Units grouped around a specific product or product line; clear task responsibilities; flexibility makes it suitable for unstable environments; costly duplication of effort
Customer organization	Units grouped to serve customer needs, such as commercial or consumer accounts at a bank; costly duplication of activities
Geographic organization	Units grouped by defined territories, districts, regions, or countries; useful for firms with varying customer needs and characteristics; used most by multinational corporations; requires large and costly staff at headquarters
Matrix organization	Blending of functional and product organizations; originated in aerospace industry; dual line of command; workers placed in teams for specific tasks; decentralized decision making; vast communications network; can cause confusion regarding authority

Staffing

Skilled individuals are the most important element of any organization, so staffing is a critical part of any manager's job. Recruitment, selection, and outplacement are the three primary staffing functions in organizations. Recruitment refers to attracting a pool of job candidates with the skills and attitudes beneficial to an organization. Advertising, visiting universities, and using private employment agencies are some of the ways in which businesses recruit employees.

During the selection process, an organization chooses the best candidate for a position. Selection tools may include applications, résumés, interviews, background checks, drug tests, and performance tests. Whatever the screening method, managers should be aware of legal and illegal activities during staff selection.

Legal and Illegal Screening Activities

Legal	*Illegal*
Ask if a person is authorized to work in the United States	Ask for proof of citizenship
Ask if a person has been convicted of a crime	Ask if a person has been arrested

Ask for proof of age after hiring	Require a birth certificate
Keep records for recording purposes about racial and ethnic identity	Ask for race, creed, or national origin on application or during interview

Staffing decisions involve more than recruiting and screening. Difficult economic times often force companies to downsize by laying off many employees at once. At such times, many firms offer outplacement services. Outplacement refers to the process of assisting dismissed workers find new jobs.

Function 3: Lead

Management positions in an organization offer the opportunity to exhibit leadership, which involves making changes and creating a vision for a firm. Successful leaders motivate others to overcome obstacles and accomplish organizational goals. At the core of effective leadership is power, the ability to influence other people to do something that they might not otherwise do. In a business setting, managers have five potential power sources.

Power Sources

Reward power	Leader controls valued rewards, such as pay raises, promotions, and bonuses.
Coercive power	Leader controls punishments that people want to avoid, such as below-average performance evaluations.
Expert power	Leader has expertise or knowledge that people trust or believe.
Referent power	Leader has personal characteristics that trigger loyalty and admiration in others.
Legitimate power	Leader has the authority to tell others what to do, so people are obligated to comply.

Classic Approaches to Understanding Leadership

Leadership in regards to management has been studied and researched over the years. The three most widely accepted classic approaches for understanding leadership are the trait approach, the behavioral approach, and the situational approach.

Trait theory was the earliest attempt to define leadership qualities. The study occurred between 1904 and 1948 and focused on more than 100 leadership traits. The trait approach attempted to uncover the personal characteristics shared by exceptional leaders. The trait theory assumes that leaders are born with characteristics such as self-assurance, intelligence, sociability, and aggressiveness. However, upon completion of the study, scholars determined that no specific characteristics were essential for someone to become a great leader. The modern perspective regarding trait theory is that some personality attributes appear to separate successful leaders from other people. Drive, integrity, self-confidence, and business knowledge distinguish leaders from followers.

The behavioral theory of leadership attempts to identify the behaviors of effective leaders. Experts have identified three general leadership behavior categories—task performance, group maintenance, and participation in decision making.

Leader Behaviors

Category	Definition	Example Behaviors
Task performance	Actions are taken to complete a task and reach a goal.	Setting goals, praising good work, giving instructions, and supervising work quality.
Group maintenance	Actions are taken to ensure group satisfaction, stability, and harmony.	Showing concern for people's feelings and expressing appreciation.
Participation in decision making	Actions are taken to involve employees in making decisions.	Autocratic leaders make decisions and announce them to employees. Democratic leaders solicit input from employees.

The Leader-Member Exchange (LMX) theory relates to group maintenance behaviors. According to the LMX theory, group maintenance behaviors such as trust, mutual respect, mutual loyalty, and open communication form the basis of satisfying personal relationships with group members.

Situational theorists assert that universal leadership traits and behaviors are nonexistent and that effective leadership varies from one situation to another. Effective leaders analyze a situation before making a decision. The Vroom model for decision making and the path-goal theory are the primary situational models considered valid for modern management.

- *Vroom model:* a situational model proposed by Victor H. Vroom that helps leaders decide how much participation to use in decision making. The model works like a funnel, asking the leader questions until reaching a recommended decision style. Decide, consult individually, consult the group, facilitate, and delegate are the five possible decision styles.

- *Path-goal theory:* a theory developed by Robert House that assesses characteristics of the followers and environmental factors before determining the appropriate leadership behavior. The four leadership behaviors are directive leadership, supportive leadership, participative leadership, and achievement-oriented leadership. Appropriate leader behaviors lead to effective performance from the followers.

Modern Theories on Leadership

While the historical views on leadership remain relevant today, contemporary experts have developed their own ideas about different leadership styles.

Leadership Styles

Charismatic leaders	Arouse excitement, hold strong moral convictions, and convey extreme self-confidence
Transformational leaders	Motivate people to focus on good of the group rather than personal interests
Transactional leaders	Use legitimate, reward, and coercive powers to give orders in exchange for benefits to followers
Level 5 leaders	Combine determination and humility to build long-term leadership
Authentic leaders	Use honesty, genuineness, reliability, and integrity to lead others; willing to sacrifice own interests
Pseudo transformational leaders	Speak about positive change for followers but power, control, wealth, and fame take priority

Motivation

An important aspect of leading is motivation, which refers to the set of forces that energize, guide, and maintain a person's efforts. Managers are responsible for motivating employees to be punctual, work well with others, and perform quality work. Setting goals for employees is a valuable motivational tool. For goals to be effective, they should be acceptable to workers, challenging, and achievable. Some of today's large organizations set stretch goals for employees. Stretch goals are especially difficult, but they are attainable. Firms have found that stretch goals push employees out of mediocrity and toward excellence.

Reinforcement is another method of encouraging or discouraging employee behavior. Organizational behavior modification attempts to change worker behavior and improve job performance by managing work conditions and applying consequences for specific actions.

- *Positive reinforcement:* give a consequence that will encourage the behavior to be repeated, such as a letter of commendation, pay raise, or positive performance evaluation
- *Negative reinforcement:* remove an unpleasant consequence, such as taking a worker off probation due to improved job performance
- *Punishment:* give an unpleasant consequence, such as criticizing an employee or assigning a worker to an undesirable task or shift
- *Extinction:* fail to give a reinforcing consequence by not complimenting an employee for doing a good job or setting unachievable performance goals

Positive reinforcement is utilized the most in business settings. Effective managers find creative ways to motivate employees by both monetary and nonmonetary means.

While reinforcement theory focuses on how the work environment motivates people's behavior, expectancy theory focuses on how people make behavioral decisions based on expected outcomes. Vroom's expectancy theory is one of the most widely accepted motivation theories, and it is based on three variables.

1. *Expectancy:* an employee's belief that increased efforts will lead to achieving performance goals
2. *Instrumentality:* an employee's belief that good job performance will lead to a specific outcome
3. *Valence:* the value that an employee places on a specific outcome

Expectancy theory proposes that employee motivation is a function of all three variables working together. The theory offers a general method of understanding the complex nature of employee motivation.

Content theories of motivation stem from the idea that people want to satisfy basic needs. The three main content theories are Maslow's hierarchy of needs, Alderfer's ERG theory, and McClelland's needs.

Content Theories of Motivation

Maslow's need hierarchy	People satisfy needs in a specific order; the needs in ascending order are physiological, safety, social, ego, and self-actualization
Alderfer's ERG theory	People have three basic sets of needs: existence, relatedness, and growth
McClelland's needs	People have three dominant needs: achievement, affiliation, and power

Function 4: Control

Control is the fourth and final function of management. A control process directs employees toward achieving organizational goals and takes corrective measures when plans go unfulfilled. A lack of controls in an organization leads to any number of problems, such as poor product quality and employee theft. Three general methods exist for achieving organizational control.

- *Bureaucratic control:* guides activities with formal rules, regulations, and authority, such as budgets and performance appraisals; best used for well-defined tasks and independent workers.

- *Market control:* guides activities with pricing mechanisms and economic information, such as evaluation based on profits and losses; best used where output can be clearly identified.

- *Clan control:* guides activities with norms, values, and trust with the assumption that the organization and the employee share the same interests; best used in environments where employees are empowered in decision making and where there is no explicit way to complete a task.

The bureaucratic, or formal, control system is the one most commonly used in organizations, although market and clan controls are valid methods for regulating employee performance. However, for the purpose of this review, the focus will be on bureaucratic control systems.

Control systems usually consist of four steps:

1. Setting performance standards
2. Measuring performance
3. Comparing performance with the standard
4. Taking corrective action

A standard is a performance target for an organizational goal. Standards clarify the desired performance level, motivate employee performance, and act as benchmarks for performance assessment. Any activity or unit within an organization—financial, legal, ethical—can have a set of expected standards. Performance standards are based on quantity, quality, time used, and cost.

Measuring performance is the second stage of the control process. Managers measure employee or unit performance by counting the number of dollars earned, products sold, and items manufactured. Written reports, oral reports, and personal observations provide management with the data needed to measure performance.

The third step in the control process involves comparing performance with the established standards. Managers analyze and evaluate performance results. According to the principle of exception, managers should focus attention on the cases that deviate significantly from the expected standard. For example, if five computer components out of every 1,000 produced on an assembly line are defective, a manager should investigate the five exceptions rather than the 995 other components. In addition, managers should not focus much time or effort on performance that is equal to or close to the standard. With the principle of exception, managers focus on the exceptions and not the norm to save valuable time.

The final step in the control process involves taking corrective action when significant deviations occur. During this step of control, adjustments are made to ensure that the planned results and goals are met. Corrective measures may be taken immediately by the manager or by subordinates involved directly with the problem. In the case of computerized manufacturing, two types of control may occur:

- *Specialist control:* employees who operate computer-numerical-control (CNC) machines notify engineering specialists about equipment problems, and the specialist corrects the issue.

- *Operator control:* trained operators repair problems as they occur, which can be more efficient than specialist control.

In addition to equipment malfunctions, corrective action may require altering a marketing approach, disciplining an employee, or providing specialized training for workers.

Managers choose from three approaches to bureaucratic control—feedforward, concurrent, and feedback.

Bureaucratic Control Approaches

Feedforward control	Focuses on preventing problems before they occur; enacted before operations start; involves policies, procedures, and rules that limit certain activities; also known as preliminary control
Concurrent control	Focuses on directing, monitoring, and modifying ongoing activities
Feedback control	Focuses on end results; uses performance data to correct deviations and guide future actions; Six Sigma is a feedback control tool used in manufacturing that aims to reduce defects

Auditing and Budgeting

A management audit is a type of control used to evaluate the effectiveness and efficiency of an organization. External audits are performed by an outside organization, such as an accounting firm. Internal audits are performed in-house to assess various elements of a firm, such as financial stability, public relations, social responsibility, and manufacturing efficiency.

Budgeting, or budgetary controlling, is a widely used control process that involves investigating what a firm has done. Results are compared with budget information for the purpose of verification and correction. Budgets connect feedforward, concurrent, and feedback controls. A budget guides the allocation of resources before an operation begins, which is a feedforward control. During the ongoing activities of an operation, budgets are monitored, which is a concurrent control. Feedback control occurs when sales and expenses are compared.

POST-TEST ANSWER SHEET

1. Ⓐ Ⓑ Ⓒ Ⓓ 13. Ⓐ Ⓑ Ⓒ Ⓓ 25. Ⓐ Ⓑ Ⓒ Ⓓ 37. Ⓐ Ⓑ Ⓒ Ⓓ 49. Ⓐ Ⓑ Ⓒ Ⓓ

2. Ⓐ Ⓑ Ⓒ Ⓓ 14. Ⓐ Ⓑ Ⓒ Ⓓ 26. Ⓐ Ⓑ Ⓒ Ⓓ 38. Ⓐ Ⓑ Ⓒ Ⓓ 50. Ⓐ Ⓑ Ⓒ Ⓓ

3. Ⓐ Ⓑ Ⓒ Ⓓ 15. Ⓐ Ⓑ Ⓒ Ⓓ 27. Ⓐ Ⓑ Ⓒ Ⓓ 39. Ⓐ Ⓑ Ⓒ Ⓓ 51. Ⓐ Ⓑ Ⓒ Ⓓ

4. Ⓐ Ⓑ Ⓒ Ⓓ 16. Ⓐ Ⓑ Ⓒ Ⓓ 28. Ⓐ Ⓑ Ⓒ Ⓓ 40. Ⓐ Ⓑ Ⓒ Ⓓ 52. Ⓐ Ⓑ Ⓒ Ⓓ

5. Ⓐ Ⓑ Ⓒ Ⓓ 17. Ⓐ Ⓑ Ⓒ Ⓓ 29. Ⓐ Ⓑ Ⓒ Ⓓ 41. Ⓐ Ⓑ Ⓒ Ⓓ 53. Ⓐ Ⓑ Ⓒ Ⓓ

6. Ⓐ Ⓑ Ⓒ Ⓓ 18. Ⓐ Ⓑ Ⓒ Ⓓ 30. Ⓐ Ⓑ Ⓒ Ⓓ 42. Ⓐ Ⓑ Ⓒ Ⓓ 54. Ⓐ Ⓑ Ⓒ Ⓓ

7. Ⓐ Ⓑ Ⓒ Ⓓ 19. Ⓐ Ⓑ Ⓒ Ⓓ 31. Ⓐ Ⓑ Ⓒ Ⓓ 43. Ⓐ Ⓑ Ⓒ Ⓓ 55. Ⓐ Ⓑ Ⓒ Ⓓ

8. Ⓐ Ⓑ Ⓒ Ⓓ 20. Ⓐ Ⓑ Ⓒ Ⓓ 32. Ⓐ Ⓑ Ⓒ Ⓓ 44. Ⓐ Ⓑ Ⓒ Ⓓ 56. Ⓐ Ⓑ Ⓒ Ⓓ

9. Ⓐ Ⓑ Ⓒ Ⓓ 21. Ⓐ Ⓑ Ⓒ Ⓓ 33. Ⓐ Ⓑ Ⓒ Ⓓ 45. Ⓐ Ⓑ Ⓒ Ⓓ 57. Ⓐ Ⓑ Ⓒ Ⓓ

10. Ⓐ Ⓑ Ⓒ Ⓓ 22. Ⓐ Ⓑ Ⓒ Ⓓ 34. Ⓐ Ⓑ Ⓒ Ⓓ 46. Ⓐ Ⓑ Ⓒ Ⓓ 58. Ⓐ Ⓑ Ⓒ Ⓓ

11. Ⓐ Ⓑ Ⓒ Ⓓ 23. Ⓐ Ⓑ Ⓒ Ⓓ 35. Ⓐ Ⓑ Ⓒ Ⓓ 47. Ⓐ Ⓑ Ⓒ Ⓓ 59. Ⓐ Ⓑ Ⓒ Ⓓ

12. Ⓐ Ⓑ Ⓒ Ⓓ 24. Ⓐ Ⓑ Ⓒ Ⓓ 36. Ⓐ Ⓑ Ⓒ Ⓓ 48. Ⓐ Ⓑ Ⓒ Ⓓ 60. Ⓐ Ⓑ Ⓒ Ⓓ

answer sheet

POST-TEST

Directions: Carefully read each of the following 60 questions. Choose the best answer to each question, and darken its letter on your answer sheet. The Answer Key and Explanations can be found following this post-test.

1. Regulating activities within an organization using pricing mechanisms is a type of
   (A) market control.
   (B) specialist control.
   (C) clan control.
   (D) operator control.

2. Which of the following persons developed the first theory regarding management functions?
   (A) Winslow Taylor
   (B) Henri Fayol
   (C) Max Weber
   (D) Henry Mintzberg

3. The process of teaching new employees the appropriate roles and behaviors needed to become effective members of a business is
   (A) organizational socialization.
   (B) cultural diagnosis.
   (C) interpersonal development.
   (D) managerial training.

4. Which of the following is the most cost-effective method of departmentalization?
   (A) Functional
   (B) Geographic
   (C) Customer
   (D) Product

5. A primary skill necessary at every level of management is
   (A) training.
   (B) technical.
   (C) conceptual.
   (D) decision-making.

6. Which of the following is characteristic of feedforward control?
   (A) Implementing transfer pricing
   (B) Monitoring ongoing data flow
   (C) Establishing rules and procedures
   (D) Evaluating performance results

7. Which theory is based on the idea that great leaders are born with self-assurance, integrity, and assertiveness?
   (A) Content theory
   (B) Path-goal theory
   (C) Trait theory
   (D) Behavioral theory

8. Labor unions traditionally focus on issues related to
   (A) salaries.
   (B) competitors.
   (C) managerial levels.
   (D) regulatory agencies.

9. Which of the following questions may legally be asked of a job candidate?
   (A) "How old are you?"
   (B) "What is your nationality?"
   (C) "May I see your proof of citizenship?"
   (D) "Have you ever been convicted of a crime?"

10. The process of different levels of managers working together to develop and implement organizational goals and strategies is
    (A) systematic management.
    (B) tactical management.
    (C) administrative management.
    (D) strategic management.

11. All of the following are informational roles of managers EXCEPT
    (A) monitor.
    (B) spokesperson.
    (C) disseminator.
    (D) figurehead.

12. Which of the following control systems is most commonly used by firms?
    (A) Clan
    (B) Market
    (C) Bureaucratic
    (D) Organizational

13. An employee's belief that increased efforts at work will lead to accomplishing performance goals is known as
    (A) equity.
    (B) expectancy.
    (C) task identity.
    (D) instrumentality.

14. Which of the following has the power to regulate X-ray machines and blood glucose meters?
    (A) Occupational Safety and Health Administration
    (B) Environmental Protection Agency
    (C) Food and Drug Administration
    (D) Centers for Disease Control and Prevention

15. Six Sigma is a tool used for
    (A) feedforward control.
    (B) feedback control.
    (C) concurrent control.
    (D) operator control.

16. Which of the following is developed to create consistency in situations repeatedly faced by an organization?
    (A) Single-use plans
    (B) Objectives
    (C) Standing plans
    (D) Scenarios

17. A sales manager who tries to make improvements in the sales department is functioning as a(n)
    (A) entrepreneur.
    (B) negotiator.
    (C) monitor.
    (D) liaison.

18. According to David McClelland, all of the following are people's primary needs EXCEPT
    (A) achievement.
    (B) power.
    (C) affiliation.
    (D) growth.

19. The process of developing a pool of job applicants is referred to as
    (A) outplacement.
    (B) assessment.
    (C) selection.
    (D) recruitment.

20. An intermediate consumer most likely purchases items from
    (A) retailers.
    (B) big box stores.
    (C) e-businesses.
    (D) wholesalers.

21. Which of the following combines aspects of feedforward, concurrent, and feedback control?

    (A) Auditing

    (B) Marketing

    (C) Budgeting

    (D) Financing

22. The extent that different work units work together to coordinate efforts is known as

    (A) integration.

    (B) organization.

    (C) configuration.

    (D) differentiation.

23. According to expectancy theory, the importance that an employee places on a specific outcome is known as

    (A) valence.

    (B) motivation.

    (C) legitimacy.

    (D) instrumentality.

24. Which of the following is the most likely managerial benefit of technological advancements implemented in a manufacturing facility?

    (A) Improved labor relations

    (B) Increased production

    (C) Lower energy costs

    (D) Diverse workforce

25. All of the following are characteristics of clan control EXCEPT

    (A) minimal direction.

    (B) employee empowerment.

    (C) shared employee norms.

    (D) specified procedures.

26. Which of the following best describes operational planning?

    (A) Short-term time frame and low level of details

    (B) Short-term time frame and high level of details

    (C) Long-term time frame and low level of details

    (D) Medium-term time frame and medium level of details

27. The Caux Principles were primarily developed to address

    (A) business ethics.

    (B) global commerce.

    (C) accounting standards.

    (D) environmental awareness.

28. Which of the following is established and implemented to help employees behave in the best interests of a business?

    (A) Customer organization

    (B) Mission statement

    (C) Control system

    (D) Tactical plan

29. Group maintenance behaviors can lead to the development of personal relationships with group members according to

    (A) LMX theory.

    (B) LPC theory.

    (C) Vroom theory.

    (D) Hersey-Blanchard theory.

30. One of the potential benefits of developing a strong organizational culture is

    (A) customer satisfaction.

    (B) economic stability.

    (C) ethics enforcement.

    (D) employee loyalty.

post-test

31. Which of the following is characterized by high-level managers making the majority of decisions?
    (A) Centralized organization
    (B) High-involvement organization
    (C) Decentralized organization
    (D) Learning organization

32. Compliance-based ethics programs are designed to
    (A) encourage ethical behavior through rewards.
    (B) create interest in social responsibility efforts.
    (C) impose punishments upon ethics violators.
    (D) comply with global business guidelines.

33. The first step in the strategic management process is
    (A) analyzing potential opportunities.
    (B) formulating a functional strategy.
    (C) assessing strengths and weaknesses.
    (D) establishing a mission statement.

34. Stretch goals are best described as
    (A) straightforward.
    (B) prolonged.
    (C) impossible.
    (D) demanding.

35. Factors outside of an organization that affect a business are known as the
    (A) supply-chain force.
    (B) external environment.
    (C) global marketplace.
    (D) peripheral culture.

36. The concept that a business should obey laws, perform ethically, and contribute positively to a community's quality of life is known as
    (A) environmental scanning.
    (B) sustainable growth.
    (C) internal strategies.
    (D) social responsibility.

37. In an automobile manufacturing corporation, the accounting department is known as a
    (A) line department.
    (B) regional department.
    (C) staff department.
    (D) product department.

38. The ability of Sony to miniaturize electronic equipment better than other organizations is an example of a
    (A) product champion.
    (B) business-level strategy.
    (C) flexible process.
    (D) core competency.

39. Management reductions in recent years have mostly affected
    (A) supervisors.
    (B) middle management.
    (C) chief executive officers.
    (D) top management.

40. Which type of consequence is exemplified when a manager fails to show appreciation to an especially helpful subordinate?
    (A) Positive reinforcement
    (B) Punishment
    (C) Negative reinforcement
    (D) Extinction

41. Overseeing the interconnected network of facilities and people that take a product from the raw material stage to distribution is known as
    (A) supply chain management.
    (B) flexible manufacturing.
    (C) egocentric management.
    (D) strategic planning.

42. Which of the following is the result of a wide span of control?
    (A) Few workers reporting to one supervisor
    (B) Few workers reporting to multiple supervisors
    (C) Many workers reporting to one supervisor
    (D) Many workers reporting to multiple supervisors

43. All of the following are types of corporate-level strategies EXCEPT
    (A) vertical integration.
    (B) implementation.
    (C) diversification.
    (D) concentration.

44. Task-specific knowledge refers to
    (A) communication skills.
    (B) analytical skills.
    (C) computer skills.
    (D) technical skills.

45. Determination and personal humility best describe
    (A) pseudo transformational leaders.
    (B) bridge leaders.
    (C) transactional leaders.
    (D) level 5 leaders.

46. Which of the following methods of departmentalization is most commonly used by multinational corporations?
    (A) Product
    (B) Geographic
    (C) Matrix
    (D) Functional

47. Management decisions to outsource manufacturing jobs to foreign countries have primarily been influenced by
    (A) trade agreements.
    (B) immigration.
    (C) labor costs.
    (D) tax laws.

48. Which of the following developed a situational model of leadership that leads to five possible decision styles?
    (A) Henri Fayol
    (B) Fred Fiedler
    (C) Abraham Maslow
    (D) Victor Vroom

49. Which of the following has most likely used a differentiation strategy in pursuit of competitive advantage?
    (A) Walmart
    (B) Toshiba
    (C) Porsche
    (D) Hoover

50. A manager's ability to understand the strategies and objectives of a business is an aspect of
    (A) decision-making skills.
    (B) conceptual skills.
    (C) interpersonal skills.
    (D) analytical skills.

51. Managers who concentrate on significant deviations from anticipated standards are most likely using the principle of
    (A) control.
    (B) accountability.
    (C) standardization.
    (D) exception.

52. Government agencies that have the power to investigate business practices are known as
    (A) prospectors.
    (B) supervisors.
    (C) regulators.
    (D) defenders.

53. All of the following are primary duties of an organization's board of directors EXCEPT
    (A) selecting the chief executive officer.
    (B) making daily operational decisions.
    (C) monitoring financial performance.
    (D) determining strategic direction.

54. Management activities such as hiring, training, and motivating workers are part of the
    (A) figurehead role.
    (B) leadership role.
    (C) monitor role.
    (D) resource allocator role.

55. Which of the following summarizes information gathered in an environmental analysis during the strategic planning process?
    (A) ABC
    (B) CRM
    (C) LCA
    (D) SWOT

56. All of the following are societal factors that indirectly influence businesses EXCEPT
    (A) birth rate.
    (B) productivity.
    (C) immigration.
    (D) life expectancy.

57. A sales manager who reaches a deal with the CEO about implementing flexible scheduling for the sales unit is acting as a
    (A) negotiator.
    (B) liaison.
    (C) figurehead.
    (D) disseminator.

58. Exchange rates and trade agreements are examples of
    (A) cooperative strategies.
    (B) direct forces.
    (C) entry barriers.
    (D) indirect forces.

59. Studying the ten roles of a manager is important to realizing that
    (A) all the roles are interconnected.
    (B) technical and general skills are both essential.
    (C) some roles are significantly more important.
    (D) levels of management are complex.

60. Which of the following is a situational factor in the path-goal theory?
    (A) Motivational methods
    (B) Characteristics of leaders
    (C) Leadership style
    (D) Characteristics of followers

ANSWER KEY AND EXPLANATIONS

1. A	13. B	25. D	37. C	49. C
2. B	14. C	26. B	38. D	50. B
3. A	15. B	27. A	39. B	51. D
4. A	16. C	28. C	40. D	52. C
5. D	17. A	29. A	41. A	53. B
6. C	18. D	30. D	42. C	54. B
7. C	19. D	31. A	43. B	55. D
8. A	20. D	32. C	44. D	56. B
9. D	21. C	33. D	45. D	57. A
10. D	22. A	34. D	46. B	58. D
11. D	23. A	35. B	47. C	59. A
12. C	24. B	36. D	48. D	60. D

1. **The correct answer is (A).** Market control uses pricing mechanisms and economic data to regulate activities in an organization. Specialist control and operator control are processes used in computerized manufacturing. Clan control is the idea that employees with shared values require fewer bureaucratic controls.

2. **The correct answer is (B).** Henri Fayol developed the first theory of professional management functions, which include planning, organizing, leading, and controlling. Taylor, choice (A), is regarded for improving industrial efficiency. Weber, choice (C), was one of the leading founders of sociology. Mintzberg, choice (D), identified the ten roles of managers.

3. **The correct answer is (A).** Organizational socialization is the process of teaching new employees the appropriate roles and behaviors needed to become effective members of a business. Managers and co-workers help new workers develop the skills necessary for acceptance into an organization. Choices (B), (C), and (D) are incorrect.

4. **The correct answer is (A).** The functional departmentalization method is the most cost effective because it uses resources efficiently. Geographic, customer, and product organizations require the duplication of many activities, so they are not cost effective.

5. **The correct answer is (D).** Decision-making skills are necessary at every level of management. Training workers and having technical skills are most important for frontline managers who deal with blue-collar workers. Top-level managers must have conceptual skills for making long-range goals, so choice (C) is incorrect.

6. **The correct answer is (C).** Establishing rules and procedures before an activity begins is characteristic of feedforward control. Monitoring ongoing data, choice (B), is an aspect of concurrent control. Feedback control involves evaluating performance results, choice (D).

7. **The correct answer is (C).** Trait theory is based on the idea that great leaders are born with characteristics such as self-assurance, integrity, and

assertiveness. Content theory, choice (A), is a motivational theory. Choices (B) and (D) are leadership theories that do not assert that people are born with leadership qualities.

8. **The correct answer is (A).** Salaries, working conditions, hiring practices, and job security are the focus of most labor unions. Labor unions remain a significant direct force in industries such as auto and steel, although only about 10 percent of U.S. workers are members. Choices (B), (C), and (D) are less important issues to labor unions.

9. **The correct answer is (D).** It is legal to ask a job candidate if he or she has been convicted of a crime; however, it is illegal to ask about arrests. Asking a person's age can only be done after hiring. It is illegal to ask about a person's nationality and for proof of citizenship.

10. **The correct answer is (D).** Strategic management is the term for the process that brings together different levels of managers to develop and implement organizational goals and strategies. Systematic management and administrative management were two classical approaches toward management that did not involve different managerial levels. Middle-level managers are sometimes referred to as tactical managers.

11. **The correct answer is (D).** The roles of monitor, disseminator, and spokesperson are informational roles performed by managers according to Mintzberg's research study. Interpersonal roles include figurehead, leader, and liaison. Therefore, choice (D) is the best answer.

12. **The correct answer is (C).** Bureaucratic control, which is also known as formal control, is the most commonly used control system within organizations. Market control systems are appropriate in situations where output can be clearly identified. Clan control is appropriate in flexible settings that allow employees to make decisions.

13. **The correct answer is (B).** According to expectancy theory, expectancy is a person's belief that increased efforts at work will lead to accomplishing performance goals. Instrumentality is the employee's belief that good job performance will lead to certain outcomes. Choices (A) and (C) are not variables in expectancy theory.

14. **The correct answer is (C).** The Food and Drug Administration (FDA) monitors medical devices, such as X-ray machines and blood glucose meters, to ensure compliance with safety standards. Choices (A) and (B) are both regulatory agencies, but neither oversees medical devices. The CDC is an agency of the U.S. Department of Health and Human Services that provides information related to disease prevention and health improvement.

15. **The correct answer is (B).** Six Sigma is a feedback control tool used to reduce defects in manufacturing. Feedback control involves using performance data to correct problems and guide future actions. Motorola developed Six Sigma, and it is used by many organizations, including hospitals and manufacturing firms like GE and Ford. Choices (A), (C), and (D) are incorrect.

16. **The correct answer is (C).** Standing plans are established for dealing with ongoing activities so that decisions can be made quickly, easily, and consistently. Standing plans often develop into company policies. Single-use plans are developed for one-time situations. Choices (B) and (D) are used

in the planning process but are not developed for the sake of consistency.

17. **The correct answer is (A).** According to Mintzberg, the entrepreneurial role of a manager involves making improvements to a unit. The negotiator bargains with others to gain benefits, and the monitor observes successes, failures, and problems that may affect the unit. As a liaison, a manager communicates with people inside and outside the organization.

18. **The correct answer is (D).** According to McClelland, people's three main needs are achievement, affiliation, and power. Growth, existence, and relatedness are people's needs according to Alderfer's theory.

19. **The correct answer is (D).** Recruitment is the process of developing a pool of job applicants through job advertisements and employment agencies. Outplacement refers to the process of assisting dismissed workers find new jobs. Selection is the process of choosing an applicant to hire into a business, which involves a series of assessments.

20. **The correct answer is (D).** An intermediate consumer purchases items from wholesalers and manufacturers to make a finished product that will be sold to final consumers. Choices (A), (B), and (C) are incorrect because final consumers purchase goods from retailers, which include big box stores like Walmart and e-businesses.

21. **The correct answer is (C).** Budgeting combines aspects of feedforward, concurrent, and feedback control. Budgets are established before a project begins, and they are monitored during a project. At the end of a project or activity, sales and expenses are compared for feedback.

22. **The correct answer is (A).** Integration refers to the extent to which different units in an organization coordinate their efforts to create a product or service. Organizations that are highly differentiated need integration to make sure that all units work together to meet goals.

23. **The correct answer is (A).** According to expectancy theory, valence refers to the importance that an employee places on a specific outcome. Vroom's expectancy theory analyzes what motivates people, so choice (B) is incorrect. Instrumentality, choice (D), is a variable in the theory that refers to an employee's belief that good work leads to a specific outcome. Choice (C) is incorrect.

24. **The correct answer is (B).** Increased production is the most likely benefit of technological advancements utilized in the workplace. Some technology may improve energy efficiency but not necessarily. Technology will have less effect on labor relations and workforce diversity.

25. **The correct answer is (D).** Clan control is characterized by minimal direction and standards, employee empowerment, and shared norms. Clan control is useful in business environments where there is more than one accepted method for completing a task. Choices (A), (B), and (C) are incorrect.

26. **The correct answer is (B).** A short-term time frame and high level of details best describe operational planning. Choice (C) describes the characteristics of strategic planning. Choice (D) describes tactical planning.

27. **The correct answer is (A).** An international group of business leaders developed the Caux Principles to address universal business ethics. The

main premise of the Caux Principles is showing human dignity and working toward the common good. Choices (B), (C), and (D) are not the focus of the Caux Principles.

28. **The correct answer is (C).** Control systems are established and implemented to help employees behave in the best interests of a business. Control systems, such as performance appraisals and raises, regulate employee performance. A mission statement is an organization's basic purpose, but it does not guide employee behavior. Choices (A) and (D) are not specifically geared toward directing the activities of employees.

29. **The correct answer is (A).** The Leader-Member Exchange (LMX) theory asserts that group maintenance behaviors, such as trust, mutual respect, mutual loyalty, and open communication, can lead to the development of personal relationships with group members. LPC theory and Hersey-Blanchard theory are situational rather than behavioral leadership theories.

30. **The correct answer is (D).** Employee loyalty and cooperation are both potential benefits of a strong organizational culture. Employees who feel like they are members of a team are more likely to remain at a job and work hard. Choices (A), (B), and (C) are less likely benefits of a strong culture within an organization.

31. **The correct answer is (A).** Top executives make the most of decisions in centralized organizations. In decentralized organizations, decision making is dispersed throughout the company. In high-involvement organizations, upper management seeks a consensus from all levels of the company. An organization

especially skilled at problem solving and creativity is known as a learning organization.

32. **The correct answer is (C).** Compliance-based ethics programs are designed to impose punishments upon ethics violators. Such programs usually involve increased monitoring of employees and the establishment of legal standards and procedures regarding ethics. In contrast, integrity-based ethics programs attempt to instill a sense of personal responsibility into employees. Choices (A), (B), and (D) do not describe compliance-based ethics programs.

33. **The correct answer is (D).** Establishing the mission, vision, and goals of the organization are the first steps in the strategic planning process. Choice (A) is the second stage of the process, and choice (C) is the third stage. Formulating a strategy, choice (B), occurs after performing a SWOT analysis in the fourth stage.

34. **The correct answer is (D).** Stretch goals are attainable but demanding goals used by firms to motivate employees to be excellent at their jobs. While stretch goals are challenging and may seem impossible, they are achievable.

35. **The correct answer is (B).** The external environment includes the direct and indirect forces that affect an organization. Direct forces include suppliers, competitors, and customers. Indirect forces include the legal system, the economy, and the global marketplace. Choices (A), (C), and (D) are incorrect.

36. **The correct answer is (D).** Social responsibility refers to the idea that corporations have economic, legal, ethical, and philanthropic responsibilities to society. Choice (A) refers

to collecting data about various forces in the management environment. Choice (B) refers to economic growth that addresses current needs without negatively affecting the needs of people in the future. Internal strategies are actions taken by businesses to avoid threats and benefit from opportunities.

37. **The correct answer is (C).** The accounting department in an automobile manufacturing corporation is a staff department. Staff departments support line departments, choice (A), which are the ones responsible for the main activities of a business. Choices (B) and (D) are incorrect.

38. **The correct answer is (D).** Sony's ability to miniaturize electronics better than other firms is an example of a core competency. Core competencies are the special skills or knowledge held by organizations that are unique and valuable. Choices (A), (B), and (C) are management terms not related to core competencies.

39. **The correct answer is (B).** Middle management has been primarily affected by corporate reductions in management staff. Supervisors are needed to directly oversee workers, while CEOs and other top-level managers are needed to guide a company into the future with long-term plans. Middle managers are more expendable in large corporations, such as IBM and Sears, where efficiency and cost effectiveness are becoming extremely important.

40. **The correct answer is (D).** Extinction is failing to provide a reinforcing consequence. Failing to show appreciation for help or failing to compliment employees for working hard are examples of extinction. Negative reinforcement may have been

tempting, but it involves removing an undesirable consequence.

41. **The correct answer is (A).** Supply chain management refers to managing an extensive network of facilities and people involved in the process of acquiring raw materials, creating products, and distributing products to customers. Tough competition has increased the need for managers to monitor costs closely at every stage of production and distribution. Choices (B), (C), and (D) are incorrect.

42. **The correct answer is (C).** With a wide span of control, many workers report to one supervisor. A narrow span of control results in a small number of workers reporting to one supervisor. In most organizations, workers should report to only one supervisor, so choices (B) and (D) are incorrect.

43. **The correct answer is (B).** The three types of corporate-level strategies include vertical integration, diversification, and concentration on a single business. Implementation is not a type of strategy. Choices (A), (C), and (D) are incorrect.

44. **The correct answer is (D).** Technical skills are task-specific. First-line managers must have strong technical skills because they are directly supervising workers, and problems associated with a task, such as nursing or accounting, arise on a daily basis. Technical skills are less important for higher-level managers. Choices (A), (B), and (C) are not task-specific knowledge.

45. **The correct answer is (D).** Level 5 leaders are characterized by determination and personal humility. Pseudo transformational leaders focus on self-interests. Bridge leaders are people who live in other cultures for a time, return home, and become leaders.

answers post-test

Transactional leaders exchange rewards or authority for people to follow them.

46. **The correct answer is (B).** Geographic organization is the most common method of departmentalization used by multinational corporations. A geographic organization groups units by geographic areas, such as territories, regions, or countries. The structure is useful when customer needs vary greatly from place to place. Choices (A), (C), and (D) are less commonly used by multinational corporations.

47. **The correct answer is (C).** The decision by many organizations to outsource jobs to other countries has been driven by low labor costs overseas, as well as an educated work force. For example, firms needing telemarketers often outsource to India where low wages pay for a skilled labor force. Choices (A), (B), and (D) have less influence on outsourcing than labor costs.

48. **The correct answer is (D).** Vroom developed a situational model of leadership that leads to five possible decision styles. Vroom's model works like a funnel with questions that lead to a recommended decision style. Fayol wrote the first theory of management. Fiedler developed the least preferred coworker (LPC) theory that asserts that a leader's style must match a situation. Maslow is known for a hierarchy of motivational needs.

49. **The correct answer is (C).** Porsche has used a differentiation strategy in seeking competitive advantage. Differentiation strategies involve being unique in an industry either through quality, marketing, or service. Walmart is an example of an organization that has used low-cost strategies to gain competitive advantage.

50. **The correct answer is (B).** Conceptual skills are needed by top-level managers to understand the objectives and strategies of a business. Determining long-term plans and predicting the benefits or problems associated with mergers, acquisitions, and investments require conceptual skills. Choices (A), (C), and (D) are skills needed by managers, but they do not relate to long-term strategic planning.

51. **The correct answer is (D).** The principle of exception indicates that managers should concentrate on deviations from a standard. Managers save time by paying less attention to cases that are close to an established standard and more attention to exceptions. The principle of exception is an important element of the control process.

52. **The correct answer is (C).** Regulators, or regulatory agencies, have the power to investigate business practices. Such agencies include the FAA, EPA, SEC, and OSHA. They monitor business compliance with workplace, product, and environmental safety laws. Choices (A), (B), and (D) are incorrect.

53. **The correct answer is (B).** Making daily operational decisions are not duties of a board of directors. A board's duties include selecting and evaluating the CEO, assessing a firm's financial performance, and deciding a firm's strategic direction. Choices (A), (C), and (D) are incorrect.

54. **The correct answer is (B).** The leadership role of a manager involves coordinating and directing the activities of workers. Staffing, motivating, and controlling employees and their work are elements of the leadership

role. Choice (A) refers to a manager's symbolic or ceremonial duties. Choice (C) refers to gathering information that may affect a unit. As a resource allocator, a manager determines how to distribute money, budget, time, and equipment.

55. **The correct answer is (D).** A SWOT analysis is a comparison of the strengths, weaknesses, opportunities, and threats that managers use to formulate strategies. It summarizes the relevant information gathered in the environmental analysis during strategic planning. ABC stands for activity-based costing, and CRM stands for customer relationship management. An LCA is a life-cycle analysis that helps determine the environmental impact of a product.

56. **The correct answer is (B).** Societal factors such as birth rate, life expectancy, and immigration affect businesses indirectly. Changes in society affect the work force, which influences how businesses function. Productivity is more closely related to technology issues than societal ones.

57. **The correct answer is (A).** The negotiator role involves bargaining with others in an organization to obtain advantages. Managers who negotiate for flexible scheduling or increased salaries are working as negotiators for the benefit of their unit. Choices (B) and (C) are both interpersonal roles that involve developing and maintaining good relationships with people. The disseminator role relates to providing information to subordinates, so choice (D) is incorrect.

58. **The correct answer is (D).** Exchange rates and trade agreements are indirect forces within the global environment. Direct forces, such as suppliers, have an immediate impact on a business, while indirect forces influence a business but not its daily operations. Barriers to entry are conditions that prevent new firms from entering an industry, such as distribution channels and government policies.

59. **The correct answer is (A).** Recognizing the existence of ten management roles helps with understanding that every role is connected to another. Neglecting one or more roles hinders employees from working effectively because each role is equally important. Choices (B) and (D) may be true, but they are not related to the ten roles identified by Mintzberg.

60. **The correct answer is (D).** Characteristics of followers and environmental factors are the two situational factors in the path-goal theory. These two factors determine the type of leadership behavior that is most appropriate given the followers and the situation. Choices (A), (B), and (C) are incorrect.

SUMMING IT UP

- Effective managers facilitate the activities within organizations through planning, organizing, leading, and controlling. Managers use the principles of supervision to guide the work of others and to help an organization accomplish its short-term needs and long-term goals.

- Most large organizations have three different levels of management—*frontline* (lower-level manager within an organization), *middle-level* (oversee frontline managers and report to top-level managers), and *top-level* or strategic managers (smallest and highest tier of management).

- The global and technical nature of modern organizations requires that managers possess a wide range of skills: technical, analytical, decision-making, conceptual, computer, communication, and interpersonal.

- The ten roles of managers identified by Canadian academic Henry Mintzberg are *figurehead, leader, liaison, monitor, disseminator, spokesperson, entrepreneur, disturbance handler, resource allocator,* and *negotiator.* Mintzberg sorted these roles into three general categories: interpersonal, informational, and decisional.

- Ethics is a system of rules that distinguishes between right and wrong. Business ethics refers to the moral principles that dictate behavior in the business realm. Ethics programs are *compliance-based* (designed by an organization's lawyers to prevent, expose, and discipline violations), *integrity-based* (designed to instill personal and ethical responsibility among employees), or somewhere in between.

- Corporate social responsibility refers to a business's obligations to society. A socially responsible company attempts to increase its positive impact and decrease its negative impact on society. Social responsibilities are divided into four major categories: economic, legal, ethical, and philanthropic.

- Internal and external environmental factors affect how an organization functions. The internal environment includes employees, office layout, management style, and bonus systems. The external environment comprises "outside" factors that have direct effects (suppliers, competitors, customers) and indirect effects (legal, political, economic, technological, social-cultural, global) on daily operations.

- In the early 1900s, Henri Fayol, a French business owner, developed the first general theory of management. Fayol's Four Functions are Plan, Organize, Lead, and Control.

- The three levels of planning are strategic, tactical, and operational.

- A SWOT analysis is a comparison of the organization's <u>s</u>trengths, <u>w</u>eaknesses, <u>o</u>pportunities, and <u>t</u>hreats; it enables managers to formulate three levels of strategy: corporate, business, and functional.

- A board of directors serves four primary duties: choosing, evaluating, rewarding, and, when necessary, replacing the CEO; assessing an organization's financial performance; deciding an organization's strategic direction; and monitoring an organization's ethical, legal, and socially responsible activities.

- Legal screening activities include asking if someone is authorized to work in the United States, if he/she has been convicted of a crime, asking for proof of age after hiring, and keeping records of racial and ethnic identity for recording purposes. Illegal screening activities include asking for proof of citizenship, asking if a person has been arrested, requiring a birth certificate, and asking for a person's race, creed, or national origin on the application or during an interview.

- The three most widely accepted classic approaches for understanding leadership are the *trait approach* (assumes leaders are born with such characteristics as self-assurance, intelligence, sociability, and aggressiveness), the *behavioral approach* (identifies behaviors of effective leaders), and the *situational approach* (asserts that universal leadership traits and behaviors are nonexistent and effective leadership varies from one situation to another).

- Vroom's expectancy theory, one of the most widely accepted motivation theories, is based on three variables: *expectancy*—employee's belief that increased efforts will lead to achieving performance goals; *instrumentality*—employee's belief that good job performance will lead to a specific outcome; and *valence*—value that an employee places on a specific outcome.

- Contemporary theories of leadership styles include *charismatic*—arouse excitement, hold strong moral convictions, and convey extreme self-confidence; *transformational*—motivate people to focus on good of the group rather than personal interests; *transactional*—use legitimate, reward, and coercive powers to give orders in exchange for benefits to followers; level 5—combine determination and humility to build long-term leadership; *authentic*—willing to sacrifice own interests and use honesty, reliability, and integrity to lead others; and *pseudo transformational*—speak about positive change but power, control, wealth, and fame take priority.

- The three main content theories are *Maslow's hierarchy of needs* (people satisfy needs in ascending order of physiological, safety, social, ego, and self-actualization), *Alderfer's ERG theory* (three basic sets of needs: existence, relatedness, and growth), and *McClelland's needs* (three dominant needs: achievement, affiliation, and power).

- The three general methods for achieving organizational control are *bureaucratic control*—guides activities with formal rules, regulations, and authority (feedforward, concurrent, and feedback); *market control*—guides activities with pricing mechanisms and economic information; and *clan control*—guides activities with norms, values, and trust that the organization and employees share the same interests.

- A management audit is a type of control used to evaluate the effectiveness and efficiency of an organization; it involves external and internal audits. Budgeting, or budgetary controlling, is a widely used control process that involves investigating what a firm has done.

Substance Abuse

chapter 4

OVERVIEW

- Diagnostic test
- Answer key and explanations
- Substance abuse: terms, theories, and costs
- Drugs: classifications and effects
- Alcohol: history, effects, and dependency
- Sedative-hypnotics
- Inhalants
- Tobacco, nicotine, and smoking
- Stimulants: cocaine and amphetamines
- Marijuana: history, effects, and medical use
- Hallucinogens
- Club drugs
- Anabolic steroids
- Antipsychotics
- Antidepressants
- Post-test
- Answer key and explanations
- Summing it up

DIAGNOSTIC TEST

Directions: Carefully read each of the following 20 questions. Choose the best answer to each question and circle your answer choice. The Answer Key and Explanations can be found following this Diagnostic Test.

1. Smoke released into the air from a lighted cigarette is known as
   (A) mainstream smoke.
   (B) nicotine smoke.
   (C) sidestream smoke.
   (D) active smoke.

2. Alcohol and tobacco are considered
   (A) opioids.
   (B) OTC drugs.
   (C) illicit drugs.
   (D) gateway drugs.

3. Valium, Ambien, and Xanax are examples of
   (A) opioids.
   (B) barbiturates.
   (C) stimulants.
   (D) benzodiazepines.

4. One of the earliest signs of withdrawal for an alcoholic is
   (A) hallucinations.
   (B) tremors.
   (C) delusions.
   (D) seizures.

5. Dr. Sigmund Freud advocated cocaine usage to treat
   (A) schizophrenia.
   (B) hallucinations.
   (C) depression.
   (D) anxiety.

6. Which region of a neuron stores neurotransmitters?
   (A) Presynaptic terminals
   (B) Cell body
   (C) Dendrites
   (D) Axon

7. One of the most common side effects of low doses of opioids is
   (A) diarrhea.
   (B) headaches.
   (C) alertness.
   (D) constipation.

8. The method of inhaling substances through rags soaked in volatile solvents is known as
   (A) snorting.
   (B) huffing.
   (C) bagging.
   (D) sniffing.

9. Which of the following was the original medical purpose of PCP?
   (A) Appetite suppressant
   (B) Sleeping aid
   (C) Anesthetic
   (D) Analgesic

10. Which of the following is the most common physiological effect of using marijuana?
    (A) Decreased blood pressure
    (B) Increased aggression
    (C) Decreased appetite
    (D) Increased heart rate

11. Frederick Serturner extracted the most potent active ingredient of opium known as
    (A) codeine.
    (B) heroin.
    (C) morphine.
    (D) methadone.

12. Cocaine is categorized as a
    (A) stimulant.
    (B) depressant.
    (C) hallucinogen.
    (D) psychotherapeutic.

13. A long-term effect known to be associated with extensive marijuana smoking is
    (A) seizures.
    (B) lung damage.
    (C) mouth cancer.
    (D) brain damage.

14. What is the alcohol content of an 80-proof bottle of whiskey?
    (A) 20 percent
    (B) 40 percent
    (C) 80 percent
    (D) 100 percent

15. Which of the following asserts that drug abuse is the result of a biological condition?
    (A) Personality predisposition model
    (B) Characterological model
    (C) Disease model
    (D) Moral model

16. Methamphetamines have effects similar to
    (A) marijuana.
    (B) heroin.
    (C) opium.
    (D) cocaine.

17. A drug interaction that involves one drug blocking the effect of another drug is known as
    (A) potentiative.
    (B) inhibitory.
    (C) additive.
    (D) synergism.

18. MDMA, GHB, and Rohypnol are examples of
    (A) club drugs.
    (B) herbal drugs.
    (C) antidepressants.
    (D) anabolic steroids.

19. Which of the following are most often prescribed for the treatment of schizophrenia?
    (A) Sedative-hypnotics
    (B) Antidepressants
    (C) Phenothiazines
    (D) Analgesics

20. Prozac is the most popular
    (A) anabolic steroid.
    (B) antidepressant.
    (C) antipsychotic.
    (D) mood stabilizer.

diagnostic test

ANSWER KEY AND EXPLANATIONS

1. C	5. C	9. C	13. B	17. B
2. D	6. A	10. D	14. B	18. A
3. D	7. D	11. C	15. C	19. C
4. B	8. B	12. A	16. D	20. B

1. **The correct answer is (C).** Sidestream smoke refers to the smoke that is released into the air from the end of a lighted cigarette. Mainstream smoke, choice (A), is the smoke that a smoker inhales directly from the mouthpiece of a cigarette. Sidestream smoke does contain high levels of nicotine, but choice (B), nicotine smoke, is not the correct terminology. Active smoking, choice (D), is the intentional inhalation of smoke by a smoker.

2. **The correct answer is (D).** Alcohol and tobacco are considered gateway drugs. Gateway drugs are typically used first by individuals who later move on to illicit drugs, such as heroin and cocaine. Choice (A) is incorrect because alcohol and tobacco are not derived from opium. Alcohol and tobacco are licit drugs, so choice (C) is incorrect. Over-the-counter (OTC) drugs, choice (B), are medicines purchased without prescriptions, such as antihistamines and aspirin.

3. **The correct answer is (D).** Benzodiazepines are CNS depressants prescribed to relieve anxiety and insomnia. Valium, Ambien, and Xanax are three popular brands of benzodiazepines commonly prescribed by doctors today. Barbiturates, choice (B), are CNS depressants like benzodiazepines, but they have the possibility of causing tolerance, dependence, and respiratory depression. Choices (A) and (C) are incorrect.

4. **The correct answer is (B).** Tremors, restlessness, and insomnia take place in the first stage of withdrawal for alcoholics. Hallucinations occur in the second stage. Stage 3 involves delusions and disorientation, and seizures are indicative of Stage 4.

5. **The correct answer is (C).** Freud recommended the use of cocaine in the treatment of depression. Physicians prescribed cocaine for a number of medical purposes until the Harrison Act of 1914 made it illegal to use or distribute cocaine. Choices (A), (B), and (D) are incorrect.

6. **The correct answer is (A).** The presynaptic terminals store neurotransmitters, which act as chemical messengers. The cell body contains the nucleus, and the dendrites are treelike branches that receive transmitter signals. The axon conducts electrical signals, so choice (D) is incorrect.

7. **The correct answer is (D).** Constipation is one of the most common side effects of opioids. Because of this side effect, opioids are used to treat severe diarrhea, so choice (A) is incorrect. Opioids relieve pain rather than cause pain, so choice (B) is incorrect. Opioids are not stimulants, so alertness is not a side effect.

8. **The correct answer is (B).** Huffing refers to holding rags or bandannas soaked in solvents such as paint thinner over the mouth and inhaling the substance. Snorting, choice (A), and sniffing, choice (D), refer to

inhaling vapors directly from a product's original container. Bagging, choice (C), occurs when a person places a solvent or other substance in a plastic bag and then inhales.

9. **The correct answer is (C).** PCP was originally intended for use as an anesthetic in the 1950s. Physicians found that patients who were given PCP as a general anesthesia experienced a range of psychological effects including depression, anxiety, and persecution. Choices (A), (B), and (D) are incorrect.

10. **The correct answer is (D).** Marijuana increases the heart rate among almost all users. Choice (A) is incorrect because marijuana's effect on blood pressure varies from slight increases to no change among users. Aggression, choice (B), is not a typical effect of marijuana because most people feel relaxed. Appetite increases with marijuana, so choice (C) is incorrect.

11. **The correct answer is (C).** Serturner extracted morphine from opium, which is the plant's most potent active ingredient. Codeine is a less potent ingredient that was extracted after Serturner's discovery. Heroin, the most potent opioid, is a combination of morphine and other chemicals, so choice (B) is incorrect. Methadone is a synthetic opioid, so choice (D) is incorrect.

12. **The correct answer is (A).** Cocaine is a stimulant that triggers excitement and paranoia among frequent users. Alcohol and sleeping pills are categorized as depressants, so choice (B) is incorrect. Hallucinogens, choice (C), alter the perceptions of users, which is not an effect of cocaine usage. Psychotherapeutic drugs, such as Prozac, are used to treat patients with extensive mental problems, so choice (D) is incorrect.

13. **The correct answer is (B).** Experts agree that long-term smoking of marijuana decreases pulmonary capabilities, causes chronic lung diseases, and raises the risk of lung cancer. Seizures and mouth cancer are not linked with smoking marijuana. Some people believe that marijuana causes brain damage, but there is no evidence to support this suspicion.

14. **The correct answer is (B).** The alcohol content of an 80-proof bottle of whiskey is 40 percent. The proof of a bottle of alcohol is printed on its label. Proof is double the alcohol percentage.

15. **The correct answer is (C).** According to the disease model of dependency, people abuse drugs and alcohol because of biological conditions. The moral model asserts that people make the choice to abuse drugs and alcohol. Choices (A) and (B) suggest that people develop chemical dependencies because their personality traits are predisposed to doing so.

16. **The correct answer is (D).** Methamphetamines are stimulants like cocaine. Methamphetamines are increasingly popular because their effects last longer than the effects of cocaine. Heroin and opium are both opioids, which bring pain relief and drowsiness. Marijuana causes relaxation instead of stimulation, so choice (A) is incorrect.

17. **The correct answer is (B).** Antagonistic or inhibitory drug interactions occur when one drug blocks the effect of another drug. Choices (A) and (D) are both terms referring to one drug enhancing the effect of another drug. Additive interactions, choice (C), are the summation of effects when similar drugs are taken.

18. **The correct answer is (A).** MDMA, GHB, and Rohypnol are all examples

of club drugs. Both GHB and Rohypnol have been used as date-rape drugs to incapacitate victims of sexual assaults. MDMA, which is known as Ecstasy, is used at raves and nightclubs to increase sensory experiences. Choices (B), (C), and (D) are incorrect.

19. **The correct answer is (C).** Phenothiazines are a group of drugs used to treat psychosis, including schizophrenia. Sedative-hypnotics treat anxiety and sleep disorders, so choice (A) is incorrect. Antidepressants, choice (B), are prescribed for patients with depression. Analgesics, choice (D), are prescribed for pain relief.

20. **The correct answer is (B).** Prozac is the most commonly prescribed antidepressant. Prozac, Paxil, and Zoloft are selective reuptake inhibitors. SSRIs are antidepressants considered safer than MAOIs and tricyclics because they have fewer adverse side effects. Choices (A), (C), and (D) are incorrect.

SUBSTANCE ABUSE: TERMS, THEORIES, AND COSTS

For thousands of years, alcohol and drugs have been used in society for medicinal and recreational purposes. Evidence suggests that substance abuse plagued societies of the past just as it does modern societies. Before addressing the different types of drugs and their unique effects, it is important to understand the terms and theories associated with substance abuse.

Terms To Know

Drugs are natural or artificial substances that improve, obstruct, or alter mind and body functions. The term *illicit drug* refers to substances that are illegal to possess, such as marijuana and cocaine. In contrast, *licit drugs* are legal and include coffee, alcohol, and tobacco. Licit drugs also include over-the-counter (OTC) drugs, which are available for purchase without a prescription, such as aspirin, cold remedies, and antihistamines. Alcohol and tobacco are considered gateway drugs because most people who abuse illicit drugs first try cigarettes and liquor.

Psychoactive drugs mainly affect the central nervous system, and they result in changes to consciousness, thought processes, and mood. Many psychoactive drugs are prescribed for physical and mental problems, but it is when such drugs are misused or abused that problems occur. Drug misuse refers to using prescribed drugs in ways other than recommended by a physician, such as taking too many pills at one time. Drug abuse occurs when a substance, either prescribed or illicit, is used in a manner that causes social, occupational, psychological, or physical problems.

Although the terms *dependence* and *addiction* often describe the same condition, medical professionals typically prefer the term *dependency*. The common use of *addiction* to describe people's overindulgence in everything from gambling to chocolate makes *dependence* a better choice. Drug dependency occurs when an individual uses a drug so often and regularly that going without it is physically and psychologically difficult and results in withdrawal symptoms. Withdrawal symptoms frequently include nausea, anxiety, muscle spasms, and sweating, but they vary with different substances.

Substance Abuse Models and Theories

Experts have analyzed and described drug addiction over the years, and three models of dependency developed as a result.

Models of Dependency

Moral model	A person chooses to abuse drugs and alcohol.
Disease model	A person abuses drugs and alcohol because of a biological condition.
Characterological or personality predisposition model	A person is inclined to develop a chemical dependency because of certain personality traits.

Although the moral model is generally considered outdated by the scientific community, many people maintain that lifestyle choices and immorality lead to drug dependency. Supporters of the disease model assert that dependency is a chronic disease that progresses with time and requires treatment and therapy. Recovery groups like Alcoholics Anonymous and Narcotics Anonymous adhere to the disease model. The fact that a number of people with chemical dependencies are also diagnosed with personality disorders supports the personality predisposition model. Consensus does not exist with regard to any of the dependency models or to the three theoretical explanations of drug dependency.

Theories of Dependency

Biological	Substance abuse stems from physical characteristics related to genetics, brain dysfunction, and biochemical patterns. People with such traits experiment with drugs and then crave them.
Psychological	The mental and emotional status of an individual leads to substance abuse. Social learning theory emphasizes that individuals learn drug use behaviors from society, family, and peers.
Sociological	Social and environmental factors influence substance abuse. Social influence theories claim that a person's daily social relationships are the cause of substance abuse. Structural influence theories assert that substance abuse occurs because of the organization of an individual's society, peer groups, and subculture.

Usage Trends and Costs of Substance Abuse

Although drug abuse occurs in all areas of society, researchers have detected certain trends. Among American college students, approximately 70 percent drink alcohol, and about 25 percent of them smoke cigarettes. A smaller number use illicit drugs: 20 percent admit to smoking marijuana, and 2 percent use cocaine. Based on race and ethnicity, Asians have the lowest percentage of illicit drug use, while Native Americans have the highest percentage. Substance abuse is also more common among men.

Researchers have also discovered that teens who use illicit drugs are more likely to know drug-abusing adults. The same adolescents typically associate with peers who use drugs, have academic difficulties, and believe their parents are not sources of support or encouragement. In general, experts believe that society, community, and family influence an individual's first use of drugs or alcohol. However, long-term usage is determined by an individual's experience with the drug. Once a person becomes truly dependent, social factors like laws, costs, and availability have very little bearing.

What Are the Costs?

Substance abuse is a costly habit to maintain. According to the National Institute on Drug Abuse, a drug addict needs $100 every day to support a narcotics habit. Unfortunately, criminal activity is the source of funds for many drug abusers. Burglary and shoplifting are the crimes primarily associated with drug abusers in need of money, and many heroin abusers become involved in prostitution. Researchers have identified at least three correlations between drugs and crime:

- Drug users commit more crimes than non-drug users.

- Violence is frequently associated with the use of narcotics, such as cocaine.

- Crimes are often committed while under the influence of drugs.

In addition to criminal activity, substance abuse affects the medical system. Diseases associated with intravenous drug use such as hepatitis B and HIV require expensive treatment. Automobile accidents, drug overdoses, and babies born with fetal alcohol syndrome require costly medical intervention as well.

Substance abuse also affects productivity in the work place. Unlike people who abuse drugs such as heroin and LSD, most alcoholics are able to hold jobs. However, alcoholics have a tendency to be late for work, have on-the-job accidents, and miss work. Many employers are requiring employees to take drug-screening tests and are making drug and alcohol assistance programs more available to employees with dependency issues.

DRUGS: CLASSIFICATIONS AND EFFECTS

Drug classification varies by the purpose of the drug. For example, a physician may categorize an amphetamine as a weight-control tool because of the drug's ability to suppress food consumption. However, a user may refer to the same drug as an upper. The following table shows the major drug categories and provides examples of the types of drugs in each category.

Drug Classifications

Category	Examples
Stimulants	Cocaine, Amphetamines, Ritalin, Caffeine
Depressants	Alcohol, Barbiturates, Sleeping Pills, Inhalants
Hallucinogens	LSD, Mescaline, Ecstasy, PCP
Opioids	Opium, Morphine, Codeine, Heroin, Methadone
Cannabis	Marijuana, THC, Hashish
Nicotine	Cigarettes, chewing tobacco, cigars
Psychotherapeutics	Prozac, Haldol

When taken in moderate doses, stimulants, such as caffeine, provide energy to users. However, powerful stimulants, such as cocaine, often trigger manic excitement and paranoia, which is why stimulants are referred to as uppers.

Depressants, known as downers, have an opposite effect of stimulants on the body. Low to medium doses lead to relaxation, a loss of inhibition, slow reaction times, and uncoordinated movements. The regular use of depressants may cause hallucinations and restlessness.

As implied by the name, hallucinogens cause users to have hallucinations and experience a distorted reality. Referred to as psychedelics, hallucinogens alter a user's perceptions, such as taste, smell, hearing, and vision. Higher amounts of hallucinogens are needed to achieve the same effects because tolerance for such drugs builds quickly.

Opioids are categorized as analgesics, painkillers, or narcotics. Low doses lead to a relaxed state, while higher doses may induce sleep. Unlike depressants that generate reckless behavior and slurred speech, opioids lead to users being in a stupor. Individuals who regularly take heroin, codeine, or morphine may become withdrawn.

The most commonly used illegal drug in the United States is marijuana, which is categorized as cannabis because it is made from the crushed parts of the Cannabis sativa plant. The main psychoactive ingredient in marijuana is delta 9-tetrahydrocannabinol (THC), which generates the "high" experienced by users.

Nicotine, which is a gateway drug, is extremely addictive and found in cigarettes, chewing tobacco, and cigars. Although nicotine is legal, it causes respiratory problems and cancer among some long-term users. Medical conditions associated with secondhand smoke have led to smoke-free buildings, businesses, and restaurants.

Psychiatrists and physicians often prescribe psychotherapeutic drugs to control mental problems in patients. Antipsychotics, such as haloperidol, are a type of psychotherapeutic drug that have a calming effect on patients and help control hallucinations. Antipsychotics are often prescribed to patients diagnosed with schizophrenia, mania, and delusional disorder. Antidepressants, such as Prozac, are psychotherapeutic drugs prescribed to patients with severe depression.

The Nervous System

As previously indicated, drugs have varying effects on the human body—excitement, relaxation, and addiction. Analyzing how the nervous system works will lead to a better understanding of the variation in drug effects.

The human body is constantly attempting to maintain internal stability, a process known as homeostasis. Homeostatic mechanisms regulate body temperature, blood pressure, and glucose concentrations, as well as many other physiological functions. The body attempts to stay the same for survival purposes—properly functioning organs and systems improve human survival. For example, a body temperature of 98.6°F is optimal because a temperature that is too high or too low causes problems in other parts of the body.

The nervous system is composed of neurons, which are specialized nerve cells that transfer messages throughout the body. All neurons consist of four regions:

- *Cell body:* contains the nucleus
- *Dendrites:* treelike branches that receive transmitter signals
- *Axon:* long extension of the cell body that conducts electrical signals
- *Presynaptic terminals:* store chemical messengers, which are known as neurotransmitters

The human brain contains billions of neurons, which are all close to each other but never touch. Neurons communicate with each other by releasing chemical messengers known as neurotransmitters. A synapse is the point of communication between a neuron sending a message and a neuron receiving a message. The small gap between one neuron and another is known as the synaptic cleft. Neurotransmitters travel across the synaptic cleft and bind to special proteins known as receptors on the outer membranes of target cells. The activation of receptors leads to a change in cell activity and is accomplished by both natural substances and drugs.

The nervous system is divided into the somatic nervous system, the autonomic nervous system, and the central nervous system. Neurons in the somatic nervous system are associated with voluntary actions, such as moving one's arms and legs, seeing, hearing, smelling, and chewing. The autonomic nervous system monitors involuntary actions, such as heart rate and blood pressure. The central nervous system consists of the brain and spinal cord and is responsible for learning, memory, and activity coordination.

As mentioned previously, neurotransmitters are chemical messengers released by neurons that have brief effects. Some drugs alter how neurotransmitters function. Certain neurotransmitters are associated with the introduction of psychoactive drugs into the nervous system, especially dopamine, acetylcholine, norepinephrine, serotonin, GABA, glutamate, and the endorphins. Many drugs that are abused, such as amphetamines and cocaine, alter dopamine neurons and cause paranoia, agitation, and euphoria. Serotonin is responsible for controlling mood, appetite, and aggressiveness, and substances such as LSD have been found to affect serotonin levels.

Drug Effects and Interactions

Physicians who prescribe medication to patients are attempting to cure an illness or relieve pain associated with a condition. In some cases, medication causes side effects, which are the unintended effects of a drug. Common side effects, such as nausea, vomiting, nervousness, breathing difficulties, dependence, and changes in cardiovascular activity, illustrate the fact that risks are associated with the consumption of any drug—over-the-counter, prescribed, and illicit. For example, morphine relieves pain, but it depresses breathing and causes constipation. Cocaine works well as a local anesthetic, but the drug's addictive nature eliminates its value in such a capacity.

Both intended and unintended effects of a substance correspond to the amount of a drug taken. Potency refers to the quantity of a drug that is required to produce an effect. In other words, a highly potent drug, such as LSD, requires a small dose to achieve a specific effect. Toxicity is a drug's capacity to harm the body, which may occur when any substance is taken in high doses. However, the consumption of extremely potent drugs, such as heroin, can cause serious damage to the body and possibly death.

The presence of one drug can affect how another drug works in the body, a process known as drug interaction. Drug interactions are categorized into three main types.

Types of Drug Interactions

Additive interactions	The summation of effects that occur when similar drugs are taken
Antagonistic interactions	One drug blocks the effect of another drug—also known as inhibitory
Potentiative interactions	One drug enhances the effect of another drug—also known as synergism

One of the most dangerous drug interactions involves any combination of depressants, alcohol, or narcotics. Since all three substances act in slowing down the breathing rate, a combination of any of them may result in one of the most common types of drug overdoses—respiratory depression. People who experience respiratory depression stop breathing and die.

An example of an antagonistic interaction often initiated by drug abusers is combining alcohol with cocaine. The cocaine chemically combines with the ethyl alcohol in the body to create an extremely potent and toxic stimulant known as cocaethylene. Cocaethylene is suspected of causing a greater sense of euphoria than cocaine alone because it increases dopamine transmission.

ALCOHOL: HISTORY, EFFECTS, AND DEPENDENCY

As illustrated in the previous section, alcohol is dangerous when combined with other substances. However, consuming alcohol by itself leads to problematic behavior, such as car accidents, risky sexual behavior, and blackouts.

History of Alcohol

Alcoholic beverages have been an aspect of society since 8000 BC and the creation of mead, a drink made from honey. Beer and berry wine were developed around 6400 BC and grape wine in 300 BC. Ancient civilizations discovered that alcohol could be made through fermentation, which is the chemical action that occurs when sugars, yeasts, and water are combined.

Distilled alcoholic beverages, such as brandy and whiskey, have alcohol concentrations greater than 15 percent. Distillation involves heating the mixture containing alcohol, collecting the vapors, and condensing the solution into a liquid once again. The process most likely originated in Arabia in 800 AD. Today, proof indicates the alcohol content of a beverage. Proof is twice the alcohol percentage, which means that a bottle of 100-proof vodka is 50 percent alcohol.

During the late eighteenth century, American citizens preferred alcoholic beverages to water partially because of water contamination issues. Much of society did not view alcohol negatively until after the Revolutionary War when distilled spirits were associated with immoral and criminal activities. The heaviest period of alcoholic consumption in the United States occurred between 1800 and 1808. The concept that people should avoid hard liquor, such as whiskey and vodka, and should only drink beer or wine in moderation was the basis of the temperance movement of the 1800s. The temperance movement eventually advocated complete abstinence from all alcoholic beverages, which led to the enactment of Prohibition laws in 1920. During Prohibition, the sale of all alcohol was illegal in America. However, Prohibition only pushed alcohol consumption underground. Speakeasies developed as places where people could purchase alcoholic drinks, and bootleggers made and sold moonshine throughout the country. The repeal of Prohibition laws in 1933 occurred for a number of reasons—lost tax revenue, enforcement difficulties, black market liquor sales, police corruption, and political pressure.

Effects of Alcohol

Previous drinking experiences, mood, attitude, expectations, and circumstances are factors in an individual's behavior while drinking. However, when a person consumes alcohol, the effect of the alcohol depends mainly upon the amount of alcohol that is concentrated in the blood system. Estimates of blood alcohol concentration (BAC) are based on an individual's gender, weight, and alcohol consumption. Blood alcohol concentration, or blood alcohol level, determines how a person behaves in response to alcohol consumption. The following table shows the correlation between BAC and behavior.

BAC and Behavior

0.05%	Reduced inhibition, decreased alertness, impaired judgment, relaxed mood
0.10%	Decreased reaction time, impaired motor skills
0.20%	Significant reduction in sensory and motor skills
0.25%	Staggering, severe motor skill disturbance
0.30%	Conscious but in a stupor
0.40%	Unconsciousness

The rate of alcohol absorption plays a significant role in BAC. Alcohol consumed on a full stomach absorbs slower than alcohol consumed on an empty stomach. Drinking water also slows the rate of alcohol absorption, while carbonated beverages increase it. Since alcohol does not distribute into fatty tissues, a lean 200-pound man will have a lower BAC than a fat 200-pound man. Body weight is a significant factor as well. A 200-pound woman who drinks one beer will have a BAC of 0.022 percent, while a 100-pound woman who drinks the same amount will have a BAC of 0.045 percent. Blood alcohol level is used as a measurement of intoxication and impairment for the legal and medical systems. A blood alcohol level greater than 0.08 percent is illegal in every state in the United States. A blood alcohol level of 0.4 percent to 0.6 percent is lethal because respiration is severely depressed.

Alcohol stays in the bloodstream until it has metabolized, or been broken down by enzymes. More than 90 percent of alcohol metabolism takes place in the liver, which is why chronic drinkers often experience liver disorders, such as alcoholic hepatitis and cirrhosis. The liver metabolizes alcohol at a constant rate, no matter how much alcohol is consumed or the size of the person drinking. In general, the number of drinks consumed is the number of hours it takes a person to metabolize the alcohol.

In addition to liver diseases, heavy alcohol use is linked to the damage of almost every organ and bodily function. Alcohol affects the digestive system by irritating tissue and damaging the stomach lining. Neurological damage is apparent because many heavy drinkers suffer from irreversible impairment to memory and judgment. However, light drinking may reduce the likelihood of heart disease perhaps because of stress reduction and increased high-density lipoproteins that carry fat through the bloodstream.

Alcohol Dependency

The socially acceptable nature of drinking lends itself to both psychological and physical dependency. The relaxation and positive feelings that occur with drinking make it routine for many people. The regular use of alcohol often leads to increased tolerance levels and decreased pharmacological effects, which may increase consumption and cause physical dependence. Alcoholics are individuals who are unable to function normally without consuming alcohol. Physical dependence becomes evident when alcohol consumption stops and withdrawal symptoms occur. Withdrawal effects from alcohol and barbiturates are more severe than effects associated with other substances. Withdrawal occurs in a progression of four stages.

- Stage 1: tremors, restlessness, insomnia, rapid heartbeat, and heavy sweating
- Stage 2: stage 1 symptoms plus hallucinations and vomiting
- Stage 3: delusions, disorientation, and fever
- Stage 4: seizures that are life-threatening in some cases

Recovering alcoholics often face a more difficult journey than other addicts, such as those using cocaine or heroin, because society finds drinking acceptable. Alcoholics Anonymous encourages addicts to stay connected with other alcoholics by attending chapter meetings and avoiding the isolation that can trigger a relapse. Some alcoholics seek help from residential treatment centers for one or two months in order to avoid relapses.

SEDATIVE-HYPNOTICS

Sedative-hypnotics, also known as central nervous system (CNS) depressants, are frequently abused substances because of their ability to reduce CNS activity, decrease the brain's level of awareness, and relieve anxiety. Within the category of CNS depressants, sedatives relieve anxiety and fear, while hypnotics induce drowsiness and sleep.

Prior to the development of CNS depressants, alcohol was commonly used to treat anxiety and nervousness. In the 1800s, bromides were introduced as a way to induce sleep, but they were later found to be highly toxic. In the early part of the twentieth century, barbiturates such as phenobarbital replaced bromides as an anti-anxiety medication. However, scientists and physicians noticed a number of problems associated with barbiturates—tolerance, dependence, and respiration depression. While many people safely took barbiturate sleeping pills, the medical community sought a better drug for the treatment of anxiety and sleep disorders.

During the 1950s, benzodiazepines were marketed as CNS depressants that offered a safe alternative to barbiturates. Benzodiazepines remain the most popular and safe CNS depressants prescribed by doctors today and include brand name drugs such as Valium, Ambien, and Xanax. Benzodiazepines are prescribed for the treatment of anxiety, neurosis, muscle relaxation, lower back pain, and insomnia. Like barbiturates, benzodiazepines increase the actions of the neurotransmitter GABA. GABA is the primary inhibitory neurotransmitter in the central nervous system and acts as the body's tranquilizer by inducing sleep and promoting calmness. Problems associated with benzodiazepines occur when they interact with other depressants, such as alcohol. Combining benzodiazepines with illicit drugs, such as heroin and cocaine, is common among substance abusers.

INHALANTS

Gasoline, paint, glue, air freshener, and nail polish are volatile substances that elicit euphoric feelings when inhaled. Although inhalant abuse may seem to be a modern trend, it actually dates back to the eighteenth century when people inhaled nitrous oxide to attain a state of drunkenness. Inhaling nitrous oxide, or laughing gas, for recreational purposes continued for many years, and the inhalant is still used for some medical procedures such as dental work. During the 1950s, the public was made aware of teenagers becoming "high" by sniffing glue. Currently, teenagers and adolescents misuse over 1,000 different products as inhalants.

Methods of inhaling vary. Sniffing or snorting refers to inhaling vapors straight from the product's original container. Bagging is the term used to describe inhaling solvents that have been placed in plastic bags. Abusers who soak rags in a solvent and hold the rag over their mouth are huffing.

There are three categories of inhalants: gaseous anesthetics, nitrites, and volatile solvents.

Inhalants

Gaseous anesthetics	Nitrous oxide ("laughing gas"), ether, chloroform
Nitrites	Amyl nitrite ("poppers")
Volatile solvents	Aerosols, toluene, butane, propane, gasoline, freon

As previously mentioned, nitrous oxide is safe to use as a light anesthetic for outpatient procedures performed by dentists and physicians. Its availability in the medical community has led to its abuse by medical professionals who have access to it. The colorless gas is found in large balloons and in cartridges called whippets that are included in containers of whipping cream. Both are sources for inhalant abusers.

Nitrites are chemicals that cause a rapid dilation of the arteries combined with a reduction in blood pressure to the brain. The result of this vasodilation is a short feeling of faintness and sometimes unconsciousness. Nitrites were sold in small vials over-the-counter in the 1960s and were "popped" between the fingers and held under the nose for inhalation. Nitrites have not been available to consumers since the early 1990s.

The most prevalent category of inhalants is volatile substances. The easy availability and low costs associated with volatile substances makes them especially appealing to children and teenagers. Some states have passed laws to limit the sale of volatile solvents to young people, but with so many kinds on the market, the effect has been minimal.

Types of Volatile Substances

Aerosols	High concentration of chemicals from spray paint and other spray cans
Toluene	Chemical found in glues, paints, and nail polish; quickly absorbed by the lungs, brain, heart, and liver
Butane and propane	Highly flammable, especially when combined with smoking; found in lighter fluid
Gasoline	Widely available and highly flammable
Freons	Found in refrigerators, airbrushes, and air conditioners; danger of freeze injuries

The initial effects of inhaling volatile chemicals are nausea, coughing, and sneezing. Low doses generate feelings of lightheadedness, disorientation, mild stimulation, and dizziness. High doses act like CNS depressants by producing relaxation, sleep, slurred speech, and possibly coma. Hypoxia, or oxygen deficiency, brain damage, suffocation, and death may occur in some cases. In addition to the short-term health effects of inhalant abuse, users may experience permanent damage. Although teenagers who abuse inhalants typically move on to other drugs or alcohol, the damage of inhalant abuse is permanent. The inhalation of high concentrations of household products that contain multiple chemicals damages vital organs that absorb the inhaled substances. In addition, young abusers of inhalants are still growing and developing, and the toxic nature of inhalants may interfere with the mental development of users.

TOBACCO, NICOTINE, AND SMOKING

Despite the fact that tobacco contributes to deaths related to cardiovascular disease and cancer, smoking remains a habit for nearly 30 percent of the U.S. population. The deadly addiction is unlikely to cease anytime soon because each day in America almost 4,000 teenagers and young adults try smoking for the first time. Tobacco will likely remain part of America's future just as it has been part of America's past.

History of Tobacco

The Indians of the New World introduced Christopher Columbus to tobacco in 1492, but the natives of Central America had likely been smoking tobacco leaves for centuries. Explorers brought tobacco back to Europe where it was initially viewed as an oddity; however, its use soon became popular. Europeans used tobacco leaves to treat over thirty different medical conditions including headaches and abscesses. Some Europeans, such as King James I, believed that tobacco was evil because of its association with Native American religion and magic. King James I attempted to curb the use of tobacco by raising the import tax on it, but tobacco continued to be popular. Across the Atlantic, the tobacco industry flourished in Virginia and became a significant export of the American colonies.

Until the late nineteenth century, pipes, chewing, and snuff were the most popular methods of using tobacco, although some people enjoyed smoking cigars. The invention of a cigarette-rolling machine in the 1880s triggered the cigarette industry and changed forever the way people used tobacco. In 1885, American tobacco companies sold 1 billion cigarettes. Cigarette sales continued to rise over the years reaching 702 billion in 1992. Although American demand for cigarettes has dropped, more than 360 billion cigarettes were smoked in the United States in 2007.

Nicotine and Its Effects

Nicotine is only one of over 4,000 chemicals in tobacco smoke, but it is the key to dependency. Nicotine is a colorless, volatile liquid alkaloid that is highly addictive. When a person smokes a cigarette, the nicotine is absorbed into the bloodstream. Nicotine entering the central nervous system triggers the release of the neurotransmitter dopamine, which causes feelings of pleasure. Within 10 seconds of smoking a cigarette, nicotine reaches the brain, which may partially explain the abuse potential. Nicotine affects the body in a number of other ways as well:

- Decreases ability of blood to carry oxygen
- Increases blood pressure, heart rate, and blood flow
- Diminishes desire to eat for a short time

Health Effects of Smoking

Although cigarette smoking has declined over the last twenty years, over 40 million adults smoke cigarettes on a regular basis. One out of every five deaths that occur in the United States can be traced to smoking—a preventable cause of death. Lung cancer, heart disease, stroke, and chronic lung disease are some of the causes of death for smokers.

The leading cause of death in the United States is cardiovascular disease, and research suggests that smoking increases a person's risk of having a heart attack. Fat deposits block the arteries of smokers and prevent blood from reaching the heart. However, the damage is not necessarily permanent. Studies have shown that people who stop smoking are able to lower their risk of heart disease over time.

Cancer is the second leading cause of death in the United States, and the risk of cancer increases with three factors:

- Number of cigarettes smoked daily
- Number of years spent smoking
- Age at which smoking began

Although lung cancer is not highly common, it can be directly linked to smoking in approximately 85 percent of all cases. Cancers of the mouth, larynx, and esophagus are associated with smoking cigars and pipes. Like heart disease, cancer risks drop when smoking ceases, although it may take many years to reach the same risk level as nonsmokers. Lung ailments, such as pulmonary emphysema, chronic bronchitis, and respiratory infections are more common among smokers than among nonsmokers.

The adverse health effects of tobacco are not limited to smokers. Passive smoking refers to the inhalation of cigarette smoke in the environment by nonsmokers. The smoker draws mainstream smoke directly from the mouthpiece of a cigarette. In contrast, sidestream smoke, which is also known as secondhand smoke, is the smoke that comes from the lighted end of a cigarette. Sidestream smoke pollutes the air of both smokers and nonsmokers, and it contains high concentrations of carbon monoxide, nicotine, and ammonia. In conditions of limited ventilation and heavy smoking, sidestream smoke is responsible for numerous respiratory tract infections among children each year.

Most people are aware that cigarette smoking during pregnancy can be detrimental to a developing fetus. Women who smoke during pregnancy have a higher risk of a still-birth and premature delivery. Babies of smokers usually have below-average weight and length because nicotine and carbon monoxide reduce the amount of oxygen and nutrients that flow to the placenta.

How to Stop Smoking

The nicotine in cigarettes is highly addictive, which makes stopping the habit extremely difficult. Nicotine gum, nicotine skin patches, self-help classes, and counseling are all methods commonly employed to help smokers stop lighting up. Regular smokers who stop smoking without the use of cessation aids, such as nicotine gum, typically experience withdrawal symptoms. Irritability, insomnia, anxiety, poor judgment, and tobacco cravings are only some of the common effects. In some cases, signs of withdrawal may appear only a few hours after quitting and may last for months. Studies indicate that smoking cessation should occur gradually rather than suddenly to avoid a relapse.

STIMULANTS: COCAINE AND AMPHETAMINES

Stimulants are substances that increase energy levels and generate a euphoric state for users. Cocaine and amphetamines are stimulants, and they are sometimes referred to as uppers. The two stimulants will be discussed separately in the next few sections.

History of Cocaine

Cocaine comes from the coca plant that grows in the Andes Mountains in South America. Citizens of the Inca Empire in Peru chewed coca leaves to provide relief from fatigue and to boost endurance for carrying loads over mountains. Coca leaves were used as currency at the time of the Spanish invasion in the sixteenth century.

During the nineteenth century, French chemist Angelo Mariani used extractions from the coca leaf in a number of products, such as cough drops, tea, and wine. Mariani's cocaine extract was advertised as a magical drug that would lift the spirits and end fatigue. The chemist even received a medal of appreciation from the Pope for Vin Mariani, a red wine created with cocaine extract. In the 1880s, Dr. W. S. Halsted, an American physician, experimented with cocaine as a local anesthetic. Dr. Sigmund Freud also advocated the use of cocaine to treat depression and morphine dependence. Most physicians realized that the regular, recreational use of cocaine was dangerous, and the Harrison Act was enacted in 1914 to regulate use and distribution of the substance.

Modern Cocaine Usage

In the early 1980s, cocaine was perceived as a safe and glamorous drug used by the wealthy and the famous. Its cost was too high for most people, until drug dealers in 1985 began selling crack, which is an inexpensive form of cocaine. Crack is a special kind of freebase cocaine smoked in a glass water pipe. Freebasing is a method of reducing the impurities in cocaine to prepare the drug for smoking. How cocaine is administered affects the drug's intensity, abuse potential, and toxicity level.

Methods of Using Cocaine

Chewing coca leaves	Least potent method; not likely to cause dependence or health issues; uncommon in United States
Intranasal (snorting cocaine powder)	Quick stimulation of CNS that lasts up to 40 minutes and is followed by "crashing"; most common administration method for recreational users
Intravenous	Delivers high amount of cocaine quickly to the brain; intense "high" that lasts up to 20 minutes followed by "crashing"; dependency likely
Smoking crack cocaine (freebasing)	Similar effects to intravenous usage but more intense; preferred by some users over intravenous because no needles required; most addictive method

Cocaine Withdrawal and Treatment

Withdrawal effects from cocaine depend on the amount of time a person has been a user and the intensity level of the abuse. Short-term withdrawal effects may include depression, insomnia, agitation, and drug cravings. Anhedonia, which is the inability to feel pleasure, is also a short-term effect of cocaine withdrawal. Long-term effects include mood swings and occasional cravings. No clear-cut treatment program exists for cocaine addicts, but many people seek help from inpatient and outpatient facilities. Most treatments attempt to curb a person's craving for cocaine and to relieve mood swings. Counseling and support groups are typical elements of treating cocaine addiction.

Amphetamines

Patented in 1932, amphetamines were initially used for the treatment of asthma because of their ability to dilate bronchial passages. People soon realized that the OTC amphetamine inhaler allowed users to stay awake for extended periods. During World War II, German, British, and Japanese soldiers used amphetamines to counteract fatigue, and U.S. soldiers used it for the same reason during the Korean War.

In the 1960s, intravenous abuse of amphetamines began because the drug offered effects similar to cocaine when injected with heroin. At the time, doctors prescribed amphetamines for depression and obesity, so legal acquisition of the drugs was not an issue. Currently, methamphetamines, which are similar in structure to amphetamines and highly addictive, are rising in popularity among drug users. Methamphetamines offer longer lasting effects than cocaine, and they can be made very easily and inexpensively in home laboratories.

In addition to alertness, amphetamines cause arousal and activate the fight-or-flight response in users. Effects associated with low doses of amphetamines include increased heartbeat, blood pressure, and breathing, as well as decreased appetite. High doses may lead to convulsions, fever, and chest pain. Heavy amphetamine usage has also been associated with behavioral stereotypy, which is the meaningless repetition of a simple activity, such as repeating a word or cleaning an object. Chronic amphetamine usage damages brain cells and reduces the number of dopamine and serotonin neurotransmitters.

Amphetamines were once prescribed for depression, fatigue, and long-term weight loss, but the Food and Drug Administration restricted amphetamine usage in 1970. Physicians may now only prescribe amphetamines for three medical conditions.

Medical Uses of Amphetamines

Narcolepsy	A condition that causes sudden sleeping; low doses of amphetamines enable narcoleptics to remain alert
Attention Deficit Hyperactivity Disorder (ADHD)	Behavioral problem in children and adolescents involving high activity levels; Ritalin is a stimulant used for treatment
Obesity	Short-term use of amphetamines in weight reduction programs; helps control appetite

Medical use of amphetamines runs the risk of abuse potential and cardiovascular toxicities. Amphetamines increase heart rate, increase blood pressure, and damage veins and arteries, which may be especially fatal for patients with hypertension or heart arrhythmia.

History of Opium

Opium is a raw plant substance that contains both morphine and codeine, and its medical and recreational use dates back thousands of years to the Middle East. The introduction of opium poppies to China and India led to significant addiction problems for the Chinese. In 1729, China banned the sale of opium, but opium continued to be smuggled from India where it was primarily grown; the British government in India encouraged the profitable cultivation and smuggling of opium to China. Trade disputes and conflicts between the Chinese and British governments triggered the Opium War, which lasted from 1839 until 1842.

In 1803, Frederick Serturner extracted and isolated the main active ingredient in opium, which was ten times more potent than the opium itself. Serturner named his extraction morphine. Thirty years later, codeine was extracted from the poppy plant. In 1874, Bayer Laboratories made changes to the morphine molecule to create heroin, which has three times the potency of morphine. Initially, the medical community was unaware of dependency issues associated with heroin, but federal laws were enacted in the early 1900s to regulate heroin.

Effects of Opioids

An opioid, also known as a narcotic, is any drug derived from opium, such as morphine and codeine, or any synthetic drug that has opium-like effects, such as oxycodone. Opioids act like two kinds of pain-suppressing neurotransmitters found naturally in the brain—enkephalins and endorphins. Although opioids are associated with drug abuse, they remain useful for therapeutic purposes because of their analgesic properties.

Medical Uses of Opioids

Morphine	Used to relieve moderate to severe pain without inducing sleep
Codeine	Used for treating mild to moderate pain and as a cough suppressant
Fentanyls	Synthetic opioids that are highly potent; used for general anesthesia and chronic pain
Oxycodone	Analgesic used for severe pain related to cancer or other lingering diseases
Dextromethorphan	Synthetic used in OTC cough medicines; high doses may cause hallucinations
Buprenorphine	Analgesic used to treat narcotic abuse and dependence; low potential for dependence
Meperidine	Synthetic drug used to treat moderate pain; associated with dependence

Constipation is one of the most common side effects of opioids, but other side effects include drowsiness, respiratory depression, nausea, and itching. In fact, opioids have been used to treat severe diarrhea, especially in patients with dysentery.

Abuse, Tolerance, and Withdrawal

Unlike morphine and codeine, which may be used for medical purposes, heroin cannot be prescribed or used in any U.S. clinics. Heroin is deadly and the most likely opioid to be abused. All opioids have the potential for abuse because they cause tolerance, dependence, and withdrawal effects. Opioids prescribed for pain relief will require increased doses to maintain the needed effect, and recreational users will need additional amounts to achieve the desired euphoria. Physical dependence on opioids is likely for people who use high doses on a regular basis.

The life of a heroin user revolves around the next dose. Heroin users often begin by sniffing heroin powder or by injecting the substance into a muscle or under the skin, a technique known as skin popping. Long-term, heavy users prefer heating powdered heroin with water and injecting it intravenously, a method known as mainlining. The use of unsterile needles and sharing needles with other users leads to hepatitis, tetanus, and AIDS. Concerns about contracting AIDS have led many users to snort or smoke heroin to avoid needle usage.

The initial stage of heroin usage brings euphoria and positive effects that encourage further abuse. Later stages require users to continue taking the drug to avoid withdrawal symptoms. Most heroin users inject themselves three or four times each day because withdrawal signs usually begin 6 hours after each dose.

The following is a list of withdrawal symptoms associated with opioid abuse:

- 6 hours after last dose—anxiety and drug cravings
- 14 hours after last dose—runny nose, perspiration, and yawning
- 16 hours after last dose—pupil dilation, tremors, hot and cold flashes, and achiness
- 24–36 hours after last dose—insomnia, nausea, and increased blood pressure, temperature, and pulse
- 36–48 hours after last dose—vomiting, diarrhea, and increased blood sugar

Each withdrawal symptom builds on the previous one, so by the final stage, a person may experience all of the effects at once. Opioid withdrawal is not typically life threatening, but it is extremely painful. Withdrawal from methadone, which is a long-lasting synthetic opioid, is associated with the first three symptoms but with less severity. Craving for methadone does not begin until 24 hours after the last dose, which is why oral methadone is often employed in the treatment of heroin dependency. Although methadone causes dependence as well, it is less addictive than heroin and easier to manage. However, buprenorphine has a lower risk of dependence than methadone and provides an alternative form of treatment for heroin addicts.

MARIJUANA: HISTORY, EFFECTS, AND MEDICAL USE

Marijuana has properties similar to a variety of substances, so it is typically given its own classification. Marijuana has been described as a depressant, hallucinogenic, and an analgesic, which makes it a unique substance. The chief psychoactive ingredient of marijuana, delta-9-tetrahydrocannabinol (THC), is found in the resin of the cannabis sativa plant, especially in the flowering tops of female plants. The woody fibers of the cannabis stem are used to make hemp cloth and rope.

History of Marijuana

Cannabis plants have been cultivated for thousands of years since the discovery that smoking the dried and crushed leaves produced intoxicating effects. Marijuana has a history of usage in India as part of religious ceremonies. The use of marijuana spread from India to the rest of the world—Asia, Africa, Europe, and the Americas. In the United States during the 1930s, public concerns were raised about marijuana as the cause of violent crimes. Although little evidence supported a link between marijuana and violence, the substance was outlawed in 1937. During the 1960s and 1970s, marijuana served as a symbol for rejecting authority, and its usage peaked in 1980.

Effects of Marijuana

Marijuana contains over 400 chemicals, but THC is the most active one. When marijuana is smoked, THC absorbs rapidly into the blood, distributes into the brain, and then redistributes to the rest of the body. Within 5 to 10 minutes, a user experiences the peak psychological and cardiovascular effects of the drug, and within 30 minutes most of the THC is out of the brain. However, reduced percentages of THC linger in a user's body for days, and large doses may take weeks to eliminate from the body. THC taken orally absorbs slowly and incompletely, so it takes longer for a user to experience its effects. The THC level in marijuana varies, but most marijuana sold by dealers in the United States has a THC content of 0.5–11 percent. Such levels are believed to be 20 percent greater than marijuana that was smoked in the 1960s and 1970s because of more efficient cultivation methods. Hashish, which is another derivative of cannabis, contains the purest version of the plant's resin. Hashish has THC levels anywhere from 3.6–25 percent, so it is a more potent version of marijuana that may generate hallucinogenic effects.

Marijuana affects both the body and the mind in a variety of ways. The primary and most consistent physiological effect of marijuana usage is an increased heart rate. Other bodily effects include reddening of the eyes and drying of the mouth and throat. Low doses of marijuana typically produce feelings of euphoria, tranquility, and relaxation. Loss of coordination and balance and slowed reaction times often accompany marijuana usage as well, which is why driving or operating heavy machinery is extremely dangerous after using marijuana. Marijuana users also experience an increased desire to eat.

The "high" experienced from smoking one marijuana cigarette usually lasts 2 or 3 hours and may be accompanied by impaired memory and an altered perception of time and events. In contrast, smoking a larger dose of marijuana may result in anxiety, panic, hallucinations, delusions, and paranoia, especially with people who are already feeling anxious or depressed.

Long-term effects of heavy marijuana usage are inconclusive. However, experts agree that long-term smoking of marijuana decreases pulmonary capabilities, causes chronic lung diseases, and raises the risk of lung cancer. Whether or not there are long-term cognitive effects of marijuana usage is a controversial subject. Amotivational syndrome refers to the idea that heavy marijuana usage reduces a person's motivation and productivity. According to the syndrome, marijuana users exhibit problems with concentration and memory, and they show signs of laziness and disinterest in normal social activities. Critics argue that there is no direct correlation between marijuana usage and amotivational syndrome, and some argue that the syndrome is nonexistent.

Frequent high doses of marijuana produce tolerance, so higher doses are needed to achieve effects of similar intensity. In addition, mild physical dependence can develop in people who often use high doses of marijuana, but physical dependence is typically very low. Mild withdrawal symptoms may include irritability, insomnia, and loss of appetite.

Medical Marijuana Use

Over the last decade, questions have arisen regarding the medical use of marijuana. Advocates of using marijuana for medical purposes assert that the substance has many possible uses. The Food and Drug Administration (FDA) approved Marinol, a legal form of synthetic THC that is available in a capsule by prescription to treat nausea associated with cancer chemotherapy and to stimulate the appetite of AIDS patients. However, marijuana legalization supporters claim that THC is more effective when it is smoked, and that medical conditions like migraines, depression, and seizures could be relieved by smoking marijuana. However, critics point out that smoking is a poor delivery system for medication because of questionable dosage regulation and possible pulmonary damage. Limited studies are available regarding the actual medical benefits or potential dangers of marijuana, so the controversy is likely to continue.

HALLUCINOGENS

For many centuries, medicine men, shamans, and mystics have used hallucinogenic plants and herbs as part of spiritual events in different cultures around the world. Hallucinogens, such as LSD, are substances that generate perceptual disturbances and produce visions for those who use them. Since many substances generate hallucinogenic effects at certain doses, the determination of whether a drug is classified as a hallucinogen has been debated for many years. In general, a drug's tendency to produce hallucinations places it in the hallucinogen category.

Within the hallucinogen classification, there are variations. Phantastica hallucinogens are those that create a fantasy world for the user, and they are divided into two categories—indole and catechol. Phantastica hallucinogens are also known as psychedelic and psychotomimetic drugs.

Phantastica Hallucinogens

Indole hallucinogens	Indole is a chemical structure found in the neurotransmitter serotonin and also in LSD and psilocybin, which is derived from the Mexican mushroom.
Catechol hallucinogens	Catecholamines include the neurotransmitters norepinephrine, epinephrine, and dopamine, and they are found in the peyote cactus, which contains mescaline.

In 1938, Dr. Albert Hofmann, a Swiss scientist, discovered lysergic acid diethylamide (LSD) while searching for active chemicals in ergot compounds. Ergot is a type of fungus that grows in rye and other plants. Hofmann's synthetic drug became one of the most widely known hallucinogenic drugs.

The effects associated with using LSD are typical of many other hallucinogenic substances, including peyote, but effects vary depending upon the individual and the environment. The following is a list of possible effects related to LSD usage:

- Hallucinations
- Heightened sensory awareness
- Enhanced emotions
- Exaggeration of perceptions
- Awareness of both fantasy world and real world
- Time distortion
- Awareness of inner thoughts

Hallucinogens such as LSD and peyote have similar effects and do not cause psychological or physical dependence. Phencyclidine (PCP), also known as angel dust, is a different kind of hallucinogen because it has a high psychological dependence. Originally developed in the 1950s as an anesthetic, PCP generates a number of unique effects:

- Numbness in low doses and general anesthesia in higher doses
- Coma, fever, seizures, and death linked to high doses
- Altered body perception and feelings of strength, power, and invincibility
- Schizophrenic-type episodes that may include violent behavior

CLUB DRUGS

Club drugs are those associated with all-night raves, parties, bars, and nightclubs. The club drug group includes MDMA (Ecstasy), GHB, and Rohypnol.

MDMA, which is known as Ecstasy or XTC, is a synthetic amphetamine that gained popularity among young adults at raves and nightclubs in England and the United States. The effects of Ecstasy include increased empathy, distortions of time, increased energy, and euphoria. A number of psychiatrists advocate the use of MDMA for the treatment of mental disorders such as fear and anxiety. Inconclusive laboratory studies of MDMA have shown that the drug may cause brain damage.

Gamma hydroxybutyrate (GHB) is found naturally in the body and has a structure similar to the inhibitory neurotransmitter GABA. GHB is a depressant that has been used as an anesthetic and a dietary supplement. Athletes have used GHB as a way to stimulate muscle growth. GHB is considered a club drug because it has been linked to date rape. Clear and odorless, GHB can be easily mixed with the beverage of an unsuspecting victim. The substance has amnesiac and sedative characteristics that make women vulnerable to sexual predators. Prosecution is often hindered by the fact that victims cannot recall details of the crime, and the substance leaves the bloodstream quickly.

Rohypnol, which is illegal in the United States, is a benzodiazepine linked to date rapes. Benzodiazepines are depressants taken for anxiety and sleep. Sexual predators dissolve the drug in a victim's drink at a party or a dance club, and sexual assault victims are unable to recall any specific details because Rohypnol blocks short-term memory.

ANABOLIC STEROIDS

Androgens are a group of hormones frequently abused by athletes. Testosterone is the primary natural androgen responsible for growth spurts during adolescence, as well as the growth of the male sex organs, body hair, muscles, and vocal cords. Anabolic steroids are a type of steroid hormone related to the male hormone testosterone. Male and female athletes have abused anabolic steroids in the attempt to build muscle mass and improve physical performance. The negative side effects of taking high doses of anabolic steroids include muscle tears, increased aggression, uncontrolled rage, headaches, insomnia, and anxiety. The use of anabolic steroids is banned from nearly all major sporting organizations.

ANTIPSYCHOTICS

A group of drugs called phenothiazines was introduced in the 1950s as a way to treat psychosis. These antipsychotics, or neuroleptics, revolutionized the mental health-care system by reducing the need for physical restraints and electroshock treatment of unmanageable patients. Antipsychotics decrease psychotic symptoms without sedation and enable patients to remain subdued enough to take care of their physical needs and to participate in social activities. Phenothiazines have been shown to help most schizophrenics, although the drugs are not a cure. Discontinuing the medication leads to a relapse of most symptoms, but the situation can be reversed by resuming treatment.

Antipsychotics are not addictive, but they have some side effects. Movement disorders similar to Parkinson's disease, such as hand tremors, muscular rigidity, and a shuffling stride, may occur with patients taking antipsychotics. However, antipsychotics developed in the last decade are less likely to have such side effects.

ANTIDEPRESSANTS

Depression is one of the most common psychiatric disorders and is characterized by sleep disturbances, diminished pleasure in normal activities, feelings of guilt and pessimism, and, in severe cases, suicidal thoughts. Antidepressant medication is typically prescribed to patients who have endogenous major depression, which is caused by either a genetic disorder or imbalanced brain chemistry. Antidepressants can be divided into three main categories.

Types of Antidepressants

Tricyclics	Side effects include drowsiness, dry mouth, and blurred vision; patients develop tolerance. Drugs in this group include Elavil, Tofranil, Sinequan, and Pamelor.
Monoamine oxidase inhibitors (MAOIs)	Limited use because of significant side effects when combined with food, wine, and other medications. Side effects include dizziness, headaches, and trembling. Drugs in this group include Nardil and Parnate.
Selective reuptake inhibitors (SSRIs)	Considered safer than other types; fewest side effects. Prozac is the most prescribed; others brands include Paxil, Zoloft, and Celexa.

Antidepressants work by making either norepinephrine or serotonin more readily available to the brain. Despite the differences between the three types of antidepressants, patients who take any of them typically do not see improvements in mood for approximately two weeks. The medication reaches a patient's brain quickly, but experts believe that repeated exposure to antidepressant medication is necessary before symptoms of depression diminish.

POST-TEST ANSWER SHEET

1. Ⓐ Ⓑ Ⓒ Ⓓ	13. Ⓐ Ⓑ Ⓒ Ⓓ	25. Ⓐ Ⓑ Ⓒ Ⓓ	37. Ⓐ Ⓑ Ⓒ Ⓓ	49. Ⓐ Ⓑ Ⓒ Ⓓ
2. Ⓐ Ⓑ Ⓒ Ⓓ	14. Ⓐ Ⓑ Ⓒ Ⓓ	26. Ⓐ Ⓑ Ⓒ Ⓓ	38. Ⓐ Ⓑ Ⓒ Ⓓ	50. Ⓐ Ⓑ Ⓒ Ⓓ
3. Ⓐ Ⓑ Ⓒ Ⓓ	15. Ⓐ Ⓑ Ⓒ Ⓓ	27. Ⓐ Ⓑ Ⓒ Ⓓ	39. Ⓐ Ⓑ Ⓒ Ⓓ	51. Ⓐ Ⓑ Ⓒ Ⓓ
4. Ⓐ Ⓑ Ⓒ Ⓓ	16. Ⓐ Ⓑ Ⓒ Ⓓ	28. Ⓐ Ⓑ Ⓒ Ⓓ	40. Ⓐ Ⓑ Ⓒ Ⓓ	52. Ⓐ Ⓑ Ⓒ Ⓓ
5. Ⓐ Ⓑ Ⓒ Ⓓ	17. Ⓐ Ⓑ Ⓒ Ⓓ	29. Ⓐ Ⓑ Ⓒ Ⓓ	41. Ⓐ Ⓑ Ⓒ Ⓓ	53. Ⓐ Ⓑ Ⓒ Ⓓ
6. Ⓐ Ⓑ Ⓒ Ⓓ	18. Ⓐ Ⓑ Ⓒ Ⓓ	30. Ⓐ Ⓑ Ⓒ Ⓓ	42. Ⓐ Ⓑ Ⓒ Ⓓ	54. Ⓐ Ⓑ Ⓒ Ⓓ
7. Ⓐ Ⓑ Ⓒ Ⓓ	19. Ⓐ Ⓑ Ⓒ Ⓓ	31. Ⓐ Ⓑ Ⓒ Ⓓ	43. Ⓐ Ⓑ Ⓒ Ⓓ	55. Ⓐ Ⓑ Ⓒ Ⓓ
8. Ⓐ Ⓑ Ⓒ Ⓓ	20. Ⓐ Ⓑ Ⓒ Ⓓ	32. Ⓐ Ⓑ Ⓒ Ⓓ	44. Ⓐ Ⓑ Ⓒ Ⓓ	56. Ⓐ Ⓑ Ⓒ Ⓓ
9. Ⓐ Ⓑ Ⓒ Ⓓ	21. Ⓐ Ⓑ Ⓒ Ⓓ	33. Ⓐ Ⓑ Ⓒ Ⓓ	45. Ⓐ Ⓑ Ⓒ Ⓓ	57. Ⓐ Ⓑ Ⓒ Ⓓ
10. Ⓐ Ⓑ Ⓒ Ⓓ	22. Ⓐ Ⓑ Ⓒ Ⓓ	34. Ⓐ Ⓑ Ⓒ Ⓓ	46. Ⓐ Ⓑ Ⓒ Ⓓ	58. Ⓐ Ⓑ Ⓒ Ⓓ
11. Ⓐ Ⓑ Ⓒ Ⓓ	23. Ⓐ Ⓑ Ⓒ Ⓓ	35. Ⓐ Ⓑ Ⓒ Ⓓ	47. Ⓐ Ⓑ Ⓒ Ⓓ	59. Ⓐ Ⓑ Ⓒ Ⓓ
12. Ⓐ Ⓑ Ⓒ Ⓓ	24. Ⓐ Ⓑ Ⓒ Ⓓ	36. Ⓐ Ⓑ Ⓒ Ⓓ	48. Ⓐ Ⓑ Ⓒ Ⓓ	60. Ⓐ Ⓑ Ⓒ Ⓓ

answer sheet

POST-TEST

Directions: Carefully read each of the following 60 questions. Choose the best answer to each question, and darken its letter on your answer sheet. The Answer Key and Explanations can be found following this post-test.

1. Amphetamines may be prescribed for which of the following medical conditions?
   (A) Depression
   (B) Asthma
   (C) Epilepsy
   (D) ADHD

2. The process used to make whiskey that involves heating an alcoholic mixture and collecting the vapors is known as
   (A) fermentation.
   (B) inhalation.
   (C) distillation.
   (D) prohibition.

3. Which of the following neurotransmitters has effects similar to morphine?
   (A) Norepinephrine
   (B) Enkephalin
   (C) Serotonin
   (D) GABA

4. The body's attempt to maintain internal stability is known as
   (A) neurotransmission.
   (B) bioavailability.
   (C) metabolism.
   (D) homeostasis.

5. A side effect of antipsychotic drugs is
   (A) short-term memory loss.
   (B) suicidal thoughts.
   (C) hand tremors.
   (D) depression.

6. The substance with the lowest possibility of physical dependency is
   (A) methadone.
   (B) marijuana.
   (C) alcohol.
   (D) codeine.

7. The most commonly used illicit drug in the United States is
   (A) barbiturates.
   (B) marijuana.
   (C) cocaine.
   (D) alcohol.

8. Which neurotransmitter is increased by benzodiazepines?
   (A) Acetylcholine
   (B) Serotonin
   (C) Dopamine
   (D) GABA

9. According to the moral model of drug dependency, people are dependent on drugs because of
   (A) peer pressure.
   (B) personal choices.
   (C) personality traits.
   (D) biological conditions.

10. The original concept behind the temperance movement was
    (A) alcohol abstinence.
    (B) marijuana legalization.
    (C) drinking in moderation.
    (D) prohibition of smoking.

11. The point of communication between two neurons is the
    (A) glial.
    (B) synapse.
    (C) dendrite.
    (D) neurotransmitter.

12. Which method of cocaine usage is the least potent?
    (A) Intranasal
    (B) Smoking
    (C) Intravenous
    (D) Chewing

13. A drug used to treat heroin addiction that has a low risk of developing dependence is
    (A) buprenorphine.
    (B) methadone.
    (C) oxycodone.
    (D) hydromorphone.

14. Which of the following was the first known abused inhalant?
    (A) Amyl nitrite
    (B) Ether
    (C) Nitrous oxide
    (D) Chloroform

15. Withdrawal symptoms are most associated with
    (A) drug misuse.
    (B) substance abuse.
    (C) psychoactive drugs.
    (D) drug dependency.

16. The primary active ingredient in marijuana is
    (A) THC.
    (B) MDMA.
    (C) cannabis.
    (D) Marinol.

17. All of the following factors increase a smoker's risk of having cancer EXCEPT
    (A) daily number of cigarettes smoked.
    (B) number of years spent smoking.
    (C) gender and body weight.
    (D) age when smoking began.

18. Prohibition laws led to
    (A) decreased criminal activity.
    (B) dependence upon narcotics.
    (C) reduction in alcohol usage.
    (D) black market alcohol sales.

19. Which of the following is an effect associated with cocaine withdrawal?
    (A) Heavy sweating
    (B) Deadening of taste buds
    (C) Life-threatening seizures
    (D) Inability to feel pleasure

20. All of the following are effects associated with LSD usage EXCEPT
    (A) hallucinations.
    (B) drowsiness.
    (C) emotionality.
    (D) self-awareness.

21. Which of the following are used to relieve anxiety and fear?
    (A) Steroids
    (B) Hypnotics
    (C) Opiates
    (D) Sedatives

22. Which of the following is most likely supported by Alcoholics Anonymous?
    (A) Moral model
    (B) Disease model
    (C) Sociological model
    (D) Predisposition model

23. Smoking cigars and pipes is closely correlated with a higher risk of
    (A) esophageal cancer.
    (B) bladder cancer.
    (C) pancreatic cancer.
    (D) breast cancer.

24. A protein to which neurotransmitters or drugs bind is a(n)
    (A) axon.
    (B) hormone.
    (C) synapse.
    (D) receptor.

25. Which of the following is an effect of inhalant usage?
    (A) Paranoia
    (B) Hallucinations
    (C) Manic excitement
    (D) Uncoordinated movements

26. A highly potent form of marijuana is
    (A) hashish.
    (B) opium.
    (C) cannabis.
    (D) hemp.

27. How soon after a dosage does a heroin addict usually experience the onset of withdrawal symptoms?
    (A) 3 hours
    (B) 6 hours
    (C) 12 hours
    (D) 24 hours

28. All of the following factors are used to estimate a person's blood alcohol level EXCEPT
    (A) alcohol consumption.
    (B) gender.
    (C) alcohol metabolism.
    (D) weight.

29. Which of the following is a group of hormones abused by athletes to increase muscle mass?
    (A) Amphetamines
    (B) Androgens
    (C) Creatines
    (D) Opiates

30. Bromide was once used to
    (A) induce sleep.
    (B) relieve pain.
    (C) treat epilepsy.
    (D) control eating.

31. Which of the following consists of the brain and the spinal cord?
    (A) Peripheral nervous system
    (B) Central nervous system
    (C) Autonomic nervous system
    (D) Somatic nervous system

32. Low doses of inhaled aerosols most often cause
    (A) dizziness.
    (B) suffocation.
    (C) sleep.
    (D) hypoxia.

33. Where does the majority of alcohol metabolism take place?
    (A) Kidneys
    (B) Pancreas
    (C) Liver
    (D) Stomach

34. The idea that drug use behaviors are established by observing family and friends is the
    (A) structural influence theory.
    (B) cultural trend theory.
    (C) social learning theory.
    (D) biological theory.

35. All of the following are effects of nicotine EXCEPT
    (A) increased desire to drink.
    (B) decreased oxygen in blood.
    (C) increased blood pressure.
    (D) decreased desire to eat.

36. The chemical structure found in both serotonin and LSD is
    (A) dopamine.
    (B) catechol.
    (C) psilocybin.
    (D) indole.

37. Which of the following is used as a cough suppressant?
    (A) Amphetamines
    (B) Codeine
    (C) Barbiturates
    (D) Morphine

38. A low dose of amphetamines would most likely result in
    (A) irregular heartbeat.
    (B) behavioral stereotypy.
    (C) increased blood pressure.
    (D) psychosis.

39. Which of the following would most likely be prescribed to a patient diagnosed as schizophrenic?
    (A) Opioids
    (B) Cannabis
    (C) Psychedelics
    (D) Antipsychotics

40. The neurotransmitter that is associated with intense euphoria is
    (A) norepinephrine.
    (B) acetylcholine.
    (C) dopamine.
    (D) GABA.

41. During which stage of alcohol withdrawal do hallucinations typically first occur?
    (A) Stage 1
    (B) Stage 2
    (C) Stage 3
    (D) Stage 4

42. Until the 1800s, the most popular way to use tobacco was by
    (A) rubbing it on the gums.
    (B) smoking cigarettes.
    (C) smoking cigars.
    (D) dipping snuff.

43. Which of the following ethnic groups accounts for the lowest percentage of illicit drug use in America?
    (A) Asians
    (B) Latinos
    (C) African Americans
    (D) Native Americans

44. Marijuana has been approved for the medical treatment of
    (A) glaucoma.
    (B) depression.
    (C) appetite stimulation in anorexics.
    (D) nausea caused by chemotherapy.

45. A method of reducing the impurities in a drug to prepare it for smoking is known as
    (A) running.
    (B) freebasing.
    (C) bingeing.
    (D) tweaking.

46. Which of the following substances causes the most severe withdrawal effects?
    (A) Nicotine
    (B) Alcohol
    (C) Cocaine
    (D) Heroin

47. A group of highly potent synthetic opioids used for general anesthesia are
    (A) amphetamines.
    (B) benzodiazepines.
    (C) fentanyls.
    (D) barbiturates.

48. One of the potential side effects related to the medical use of amphetamines is
    (A) Alzheimer's disease.
    (B) neuromuscular damage.
    (C) Parkinson's disease.
    (D) cardiovascular damage.

49. Which of the following is a colorless, volatile liquid alkaloid that is highly addictive?
    (A) Nicotine
    (B) Heroin
    (C) Alcohol
    (D) Toluene

50. The criminal activity most associated with heroin addicts is
    (A) carjacking.
    (B) forgery.
    (C) smuggling.
    (D) prostitution.

51. Which neurotransmitter is most affected by LSD?
    (A) Dopamine
    (B) Glutamate
    (C) Serotonin
    (D) Endorphins

52. Which of the following has the fewest side effects in the treatment of moderate to severe depression?
    (A) MAOIs
    (B) Lithium
    (C) SSRIs
    (D) Tricyclics

53. A person who smokes one marijuana cigarette will most likely experience
    (A) agitation.
    (B) relaxation.
    (C) hallucinations.
    (D) alertness.

54. Which of the following increases the rate at which alcohol is absorbed in the body?
    (A) Soda
    (B) Food
    (C) Water
    (D) Coffee

55. Side effects of high doses of anabolic steroids may include all of the following EXCEPT
    (A) uncontrolled rage.
    (B) frequent headaches.
    (C) visual hallucinations.
    (D) increased aggression.

56. All of the following are associated with employees who abuse alcohol EXCEPT
    (A) criminal activity.
    (B) absenteeism.
    (C) accidents.
    (D) tardiness.

57. Which neurotransmitters are made more available to the brain with antidepressant medication?
    (A) Serotonin and dopamine
    (B) Acetylcholine and dopamine
    (C) Norepinephrine and serotonin
    (D) Glutamate and norepinephrine

58. Which of the following is an opioid?
    (A) Ritalin
    (B) Codeine
    (C) Prozac
    (D) Ecstasy

59. Research studies have suggested that MDMA may cause
(A) brain damage.
(B) seizures.
(C) lung damage.
(D) amnesia.

60. Combining depressants, alcohol, and narcotics often leads to
(A) cocaethylene.
(B) muscular rigidity.
(C) psychotic behavior.
(D) respiratory depression.

ANSWER KEY AND EXPLANATIONS

1. D	13. A	25. D	37. B	49. A
2. C	14. C	26. A	38. C	50. D
3. B	15. D	27. B	39. D	51. C
4. D	16. A	28. C	40. C	52. C
5. C	17. C	29. B	41. B	53. B
6. B	18. D	30. A	42. D	54. A
7. B	19. D	31. B	43. A	55. C
8. D	20. B	32. A	44. D	56. A
9. B	21. D	33. C	45. B	57. C
10. C	22. B	34. C	46. B	58. B
11. B	23. A	35. A	47. C	59. A
12. D	24. D	36. D	48. D	60. D

1. **The correct answer is (D).** Amphetamines may be prescribed for Attention Deficit Hyperactivity Disorder (ADHD), narcolepsy, and obesity. In the past, amphetamines were prescribed for depression and asthma, but the FDA ended that practice in 1970.

2. **The correct answer is (C).** Distillation is the process of making a concentrated spirit, such as brandy or whiskey, by heating the mixture, collecting the vapors, and condensing the vapors back to a liquid form. Fermentation, choice (A), is used to make beer and wine and involves a combination of yeast, sugar, and water but no heat. Prohibition, choice (D), was the period from 1920–1933 when alcohol was illegal in the United States. Choice (B) is a distracter.

3. **The correct answer is (B).** Enkephalins are neurotransmitters that occur naturally in the brain, and they suppress pain like opioids. Choice (A) regulates appetite and waking. Choice (C) is a neurotransmitter important in impulsivity and depression. GABA, choice (D), is an inhibitory neurotransmitter.

4. **The correct answer is (D).** Homeostasis refers to the body's attempt to maintain internal stability. The human body functions better when bodily functions, such as temperature, glucose levels, and blood pressure, stay at constant levels. Choices (A), (B), and (C) are not related to homeostasis.

5. **The correct answer is (C).** One of the side effects of antipsychotic drugs is movement disorders similar to Parkinson's disease. Hand tremors, muscular rigidity, and a shuffling walk occur in about 20 percent of patients taking phenothiazines. Choices (A), (B), and (D) are not common side effects of antipsychotic drugs.

6. **The correct answer is (B).** Marijuana has a very low physical dependency level. Methadone has a high physical dependency level, so choice (A) is incorrect. Both alcohol and codeine have moderate dependency levels.

7. **The correct answer is (B).** Marijuana is the most commonly used illegal drug in the United States. Alcohol is a legal substance abused by many people, so choice (D) is incorrect.

Choices (A) and (C) are illicit drugs, but they are not used as commonly as marijuana.

8. **The correct answer is (D).** GABA is increased by benzodiazepines in the body. GABA is the body's main inhibitory neurotransmitter and works to induce sleep and calmness. Benzodiazepines, such as Valium, are prescribed as sedatives, and they increase GABA activity. Choices (A), (B), and (C) are not directly linked to benzodiazepines.

9. **The correct answer is (B).** Lifestyle choices and immorality are the reason people become drug dependent, according to the moral model. Peer pressure is a sociological reason for drug dependency, so choice (A) is incorrect. Choice (C) refers to the personality predisposition model, and choice (D) refers to the disease model of dependency.

10. **The correct answer is (C).** The temperance movement of the 1800s began as an attempt to encourage moderate drinking of beer and wine when the consumption of hard liquor was associated with criminal activity. The movement later advocated abstinence from all alcohol, so choice (A) is close but incorrect. Choice (B) is not related to the temperance movement. Prohibition laws of 1920 outlawed alcohol in the United States and developed out of the temperance movement, so choice (D) is incorrect.

11. **The correct answer is (B).** The synapse is the junction or communication point between two neurons. Glial cells are the cells in the nervous system that do not communicate with other cells, so choice (A) is incorrect. The treelike branches on neurons that receive transmitter signals are the dendrites, so choice (C) is incorrect.

Neurotransmitters are released by neurons, so choice (D) is incorrect.

12. **The correct answer is (D).** Chewing coca leaves is the least potent way to use cocaine. The potency of the coca leaves is diminished by the stomach and liver before it reaches the central nervous system. Snorting is more potent than chewing, but intravenous use and smoking crack are the most addictive methods.

13. **The correct answer is (A).** Buprenorphine is used to treat heroin addiction because it has a low risk of developing addiction. Methadone is also used to treat narcotic addiction, but it has a high rate of addiction—less than heroin but more than buprenorphine. Oxycodone treats pain and has been abused in recent years. Hydromorphone is morphine-based and is not used for treating narcotic addictions.

14. **The correct answer is (C).** Nitrous oxide, known as "laughing gas," was first abused in the eighteenth century. People inhaled the substance to achieve a quick state of drunkenness. Ether and chloroform are two other types of gaseous anesthetics, but they were not used first. Amyl nitrite became popular in the 1960s.

15. **The correct answer is (D).** Withdrawal symptoms are most associated with drug dependency, which means that a person uses a drug so frequently that going without it causes physical and psychological problems. Drug misuse, choice (A), refers to using a prescription drug incorrectly, which is not likely to lead to withdrawal symptoms. Substance abuse, choice (B), may lead to dependency, but the abuse of alcohol or drugs does not necessarily cause withdrawal symptoms. Psychoactive drugs, choice (C), only

lead to withdrawal symptoms if a person becomes dependent on them.

16. **The correct answer is (A).** THC, which is delta-9-tetrahydrocannabinol, is the main active ingredient in marijuana. MDMA is an amphetamine derivative, so choice (B) is incorrect. THC is in the cannabis sativa plant, so choice (C) is incorrect. Marinol is a synthetic THC prescribed for the treatment of nausea in cancer patients.

17. **The correct answer is (C).** Gender and body weight are less likely to affect a smoker's risk of cancer. A smoker's risk of cancer increases with the number of cigarettes smoked on a daily basis, the number of years spent smoking, and the age when smoking began.

18. **The correct answer is (D).** Bootlegging and black market liquor sales increased during Prohibition because these were the only ways to acquire alcohol between 1920 and 1933. Criminal activity and corruption increased during Prohibition, so choice (A) is incorrect. Alcohol consumption did not decrease during Prohibition because people who wanted to drink went to speakeasies or bootleggers, so choice (C) is incorrect. Narcotics usage did not change because of Prohibition, so choice (B) is incorrect.

19. **The correct answer is (D).** Anhedonia, which is the loss of pleasure, is a short-term effect of cocaine withdrawal. Choices (A) and (C) are associated with alcohol withdrawal. Heavy smokers lose some sensitivity in their taste buds, so choice (B) is incorrect.

20. **The correct answer is (B).** Hallucinations, heightened emotions, and self-awareness are typical effects of LSD usage. Drowsiness is not a typical effect of LSD, although numbness may occur with the use of PCP, which is another hallucinogen. Therefore, choices (A), (C), and (D) are incorrect.

21. **The correct answer is (D).** Sedatives are CNS depressants used to relieve anxiety and fear. Hypnotics are also CNS depressants, but they are intended to help people sleep. Choices (A) and (C) are not drugs used for the relief of nervousness or anxiety.

22. **The correct answer is (B).** Alcoholics Anonymous (AA) and Narcotics Anonymous advocate the disease model, which asserts that people abuse drugs and alcohol because of biological conditions. Choices (A) and (D) are two other dependency models that are less likely to be supported by AA. Sociological theories of drug dependency suggest that social relationships lead to substance abuse.

23. **The correct answer is (A).** Cancers of the esophagus, mouth, and larynx are more common among pipe and cigar smokers. Cigarette smoking increases the risk of lung, bladder, pancreas, and kidney cancer, but cigar and pipe smoking is more likely to lead to esophageal cancer.

24. **The correct answer is (D).** Receptors are special proteins to which neurotransmitters and drugs bind, which causes the cell function to change. The axon is part of the neuron, so choice (A) is incorrect. Hormones are chemical messengers released by glands, so choice (B) is incorrect. The synapse is the location at which two neurons communicate, so choice (C) is incorrect.

25. **The correct answer is (D).** Uncoordinated movements and slurred speech are the typical effects associated with inhalant usage. Inhalants are categorized as depressants because they have similar effects to the use of

alcohol and barbiturates. Choices (A) and (C) are effects of stimulants, such as cocaine and amphetamines. Choice (B) is linked to using hallucinogens, such as Ecstasy and LSD.

26. **The correct answer is (A).** Hashish is a potent form of marijuana that contains high levels of THC and may cause hallucinations. Opium is not a form of marijuana, so choice (B) is incorrect. The wood stem of the cannabis plant is used to make hemp cloth and rope, so choices (C) and (D) are incorrect.

27. **The correct answer is (B).** Six hours after a dose, a heroin addict is likely to experience anxiety and cravings, which are the first signs of withdrawal. Most heavy users inject themselves every 4 to 6 hours to avoid the unpleasant effects of withdrawal, which can last for two days.

28. **The correct answer is (C).** The amount of alcohol consumed and the gender and weight of an individual are factors used to estimate a person's blood alcohol level. Alcohol metabolism refers to the way alcohol is broken down by enzymes in the body. Alcohol metabolism occurs at a constant rate no matter a person's weight or gender.

29. **The correct answer is (B).** Androgens are hormones abused by athletes that are found in anabolic steroids. Athletes have used both amphetamines and creatine, but neither one is a hormone. Opiates are not hormones, so choice (D) is incorrect.

30. **The correct answer is (A).** Bromide salts were once used to induce sleep and a hypnotic state. However, bromide was found to be toxic and was replaced by barbiturates as a way to relieve anxiety and insomnia. Choices (B), (C), and (D) are incorrect.

31. **The correct answer is (B).** The central nervous system consists of the brain and spinal cord and is responsible for learning and memory. The autonomic nervous system controls involuntary actions of the body like blood pressure. The somatic nervous system controls voluntary actions like chewing. The autonomic and somatic nervous systems comprise the peripheral nervous system, so choices (A), (C), and (D) are incorrect.

32. **The correct answer is (A).** Dizziness and lightheadedness usually occur with low doses of aerosols such as spray paint. Sleep occurs with high doses, so choice (C) is incorrect. Suffocation and hypoxia can occur in some cases, especially when extremely large doses are inhaled.

33. **The correct answer is (C).** The liver metabolizes over 90 percent of all alcohol that a person consumes, which is why liver problems occur among heavy drinkers. Alcohol damages all organs of the body when consumed in large amounts over many years, but choices (A), (B), and (D) are incorrect.

34. **The correct answer is (C).** According to the social learning theory, individuals learn drug use behaviors from family and friends. Choice (A), structural influence theory, points to the organization of a society or subculture as the greatest influence on an individual's drug use. Biological theories, choice (D), suggest that substance abuse derives from genetics and biological conditions. Choice (B) is a distracter.

35. **The correct answer is (A).** Nicotine increases blood pressure, heart rate, and blood flow. The desire to eat decreases with smoking, at least for a short time. The ability of blood to carry oxygen is decreased by nicotine,

so choice (B) is incorrect. Although smokers may drink alcohol while smoking, there is no indication that nicotine increases the desire to drink.

36. **The correct answer is (D).** Indole is a chemical structure found in LSD and serotonin. Indole is also found in psilocybin, which is derived from the Mexican mushroom. Catechol hallucinogens include peyote but not LSD, so choice (B) is incorrect.

37. **The correct answer is (B).** Codeine is used for treating moderate pain and as a cough suppressant. Morphine is another opioid used to relieve pain without inducing sleep. Amphetamines and barbiturates are not used for cough suppression, so choices (A) and (C) are incorrect.

38. **The correct answer is (C).** Low doses of amphetamines typically increase blood pressure and heartbeat. An irregular heartbeat would be more likely with a high dose of the substance, so choice (A) is incorrect. Choices (B) and (D) are also more common with heavy amphetamine usage rather than limited or light usage.

39. **The correct answer is (D).** Antipsychotics are often prescribed to patients with schizophrenia because such drugs have a calming effect on patients. Choice (A) is incorrect because opioids are prescribed for pain relief. Some doctors prescribe marijuana or cannabis, choice (B), for pain relief but not for schizophrenia. Psychedelics, choice (C), cause people to hallucinate, which is what a schizophrenic is trying to lessen.

40. **The correct answer is (C).** Dopamine is associated with mood elevation, and many abused drugs alter the dopamine neurons of the body. Choice (A) is associated with arousal and attentiveness.

Choice (B) is linked to mild euphoria, excitability, and insomnia. Choice (D), GABA, which is linked to alcohol and barbiturates, causes depression and drowsiness.

41. **The correct answer is (B).** Hallucinations usually first appear in the second stage of alcohol withdrawal. Stage 1 involves tremors and restlessness, while Stage 3 involves disorientation. Seizures are symptomatic of the fourth stage of alcohol withdrawal.

42. **The correct answer is (D).** Dipping snuff, chewing tobacco, and smoking pipes were the most popular methods of using tobacco. Native Americans often made syrup out of tobacco and rubbed it on their gums. Some people enjoyed cigars, but snuff was considered fashionable. Cigarettes did not become popular until the late 1800s, when a cigarette-rolling machine was invented.

43. **The correct answer is (A).** Asians have the lowest percentage of illicit drug use, while Native Americans have the highest. Latinos and African Americans are both more frequent users than Asians but less frequent users than Native Americans.

44. **The correct answer is (D).** Nausea caused by chemotherapy may be treated with Marinol, a synthetic THC. Marinol may also be given to AIDS patients to help with appetite stimulation, but not to anorexics, choice (C). Marijuana may be beneficial to the treatment of patients with glaucoma, choice (A), and depression, choice (B), but the FDA has not given approval for such use.

45. **The correct answer is (B).** Freebasing refers to the method of reducing the impurities in a drug to prepare it for smoking. Freebasing cocaine results in crack. A run, choice (A), is

the intense use of a stimulant over a few days; a binge, choice (C), is similar but for a shorter duration. Tweaking, choice (D), refers to the repeated use of methamphetamines to maintain a high.

46. **The correct answer is (B).** Withdrawal effects from alcohol and barbiturates are more severe than effects associated with other substances. Withdrawal from alcohol may involve tremors, hallucinations, delusions, and seizures. Withdrawal issues occur with nicotine, cocaine, and heroin, but they are not as severe as the withdrawal symptoms experienced by alcoholics.

47. **The correct answer is (C).** Fentanyls are highly potent synthetic opioids used for general anesthesia and chronic pain. Overdoses of even small doses of fentanyls have been known to cause fatal respiratory depression. Choices (B) and (D) are depressants, and choice (A) is classified as a stimulant.

48. **The correct answer is (D).** Cardiovascular damage is a potential side effect of therapeutic amphetamine usage. Amphetamines increase heart rate, increase blood pressure, and may damage veins and arteries. Patients with a history of heart attacks, hypertension, or heart arrhythmia are at an even higher risk of cardiovascular damage. Choices (A), (B), and (C) are not side effects known to be associated with amphetamine usage.

49. **The correct answer is (A).** Nicotine is a colorless, volatile liquid alkaloid that is highly addictive and found in tobacco. Heroin, choice (B), is addictive, but it is not a liquid alkaloid. Alcohol, choice (C), is addictive for some people, but not everyone. Toluene, choice (D), is a chemical found in glues and paints.

50. **The correct answer is (D).** The high cost of heroin leads many female users to become involved in prostitution to support the habit. Burglary and shoplifting are also crimes typically committed by drug addicts in need of quick cash. Carjacking, forgery, and smuggling are crimes less associated with heroin addicts because they do not necessarily offer quick rewards.

51. **The correct answer is (C).** Hallucinogenic drugs like LSD affect serotonin pathways in the body. Serotonin controls mood, appetite, and aggression. Cocaine and amphetamines affect dopamine levels, so choice (A) is incorrect. Cocaine has also been linked to changes in glutamate transmission, so choice (B) is incorrect. Drugs derived from opium affect endorphins, so choice (D) is incorrect.

52. **The correct answer is (C).** Selective reuptake inhibitors (SSRIs) are considered the safest antidepressant medication with the fewest side effects. Both tricyclics and MAOIs are antidepressant medications, but they both have significant side effects. Lithium is a mood stabilizer used for the treatment of bipolar patients.

53. **The correct answer is (B).** The typical effects of smoking one marijuana cigarette include relaxation and euphoria. Smoking higher doses may result in hallucinations, anxiety, delusions, and panic in some users. Choices (A), (C), and (D) are incorrect.

54. **The correct answer is (A).** Carbonated beverages increase the rate that alcohol is absorbed in the body. Water and food decrease the rate of absorption, so choices (B) and (C) are incorrect. Coffee is falsely linked to the metabolism of alcohol, but it does not affect alcohol absorption.

55. **The correct answer is (C).** Negative side effects of taking high doses of anabolic steroids include uncontrolled rage, headaches, aggression, anxiety, and insomnia. Visual hallucinations are not known side effects associated with anabolic steroid usage.

56. **The correct answer is (A).** Being absent from work or frequently late are typical characteristics of alcoholic employees. Employees who have alcohol or drug abuse issues are also involved in more accidents than employees who do not abuse drugs or alcohol. Therefore, the correct answer is choice (A). Unlike individuals who abuse narcotics, most alcoholics are able to support themselves with employment instead of criminal acts.

57. **The correct answer is (C).** Antidepressants trigger either norepinephrine or serotonin in the brain to help relieve depression symptoms. Dopamine is made more available by cocaine and causes euphoria and agitation, so choices (A) and (B) are incorrect. Glutamate is found throughout the body and is not specifically triggered by antidepressants.

58. **The correct answer is (B).** Codeine is an opioid, which is a category of drugs that relieves pain. Ritalin is a stimulant, so choice (A) is incorrect. Prozac is a psychotherapeutic, so choice (C) is incorrect. Ecstasy is a hallucinogen, so choice (D) is incorrect.

59. **The correct answer is (A).** Laboratory experiments have indicated that MDMA may cause brain damage. Seizures, amnesia, and lung damage are not side effects linked to MDMA, which is also known as Ecstasy.

60. **The correct answer is (D).** Respiratory depression may occur as a result of combining depressants, alcohol, and narcotics, which all slow down the breathing rate. Respiratory depression means that a person stops breathing completely; it is a common result of many drug overdoses. Choice (A) is the substance created in the body when a person combines cocaine and alcohol. Choices (B) and (C) are not likely results of combining depressants, alcohol, and narcotics.

answers post-test

SUMMING IT UP

- Drugs are natural or artificial substances that improve, obstruct, or alter mind and body functions. Illicit drugs, such as marijuana and cocaine, are illegal to possess. Licit (legal) drugs include coffee, alcohol, tobacco, and over-the-counter (OTC) drugs like cold remedies. Alcohol and tobacco are considered gateway drugs because most illicit drug abusers first try cigarettes and liquor.

- Psychoactive drugs mainly affect the central nervous system, and they result in changes to consciousness, thought processes, and mood.

- Drug dependency occurs when one uses a drug so often that going without it is physically and psychologically difficult and results in such withdrawal symptoms as nausea, anxiety, muscle spasms, and sweating. The three models of dependency are *moral*, *disease*, and *characterological or personality predisposition*. Theories of dependency are *biological, psychological,* and *sociological*.

- Burglary and shoplifting are the crimes primarily committed by drug abusers in need of money. Many heroin abusers become involved in prostitution.

- Drug classifications are *stimulants* (cocaine, amphetamines, Ritalin, caffeine), *depressants* (alcohol, barbiturates, sleeping pills, inhalants), *hallucinogens* (LSD, Mescaline, Ecstasy, PCP), *opioids* (opium, morphine, codeine, heroin, methadone), *cannabis* (marijuana, THC, hashish), *nicotine* (cigarettes, chewing tobacco, cigars), and *psychotherapeutics* (Prozac, Haldol).

- The human body constantly attempts to maintain internal stability, a process known as homeostasis. Homeostatic mechanisms regulate body temperature, blood pressure, and glucose concentrations, as well as many other physiological functions.

- The nervous system is composed of neurons, which are specialized nerve cells that transfer messages throughout the body. The brain's billions of neurons communicate with each other by releasing chemical messengers known as neurotransmitters. The nervous system is divided into the somatic, autonomic, and central nervous systems.

- The three main types of drug interactions are: additive, antagonistic, and potentiative. Any combination of depressants, alcohol, or narcotics can lead to respiratory failure and death.

- Blood alcohol concentration (BAC) estimates are based on a person's gender, weight, and alcohol consumption. A blood alcohol level greater than 0.08 percent is illegal in every U.S. state. A blood alcohol level of 0.4–0.6 percent is often lethal, as breathing can stop.

- Withdrawal effects from alcohol and barbiturates are more severe than withdrawal from other substances. The four states of withdrawal start with tremors, insomnia, and rapid heartbeat and end with life-threatening seizures.

- Sedative-hypnotics, also known as central nervous system (CNS) depressants, reduce CNS activity, decrease the brain's level of awareness, and relieve anxiety.

- Inhalant abuse dates back to the eighteenth century, when nitrous oxide was inhaled to become "drunk." Inhaling methods include sniffing or snorting, bagging, and huffing. The three categories of inhalants are gaseous anesthetics, nitrites, and volatile solvents.

- Nicotine is a colorless, volatile liquid alkaloid that is highly addictive. Nicotine decreases ability of blood to carry oxygen; increases blood pressure, heart rate, and blood flow; and diminishes one's desire to eat for a short time.

- Passive smoking refers to the inhalation of cigarette smoke in the environment by nonsmokers. Mainstream smoke is drawn in directly from the mouthpiece of a cigarette. Sidestream or secondhand smoke comes from the lighted end of a cigarette.

- Stimulants (uppers) increase energy levels and generate a euphoric state for users. Cocaine and amphetamines are stimulants. Cocaine use includes chewing coca leaves, snorting, intravenous, and smoking crack cocaine. Amphetamines can increase heart rate and blood pressure and damage veins and arteries.

- Opioids or narcotics are drugs derived from opium that suppress pain and include morphine, codeine, Fentanyl, oxycodone, Dextromethorphan, Buprenorphine, and Meperidine. Heroin is the most likely opioid to be abused and can be deadly.

- Marijuana, a depressant, hallucinogenic, and analgesic, is a unique substance. Its chief psychoactive ingredient, delta-9-tetrahydrocannabinol (THC), is found in the resin of the cannabis sativa plant.

- Hashish, another derivative of cannabis, has THC levels of 3.6–25 percent, making it a more potent version of marijuana that may generate hallucinogenic effects.

- Hallucinogens, such as LSD, are substances that generate perceptual disturbances and produce visions for those who use them. Phantastica hallucinogens create a fantasy world for the user and are divided into two categories: indole and catechol.

- Club drugs are those associated with all-night raves, parties, bars, and nightclubs. The club drug group includes MDMA (Ecstasy), GHB, and Rohypnol.

- Anabolic steroids are related to the male hormone testosterone and have been abused by athletes wanting to build muscle mass and improve physical performance. Negative side effects include muscle tears, uncontrolled rage, insomnia, and anxiety.

- Phenothiazines, antipsychotic drugs, revolutionized the mental health-care system in the 1950s by reducing the need for physical restraints and electroshock treatment. Antipsychotics decrease psychotic symptoms without sedation, and patients can participate in social activities. Phenothiazines help most schizophrenics but are not a cure.

- Antidepressants can be divided into three main categories: tricyclics, monoamine oxidase inhibitors (MAOIs), and selective reuptake inhibitors (SSRIs).

Business Mathematics

chapter 5

OVERVIEW

- Diagnostic test
- Answer key and explanations
- Number sense: fractions, decimals, and percentages
- Algebraic concepts
- Statistics
- Business applications
- Financial mathematics
- Post-test
- Answer key and explanations
- Summing it up

DIAGNOSTIC TEST

Directions: Carefully read each of the following 20 questions. Choose the best answer to each question and circle your answer choice. The Answer Key and Explanations can be found following this Diagnostic Test.

1. Use the quadratic equation to solve for x where $x^2 + 4x - 21$.
   - **(A)** $-2 \pm 2\sqrt{17}$
   - **(B)** 3, −7
   - **(C)** 3, 7
   - **(D)** − 3, $2 + 2\sqrt{17}$

2. The science teacher asked each student in the science class to measure the temperature in degrees Fahrenheit for the classroom. For various reasons, not all of the students came up with the same answer. The students' measurements were 72, 74, 72, 70, 68, and 76. What was the mean ± the standard deviation?
   - **(A)** $72 \pm 2\sqrt{2}$
   - **(B)** $72 \pm 4\sqrt{2}$
   - **(C)** 72 ± 8
   - **(D)** 74 ± 8

183

3. A data set consists of the values (45, 3, 7, 26, 12, 9, 57, 3, 12). Which number in the group would be the value of the lowest quartile?

(A) 3

(B) 7

(C) 9

(D) 12

4. The number of people employed by the city in 1980 was 220. In 1990, there were 440 employees. In 2000, the number had grown to 880. What is the index number for city employment in 2000 relative to 1980?

(A) 4

(B) 20

(C) 400

(D) 800

5. A semiconductor company buys a tool for 2 million dollars and will depreciate it over five years. Its residual value is $500,000. How much does the tool depreciate per year?

(A) $100,000

(B) $300,000

(C) $400,000

(D) $500,000

6. Janet purchases a vacuum for $1500 from a janitorial supply store. The credit terms are 5/10, n/20. How much would she pay if she paid her bill in 15 days?

(A) $75

(B) $1487

(C) $1475

(D) $1500

7. Sarah marked up the prices of dresses in her shop. Her average selling price is $80 per dress, and her average cost is $60. What is her average % markup?

(A) 20%

(B) 33%

(C) 66%

(D) 75%

8. A town's budget is $600,000. The total assessed property value is 30 million dollars. What tax rate can the city council choose so that it raises exactly the amount it needs for the city's budget?

(A) 2%

(B) 3%

(C) 4%

(D) 20%

9. Colleen is in charge of selling calendars. The cost equation for her company's newest calendar is $C(x) = 0.5x + 1000$ in dollars. For what price must she sell the calendars, if she wishes to break even at 1000 units?

(A) $1.50

(B) $2.00

(C) $15

(D) $1500

10. If the total cost for manufacturing large screen TVs is $C(x) = 200x + 50,000$ in dollars, what is the fixed cost to manufacture 500 TVs?

(A) $200

(B) $50,000

(C) $100,000

(D) $150,000

11. Solve the equation for q, where $5q - 3 = 7$.

(A) $\frac{4}{5}$

(B) 2

(C) 5

(D) 7

12. Martin purchased a new truck for $15,000 on an installment plan. He agreed to pay $300 monthly for 5 years with a down payment of $500. What is the deferred payment price for Martin's truck?

    (A) $18,500

    (B) $20,000

    (C) $22,500

    (D) $24,500

13. A woman takes out a loan from her local bank for $1000. She will repay the money in two years at a rate of 10%. How much interest will she pay?

    (A) $20

    (B) $200

    (C) $2000

    (D) $20,000

14. A large group of sales people attended a weekend sales conference, where an 18-round golf tournament was held in the afternoon. The winner of the tournament shot a 72, but his boss unfortunately had the worst score of the day at 114. The average score was a 94, with most golfers scoring a 96. What was the mode score for the tournament?

    (A) 42

    (B) 94

    (C) 95

    (D) 96

15. Tara created the following trend analysis table to track her company's cookie sales. Her base year for comparison was 2007, when the company sold $40,000 in cookies. What was the company's sales for 2006?

Year:	2006	2007	2008	2009
Sales:	90%	100%	120%	80%

    (A) $26,000

    (B) $30,000

    (C) $36,000

    (D) $40,000

16. Which type of loan requires periodic payments with a final payment at the end of the loan period?

    (A) Adjustable loan

    (B) Single payment loan

    (C) Balloon payment loan

    (D) Noninterest bearing simple loan

17. A woman has $3.00 in quarters and dimes. She notices that she has twice as many quarters as dimes. How many quarters and how many dimes does she have?

    (A) 5 dimes, 10 quarters

    (B) 10 dimes, 8 quarters

    (C) 3 dimes, 6 quarters

    (D) None of the above

18. What would be the monthly payment if you borrowed $25,000 for five years at 6 percent annual interest?

    (A) $483.32

    (B) $523.56

    (C) $635.55

    (D) $695.76

19. Jonah wishes to save for his daughter's college fund. If he deposits $200 at the end of each month and earns 6.0% compounded monthly for 18 years, how much will he have in his account at the end of this time?

(A) $71,112.67

(B) $73,118.85

(C) $75,120.45

(D) $77,470.64

20. A test was given to 480 students and 468 passed. What percentage of students did NOT pass the test?

(A) 0.025%

(B) 2.5%

(C) 0.975%

(D) 97.5%

ANSWER KEY AND EXPLANATIONS

1. B	5. B	9. A	13. B	17. A
2. A	6. D	10. B	14. D	18. A
3. B	7. B	11. B	15. C	19. D
4. C	8. A	12. A	16. C	20. B

1. **The correct answer is (B).** Using the quadratic equation with $a = 1$, $b = 4$, and $c = -21$:

$$x = \frac{-(4) \pm \sqrt{(4)^2 - 4(1)(-21)}}{2(1)}$$

$$x = \frac{-4 \pm \sqrt{16 + 84}}{2}$$

$$x = \frac{-4 \pm \sqrt{100}}{2}$$

$$x = \frac{-4 \pm 10}{2}$$

Now solve for both the negative and the positive solution:

$$x = \frac{-4 + 10}{2} \qquad x = \frac{-4 - 10}{2}$$

$$x = \frac{6}{2} \qquad x = \frac{-14}{2}$$

$$x = 3 \qquad x = -7$$

The answer is $x = 3, -7$.

2. **The correct answer is (A).** First, calculate the mean:

$$\text{avg} = \frac{72 + 74 + 72 + 70 + 68 + 76}{6}$$

$$\text{avg} = \frac{432}{6}$$

$$\text{avg} = 72$$

Next, use the equation for standard deviation:

$$stdev = \sqrt{\sum_{i=1}^{n} \frac{(x_i - \bar{x})^2}{n-1}}$$

$$= \sqrt{\frac{(72-72)^2 + (74-72)^2 + (72-72)^2 + (70-72)^2 + (68-72)^2 + (76-72)^2}{6-1}}$$

$$= \sqrt{\frac{0+4+0+4+16+16}{5}}$$

$$= \sqrt{\frac{40}{5}}$$

$$= \sqrt{8}$$

$$= \sqrt{(4)(2)}$$

$$= 2\sqrt{2}$$

The mean and standard deviation is $72 \pm 2\sqrt{2}$.

3. **The correct answer is (B).** First, arrange the numbers from lowest to highest:

$$(3, 3, 7, 9, 12, 12, 26, 45, 57)$$

We have nine entries. Using the equation for percentile, we can find the value of the lowest quartile:

$$n = \frac{N}{100}p + 0.5$$

$$= \frac{9}{100}(25) + 0.5$$

$$= 2.25 + 0.5$$

$$= 2.75$$

Round this number to the nearest integer = 3. The third value in our ranked data is 7.

4. **The correct answer is (C).** To calculate the index number, divide the number of employees in the year 2000 by those in 1980 and multiply by 100.

$$= \left(\frac{880}{220}\right)100$$

$$= (4)100$$

$$= 400$$

The index is 400.

5. **The correct answer is (B).** Use the equation:

$$\text{Depreciation} = \frac{\text{Cost} - \text{Residual Value}}{\text{Estimated Useful Life}}$$

And solve:

$$= \frac{2,000,000 - 500,000}{5}$$

$$= \frac{1,500,000}{5}$$

$$= 300,000$$

The tool depreciates $300,000 per year.

6. **The correct answer is (D).** The 5/10 means a 5% discount if net is paid in 10 days. Otherwise, net is due in 20 days. Janet did not pay her bill in 10 days, so she receives no discount. She will pay the full amount.

7. **The correct answer is (B).** Using the equation for Selling Price = (Total Cost) (1 + % markup). We can calculate the % markup as x:

$$80 = 60(1 + x)$$

$$1 + x = \frac{80}{60}$$

$$x = \frac{80}{60} - 1$$

$$x = \frac{4}{3} - 1$$

$$x = \frac{4}{3} - \frac{3}{3}$$

$$x = \frac{1}{3}$$

$$x = 33\%$$

33% is the average markup.

8. **The correct answer is (A).** Using the equation:

$$\text{Tax Rate} = \frac{\text{Budget Needed}}{\text{Total Assessed Value}}, \text{ we can solve for the tax rate:}$$

$$= \frac{600,000}{30,000,000}$$

$$= \frac{6}{300}$$

$$= \frac{1}{50}$$

$$= 0.020$$

The city will need a 2% tax rate.

9. **The correct answer is (A).** To solve this problem, first set the cost of manufacturing equation equal to the equation for revenue. The equation for revenue is $R(x) = px$, where p is the price.

Set $x = 1000$ and solve:

$$(p)(1000) = 0.5(1000) + 1000$$
$$(p)(1000) = 500 + 1000$$
$$p = \frac{1500}{1000}$$
$$p = 1.5$$

Colleen must sell her calendars for $1.50.

10. **The correct answer is (B).** The fixed cost does not change no matter how many TVs are manufactured. If we set $x = 0$, we can see that the fixed cost is:

$$= 200(0) + 50,000$$
$$= 50,000$$

$50,000 is the fixed cost.

11. **The correct answer is (B).** Solving linear equations requires that you isolate the variable q:

$$5q - 3 = 7$$
$$5q - 3 + 3 = 7 + 3$$
$$5q = 10$$
$$\frac{5q}{5} = \frac{10}{5}$$
$$q = 2$$

The value of q is 2.

12. **The correct answer is (A).** The Deferred Payment Price = Total of All Payments + Down Payment. The total of all payments is $(12)(5)(300) = \$18,000$. Add to this the $500 down payment and the total deferred payment price is $18,500.

13. **The correct answer is (B).** To calculate interest, use the equation $i = PVrt$.

$$i = (1000)(0.1)(2)$$
$$= 200$$

The woman will pay $200 in interest.

14. **The correct answer is (D).** The mode is the most frequently occurring value and is stated to be 96.

15. **The correct answer is (C).** To find the percentage, we divide the year's sales by the base year sales. We know $40,000 was the total sales in 2007, so we can solve where x = sales in 2006:

$$\frac{x}{40,000} = 0.9$$
$$x = 40,000(0.9)$$
$$x = 36,000$$

The company's sales in 2006 totaled $36,000.

16. **The correct answer is (C).** A balloon payment requires periodic payments of principal and interest for a period of time. After the last payment is made, the remaining principal and interest are owed in one large payment.

17. **The correct answer is (A).** Let q = the number of quarters and d = the number of dimes. We know that there are twice as many quarters as dimes.

$$q = 2d$$

We also know that the total number of dimes and quarters equals $3.00. We can solve for cents, so that we don't have to use decimals:

$$10d + 25q = 300$$

All that is required now is to substitute the first equation into the second and solve for the number of dimes:

$$10d + 25q = 300$$
$$10d + 25(2d) = 300$$
$$10d + 50d = 300$$
$$60d = 300$$
$$d = 5$$

If there are 5 dimes, then, using the first equation, we know there are 10 quarters.

18. **The correct answer is (A).**

Use the equation $PMT_{\text{Amort}} = \dfrac{PV\left(\dfrac{r}{m}\right)}{1 - \left(1 + \dfrac{r}{m}\right)^{-mt}}$ to solve:

$$
\begin{aligned}
PMT_{\text{Amort}} &= \frac{25{,}000\left(\dfrac{0.06}{12}\right)}{1 - \left(1 + \dfrac{0.06}{12}\right)^{-(5)(12)}} \\[2mm]
&= \frac{25{,}000\,(0.005)}{1 - \left(1 + 0.005\right)^{-60}} \\[2mm]
&= \frac{125}{1 - \left(1.005\right)^{-60}} \\[2mm]
&= \frac{125}{1 - 0.741372} \\[2mm]
&= 483.32
\end{aligned}
$$

The monthly payment is $483.32.

19. **The correct answer is (D).**

Use the equation $FV_{OA} = PMT\left[\dfrac{\left(1 + \dfrac{r}{m}\right)^{tm} - 1}{\dfrac{r}{m}}\right]$ to solve:

$$= 200\left[\dfrac{\left(1 + \dfrac{0.06}{12}\right)^{216} - 1}{\dfrac{0.06}{12}}\right]$$

$$= 200\left[\dfrac{\left(1 + 0.005\right)^{216} - 1}{0.005}\right]$$

$$= 200\left[\dfrac{\left(1.005\right)^{216} - 1}{0.005}\right]$$

$$= 200\left[\dfrac{2.936766 - 1}{0.005}\right]$$

$$= 77,470.64$$

Jonah will save $77,470.64.

20. **The correct answer is (B).**

First, you need to find the number of students who didn't pass:

$$480 - 468 = 12$$

Next, divide the number of students who did not pass by the total number of students. Multiply this number by 100 to make it a percentage:

$$= \left(\dfrac{12}{480}\right)100$$
$$= (0.025)100$$
$$= 2.5\%$$

2.5% of the students did not pass the test.

NUMBER SENSE: FRACTIONS, DECIMALS, AND PERCENTAGES

When describing a baseball batting average, the chance of rain, or the odds of winning at poker, you are using a number to describe a part of a whole. There are three common ways to represent this relationship using numbers: fractions, decimals, and percentages. The following are some examples:

- Fraction = $\frac{3}{4}$, 3/4 = three fourths, three over four, three divided by four, 3:4, three to four

- Decimal = 0.75 = zero point seven five, seventy-five hundredths, point seven five

- Percentage = 75% = seventy-five percent, 75 out of 100

The fraction 3/4 tells us that there are 3 equal parts of a whole that contains 4 total parts. It's important to remember that the top part of the fraction, 3 in this example, is called the numerator, and the bottom part, 4 in this example, is called the denominator.

When adding or subtracting fractions, the denominator must be the same number. Multiplying by 1 expressed as a fraction $\frac{n}{n}$ can create the common denominator.

Example 1: Show use of $\frac{n}{n}$ to create common denominator, and to simplify.

Solution:

$$\text{Addition} \quad \frac{3}{4} + \frac{1}{8} = \frac{3}{4}\left(\frac{2}{2}\right) + \frac{1}{8} \qquad \text{Reduction} \quad \frac{10}{15} = \frac{(2)(5)}{(3)(5)}$$

$$= \frac{6}{8} + \frac{1}{8} \qquad\qquad = \frac{2}{3}\left(\frac{5}{5}\right)$$

$$= \frac{7}{8} \qquad\qquad\qquad = \frac{2}{3}$$

The decimal 0.75 tells us that there are 75 out of 100 or $75 \div 100 = 0.75$. Decimals are most commonly used in spreadsheets or when using calculators. Some fractions, such as 1/3, are represented as a repeating decimal, or 0.333..., where the decimal is rounded up or down where appropriate. Sometimes, extra zeros are added to the end of decimals. For example, 0.750 means 750 out of 1000. The extra zero doesn't change the value of the decimal.

Percentage means "per cent" or "out of 100." For example, 45% means 45 out of 100. To convert a decimal to a percentage, you must multiply the decimal by 100.

Example 2: A pie has 2 pieces left out of an original 8 pieces.

Solution: 2 out of 8 = $\frac{2}{8}$, or $\frac{1}{4}$, $1 \div 4 = 0.25$, $0.25 \times 100 = 25\%$

ALGEBRAIC CONCEPTS

Linear Equations and Inequalities

Linear equations are equations of a straight line. They are usually presented in the form $y = mx + b$ where m is the slope and b is the point where the line intercepts the y-axis.

To solve linear equations, you are simply trying to find the value of the variable that makes the equation true. The best way to do this is to isolate the variable on the left-hand side of the equation using addition, subtraction, multiplication, and division. Table 1: Rules for Exponential Equations 1 contains rules for exponents that will assist you in solving these problems.

Table 1: Rules for Exponential Equations

Product	$a^m a^n = a^{m+n}$
Product of a power	$(a^m)^n = a^{mn}$
Quotient to a power	$\left(\dfrac{a}{b}\right)^n = \dfrac{a^n}{b^n}$
Quotient	$\dfrac{a^m}{a^n} = a^{m-n}$
Zero exponent	$a^0 = 1$
Negative exponent	$a^{-n} = \dfrac{1}{a^n}$
Inversion	$\left(\dfrac{a}{b}\right)^{-n} = \left(\dfrac{b}{a}\right)^n$

Example 3: Solve the linear equation $3x + 5 = -4$.

Solution: To solve this problem, we need to find the value of x. We do this by subtracting 5 from both sides of the equation and then multiplying by 1/3.

$$3x + 5 = -4$$
$$3x + 5 - 5 = -4 - 5$$
$$3x = -9$$
$$\frac{1}{3}(3x) = \frac{1}{3}(-9)$$
$$\left(\frac{3}{3}\right)x = \frac{-9}{3}$$
$$x = \frac{(-3)(3)}{3}$$
$$x = -3$$

An inequality is a math statement where instead of an equal sign being used, the equation uses one of the following: a "greater than" symbol (>), a "less than" symbol (<), a "greater than or equal to" symbol (≥), or a "less than or equal to" symbol (≤). Solving inequalities is very similar to solving linear equalities except for one simple rule:

Inequality Rule: The inequality sign has to be flipped whenever you multiply or divide by a negative number.

Example 4: Solve $-3 - 5x < 7$.

Solution:

$$-3 - 5x < 7$$
$$-3 - 5x + 3 < 7 + 3$$
$$-5x < 10$$
$$-5x\left(\frac{1}{-5}\right) > 10\left(\frac{1}{-5}\right)$$
$$x > -2$$

Notice that the < sign was reversed because we multiplied by a negative number to isolate x.

Simultaneous Linear Equations

Many problems will require you to deal with more than one equation having more than one variable, which is called simultaneous equations. The goal is to find the values for the variables that make the equation true.

There are several ways to solve simultaneous equations. The easiest, and probably the most popular, method is the substitution method. This method involves using the following procedure:

Step 1: Solve one equation for one of the variables in terms of the other variable.

Step 2: Substitute the equation from step 1 into the other equation, resulting in an equation that contains only one variable.

Step 3: Find the solution to the equation obtained in step 2. This gives you the value of one variable.

Step 4: Use the value obtained in step 3 in the remaining equation to solve for the second variable.

Example 5: Solve the simultaneous equations to find the values of x and y.

$$\begin{cases} 5x + y = 13 \\ x - 2y = 7 \end{cases}$$

Solution:

Step 1: We can solve the first equation for y. Subtract $5x$ from both sides:

$$5x + y = 13$$
$$5x + y - 5x = 13 - 5x$$
$$y = 13 - 5x$$

Step 2: Substitute this value of y into the second equation and solve for x:

$$x - 2y = 7$$
$$x - 2(13 - 5x) = 7$$

Step 3: Now solve the equation from step 2:

$$x - 2(13 - 5x) = 7$$
$$x + (-2)(13) + (-2)(-5)x = 7$$
$$x - 26 + 10x = 7$$
$$(10 + 1)x - 26 = 7$$
$$11x - 26 + 26 = 7 + 26$$
$$11x = 33$$
$$x = 3$$

Step 4: Substitute this value of x into either equation (we'll use equation 2) and solve:

$$(3) - 2y = 7$$
$$3 - 2y - 3 = 7 - 3$$
$$-2y = 4$$
$$-2y\left(-\frac{1}{2}\right) = 4\left(-\frac{1}{2}\right)$$
$$y = -2$$

Our solution is $x = 3$ and $y = -2$. Using substitution, we have shown how to solve simultaneous equations.

Quadratic Equations and Functions

A quadratic equation is one that contains a variable of the second order. For example, $2x^2 - 3x + 5$ is a quadratic.

A quadratic equation is often solved by finding where the equation equals zero. There are several ways to solve quadratic equations, but by far the easiest method involves using the quadratic formula.

If $ax^2 + bx + c = 0$, where $a \neq 0$, then the roots of the equation are given by:

$$x = \frac{-b \pm \sqrt{b^2 - 4ac}}{2a}$$

Example 6: Solve $2x^2 + 12x + 10 = 0$.

Solution: Letting $a = 2$, $b = 12$, and $c = 10$, we can solve:

$$x = \frac{-(12) \pm \sqrt{(12)^2 - 4(2)(10)}}{2(2)}$$

$$x = \frac{-12 \pm \sqrt{(12)^2 - 4(2)(10)}}{2(2)}$$

$$x = \frac{-12 \pm \sqrt{144 - 80}}{4}$$

$$x = \frac{-12 \pm \sqrt{64}}{4}$$

$$= \frac{-12 \pm \sqrt{64}}{4}$$

$$= \frac{-12 \pm 8}{4}$$

Now solve for both the negative and positive solutions:

$$x = \frac{-12 + 8}{4} \qquad x = \frac{-12 - 8}{4}$$

$$x = \frac{-4}{4} \qquad x = \frac{-20}{4}$$

$$x = -1 \qquad x = -5$$

The answer is $x = -1$ and $x = -5$.

Extrapolation and Interpolation

When you "connect the dots," in a way you are interpolating. Interpolation is a method of fitting a line or other data points between two known points. There are several methods for constructing the line between points. The nearest-neighbor method is very simple and just uses the value of the point nearest to it. Linear interpolation draws a straight line. Curved interpolation is achieved by using polynomial and other advanced equations.

Interpolation often requires creating a missing value in a spreadsheet. For example, given the table below, you can interpolate the missing y_2-value with the equation provided. The only requirement is that the x and y data are both ranked in the same ascending or descending order:

x_1	y_1
x_2	
x_3	y_3

$$y_2 = \frac{(x_2 - x_1)(y_3 - y_1)}{(x_3 - x_1)} + y_1$$

When you need to construct new data points outside of your known data points, you can use extrapolation. Extrapolation allows data to be created based on the trend of the known data. Extrapolation is less reliable than interpolation with greater uncertainty and should be used with care. Like interpolation, there are various methods to achieve linear or curved projections.

Graphing Equations and Evaluating Functions

Evaluating a function requires finding the values that are true for the function. Often, you will evaluate a function or equation in order to graph the points so that you can know what the function looks like.

The steps for evaluating an equation(s) are as follows:

Step 1: Find ordered pairs that satisfy the equation. Pick values for x and solve for y. The best values to pick for x depend on the equation.

Step 2: Plot the values on the coordinate plane.

Step 3: Connect the dots using extrapolation and interpolation. If you don't have enough points to clearly graph the equation, create more pairs.

Step 4: Repeat steps 1 through 3 for the next equation.

Example 7: Evaluate the function $f(x) = x^2 + 2x + 2$.

Step 1: Choose values for x and solve for $f(x)$ or y. Insert -3 into the equation and solve:

$$(-3)^2 + 2(-3) + 2 = 5$$

Repeat for other points:

x	−3	−1	0	1	2
y	5	1	2	5	10

Steps 2 and 3: Graph the points and draw a fitted curve using extrapolation and interpolation:

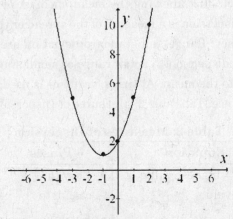

Figure 1: Plot of $f(x) = x^2 + 2x + 2$

STATISTICS

Central Tendency

Mean, median, and mode are different methods of measuring the central tendency, or the "middle," of a data set. Mean, or average, is the most popular measure because it can be calculated easily. Median is the middle point when you sort the data from lowest to highest. Mode is the most common or frequently occurring value in a data set. TaTable 2: Central Tendency Calculationsshows the different measurements along with pluses and minuses.

Table 2: Central Tendency Calculations

	Equation	Pluses	Minuses
Mean	$\text{avg} = \dfrac{x_1 + x_2 + \dots x_n}{n}$	• Easy to calculate • Most common method	• Influenced by outliers* in data
Median	Odd data points = middle value of a sequence Even data points = average of two middle points	• Good for eliminating outliers in data	• Can be inconvenient to calculate
Mode	Most frequently occurring value	• Good for well formed normal data • Good when you want to know the most common value	• Not good for sparsely populated data

*A statistical value that is outside other values in a set of data

Dispersion

Data is not always exact. Just knowing the mean, median, or mode of the data isn't always the full story. Dispersion is a measure of the spread or the deviation of the data from the central tendency. Range and standard deviation are the two most popular methods for measuring dispersion. A small range or small standard deviation means that the data are close to the mean. At times, variance is used. Standard deviation is the square root of variance. TabTable 3: Measures of Dispersionhows the equations.

Table 3: Measures of Dispersion

	Equation	Pluses	Minuses
Range	Range = highest value − lowest value	• Easy to calculate • Easily understood	• Only uses two data points • Influenced by outliers
Standard Deviation	$$\text{sd} = \sqrt{\sum_{i=1}^{n} \frac{(x_i - \bar{x})^2}{n-1}}$$ x_i = data point $\bar{x}$ = data average n = sample number	• Very popular method	• More difficult to calculate

Normal distribution is one of the most important data distributions. The data is spread symmetrically about the mean. FigurFigure 2: Normal Distributionws the graph of a normal distribution. Each vertical line is one standard deviation from the mean. The mean ± 1 standard deviation represents 68 percent of the data. Said another way, 68 percent of the data will fall within ± 1 sigma. The mean ± 2 standard deviation represents 95 percent of the data. Lastly, ± 3 sigma (sometimes called 6 sigma) represents 99.7 percent of the data.

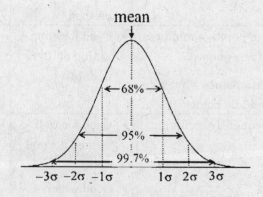

Figure 2: Normal Distribution

The standard error is a way of measuring the sampling fluctuation in a set of data. Sampling fluctuation is how much a statistic fluctuates from sample to sample. Sampling error can be calculated with the following equation:

$$SE_{\bar{x}} = \frac{\sigma}{\sqrt{n}}$$

Where:

σ = standard deviation

n = number of samples

Statistical Significance

Statistical significance is a measure of the reliability of a result or how confident you are that the outcome of an experiment happened by chance or not. In other words, did the result you obtained occur by chance or is the result statistically significant? The level of significance is indicated by the symbol α. For example, if there is a 1-in-100 chance an event could occur, then $\alpha = 1/100$, or 0.01.

For example, if we believed one group of kids cheated on a test and another group did not, we'd look to see if the average grades by the two groups for this test were significantly different. The measures that would help us make this decision would be:

1. The mean of the two groups are greater. A greater difference between the mean shows greater significant difference.

2. The measurement uncertainty or "noise" is smaller. A lower standard deviation increases significance.

3. The sample size is larger. The larger a sample size, the greater chance the data will be accurate and less susceptible to outliers.

There is always the possibility that a mistake can be made when testing for significance. Two types of errors can occur:

- A Type I error occurs when you assume that something is true when in fact it is false.
- A Type II error occurs when you believe something to be false when in fact it is true.

Probability Distributions and Expected Value

When you roll dice, flip a coin, or count the number of cars that drive past your house each hour, these measures are random variables. A random variable is something that changes every time it is tested. The results of a random variable can be placed into groups of expected outcomes. The chance that a result falls into one of these groups or bins is its probability.

Example 8: Maurice believes a six-sided die isn't evenly weighted and not rolling fairly. To test his belief, he rolls the die 1,000 times. A 1 came up 150 times. A 2 was rolled 160 times. 3, 4, and 5 all came up 170 times each, and 6 came up 180 times. Create a probability table for the random variable.

Solution: The probability is calculated by dividing each roll count by the total number of rolls. The probability a 1 is rolled is 150/1000, or 0.15. The probability for each roll is calculated and placed in the following table.

x	1	2	3	4	5	6
$P(x)$	0.15	0.16	0.17	0.17	0.17	0.18

If the random variables can take on the values $x_1, x_2, x_3, x_4 \dots x_n$ and the probability for each outcome is $p_1, p_2, p_3, p_4, \dots p_n$, then the expected value is

$$E(x) = x_1p_1 + x_2p_2 + x_3p_3 + x_4p_4 + \dots + x_np_n$$

Example 9: Using the die from Example 8, what is the expected value when you roll the die? What would be the expected value of a fair and evenly weighted six-sided die?

Solution: Use the expected value equation to solve:

$$E(x) = (0.15)(1) + (0.16)(2) + (0.17)(3) + (0.17)(4) + (0.17)(5) + (0.18)(6)$$
$$= 0.15 + 0.32 + 0.51 + 0.68 + 0.85 + 1.08$$
$$= 3.59$$

If the die were weighted evenly, then the probability of rolling any number would be the same: 1/6.

$$E(x) = \left(\frac{1}{6}\right)(1) + \left(\frac{1}{6}\right)(2) + \left(\frac{1}{6}\right)(3) + \left(\frac{1}{6}\right)(4) + \left(\frac{1}{6}\right)(5) + \left(\frac{1}{6}\right)(6)$$
$$= 3.5$$

The unevenly weighted die is more likely to roll a higher number than the evenly weighted die.

Weighted Averages

An average where each value is given a different importance or weight is the weighted average. If we let w_i be the weight of each value, we have the following equation:

$$\text{Weighted Average } (x) = \frac{w_1x_1 + w_2x_2 + \dots + w_nx_n}{w_1 + w_2 + \dots + w_n}$$

Example 10: Tests count for 70% of a student's grade in a senior algebra class, homework 10%, attendance 5%, and quizzes 15%. If Maria has a test average of 88, a homework average of 95, a quiz average of 95, and perfect attendance, what is her overall grade in this class?

Solution: Use the weighted average equation:

$$\text{Grade} = \frac{(70)(88) + (10)(95) + (15)(95) + (5)(100)}{70 + 10 + 5 + 15}$$

$$= \frac{9035}{100}$$

$$= 90.35$$

Percentiles

The amount of data that falls above or below a given value is called the percentile. For example, 30% of the data should fall below the 30th percentile. The median is actually the 50% percentile, as there are as many values above 50% as there are below.

There is no one method for calculating percentiles. However, a widely accepted method to estimate the percentile is:

1. Rank the data set by ordering the values from smallest to largest.

2. Determine the number of data points N.

3. Calculate n using the equation below where p is the percentile:

$$n = \frac{N}{100}p + \frac{1}{2}$$

4. Round this number to the nearest integer.

5. The nth value of your ranked data will be the number that represents that percentile.

BUSINESS APPLICATIONS

Index Numbers

Index numbers are used to compare data of different sizes. Index numbers show the relative changes in a variable. Index numbers are calculated just like percentages.

$$\text{Index Number} = \frac{\text{Current Value of the Indicator}}{\text{Base Period Value of the Indicator}} \times 100$$

Example 11: A house in Valley Oaks just sold for $250,000. In 1990, the same house sold for $125,000. What is the index number for the house relative to 1990?

Solution: Divide $250,000 by $125,000 multiplied by 100 for an index of 200.

Interest

Interest is the fee paid when someone uses someone else's money. You pay interest when you borrow money. The bank pays you interest to use your money when you deposit it in an account. The amount of the loan or original deposit is the principal. There are several methods to calculate interest.

Simple interest is calculated on the principal amount; the interest is never added back into the principal. It is the most basic method for calculating return. It is a fixed, non-growing return. The equation for simple interest is:

$$i = PVrt$$

Where:

PV = principal or present value ($)

r = annual interest rate (decimal)

t = number of years (in years)

The future value, or maturity value, at the end of t years for simple interest FV is:

$$FV = PV(1 + rt)$$

Where:

i = interest rate per period (decimal)

m = compounding periods per year (number)

The present value P of simple interest is:

$$PV = \frac{FV}{1 + rt}$$

Compound interest adds the interest to the principal at a predetermined period. When the interest is added to the principal, the annual returns will grow every period. The present value of compound interest is:

$$PV = \frac{FV}{\left(1 + \dfrac{r}{m}\right)^{mt}}$$

The future value of compound interest is:

$$FV = PV\left(1 + \frac{r}{m}\right)^{mt}$$

Continuous interest is the answer to the question "What happens if you compound interest at an infinitely small time frame?" The future value of continuous interest is:

$$FV = PVe^{rt}$$

Depreciation and Salvage Value

For accounting purposes, a company needs to know how much it is worth. The worth of a company is its assets. A company's buildings, tools, and other objects are part of its assets. Unfortunately, these assets get less valuable over time as they wear out and age. Depreciation is the process of putting a value to the company's changing assets.

The equation for depreciation is:

$$\text{Depreciation} = \frac{\text{Cost} - \text{Residual Value}}{\text{Estimated Useful Life}}$$

The cost is what the company paid for the item. The estimated useful life is how long the company believes the item has value. The residual value or salvage value is what the item is worth when it is fully depreciated.

Discounts and Credit Terms

The conditions under which the loan is given are the credit terms. One type of credit term is a cash discount, which is an incentive offered to purchasers of a product for payment within a specified period. The credit period is the amount of time to pay off the loan.

Invoices often include the credit term for when the customer must pay and define the sales discount if one was included. For example, the terms for a discount are usually written in the form of 2/15, *n*/30. This means that there is a 2% discount if paid in 15 days, or the net is due in 30 days.

Example 12: A man purchases $100 worth of merchandise with credit terms 5/10, *n*/30. If he pays in 8 days, what does he owe?

Solution: 5% of $100 is $5, which is subtracted from $100. The man owes $95.

Installment Purchases

Installment purchases are a form of credit where payments are made in installments over a fixed period, usually monthly. The lender owns the item until it is paid off, but the buyer gets to use the product.

The amount financed is the borrowed amount, and the down payment is what is paid up front:

$$\text{Amount Financed} = \text{Cash Price} - \text{Down Payment}$$

The finance charge is the total of the payments minus the amount financed:

$$\text{Total Finance Charge} = \text{Total of All Payments} - \text{Amount Financed}$$

The deferred payment price is what the item really costs:

$$\text{Deferred Payment Price} = \text{Total of All Payments} + \text{Down Payment}$$

The monthly payment can be calculated using the formula:

$$\text{Monthly Payment} = \frac{\text{Finance Charge} + \text{Amount Financed}}{\text{Number of Payments}}$$

Markup and Markdown

The selling price for an item is not the cost the seller paid for it. For the seller to make money, the seller needs to add markup to the price of the item. Markup allows the seller to make a profit on his sale as well as pay for labor costs, property rental, taxes, and other expenses that are required to operate the business.

Selling Price = Cost + Markup

or:

Selling Price = Cost(1 + % Markup)

Markdown is the amount a seller discounts a product to encourage sales:

$$\text{Markdown \%} = \frac{\text{Dollar Markdown}}{\text{Original Selling Price}} \times 100$$

Taxes

Governments use taxes to raise revenue. Sales taxes are usually added as a percentage of the sale price. Other taxes include excise tax, which is a fixed or percentage tax placed on luxury and nonessential items such as tobacco.

Property tax is a tax placed on the value of property. The value the government assigns to a property is its assessed value. Generally, the amount of property tax is based on a tax rate. The tax rate is often based on budget needs:

$$\text{Tax Rate} = \frac{\text{Budget Needed}}{\text{Total Assessed Value}}$$

The amount of property tax paid is:

Property Tax = Tax Rate × Total Assessed Value

Cost Calculations

There are two types of costs—fixed costs and variable costs. Fixed costs are expenses that do not increase or decrease with the number of products produced. On the other hand, variable costs increase with the number of units produced. Total cost is the sum of fixed and variable costs.

$C(x)$ represents the total cost of manufacturing x number of items, m represents the cost per unit or marginal cost, and F represents the total fixed costs:

$$C(x) = mx + F$$

Example 13: If the total cost for manufacturing watches is $C(x) = 3x + 500$, what would the fixed costs be? What would be the cost of manufacturing 1000 watches?

Solution: For fixed cost, let $x = 0$ and solve for $C(x)$:

$$C(0) = 3(0) + 500$$
$$= 500$$

Fixed cost = $500. For 1000 watches, let $x = 1000$ and solve:

$$C(1000) = 3(1000) + 500$$
$$= 3500$$

Total cost = $3500

The average cost to manufacture is the total cost divided by the number of units manufactured. For example, the average cost of watches for 1000 watches manufactured would be 3500/1000, or $3.50 per cup.

Break-even Analysis

Break-even is the point where the revenue generated by a product will equal the cost of manufacturing. After the break-even point, a product can produce a profit. Like cost, we can plot revenue where $R(x) = px$, with p being the marginal revenue, or how much money is made per item. Profit is the revenue minus the cost:

$$\text{Profit} = \text{Revenue} - \text{Cost}$$

Example 14: Graph the break-even point if the fixed cost to manufacture a toothbrush is $10,000, and the marginal cost is $2 per item. The toothbrush can be sold for $4 per item. Next, find the break-even point without graphing. What would the profit be if 20,000 items were sold?

Solution: Plot the two lines and find the intersect point. $C(x) = 2x + 10,000$ and $R(x) = 4x$:

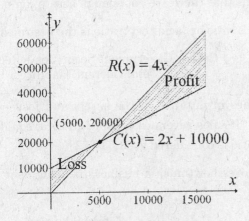

Figure 3: Break-even Graph

You can see that the break-even point occurs at the manufacturing of 5000 units. To find the solution without graphing, we need to set the two equations equal to each other:

$$C(x) = R(x)$$
$$2x + 10,000 = 4x$$
$$2x = 10,000$$
$$x = 5000$$

Again, we arrive at the solution of 5000 units to break even. Next, find the profit if 15,000 units are sold:

$$P(x) = R(x) - C(x)$$
$$P(20,000) = 4(20,000) - \big(2(20,000) + 10,000\big)$$
$$= 80,000 - 40,000 - 10,000$$
$$x = 30,000$$

The profit for selling 20,000 units would be $30,000.

Financial Ratio Calculation and Analysis

The relationship of one number to another can be expressed with a ratio. Companies use ratios to compare various measures from one year to another to spot trends. Ratios can be used to compare one company to another.

Here are some examples of common financial ratios.

Current Ratio—Best measure of financial strength:

$$\text{Current Ratio} = \frac{\text{Total Current Assets}}{\text{Total Current Liabilities}}$$

The main question answered by this ratio is, "Does the business have enough current assets to meet the payment schedule of its current debts?" A healthy ratio is 2 to 1. A ratio below 1 to 1 means that there are not enough assets compared to debts.

Quick Ratio—The quick ratio or "acid-test" ratio is the best measure of liquidity:

$$\text{Quick Ratio} = \frac{\text{Cash} + \text{Government Securities} + \text{Receivables}}{\text{Total Current Liabilities}}$$

The quick ratio excludes inventories in the assets and focuses on liquid assets. It answers the question, "If sales revenues dropped to zero, could the business pay its current debt?" A 1:1 ratio is considered good.

Leverage Ratio—Measures how much a business is using debt financing as opposed to their equity:

$$\text{Leverage Ratio} = \frac{\text{Total Liabilities}}{\text{Net Worth}}$$

This ratio answers the question, "How much does this business rely on credit?" The higher this ratio, the more trouble this business could be in if credit becomes difficult to obtain.

Many other ratios exist. You can find these ratios in finance books or on the Internet.

Trend analysis uses ratios to uncover changes from year to year. A base year is required for each metric. Each individual value is then divided by the base value. Trend analysis is a form of normalization expressed as a percentage. See the example below of how to use trend analysis for sales from year to year.

Example 15: Use trend analysis to compare the sales from various years using 2007 as the base year. 2006 = $20,000; 2007 = $22,000; 2008 = $25,000; 2009 = $18,000.

Solution: Divide each year's sales by $22,000.

Year:	2006	2007	2008	2009
Sales:	$= \dfrac{20,000}{22,000}$ $= 91\%$	$= \dfrac{22,000}{22,000}$ $= 100\%$	$= \dfrac{25,000}{22,000}$ $= 114\%$	$= \dfrac{18,000}{22,000}$ $= 82\%$

Promissory Notes and Other Loans

The promissory note is a contract between a borrower and a lender that puts loan information in writing. Many lenders require a signed promissory note from a borrower when lending money. The note states that the borrower will repay the money at a fixed interval. The note can be interest bearing or noninterest bearing depending on whether interest is included or not. The note will include the names of the parties, the amount of the loan, the interest rate if any, and the payment schedule. Other information may be included as well. A promissory note differs from an IOU, which only states that a debt exists.

A loan that is repaid at one time is called a single payment. With amortized payments, you pay a set amount each period, usually a month or a year, until the loan is paid in full. A balloon payment requires periodic payments of principal and interest for a set amount of time. After the last payment, the remaining principal and interest are owed in one large payment. Another type of balloon payment is the interest-only balloon payment. With this type of balloon payment, you pay the lender regular payments of only the interest and then one final balloon payment of all of the principal and remaining interest.

Interpretation of Graphical Representations

Graphs are a valuable method for giving data meaning. With computers, it's very easy to create nice-looking graphs, but it's also very easy to create bad graphs. It's important to choose the right graph and use it in the correct way. If a graph doesn't clearly convey the meaning of the numbers, then it is not serving its purpose.

There are many types of graphs:

- *Bar graph:* bars help show changes that have occurred over a period.
- *Line Graph:* lines connect data points to show changes over time.
- *Scatter Plot:* two variables are plotted against each other usually without lines.
- *Pie Chart:* a circle is sliced into pieces that represent parts of the whole.

Here are a few rules to making a good graph:

1. The graph should have a title that clearly states what the graph is about.
2. The x-axis should be the independent variable and the y-axis the dependent variable.
3. Label and number the axes.
4. A key should identify each line type.
5. Avoid fancy 3-D effects, and use pie charts as infrequently as possible.

Graphs can be used to misrepresent information. For example, numbers can be left off the axes to avoid clearly showing what is happening with the data. The y-axis might not begin with a zero value, and changes might be exaggerated by not showing a full scale on the y-axis. Fancy 3-D effects can also be used to hide data in the background or to distort the relative size of the data. As a rule of thumb, pie charts should rarely be used. Often the size of the pie slice is difficult to compare especially when the percentages are not included.

Unit Conversions

It is often necessary to convert units when working with data. Changing inches to centimeters is a common conversion. Changing one currency to another requires some knowledge in converting units.

The best method for converting units is to set up the conversion in a table as shown below. Do not take shortcuts when doing a conversion, no matter how simple a conversion may seem.

In the table below, dollars per hour are being converted to yen per day. Notice that units are kept with the numbers and canceled. The use of this type of table helps you keep up with the units and make certain you are multiplying and dividing by the correct amounts.

$$\frac{5\ \text{dollars}}{\text{hour}} \quad \frac{95\ \text{yen}}{1\ \text{dollar}} \quad \frac{24\ \text{hours}}{1\ \text{day}} = \frac{(5)(95)(24)\ \text{yen}}{\text{day}} = 11{,}400 \text{ yen per day}$$

Investment Performance Measures

The P/E ratio, or price-to-earnings ratio, is the measure of a company's current share price compared to its per-share earnings. For example, if a company is trading at $20 a share and the earnings for the last year were $2 per share, the P/E ratio would be 10.0. The higher the P/E ratio, the more demand there is for a stock. The P/E ratio's unit is in years, as it refers to the number of years it will take to pay back the stock purchase price.

$$\text{P/E Ratio} = \frac{\text{Price per Share}}{\text{Annual Earnings per Share}}$$

The rate of return, or ROR, is a measure of the money gained or lost on an investment relative to the money invested. It is also known as return on investment, or ROI. The single-period arithmetic return is:

$$\text{Rate of Return} = \frac{\text{Final Value} - \text{Initial Value}}{\text{Initial Value}}$$

Stock yield, or current dividend yield, percentage tells stockholders what the dividend per share is returning:

$$\text{Stock Yield} = \frac{\text{Annual Dividend per Share}}{\text{Current Share Price}}$$

Cost Minimization and Value Optimization

In the discussion of the break-even point, it is clear that the higher the price you receive for a product, the fewer units you need to produce to break even. However, the higher the price, the fewer units you will sell and the longer it will take to break even. So how do you set a price?

Obviously, to make a profit, the selling price must be above the cost of the unit. The lower the cost of the unit, the more money can be made when it is sold. For many products with stiff price competition, finding ways to lower costs is the only way to make a profit and survive in the market place.

The product's value is what the customer thinks the product or service is worth. The more the customer thinks the product is worth, the more the customer is willing to pay. The value of a product can be increased any number of ways. Advertising makes a product more desirable in the eye of the consumer. Improving quality or adding additional features can also increase value by distinguishing a product from a competitor's product.

FINANCIAL MATHEMATICS

Annuities—Present and Future Value

An annuity is a stream of fixed payments or receipts made over a specified period. An ordinary annuity is one where the payment is made at the end of the payment period. The equation for calculating the present value of an ordinary annuity, where PMT is the periodic payment, is:

$$PV_{OA} = PMT \left[\frac{1 - \dfrac{1}{\left(1 + \dfrac{r}{m}\right)^{tm}}}{\dfrac{r}{m}} \right]$$

The annuity can be calculated based on the present value of the loan:

$$PMT_{OA} = PV \left[\frac{\dfrac{r}{m}}{\left(1 + \dfrac{r}{m}\right)^{mn} - 1} \right] \left(1 + \frac{r}{m}\right)^{mn}$$

The future value of an ordinary annuity can be calculated:

$$FV_{OA} = PMT \left[\frac{\left(1 + \dfrac{r}{m}\right)^{mn} - 1}{\dfrac{r}{m}} \right]$$

With an annuity due, the payment is made at the beginning of the payment period. The equation for the present value of an annuity due is:

$$PV_{AD} = PMT \left[\frac{1 - \dfrac{1}{\left(1 + \dfrac{r}{m}\right)^{tm}}}{\dfrac{r}{m}} \right] \left(1 + \frac{r}{m}\right)$$

Where:

PV_{OA} = present value of an ordinary annuity

PMT_{OA} = amount of each payment

PV_{AD} = present value of an ordinary annuity

r = yearly nominal interest rate (in decimal, or % ÷ 100)

t = number of years

m = number of periods per year

PMT = periodic payment

Important Note: $\frac{r}{m}$ replaces i, the annual interest, in the equations in this section, so that you will clearly understand what interest is used in the calculation.

The future value of an ordinary annuity is the value of expected periodic payments after a period of time:

$$FV_{OA} = PMT\left[\frac{\left(1 + \frac{r}{m}\right)^{tm} - 1}{\frac{r}{m}}\right]$$

The future value can be calculated for an annuity due:

$$FV_{AD} = PMT\left[\frac{\left(1 + \frac{r}{m}\right)^{tm} - 1}{\frac{r}{m}}\right]\left(1 + \frac{r}{m}\right)$$

Amortization

A loan is amortized if the principal and interest are paid by a sequence of equal periodic payments. It is a process of reducing the balance of a loan by a periodic payment. The following equation can be used to calculate the payment for an amortization loan made at the end of each period:

$$PMT_{\text{Amort}} = \frac{PV\left(\frac{r}{m}\right)}{1 - \left(1 + \frac{r}{m}\right)^{-mt}}$$

Banks use amortization tables because they require exact calculations; however, the remaining balance of an amortization can be approximated by the following equation:

$$y_{\text{Amort}} = PMT\left[\frac{1 - \left(1 + \frac{r}{m}\right)^{-(mt-x)}}{\frac{r}{m}}\right]$$

Where:

x = number of payments made

You can calculate the amount of the total interest paid on a loan with the following calculation:

Amount Paid in Interest = Total Payments Made − Amount of the Loan

Annual Percentage Rate

The annual percentage rate, or APR, is a term created to help convey what the annual cost of the loan will be in a percentage. Nominal APR is a simple-interest rate for a year. Effective APR, or EAR, includes fees such as participation fees, loan origination fees, monthly service fees, or late charges. The effective APR is the true annual interest rate paid when it is all said and done.

Effective Annual Rate

The effective rate is the actual rate that you earn on an investment or pay on a loan when interest is compounded more than once a year. The effective interest rate does not incorporate one-time charges or front-end fees.

The effective rate of an investment will always be higher than the nominal or stated interest rate. The equation for effective rate of compounded interest r_E is:

$$r_E = \left(1 + \frac{r}{m}\right)^m - 1$$

The effective rate for continuous interest is:

$$r_E = e^r - 1$$

Note: With these types of problems, you will be working with numbers raised to very large powers. It is not uncommon for hand calculators, spreadsheets, or calculators from Web sites to be off by a few cents.

POST-TEST ANSWER SHEET

1. Ⓐ Ⓑ Ⓒ Ⓓ
2. Ⓐ Ⓑ Ⓒ Ⓓ
3. Ⓐ Ⓑ Ⓒ Ⓓ
4. Ⓐ Ⓑ Ⓒ Ⓓ
5. Ⓐ Ⓑ Ⓒ Ⓓ
6. Ⓐ Ⓑ Ⓒ Ⓓ
7. Ⓐ Ⓑ Ⓒ Ⓓ
8. Ⓐ Ⓑ Ⓒ Ⓓ
9. Ⓐ Ⓑ Ⓒ Ⓓ
10. Ⓐ Ⓑ Ⓒ Ⓓ
11. Ⓐ Ⓑ Ⓒ Ⓓ
12. Ⓐ Ⓑ Ⓒ Ⓓ

13. Ⓐ Ⓑ Ⓒ Ⓓ
14. Ⓐ Ⓑ Ⓒ Ⓓ
15. Ⓐ Ⓑ Ⓒ Ⓓ
16. Ⓐ Ⓑ Ⓒ Ⓓ
17. Ⓐ Ⓑ Ⓒ Ⓓ
18. Ⓐ Ⓑ Ⓒ Ⓓ
19. Ⓐ Ⓑ Ⓒ Ⓓ
20. Ⓐ Ⓑ Ⓒ Ⓓ
21. Ⓐ Ⓑ Ⓒ Ⓓ
22. Ⓐ Ⓑ Ⓒ Ⓓ
23. Ⓐ Ⓑ Ⓒ Ⓓ
24. Ⓐ Ⓑ Ⓒ Ⓓ

25. Ⓐ Ⓑ Ⓒ Ⓓ
26. Ⓐ Ⓑ Ⓒ Ⓓ
27. Ⓐ Ⓑ Ⓒ Ⓓ
28. Ⓐ Ⓑ Ⓒ Ⓓ
29. Ⓐ Ⓑ Ⓒ Ⓓ
30. Ⓐ Ⓑ Ⓒ Ⓓ
31. Ⓐ Ⓑ Ⓒ Ⓓ
32. Ⓐ Ⓑ Ⓒ Ⓓ
33. Ⓐ Ⓑ Ⓒ Ⓓ
34. Ⓐ Ⓑ Ⓒ Ⓓ
35. Ⓐ Ⓑ Ⓒ Ⓓ
36. Ⓐ Ⓑ Ⓒ Ⓓ

37. Ⓐ Ⓑ Ⓒ Ⓓ
38. Ⓐ Ⓑ Ⓒ Ⓓ
39. Ⓐ Ⓑ Ⓒ Ⓓ
40. Ⓐ Ⓑ Ⓒ Ⓓ
41. Ⓐ Ⓑ Ⓒ Ⓓ
42. Ⓐ Ⓑ Ⓒ Ⓓ
43. Ⓐ Ⓑ Ⓒ Ⓓ
44. Ⓐ Ⓑ Ⓒ Ⓓ
45. Ⓐ Ⓑ Ⓒ Ⓓ
46. Ⓐ Ⓑ Ⓒ Ⓓ
47. Ⓐ Ⓑ Ⓒ Ⓓ
48. Ⓐ Ⓑ Ⓒ Ⓓ

49. Ⓐ Ⓑ Ⓒ Ⓓ
50. Ⓐ Ⓑ Ⓒ Ⓓ
51. Ⓐ Ⓑ Ⓒ Ⓓ
52. Ⓐ Ⓑ Ⓒ Ⓓ
53. Ⓐ Ⓑ Ⓒ Ⓓ
54. Ⓐ Ⓑ Ⓒ Ⓓ
55. Ⓐ Ⓑ Ⓒ Ⓓ
56. Ⓐ Ⓑ Ⓒ Ⓓ
57. Ⓐ Ⓑ Ⓒ Ⓓ
58. Ⓐ Ⓑ Ⓒ Ⓓ
59. Ⓐ Ⓑ Ⓒ Ⓓ
60. Ⓐ Ⓑ Ⓒ Ⓓ

answer sheet

POST-TEST

Directions: Carefully read each of the following 60 questions. Choose the best answer to each question, and darken its letter on your answer sheet. The Answer Key and Explanations can be found following this post-test.

1. If Leon ate one third of an apple pie, one fourth of a cherry pie, and one fourth of a pecan pie, how much total pie did Leon eat?

   (A) $\frac{1}{6}$

   (B) $\frac{3}{11}$

   (C) $\frac{5}{12}$

   (D) $\frac{5}{6}$

2. A concrete mixer is purchased from a hardware store on installments. Who legally owns the concrete mixer if the second payment is missed by the buyer?

   (A) The buyer

   (B) The hardware store

   (C) The bank

   (D) None of the above

3. What is an amortized loan?

   (A) A loan where only interest is paid

   (B) A loan repaid in a one-time payment of both interest and principal

   (C) A loan where payments are made each period to pay off interest and principal

   (D) None of the above

4. What is the effective annual interest rate for a continuously compounded interest rate of 12%?

   (A) 1.0%

   (B) 12.0%

   (C) 12.68%

   (D) 12.75%

5. Which of the following defines P/E ratio?

   (A) Performance-to-equity ratio

   (B) Price-to-earnings ratio

   (C) Profit-to-expense ratio

   (D) Principal-to-equity ratio

6. Crystal is looking at credit cards and notices that the APR on her credit card is 19.2%. What is the monthly interest rate?

   (A) 1.6%

   (B) 1.75%

   (C) 20.98%

   (D) 21.17%

7. Solve the equation $3x^2 - 3x + \frac{1}{2} = 0$.

   (A) $x = -\frac{1}{2} \pm \frac{\sqrt{3}}{2}$

   (B) $x = -\frac{1}{6} \pm \frac{\sqrt{3}}{6}$

   (C) $x = \frac{1}{2} \pm \frac{\sqrt{3}}{2}$

   (D) $x = \frac{1}{2} \pm \frac{\sqrt{3}}{6}$

8. What is wrong with the graph below?

Company ABC Profits

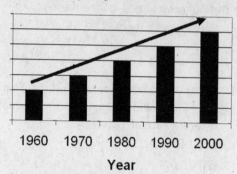

Year

(A) The arrow is distracting from the true data trend.

(B) The data would be better represented with a line chart.

(C) The y-axis label and values are missing.

(D) There is nothing wrong with the graph.

9. What would be the best linear extrapolation of the points (0,1) and (1,3)?

(A) (3,6)

(B) (−1,−1)

(C) (2,6)

(D) (−3,−3)

10. A boy is in the 75th percentile for his height at his current age. What do we know about the boy?

(A) He is 75% shorter than he should be for his age.

(B) He will grow another 25%.

(C) He is taller than 75% of the boys his age.

(D) He is 75% shorter than other boys his age.

11. Which of the following functions best represents the plot in the graph below?

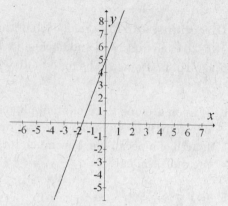

(A) $f(x) = -3.5x - 5$

(B) $f(x) = 3x + 5$

(C) $f(x) = 5x + 3$

(D) $f(x) = 5x + 5$

12. What is the difference between the mean and median for the data points (4, 3, 6, 3, 7, 4, 5, 9, 4)?

(A) 0

(B) 1

(C) 2

(D) 3

13. How would the credit terms be notated for a 2% discount in 20 days and net due in 30 days?

(A) 20/2, 30/n

(B) 2-20/n-30

(C) 2/20, n/30

(D) 1 + n/3

14. What is a promissory note?

(A) An IOU

(B) A contract between a borrower and a lender

(C) A coupon promising a discount

(D) All of the above

15. Dariya works at a carnival at a booth where children throw darts at balloons to win a prize. The children toss a dart until they successfully pop a balloon. When popped, each balloon reveals a prize number 1 through 4, where 4 is the most expensive prize and 1 is the least expensive. Dariya needs to prepare 100 balloons so the expected outcome if the balloons are popped at random is 1.5. She is told that there must be one #4 price and ten #3 prizes. How many of each balloon must she prepare from 1 to 4?

(A) 70, 19, 10, 1

(B) 50, 39, 10, 1

(C) 62, 27, 10, 1

(D) 60, 29, 10, 1

16. Bryan wishes to prepare for his future retirement in 10 years. He deposits $85,000 at the end of each year for 10 years into an account paying 8% annually. How much will be in his account at the end of the 10 years?

(A) $850,450.12

(B) $1,004,565.34

(C) $1,231,357.81

(D) $1,321,577.14

17. What is the percent chance that three coins when flipped will all turn up heads?

(A) 8 percent

(B) 12.5 percent

(C) 25 percent

(D) 33 percent

18. A piano in the music store wasn't selling at $9500, so the shop owner decided to mark it down to $6950. What would be the markdown % for the piano?

(A) 20%

(B) 25%

(C) 27%

(D) 30%

19. A manufacturer estimates that he will sell 10,000 widgets. He knows that with only minor changes to his current tool set in his plant he can make widgets at $4 per unit, with a fixed cost of $9800. How much additional fixed cost could the manufacturer spend on top of the $9800, if the extra fixed costs achieved a variable cost of $3.50 per unit?

(A) $5000

(B) $5500

(C) $6000

(D) $6500

20. The percentage markup on a dress is 85%, and the dress is priced to sell at $185. What is the cost of the dress?

(A) $45.94

(B) $85.00

(C) $100.00

(D) $157.25

21. If a company's current ratio is 2:1, what do you know about the company?

(A) Its total current assets are half the total current liabilities.

(B) The total liabilities are twice the net worth.

(C) There are enough assets compared to debts.

(D) Total cash, securities, and receivables are twice the current liabilities.

22. Elias searched the Internet for basketball prices and was amazed at how many different prices he found. He found the following prices: $19.17, $22.50, $12.95, $16.99, $17.50, $18.25, $16.99. What is the 50th percentile for these prices?

(A) $12.95

(B) $16.99

(C) $17.50

(D) $17.76

23. The index number for stock XYZ in 2000 was 250 relative to the price in 1970. If the stock was $12 per share in 1970, what was the price in 2000?

(A) $12

(B) $15

(C) $24

(D) $30

24. A company buys a dump truck for $100,000, and its salvage value is $20,000. If the company depreciates the truck over 8 years, what is its depreciation?

(A) $8000

(B) $10,000

(C) $12,000

(D) $20,000

25. Solve the liner equations:

$$\begin{cases} 2x + y = 5 \\ 5x + 5y = 5 \end{cases}$$

(A) (2,3)

(B) (4,−3)

(C) (2,1)

(D) (5,−5)

26. The credit terms for a $1000 purchase are written 3/10, n/20. If the customer pays in 8 days, what will the customer pay?

(A) $30

(B) $970

(C) $990

(D) $1000

27. The total assessed value of property in the city of Cape Watertown is 32.5 million dollars. If their tax rate was 0.0648 per dollar, how much revenue will they raise through property tax?

(A) $2,106,000

(B) $2,215,450

(C) $2,420,655

(D) $3,250,000

28. Who sets the assessed value for property?

(A) The market

(B) The property owner

(C) The owner of properties mineral rights

(D) The assessor's office

29. If the total manufacturing cost for widgets is $C(x) = 0.17x + 50,000$, what is the cost of manufacturing 1500 widgets?

(A) $255.00

(B) $49,745

(C) $50,255

(D) $75,500

30. Solve $x^2 − 6x + 5 = 0$.

(A) (1,−0.833)

(B) (−1,−5)

(C) (5,1)

(D) (1,−1.2)

31. What would be the fixed cost to manufacture dolls if the cost per unit was $1.45 and 10,000 dolls cost $16,200?

(A) $1450

(B) $1620

(C) $1650

(D) $1700

32. If the cost for a product is $C(x) = 1.2x + 1274$ and the product is sold for $R(x) = 6x$, how many units will need to be sold in order to break even?

(A) 263

(B) 264

(C) 265

(D) 266

33. If the standard error is 2 for a set of data where the mean is 250 and the standard deviation is 20, what is the number of data points?

(A) 40

(B) 100

(C) 250

(D) 500

34. Given the graph below, what is the number of units needed to break even, and what is the profit/cost for that number of units?

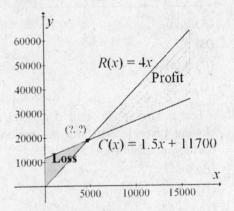

(A) 4680, $18,720

(B) 4000, $11,700

(C) 4680, $11,700

(D) 4000, $11,700

35. The following chart shows Company A's expenses from year to year. If the trend analysis is based on 2008, where expenses were $243,000, what were the expenses for 2005?

Year:	2005	2006	2007	2008	2009
Expenses:	85%	90%	95%	100%	72%

(A) $36,450

(B) $201,250

(C) $206,550

(D) $285,882

36. Solve the linear equation $3x - 10 = 23$.

(A) 3

(B) 4.33

(C) 9

(D) 11

37. Examine the pie chart below. If the average budget of the people represented in this graph is $3000 per month, how much does the average person spend on food per month?

Where does your dollar go?

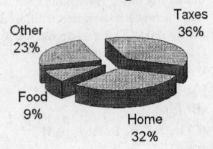

(A) $270

(B) $300

(C) $333

(D) The pie chart does not contain enough information to solve.

38. Given the following spreadsheet, what would be the best linear interpolated value for the unknown cell x?

1	45
7	x
15	89

(A) 53.45

(B) 62

(C) 63.86

(D) 67

39. A businesswoman spent 2940 Euros during a one-week business trip in Sicily. What is her cost in U.S. dollars per day if 1 Euro = U.S. $1.42?

(A) $207.04

(B) $295.77

(C) $420.00

(D) $596.40

40. A researcher presented a paper at a conference that showed that El Niño was responsible for increased onion production in New Mexico. However, after the paper was published, numerous other researchers showed that there was no significant difference in his data. The researcher gave a retraction at a later conference. What type of error was this?

(A) Type I

(B) Type II

(C) Both Type I and Type II

(D) It was not an error.

41. The temperature outside is 18° Celsius, where C is Celsius and F is Fahrenheit and the conversion equation is: $C = \dfrac{5}{9}(F - 32)$. What is the temperature in Fahrenheit?

(A) 64.3°

(B) 66.8°

(C) 68.3°

(D) 72.0°

42. Milo's final grades for the semester are shown in the table below. An A = 4 points, a B = 3 points, and a C = 2 points. What would be Milo's grade point average if the classes are weighted against their credit hours?

Class	Credit hours	Grade
English	3	A
Algebra	3	B
Physics	4	B
Chemistry	4	C
Phys. Ed.	2	A

(A) 2.75

(B) 2.85

(C) 3.06

(D) 3.20

43. What is the stock yield if a stock's closing price is $45 and its annual dividend per share is $2?

(A) 4.4%

(B) 8.8%

(C) 22.5%

(D) 44%

44. What is a sure way to decrease the time it takes to sell enough units to break even?

(A) Lower the cost to manufacture

(B) Decrease the sale price

(C) Lower the sale price

(D) None of the above

45. What is the future value of $1800 compounded monthly at 9.5% interest for 8 years?

(A) $3543.37

(B) $3845.40

(C) $3837.41

(D) $4225.98

46. A woman wishes to give $50 at the end of each month to a charity for two years. The interest rate that can be earned on the money is 12%. What is the present value of this gift?
    (A) $1054.20
    (B) $1062.17
    (C) $1200.00
    (D) $1450.69

47. Before the professor handed out the grades on the last exam, he wrote on the board that the class average was 78 with a standard deviation of 7. He also noted that the distribution of the grades was normal. Based on this information, which of the following statements is most likely true?
    (A) No more than 68% of the students scored between a 71 and 85.
    (B) No more than 34% of the students scored above a 78.
    (C) No more than 95% of the students' scores are between 57 and 99.
    (D) No one could have scored a 100.

48. A car costs $20,000. Francis will pay a $5000 down payment and then monthly payments for three years with an interest of 10%. What is the amount of each payment?
    (A) $430.09
    (B) $445.22
    (C) $484.01
    (D) $501.25

49. If the depreciation of a $20,000 widget is $2000 and it depreciates over 7 years, what is its salvage value?
    (A) $2000
    (B) $3000
    (C) $6000
    (D) $14,000

50. What interest would be earned if $500 were invested for 5 years at 8% simple interest?
    (A) $200.00
    (B) $225.65
    (C) $250.26
    (D) $500.00

51. A family buys a house for $265,000 with a down payment of $25,000. The family takes out a 15-year mortgage at an interest rate of 5.5%. Find the amount of the monthly payment required to amortize this loan.
    (A) $1362.69
    (B) $1961.00
    (C) $2117.34
    (D) $2251.67

52. If Susie buys a blanket from an infomercial on TV and pays 3 easy payments of $19.95 along with a one-time down payment to upgrade to thicker cotton for $7.50, what is the deferred payment price of the blanket?
    (A) $19.95
    (B) $27.45
    (C) $59.85
    (D) $67.35

53. The local high school held a musical and raised $988.75 from admissions. If the tickets were $3.50 for adults and $1.75 for children and 335 tickets were sold, how many of the tickets were for adults and how many were for children?
    (A) 105 adult, 235 children
    (B) 132 adult, 124 children
    (C) 200 adult, 100 children
    (D) 230 adult, 105 children

54. The following table of index values for widgets is relative to 1970. If the price of widgets were $8 in 1960, what was the price of widgets in 2000?

Year	1960	1970	1980	1990	2000
Index	80	100	120	140	180

(A) $12.5

(B) $18.0

(C) $22.5

(D) $24.5

55. A family pays 360 payments of $902.43 on a house mortgage. The original loan was for $250,000. How much was the total interest paid on this loan?

(A) $65,145.55

(B) $68,512.50

(C) $70,450.55

(D) $74,874.80

56. If a credit card company charges 1% per month, what is the APR?

(A) 1.0%

(B) 12.0%

(C) 12.06%

(D) 14.36%

57. Solve the inequality: $-3x + 4 < 5x + 7$.

(A) $x < \dfrac{3}{8}$

(B) $x > \dfrac{3}{8}$

(C) $x > -\dfrac{3}{8}$

(D) $x < -\dfrac{3}{8}$

58. If the nominal annual interest rate is 18%, what is the effective annual interest rate?

(A) 1.5%

(B) 19.56%

(C) 19.72%

(D) 21.6%

59. In baseball, a batting average is the number of hits divided by the number of times at bat rounded to 3 decimals. What would the batting average be of a player who got 154 hits out of 403 at bats?

(A) 0.382

(B) 0.403

(C) 2.62

(D) 154

60. In the month of April, it rained a total of 22 days. What was the percentage of days that it rained for that month?

(A) 7.3%

(B) 72%

(C) 73%

(D) 79%

ANSWER KEY AND EXPLANATIONS

1. D	13. C	25. B	37. A	49. C
2. B	14. B	26. B	38. C	50. A
3. C	15. C	27. A	39. D	51. B
4. D	16. C	28. D	40. A	52. D
5. B	17. B	29. C	41. A	53. D
6. A	18. C	30. C	42. C	54. B
7. D	19. A	31. D	43. A	55. D
8. C	20. C	32. D	44. A	56. B
9. B	21. C	33. B	45. C	57. C
10. C	22. C	34. A	46. B	58. B
11. B	23. D	35. C	47. A	59. A
12. B	24. B	36. D	48. C	60. C

1. **The correct answer is (D).** Find a common denominator and add the two fractions together:

$$= \frac{1}{3} + \frac{1}{4} + \frac{1}{4}$$
$$= \frac{1}{3}\left(\frac{4}{4}\right) + \frac{1}{4}\left(\frac{3}{3}\right) + \frac{1}{4}\left(\frac{3}{3}\right)$$
$$= \frac{4}{12} + \frac{3}{12} + \frac{3}{12}$$
$$= \frac{10}{12}$$
$$= \frac{5}{6}$$

Leon ate five sixths of a pie.

2. **The correct answer is (B).** The lender owns a purchase made on installments until the full price is paid.

3. **The correct solution is (C).** An amortized loan is a loan where payments are made each period, usually monthly, to pay off interest and principal.

4. **The correct answer is (D).** We can solve using the effective interest rate for continuous interest which is $r_E = e^r - 1$:

$$r_E = e^{0.12} - 1$$
$$r_E = 0.1275$$

The effective interest rate is 12.75%.

5. **The correct answer is (B).** The P/E ratio is the price-to-earnings ratio of a company's current share price compared to its per-share earnings.

6. **The correct answer is (A).** The monthly interest rate is the APR ÷ 12, or monthly interest = 19.2 ÷ 12 = 1.6%.

7. **The correct answer is (D).** Use the quadratic equation to solve: $x = \dfrac{-b \pm \sqrt{b^2 - 4ac}}{2a}$ where $a = 3$, $b = -3$, and $c = \dfrac{1}{2}$.

$$x = \frac{-(-3) \pm \sqrt{(-3)^2 - 4(3)\left(\frac{1}{2}\right)}}{2(3)}$$

$$x = \frac{3 \pm \sqrt{9 - 6}}{6}$$

$$x = \frac{3 \pm \sqrt{3}}{6}$$

Now solve for both the negative and positive:

$$x = \frac{3 + \sqrt{3}}{6} \qquad x = \frac{3 - \sqrt{3}}{6}$$

$$x = \frac{3}{6} + \frac{\sqrt{3}}{6} \qquad x = \frac{3}{6} - \frac{\sqrt{3}}{6}$$

$$x = \frac{1}{2} + \frac{\sqrt{3}}{6} \qquad x = \frac{1}{2} - \frac{\sqrt{3}}{6}$$

The solution is $x = \dfrac{1}{2} \pm \dfrac{\sqrt{3}}{6}$.

8. **The correct answer is (C).** The y-axis label and values are missing.

9. **The correct answer is (B).** If you graph (0,1) and (1,3), you will see that only the solution (−1,−1) falls on the line created by these two points. The other choices do not fall in the line created by (0,1) and (1,3).

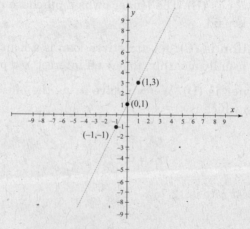

10. **The correct answer is (C).** 75th percentile means that the boy is taller than 75% of boys his age.

11. **The correct answer is (B).** First, evaluate the plot and determine the obvious points. For example, the line goes through the y-axis at 5 when $x = 0$, so we know (0,5) is one of the line's points. If we evaluate the functions, we can see that answer choices (A) and (C) do not fit this point. The next point we can evaluate is the point where the line crosses the x-axis. At this point, we know that $y = 0$. Substitute 0 for y in answer choices (B) and (D) and solve for x:

$$
\begin{array}{cc}
\text{B} & \text{D} \\
f(x) = 3x + 5 & f(x) = 5x + 5 \\
0 = 3x + 5 & 0 = 5x + 5 \\
-5 = 3x & -5 = 5x \\
\dfrac{-5}{3} = x & \dfrac{-5}{5} = x \\
x \approx -1.67 & x = -1
\end{array}
$$

The graph shows the line crossing the x-axis somewhere between -1 and -2, so the plot represents the function in choice (B), $f(x) = 3x + 5$.

12. **The correct answer is (B).** Rank the points from smallest to largest:

$$3, 3, 4, 4, 4, 5, 6, 7, 9$$

The median is the middle value, or 4. The mean or average is found by dividing the sum of the terms by the number of terms:

$$
\begin{aligned}
\text{avg} &= \frac{3 + 3 + 4 + 4 + 4 + 5 + 6 + 7 + 9}{9} \\
&= \frac{45}{9} \\
&= 5
\end{aligned}
$$

The median of the terms is 5. The difference between the mean and the median is $5 - 4 = 1$.

13. **The correct answer is (C).** 2/20, n/30 is the correct notation for credit terms.

14. **The correct answer is (B).** A promissory note is a contract between a borrower and a lender often required for a loan.

15. **The correct answer is (C).** With this type of problem, the first steps should be to create as many equations as can be found in the given information. Using these equations, you can solve the problem.

We know the probability for hitting a #4 prize balloon is 1 in 100, or 0.01. The probability for hitting a #3 prize is 10 in 100, or 0.1. Using the equation for expected value, with the number of balloons as n_1 through n_4, we can create our first equation:

$$Ex_{\text{balloons}} = p_1 1 + p_2 2 + p_3 3 + p_4 4$$

$$1.5 = \left(\frac{n_1}{100}\right)1 + \left(\frac{n_2}{100}\right)2 + \left(\frac{10}{100}\right)3 + \left(\frac{1}{100}\right)4$$

$$1.5 = \left(\frac{n_1}{100}\right)1 + \left(\frac{n_2}{100}\right)2 + (0.1)3 + (0.01)4$$

$$1.5 = \left(\frac{n_1}{100}\right) + \left(\frac{n_2}{50}\right) + 0.34$$

$$1.16 = \left(\frac{n_1}{100}\right) + \left(\frac{n_2}{50}\right)$$

We also know that the total number of balloons = 100, so we can create a second equation:

$$\text{total} = n_1 + n_2 + n_3 + n_4$$

$$100 = n_1 + n_2 + 10 + 1$$

$$100 = n_1 + n_2 + 11$$

$$89 = n_1 + n_2$$

Now we have two equations and two unknowns. We can solve the second equation for n_1:

$$89 = n_1 + n_2$$

$$n_1 = 89 - n_2$$

Substitute this value of n_1 into the first equation:

$$1.16 = \left(\frac{89 - n_2}{100}\right) + \left(\frac{n_2}{50}\right)$$

$$1.16 = \frac{89}{100} - \frac{n_2}{100} + \frac{n_2}{50}$$

$$1.16 = 0.89 - \frac{n_2}{100} + \frac{2n_2}{100}$$

$$1.16 = 0.89 + \frac{(2-1)n_2}{100}$$

$$1.16 = 0.89 + \frac{n_2}{100}$$

$$1.16 - 0.89 = \frac{n_2}{100}$$

$$0.27 = \frac{n_2}{100}$$

$$n_2 = 27$$

Now that we know we have 27 #2 balloons, we can solve using the second equation:

$$89 = n_1 + n_2$$
$$89 = n_1 + 27$$
$$89 - 27 = n_1$$
$$n_1 = 62$$

So, she must prepare 62 #1 balloon prizes and 27 #2 balloons.

You can check just to make sure that the total of all balloons does, in fact, equal 100:

$$62 + 27 + 10 + 1 = 100$$

16. **The correct answer is (C).** We can solve using the calculation for the future value of an ordinary annuity equation:

$$FV_{OA} = PMT \left[\frac{\left(1 + \frac{r}{m}\right)^{mn} - 1}{\frac{r}{m}} \right]$$

Where $r = 0.08$, $m = 1$, $t = 10$, and $PMT = 85,000$

$$FV_{OA} = 85,000 \left[\frac{\left(1 + \frac{0.08}{1}\right)^{(1)(10)} - 1}{\frac{0.08}{1}} \right]$$

$$= 85,000 \left[\frac{(1.08)^{10} - 1}{0.08} \right]$$

$$= 85,000 \left[\frac{(1.08)^{10} - 1}{0.08} \right]$$

$$= 85,000 [14.48656]$$

$$= 1,231,357.81$$

The future value in his account will be \$1,231,357.81.

17. **The correct answer is (B).** We first need to determine the total number of possible throws:

1	TTT
2	TTH
3	THT
4	THH
5	HTT
6	HTH
7	HHT
8	HHH

We can see that there are 8 possible tosses of three coins. Only one of the tosses in 8 will come up "head, head, head," so 1/8 = 12.5 percent.

18. **The correct answer is (C).** First, calculate the markdown. 9500 – 6950 = 2550.

Using the equation for markdown, $\text{Markdown \%} = \dfrac{\text{Markdown Price}}{\text{Original Selling Price}} \times 100$, we can solve:

$$MD\% = \frac{2550}{9500}(100)$$
$$= 26.84$$
$$= 27\%$$

The markdown is 27%.

19. **The correct answer is (A).** Use the equation for total cost $C(x) = mx + F$, where $C(x)$ = total cost, m = variable cost, and F = fixed cost:

$$4.0(10,000) + 9,800 = 3.5(10,000) + (9800 + x)$$
$$40,000 + 9800 = 35,000 + 9800 + x$$
$$49,800 = 44,800 + x$$
$$49,800 - 44,800 = x$$
$$5000 = x$$

The manufacturer can spend up to $5000 for additional fixed costs.

20. **The correct solution is (C).** Use the equation Selling Price = Cost (1 + % Markup), and solve for cost:

$$185 = \text{Cost}(1 + 0.85)$$
$$\text{Cost} = \frac{185}{1.85}$$
$$\text{Cost} = 100$$

The cost is $100.00.

21. **The correct answer is (C).** The equation for current ratio is:

$$\text{Current Ratio} = \frac{\text{Total Current Assets}}{\text{Total Current Liabilities}}$$

We know a 2:1 ratio means there are twice the current assets as total current liabilities. A ratio of 2:1 is considered healthy.

22. **The correct answer is (C).** The 50th percentile is the center value. Rank the prices from smallest to largest, and $17.50 is the center value.

23. **The correct answer is (D).** Use the equation for index number to calculate the current price in 2000:

$$\text{Index Number} = \frac{\text{Current Value of the Indicator}}{\text{Base Period Value of the Indicator}} \times 100$$

$$250 = \frac{x}{12}(100)$$

$$x = \frac{(250)(12)}{100}$$

$$x = \frac{3000}{100}$$

$$x = 30$$

The price in 2000 was $30.

24.   **The correct answer is (B).** Use the equation to solve for the depreciation:

$$\text{Depreciation} = \frac{\text{Cost} - \text{Residual Value}}{\text{Estimated Useful Life}}$$

$$D = \frac{100,000 - 20,000}{8}$$

$$D = \frac{80,000}{8}$$

$$D = 10,000$$

The depreciation is $10,000.

25. **The correct answer is (B).** Solve the first equation for y:

$$2x + y = 5$$

$$y = 5 - 2x$$

Substitute this value of y into the second equation:

$$5x + 5(5 - 2x) = 5$$

$$5x + 25 - 10x = 5$$

$$-5x = 5 - 25$$

$$-5x = -20$$

$$x = 4$$

Substitute this value of x into the first equation:

$$2(4) + y = 5$$

$$8 + y = 5$$

$$y = 5 - 8$$

$$y = -3$$

The solution is (4,−3).

26. **The correct answer is (B).** A 3% discount is $(0.03)(1000) = 30$. We then subtract this from 1000. $1000 - 30 = 970$. The discounted price is $970.

27. **The correct answer is (A).** The equation Property Tax = Tax Rate × Total Assessed Value can be used to calculate the Budget:

$$\text{Tax} = (0.0648)(32,500,000)$$

$$= 2,106,000$$

The city will raise $2,106,000.

28. **The correct answer is (D).** Although the market plays a strong role in the assessed value for property, the government sets the final assessed value.

29. The correct answer is (C). For 1500 widgets, let $x = 1500$ and solve:

$$C(1500) = 0.17(1500) + 50,000$$
$$= 50,255$$

Total cost = $50,255

30. The correct answer is (C). Use the quadratic equation to solve:

$x = \dfrac{-b \pm \sqrt{b^2 - 4ac}}{2a}$, where $a = 1$, $b = -6$, and $c = 5$.

$$x = \frac{-(-6) \pm \sqrt{(-6)^2 - 4(1)(5)}}{2(1)}$$

$$x = \frac{6 \pm \sqrt{36 - 20}}{2}$$

$$x = \frac{6 \pm \sqrt{16}}{2}$$

$$x = \frac{6 \pm 4}{2}$$

Now solve for both the negative and positive:

$$x = \frac{6 + 4}{2} \qquad x = \frac{6 - 4}{2}$$
$$x = 5 \qquad\qquad x = 1$$

The solution is $x = 5$ and 1.

31. The correct answer is (D). To solve, we would evaluate the following equation for C(x) = 16,200, x = 10,000 and m = 1.45 and find the value of fixed cost:

$$C(x) = m(x) + Fc$$
$$16,200 = 1.45(10,000) + Fc$$
$$Fc = 16,200 - 1.45(10,000)$$
$$Fc = 16,200 - 14,500$$
$$Fc = 1700$$

The fixed cost is $1700.

32. The correct answer is (D). To find the solution, we need only to set the two equations equal to each other and solve for x:

$$C(x) = R(x)$$
$$1.2x + 1274 = 6x$$
$$1.2x - 6x = -1274$$
$$(1.2 - 6)x = -1274$$
$$-4.8x = -1274$$
$$x = 265.4167$$

To break even, they need to make just a little more than 265 units, so to break even they need 266 units.

33. **The correct answer is (B).** Use the equation for standard error $SE_{\bar{x}} = \dfrac{\sigma}{\sqrt{n}}$ to solve for n:

$$2 = \frac{20}{\sqrt{n}}$$
$$\sqrt{n} = \frac{20}{2}$$
$$\sqrt{n} = \frac{20}{2}$$
$$\sqrt{n} = 10$$
$$\left(\sqrt{n}\right)^2 = 10^2$$
$$n = 100$$

There are 100 data points.

34. **The correct answer is (A).** To find the solution, we need to set the two equations equal to each other and solve for x:

$$C(x) = R(x)$$
$$1.5x + 11,700 = 4x$$
$$1.5x - 4x = -11,700$$
$$(1.5 - 4)x = -11,700$$
$$-2.5x = -11,700$$
$$x = 4680$$

To break even they need to make just more than 4680 units. Now calculate $R(x) = 4(4680) = 18,720$.

35. **The correct answer is (C).** To solve, multiply the base year expenses by the 2005 percentage: $(0.85)(243,000) = 206,550$.

36. **The correct answer is (D).** To solve the linear equation, add 10 to both sides and then divide by 3:

$$3x - 10 = 23$$
$$3x - 10 + 10 = 23 + 10$$
$$3x = 33$$
$$\frac{1}{3}(3x) = \frac{1}{3}(33)$$
$$\left(\frac{3}{3}\right)x = \frac{33}{3}$$
$$x = 11$$

The solution is 11.

37. **The correct answer is (A).** If 9% of the budget goes to food, then $(0.09)(3000) = \$270$ per month.

38. The correct answer is (C). Use the equation for linear interpolation:

$$y_2 = \frac{(x_2 - x_1)(y_3 - y_1)}{(x_3 - x_1)} + y_1$$

$$x = \frac{(7-1)(89-45)}{(15-1)} + 45$$

$$x = \frac{(6)(44)}{(14)} + 45$$

$$x = 18.857 + 45$$

$$x = 63.86$$

The interpolated value is 63.86.

39. The correct answer is (D). Use a conversion table form to convert and cancel units:

2940 ~~Euro~~	1.42 dollar	1 ~~week~~
1 ~~week~~	1 ~~Euro~~	7 day

$$= \frac{(2940)(1.42)\ \text{Euro}}{7\ \text{day}} = 596.40 \text{ dollars per day}$$

The businesswoman spends $586.40 per day.

40. The correct answer is (A). A Type I error is when you believe something is true and it is not. The researcher believed his data showed a significant difference when there was none.

41. The correct answer is (A). Use the equation to make the conversion:

$$18 = \frac{5}{9}(F - 32)$$

$$18 = (0.556)F - (0.556)(32)$$

$$18 = 0.556F - 17.778$$

$$0.556F = 18 + 17.778$$

$$0.556F = 35.778$$

$$F = 64.34$$

The temperature is 64.3° Fahrenheit.

42. The correct answer is (C). Use the weighted average equation:

$$GPA = \frac{(3)(A) + (3)(B) + (4)(B) + (4)(C) + (2)(A)}{3 + 3 + 4 + 4 + 2}$$

$$= \frac{(3)(4) + (3)(3) + (4)(3) + (4)(2) + (2)(4)}{3 + 3 + 4 + 4 + 2}$$

$$= \frac{12 + 9 + 12 + 8 + 8}{16}$$

$$= \frac{49}{16}$$

$$= 3.06$$

The GPA is 3.06.

43. The correct answer is (A). Use the following equation to calculate the stock yield:

$$\text{Stock Yield} = \frac{\text{Annual Dividend per Share}}{\text{Current Share Price}}$$

Solve:

$$SY = \frac{2}{45}$$
$$SY = 0.044$$
$$SY = 4.4\%$$

The stock yield is 4.4%.

44. The correct answer is (A). Increasing the price will lower the number of units it takes to break even, but the increased price could slow sales. Lowering the fixed or variable cost of manufacture will decrease the number of units to break even. The price will not have to be raised with reduced cost, so the time it takes to break even will be reduced.

45. The correct answer is (C). Use the equation $FV = PV\left(1 + \dfrac{r}{m}\right)^{mt}$ to solve for the future value:

$$FV = 1800\left(1 + \frac{0.095}{12}\right)^{(12)(8)}$$
$$= 1800\left(1 + 0.0079167\right)^{96}$$
$$= 1800\left(1.0079167\right)^{96}$$
$$= 1800(2.1319)$$
$$= 3837.41$$

The future value is $3837.41.

46. The correct answer is (B). We can solve using the calculation for an ordinary annuity present value:

$$PV_{OA} = PMT\left[\frac{1 - \dfrac{1}{\left(1 + \dfrac{r}{m}\right)^{tm}}}{\dfrac{r}{m}}\right]$$

Where $r = 0.12$, $m = 12$, $t = 2$, and $PMT = \$50$:

$$PV_{OA} = 50\left[\frac{1 - \dfrac{1}{\left(1 + \dfrac{0.12}{12}\right)^{(2)(12)}}}{\dfrac{0.12}{12}}\right]$$

$$= 50\left[\frac{1 - \dfrac{1}{(1.01)^{24}}}{0.01}\right]$$

$$= 50\left[\frac{1 - \dfrac{1}{1.12697}}{0.01}\right]$$

$$= 50\left[\frac{0.212434}{0.01}\right]$$

$$= 50(21.24339)$$

$$= 1062.17$$

The present value of the gift is $1062.17.

47. **The correct answer is (A).** The distribution is normal, so we know that half of the students most likely scored above the average, 78, so choice (B) is incorrect. The correct percentage of students that scored between 57 and 99, or mean ± 3 standard deviations, is 99.7%, thus choice (C) is incorrect. It is possible that someone scored outside the ± 3 sigma limits and could have scored a 100 on the test, thus choice (D) is incorrect. The distribution of the grades was normal, so the students can correctly assume that 68% of the students scored between the mean ± 1 standard, 71 and 85, so choice (A) is correct.

48. **The correct answer is (C).** We can solve using the calculation for an ordinary annuity equation for payments:

$$PMT_{OA} = PV\left[\frac{\dfrac{r}{m}}{\left(1 + \dfrac{r}{m}\right)^{mn} - 1}\right]\left(1 + \dfrac{r}{m}\right)^{mn}$$

Where $r = 0.10$, $m = 12$, $t = 3$, and $PV = \$20,000 - \$5000 = \$15,000$:

$$PMT_{OA} = 15,000 \left[\frac{\frac{0.1}{12}}{\left(1 + \frac{0.1}{12}\right)^{(12)(3)} - 1} \right]\left(1 + \frac{0.1}{12}\right)^{(12)(3)}$$

$$PV_{OA} = 15,000 \left[\frac{0.008333}{(1 + 0.008333)^{36} - 1} \right](1 + 0.008333)^{36}$$

$$= 15,000 \left[\frac{0.008333}{(1.008333)^{36} - 1} \right](1.008333)^{36}$$

$$= 15,000 \left[\frac{0.008333}{0.348166} \right]1.348166$$

$$= 15,000(0.023934)1.348166$$

$$= 484.01$$

The monthly payment of 484.01 will be needed.

49.   **The correct answer is (C).** Use the equation to solve for salvage value:

$$\text{Depreciation} = \frac{\text{Cost} - \text{Residual Value}}{\text{Estimated Useful Life}}$$

$$2000 = \frac{20,000 - x}{7}$$

$$(2000)(7) = 20,000 - x$$

$$14,000 = 20,000 - x$$

$$14,000 - 20,000 = -x$$

$$-6000 = -x$$

$$x = 6000$$

The salvage value is $6000.

50. **The correct answer is (A).** Use the equation $i = PVrt$ to solve for $i =$ $(500)(0.08)(5) = \$200$.

51. **The correct answer is (B).** We can solve using the equation for amortization:

$$PMT_{\text{Amort}} = \frac{PV\left(\frac{r}{m}\right)}{1 - \left(1 + \frac{r}{m}\right)^{-mt}}$$

Where $r = 0.055$, $m = 1$, $t = 15$, and $PMT = 265{,}000 - 25{,}000 = 240{,}000$:

$$PMT_{\text{Amort}} = \frac{PV\left(\dfrac{r}{m}\right)}{1 - \left(1 + \dfrac{r}{m}\right)^{-mt}}$$

$$= \frac{240{,}000\left(\dfrac{0.055}{12}\right)}{1 - \left(1 + \dfrac{0.055}{12}\right)^{-(12)(15)}}$$

$$= \frac{240{,}000\left(0.00458333\right)}{1 - \left(1.00458333\right)^{-180}}$$

$$= \frac{1099.92}{1 - 0.439061786}$$

$$= 1961.00$$

The monthly payment is $1961.00.

52. **The correct answer is (D).** Use the equation Deferred Payment Price = Total of All Payments + Down Payment to solve. DPP = 3(19.95) + 7.50 = $67.35.

53. **The correct answer is (D).** To solve this problem, let a = number of adult tickets sold and c = number of children's tickets sold. We know $1.75c + 3.5a = 988.75$ and $c + a = 335$:

First, solve the second equation for c:

$$c + a = 335$$
$$c = 335 - a$$

Substitute this value into the first equation:

$$1.75(335 - a) + 3.5a = 988.75$$
$$586.25 - 1.75a + 3.5a = 988.75$$
$$(-1.75 + 3.5)a = 988.75 - 586.25$$
$$1.75a = 402.5$$
$$a = 230$$

Use this value of a and substitute it into the second equation:

$$c + a = 335$$
$$c + 230 = 335$$
$$c = 335 - 230$$
$$c = 105$$

The high school sold 230 adult tickets and 105 children's tickets.

54. The correct answer is (B). First, solve using the equation

$\text{Index Number} = \dfrac{\text{Current Value}}{\text{Base Period Value}} \times 100$ for 1960 to get the 1970 base value:

$$80 = \frac{8}{x}(100)$$
$$x = \frac{(10)(100)}{80}$$
$$x = 10$$

The base value for 1970 is $10. Using this value, we can find the price in 2000:

$$180 = \frac{x}{10}(100)$$
$$x = \frac{(10)(180)}{100}$$
$$x = 18$$

The price of widgets in 2000 was $18.

55. The correct answer is (D). First, calculate the total amount paid on the loan:

$$(360)(902.43) = 324{,}874.8$$

Next, find the total amount of interest:

$$\text{total} = 324{,}874.80 - 250{,}000$$
$$= 74{,}874.80$$

The total interest paid is $74,874.80.

56. The correct answer is (B). The APR is the monthly rate multiplied by 12, or $1\% \times 12 = 12\%$.

57. The correct answer is (C). To solve this inequality, you need to isolate x on one side of the equation:

$$-3x + 4 < 5x + 7$$
$$-3x - 5x + 4 < 5x - 5x + 7$$
$$(-3 - 5)x + 4 < 7$$
$$-8x + 4 < 7$$
$$-8x + 4 - 4 < 7 - 4$$
$$-8x < 3$$
$$x > -\frac{3}{8}$$

Remember that you flip the inequality sign if you multiply or divide by a negative number.

58. The correct answer is (B). To solve, use the equation:

$$r_E = \left(1 + \frac{r}{m}\right)^m - 1$$

$$r_E = \left(1 + \frac{0.18}{12}\right)^{12} - 1$$

$$r_E = \left(1 + 0.015\right)^{12} - 1$$

$$r_E = \left(1.015\right)^{12} - 1$$

$$r_E = 0.195618$$

The effective interest rate = 19.56%.

59. The correct answer is (A). Divide 403 into 154 and round to three digits:

$$= \frac{154}{403}$$

$$= 0.382133$$

$$= 0.382$$

The batting average is 0.382.

60. The correct answer is (C). There are 30 days in the month of April. If it rained for 22 days, then the percentage of days that it rained is:

$$= \frac{22}{30} \times 100$$

$$= 73.33\%$$

It rained 73% of the days in April.

SUMMING IT UP

- There are three common ways to use numbers to describe a part of a whole: fractions, decimals, and percentages. Percentage means "per cent" or "out of 100."

- Linear equations are equations of a straight line and usually appear as $y = mx + b$ where m is the slope and b is the point where the line intercepts the y-axis.

- An inequality is a math statement where instead of an equal sign being used, the equation uses one of the following symbols: "greater than" (>), "less than" (<), "greater than or equal to" ($\geq$), or "less than or equal to" ($\leq$).

- Equations having more than one variable are simultaneous equations. The substitution method is the easiest way to solve simultaneous equations.

- A quadratic equation contains a variable of the second order, for example, $3x^2 - 2x + 5$. Solve quadratic equations by finding where the equation equals zero.

- Interpolation is a method of fitting a line or other data points between two known points. Linear interpolation draws a straight line. Curved interpolation uses polynomial and other advanced equations. Extrapolation creates data based on the trend of known data; it is less reliable than interpolation.

- Evaluating a function requires finding the values that are true for the function. Graphing the points helps you know what the function looks like.

- Mean, median, and mode are methods of measuring the central tendency, or the "middle," of a data set.

- Dispersion is a measure of the spread or the deviation of the data from the central tendency. Range and standard deviation are two methods for measuring dispersion. A small range or small standard deviation means that the data are close to the mean.

- Statistical significance is a measure of the reliability of a result. The level of significance is indicated by the symbol α. Type I errors occur when one assumes that something is true when it is false; Type II errors occur when one believes something to be false when it is true.

- The standard error is a way of measuring the sampling fluctuation in a set of data. Sampling fluctuation is how much a statistic fluctuates from sample to sample.

- A random variable is something that changes every time it is tested. The results of a random variable can be placed into groups of expected outcomes. The chance that a result falls into one of these groups or bins is its probability.

- An average where each value is given a different importance or weight is the weighted average.

- A percentile is the amount of data that falls above or below a given value. For example, 30% of the data falls below the 30th percentile. The median is the 50% percentile, as there are as many values above 50% as there are below.

- Index numbers are used to compare data of different sizes.

- Interest is the fee paid when someone uses someone else's money. Principal is the amount of the loan or original deposit. Simple interest is calculated on the principal amount; the interest is never added back into the principal. Compound interest adds the interest to the principal at a predetermined period.

- Depreciation is the process of putting a value to a company's changing assets. The cost is what the company paid for the item, the estimated useful life is how long the company believes the item has value, and the residual or salvage value is what the item is worth when fully depreciated.

- A cash discount is an incentive offered to purchasers of a product for payment within a specified period. The credit period is the amount of time to pay off the loan. The terms for a discount are usually written in the form of 2/15, n/30. This means that there is a 2% discount if paid in 15 days, or the net is due in 30 days.

- Installment purchases are a form of credit where payments are made in parts over a fixed period of time. Until it is paid off, the lender owns the item, but the buyer can use it. The borrowed amount is the amount financed. The down payment is what is paid up front. The finance charge is the total of the payments minus the amount financed. The deferred payment price is what the item really costs.

- Markup allows the seller to make a profit on his sale as well as pay for labor costs, property rental, taxes, and other expenses that are required to operate the business. Markdown is the amount a seller discounts a product to encourage sales.

- Sales tax is usually added as a percentage of the sale price. Excise tax is a fixed or percentage tax placed on luxury and nonessential items. Property tax is a tax placed on the value of property. The value the government assigns to a property is its assessed value.

- Break-even is the point where the revenue generated by a product equals the cost of manufacturing. After the break-even point, a product can produce a profit. Profit is the revenue minus the cost.

- Ratios are used by companies to compare various measures from one year to another to spot trends. Common financial ratios include current ratio, quick or "acid test" ratio, and leverage ratio. Trend analysis ratios uncover changes from year to year and are expressed as percentages.

- The promissory note is a contract between a borrower and a lender that puts loan information in writing.

- A single payment loan is repaid at one time. With amortized payments, you pay a set amount each period until the loan is paid in full. A balloon payment requires periodic payments of principal and interest for a set amount of time, and after the last payment, the remaining principal and interest are owed in one large payment.

- Graphs are a valuable method for giving data meaning, but it must clearly convey the meaning of the numbers. Types of graphs include bar graphs, line graphs, scatter plots, and pie charts.

- The P/E (price-to-earnings) ratio is the measure of a company's current share price compared to its per-share earnings. The rate of return (ROR) or return on investment (ROI) is a measure of the money gained or lost on an investment relative to the money invested. Stock yield, or current dividend yield, percentage tells stockholders what the dividend per share is returning.

- To make a profit, the selling price must be above the cost of the unit. The lower the cost of the unit, the more money can be made when it is sold. The product's value is what the customer thinks the product or service is worth.

- An annuity is a stream of fixed payments or receipts made over a specified period. An ordinary annuity is one where the payment is made at the end of the payment period. The future value of an ordinary annuity is the value of expected periodic payments after a period of time.

- A loan is amortized if the principal and interest are paid by a sequence of equal periodic payments. It is a process of reducing the balance of a loan by a periodic payment. Amount paid in interest = total payments made − amount of the loan.

- The annual percentage rate (APR) conveys what the annual cost of the loan will be in a percentage. Nominal APR is a simple-interest rate for a year. Effective APR (EAR) includes participation fees, loan origination fees, monthly service fees, or late charges and is the true annual interest rate paid.

Principles of Public Speaking

OVERVIEW

- Diagnostic test
- Answer key and explanations
- Ethical considerations in public speaking
- Audience analysis and adaptation
- Speech topics and purposes
- Research, content, and organization
- Delivering a speech so an audience will listen
- Criticizing and evaluating speeches
- Post-test
- Answer key and explanations
- Summing it up

DIAGNOSTIC TEST

Directions: Carefully read each of the following 20 questions. Choose the best answer to each question and circle your answer choice. The Answer Key and Explanations can be found following this Diagnostic Test.

1. Which of the following refers to current, popular opinions about issues and trends?
   - **(A)** Conventional wisdom
   - **(B)** Political correctness
   - **(C)** Audience attitude
   - **(D)** Cultural factors

2. What is the general purpose of a persuasive speech?
   - **(A)** To provide new information
   - **(B)** To increase understanding
   - **(C)** To amuse with wittiness
   - **(D)** To change attitudes

3. Which of the following would be the best resource to use for finding out the state bird of Kansas?
   - **(A)** Gazetteer
   - **(B)** Dictionary
   - **(C)** Periodical
   - **(D)** Newspaper

4. Which of the following is an example of plagiarism in a speech?

(A) Using and acknowledging statistics from a government agency

(B) Changing key words from a speech found in the public domain

(C) Paraphrasing information and citing the source

(D) Crediting unique ideas to the original source

5. Attacks against the intelligence and integrity of a politician rather than the politician's actions exemplify which of the following?

(A) Hasty generalization

(B) False cause

(C) Ad hominem

(D) Bandwagon

6. The process of creating a common bond with an audience based on similar values and experiences is known as which of the following?

(A) Orientation

(B) Centeredness

(C) Stereotyping

(D) Identification

7. Which organizational pattern would be most appropriate for a speech explaining how to make a quilt?

(A) Causal

(B) Topical

(C) Temporal

(D) Structure-function

8. Which of the following is another term for literal and objective word meanings?

(A) Connotative

(B) Generic

(C) Denotative

(D) Imagery

9. Which of the following best describes the goal of speech criticism given in a classroom setting?

(A) Provide constructive feedback

(B) Identify speaker shortcomings

(C) Compare different speech purposes

(D) Reveal weakest supporting materials

10. Which of the following speech organization patterns was first developed as a model for sales presentations?

(A) Pro-and-con

(B) Cause-effect

(C) Statement of reasons

(D) Motivated sequence

11. Which of the following is the first step of the listening process?

(A) Understanding

(B) Answering

(C) Receiving

(D) Retaining

12. The speed at which people speak is known as which of the following?

(A) Rate

(B) Tone

(C) Pitch

(D) Volume

13. Which of the following is a function of speech introductions?

(A) Explain visual aids

(B) Establish credibility

(C) Summarize the main points

(D) Indicate how listeners should respond

14. Which of the following elements of a speech is most often phrased as an infinitive statement?

(A) Topic

(B) Thesis

(C) Main idea

(D) Specific purpose

15. Specific instances that illustrate larger groups of people or events are characterized as which of the following?
    (A) Examples
    (B) Narratives
    (C) Statistics
    (D) Testimonies

16. Words and phrases that link ideas within a speech to show relationships between concepts are known as which of the following?
    (A) Parallelisms
    (B) Connectives
    (C) Commentaries
    (D) Supporting materials

17. Which of the following is one of the principles of effective speech criticism?
    (A) Be subjective
    (B) Stress the negative
    (C) Be specific
    (D) Ask many questions

18. Which of the following would be most appropriate in a speech conclusion?
    (A) Introducing a new idea
    (B) Telling an old joke
    (C) Listing credentials
    (D) Restating the thesis

19. The production of syllables and words based on accepted standards is known as which of the following?
    (A) Pronunciation
    (B) Articulation
    (C) Expression
    (D) Accent

20. Which type of argument is being used in a statement such as "fever and a rash indicate an allergic reaction"?
    (A) Argument from causation
    (B) Argument from example
    (C) Argument from analogy
    (D) Argument from sign

ANSWER KEY AND EXPLANATIONS

1. A	5. C	9. A	13. B	17. C
2. D	6. D	10. D	14. D	18. D
3. A	7. C	11. C	15. A	19. A
4. B	8. C	12. A	16. B	20. D

1. **The correct answer is (A).** Conventional wisdom is the term used to describe current, popular opinions about issues, trends, topics, styles, and society. An understanding of conventional wisdom can provide a starting point for speech topics and is a useful tool in audience analysis. Audience attitude, choice (C), and cultural factors, choice (D), are aspects to consider when preparing a speech. Political correctness, choice (B), refers to the use of terminology that is nonoffensive.

2. **The correct answer is (D).** The general purpose of a persuasive speech is to change the attitudes, opinions, and feelings of audience members. Choices (A) and (B) describe the general purpose of informative speeches. Choice (C) describes the purpose of a speech intended to entertain an audience.

3. **The correct answer is (A).** Gazetteers are geographical dictionaries that serve as useful resources for facts such as mountain heights, state flowers, state birds, and island sizes. Periodicals and newspapers are resources for current events; dictionaries provide not only definitions but also word origins.

4. **The correct answer is (B).** Changing key words or using unique ideas from another person's speech is an example of plagiarism, even if the speech is old enough to be considered part of the public domain. Plagiarism involves stealing or passing off ideas as original ones rather than crediting the source. Choices (A), (C), and (D) are not plagiarism because all sources are cited.

5. **The correct answer is (C).** Ad hominem is a reasoning fallacy that occurs when a speaker attacks the character rather than the actions or opinions of a person. False cause fallacies, choice (B), occur when an incorrect connection is made between a cause and an effect. Hasty generalizations, choice (A), are fallacies that offer generalizations without solid evidence. Bandwagon, choice (D), is a fallacy that makes the connection between popularity and desirability, and it is used most often in advertising.

6. **The correct answer is (D).** Identification occurs when a speaker forms a bond with an audience by pointing out similar values and experiences, which increases speaker credibility. Identifying with audience members is an aspect of choice (B); however, audience-centeredness is the process of keeping the audience in mind throughout a speech. Performance orientation and communication orientation are related to speaker anxiety, so choice (A) is incorrect. Choice (C) refers to making judgments about groups of people based on certain traits.

7. **The correct answer is (C).** A temporal pattern is most appropriate for informative speeches that explain a process, such as how to make a quilt or how to train a puppy. Choice (A) is useful for speeches that discuss a cause-effect relationship. Choice

(B) is appropriate for speeches that analyze the parts of a whole. Choice (D) is useful when a speaker wants to point out the structural and functional aspects of something.

8. **The correct answer is (C).** Denotative meanings are those that are literal and objective and the ones found in the dictionary. In contrast, connotative meanings are those suggested by word associations, so choice (A) is incorrect. Generic language refers to noninclusive words, such as police officer. Imagery is vivid language that creates word images for an audience, so choice (D) is incorrect.

9. **The correct answer is (A).** Providing constructive feedback to help speakers improve their skills is the primary objective of speech criticism. Criticism involves identifying both positive and negative aspects of a speech, not just the weaknesses, so choices (B) and (D) are incorrect. Criticism involves comparing a speech to the accepted standard, so choice (C) is incorrect.

10. **The correct answer is (D).** Alan Monroe developed the motivated sequence pattern during the 1930s as a technique for giving sales presentations. Since then, the pattern has been used in political speeches and advertisements. The statement of reasons pattern is a persuasive speech structure, but it was not initially developed for sales presentations. Choices (A) and (B) are both useful for informative and persuasive speeches, but neither was created for the purpose of sales presentations.

11. **The correct answer is (C).** Receiving a message is the first step in the five-step listening process. In contrast, hearing begins and ends with receiving a message. After a message is received, a person then understands, retains, evaluates, and answers, so choices (A), (B), and (D) are incorrect.

12. **The correct answer is (A).** Rate is the speed at which people speak, and it averages 150 words per minute. Tone is related to vocal quality, so choice (B) is incorrect. Pitch is the highness or lowness of a voice, and volume is the degree of loudness.

13. **The correct answer is (B).** Establishing speaker credibility is one of the primary functions of a speech introduction. Credibility refers to the audience's perception of a speaker's qualifications about a specific topic. Choices (C) and (D) are functions of speech conclusions. Visual aids, choice (A), in introductions may be used to gain listener attention, but explaining them is not the purpose of an introduction.

14. **The correct answer is (D).** The specific purpose statement of a speech is an infinitive, such as *to inform my audience about the benefits of strength training*. A speech topic is most likely a phrase or group of words, so choice (A) is incorrect. The thesis statement is a complete sentence, and main ideas are most often phrased as complete sentences as well.

15. **The correct answer is (A).** Examples are used in speeches to illustrate larger groups of people or events, and they may be real or hypothetical. Narratives are stories that are often used in speeches to illustrate abstract points. Statistics are a type of supporting material that uses numerical data. Testimonies are expert opinions that support claims in a speech.

16. **The correct answer is (B).** Connectives are words and phrases that link ideas in a speech and help illustrate relationships between concepts. Transitions, signposts, and previews are

types of connectives used by public speakers. Supporting materials are examples, statistics, and narratives that support the main points in a speech, so choice (D) is incorrect.

17. **The correct answer is (C).** Being as specific as possible when giving speech criticism helps a speaker understand particular strengths and weaknesses of a presentation and thus improve his or her public speaking skills. Criticism should be objective and devoid of biases rather than subjective, so choice (A) is incorrect. Emphasis should be given to the positive elements of a speech rather than the negative, so choice (B) is incorrect. Questions, choice (D), may be asked after a speech, but they are not a key element of criticism.

18. **The correct answer is (D).** Restating the thesis, or central idea, of the speech is appropriate in a conclusion because it reminds the audience about the specific purpose of the presentation. Introducing a new idea is a common mistake because the focus of the conclusion should be on concepts already developed in the speech. Telling a joke is inappropriate for most speeches, and speaker credentials should be established during the introduction, which means choices (B) and (C) are incorrect.

19. **The correct answer is (A).** Pronunciation is the production and formation of syllables and words based on accepted standards. Articulation refers to using the speech organs, such as the tongue, vocal cords, and lips to produce individual sounds. Choices (C) and (D) are incorrect even though speakers often have noticeable accents or expressions common to a particular region.

20. **The correct answer is (D).** An argument from sign cites information that signals a claim. A fever and a rash typically accompany allergic reactions, so they are signs of an allergic reaction. The rash and fever did not cause the allergic reaction, so choice (A) is incorrect. An argument from example, choice (B), supports a claim with examples, while an argument from analogy, choice (C), supports a claim with a comparable situation.

ETHICAL CONSIDERATIONS IN PUBLIC SPEAKING

Ethics is the area of philosophy that addresses issues of morality, fairness, and justice, and it plays a significant role in public speaking. Public speakers face ethical dilemmas at nearly every stage of the speechmaking process—from selecting a topic to presenting the final message. A speaker's character, which Aristotle referred to as ethos, is a critical component of public speaking. Although the First Amendment protects freedom of speech, public speakers must make moral considerations when addressing audiences. Are the goals of the speech ethically sound? Is the subject matter appropriate for the audience? Is the information accurate and appropriately cited?

The ethical nature of rhetorical communication can be viewed as ends and means or credibility-centered. Public speakers often justify the use of any means necessary to achieve a particular end; however, this approach assumes that the speaker rather than the listener knows what is best. An ends-and-means approach may involve deceit, emotional appeals, or name-calling. Emotional appeals, which Aristotle called pathos, evoke strong feelings from listeners, such as anger, sadness, happiness, fear, or sympathy. Although emotional appeals are appropriate in some situations, they are immoral in others, such as Hitler's use of hatred toward Jews to encourage German support of his actions. Another ends-and-means approach involves name-calling, which refers to using language in a speech that degrades people based on sexual orientation, religion, or ethnicity.

In contrast, speakers who adhere to credibility-centered ethics use sound reasoning, examine all available evidence, credit sources, and avoid immoral emotional appeals. According to credibility-centered ethics, the effectiveness of a speech is diminished by the loss of a speaker's credibility with an audience.

Plagiarism

One of the most unethical actions taken by a public speaker is plagiarism. Plagiarism occurs when a writer or a speaker presents the ideas or words of another person as their own in one of three ways:

- Global plagiarism
- Patchwork plagiarism
- Incremental plagiarism

Global plagiarism occurs when an entire speech is stolen from one source, and a speaker presents the work as original. As the name implies, patchwork plagiarism involves stealing from multiple sources rather than a single source. A speaker who employs patchwork plagiarism copies word for word from two or three sources and then combines the information into a single speech. Global and patchwork plagiarism are blatantly unethical because entire sentences and paragraphs are stolen verbatim from one or more sources. Incremental plagiarism is more subtle, yet it remains unethical. Incremental plagiarism occurs most often in conjunction with quotations and paraphrases. Paraphrased information and direct quotations are appropriate and useful in a speech, but citations are necessary. Direct quotations incorporated into a speech must be attributed to the original speaker; otherwise, the information has been plagiarized. Similarly, paraphrasing or summarizing the unique ideas of another person is considered plagiarism unless the original source is cited during the speech.

AUDIENCE ANALYSIS AND ADAPTATION

Public speakers who take the time to determine the background, beliefs, and knowledge of audience members can tailor informative and persuasive speeches and improve communication. The audience should be the primary consideration during the speechmaking process and the speech presentation, a concept known as audience-centeredness.

Effective speakers focus on and identify with listeners. Audience identification is the process of forming a bond with listeners by pointing out common beliefs, experiences, and goals. How can a speaker know about the attitudes of an audience? Audience analysis is the process of acquiring information about an audience in order to adapt a speech. Speakers can learn about listeners in a number of ways:

- Conventional wisdom
- Direct observation
- Questionnaires
- Demographic audience analysis
- Situational audience analysis

Conventional wisdom, which is the popular opinion about issues and trends, provides speakers with a general idea about societal attitudes and interests and is particularly useful during the process of selecting a speech topic. A speaker can also gather information about an audience through direct observation. Inferences about economic status and interests can be made based on clothing and appearance, although stereotyping should be carefully avoided. Questionnaires distributed via e-mail prior to a speech can help a speaker determine the attitudes and knowledge base of audience members regarding a particular topic—a method often used for classroom speeches.

The two most useful ways to learn about an audience prior to a speech are through a demographic audience analysis and a situational audience analysis. A demographic audience analysis is a method of learning about listeners based on demographic factors, including age, gender, religion, sexual orientation, ethnicity, economic status, occupation, education, and organizational membership.

The age of audience members has a significant impact on many aspects of a speech. For example, an older audience would most likely be more interested in a speech about estate planning than dating issues. In addition to guiding the speech topic, age also affects the information presented in the speech. An older audience would most likely understand historical references to World War II or the Great Depression, while a younger audience may require additional background information. In addition, age affects attitudes. Older people have had a longer time to develop opinions about various topics, and their beliefs are steadfast. In contrast, opinions held by young people change with time and experience.

With regard to gender, religion, and sexual orientation, effective public speakers avoid using sexist language or assuming that all audience members are heterosexual or hold similar religious beliefs. Just like modern society, today's audiences are diverse, and experienced public speakers use inclusive examples and language. A demographic audience analysis helps a speaker anticipate how listeners will react to a speech and provides the basis for a situational audience analysis.

A situational audience analysis considers the characteristics of a particular audience, such as size, physical setting, occasion, and time. The size of an audience affects speech delivery; a small audience can be addressed informally, while a large audience requires more structure. Moreover, a large audience prevents a speaker from assessing how listeners are responding to a speech because of the distance between the speaker and each audience member. Flexibility during speech presentation is essential to adapting to audience size, which may be unknown until moments before the speech begins. The setting of a speech may be a classroom, an overcrowded auditorium, or a large dining hall, and unpleasant settings require speakers to remain energetic in order to hold the interest of listeners.

The time and occasion of a speech are important situational factor to consider. The tone and content of a pep-rally speech is very different from that of a presentation to stockholders, and speakers should consider the occasion in advance. Time is another situational factor and refers to both the time of day and the length of the speech. Speakers often find listeners attentive in the morning and tired late in the afternoon, which is a consideration when determining the length of a speech.

A situational audience analysis not only addresses the physical aspects of an audience but also the anticipated viewpoint of an audience towards a topic. Audience knowledge of a subject plays a major role in the language and terminology used in a speech. For example, a physician addressing a medical convention would not need to explain medical terms, but a physician addressing a group of high school students would need to explain concepts in a more basic manner. Audience attitude refers to the mindset of listeners regarding a topic, and a speaker who is aware of an audience's attitude can adapt a speech to address possible concerns and objections.

The purpose of audience analysis is audience adaptation, which means modifying a message to make it appropriate for a specific audience. Audience adaptation occurs when preparing the speech and when presenting the speech. During the speechmaking process, the information gained from the audience analysis directs topic selection, determines examples to use, and guides the phrasing of introductions and conclusions.

Audience-centeredness and audience adaptation go hand in hand. Every stage of the speechmaking process should consider audience response to the message. During the writing phase, a speaker modifies a speech to make it as coherent and appropriate as possible for the given audience. During speech presentations, effective speakers make adaptations based on audience feedback. For example, a speaker who presents a concept and notices confused looks on the faces of many listeners may review the idea again or rephrase the information in a different way. Successful public speakers use audience analysis to adapt to audiences both before and during speeches.

SPEECH TOPICS AND PURPOSES

Before the speechmaking process can begin, a speaker needs to determine the purpose of the speech. Three general purposes exist for making a speech:

- To inform
- To persuade
- To entertain

An informative speech increases audience awareness and knowledge about a specific subject. Informative speeches do not attempt to persuade listeners to respond or act upon newly acquired knowledge. However, the purpose of a persuasive speech is to change the attitudes, behaviors, feelings, and beliefs of listeners. The purpose of an entertaining speech is to amuse the audience with the speaker's humor and cleverness.

In conjunction with determining the purpose of a speech, topic selection needs to occur. Generating ideas for potential speech topics can be accomplished in many different ways. Surveys, such as the Gallup Poll, may provide topic ideas related to current issues, trends, or problems. Newspapers and magazines, such as *Time* and *Forbes*, provide information about current events and issues about which people are concerned. Brainstorming, which involves jotting down a list of topics in a short amount of time, is another useful tool in generating a speech topic. A tree diagram is a method of limiting a speech topic by repeatedly dividing a topic into smaller parts until arriving at a manageable topic. Topoi, a method based on ancient rhetoric techniques, involves asking and answering questions to generate topic ideas.

After developing a list of general topic ideas, all possible speech subjects should be evaluated to determine which one is most appropriate:

- Topics should be interesting to the speaker; otherwise, a lack of enthusiasm will be apparent to listeners.
- Topics should be interesting and useful to the audience, which can be determined through an audience analysis.
- Topics should be ethically appropriate and maintain a goal of improving society.
- Topics should be appropriate for the specific occasion, which means that the speech should meet audience expectations, be relevant, and be narrow in scope.

In general, topics that are interesting and appropriate for the speaker, the audience, and the occasion make the most effective speeches.

After establishing a topic and a general purpose, it is time to determine the specific purpose of a speech, which is the speaker's goal. The specific purpose statement should focus on one clear idea and be stated in a brief infinitive phrase. A properly phrased specific purpose statement includes three key elements:

- General purpose
- Intended audience
- Exact goal

To inform my audience about the signs of skin cancer is an example of a specific purpose statement for an informative speech. *To persuade my audience to stop texting while driving* is an example of a specific purpose statement for a persuasive speech. Specific purpose statements guide the direction of the speech, and they serve as one of the most critical early steps of the speechmaking process.

The specific purpose statement leads into the thesis statement, which is the central idea or theme of the speech. The thesis of an informative speech summarizes what a speaker wants an audience to learn. Residual message is the term used to describe what a speaker hopes listeners will remember from a speech. *There are three primary causes of heart disease* is an example of a thesis statement for an informative speech. *All high school athletes should be drug-tested* is an example of a thesis statement for a persuasive speech. The thesis statement of an informative speech should be neutral, and the thesis statement of a persuasive speech should express a clear opinion.

The formation of the specific purpose statement occurs early in the speech process, but the thesis statement typically develops after research and analysis of the topic. A well-written thesis statement helps develop main ideas for a speech because it infers a question. In the previous informative speech thesis, the main ideas of the speech might be the three main causes of heart disease. Similarly, the reasons for drug testing all high school athletes would be presented in the body of the speech.

In addition to generating key ideas, a speech thesis focuses audience attention. For informative speeches, the thesis sentence is most often stated early in the presentation. For persuasive speeches, the time to introduce your thesis statement depends on the audience. If an audience analysis has determined that listeners are neutral or positive towards the speech topic, then clearly stating the thesis early in the presentation is appropriate. If the audience of a persuasive speech is most likely hostile to the speaker's position, then arguments and evidence should be provided before gradually presenting the thesis.

RESEARCH, CONTENT, AND ORGANIZATION

Once a topic and the specific purpose of a speech have been determined, research of the subject matter needs to occur. If the speech topic is an area familiar to the writer, then life stories and personal experiences make excellent additions to any presentation. However, most speeches cannot rely solely on the expertise of the speaker, so supplemental information needs to be gathered.

Research: Library versus the Internet

Even in the age of the Internet, the library remains the primary place to seek information for a speech using a number of different library sources—both paper and electronic:

- Books
- Periodical databases
- Newspapers
- Encyclopedias
- Government publications
- Quotation books

- Biographical aids
- Atlases and gazetteers

If the topic of a speech has been a significant issue for at least six months, then it is highly likely that information can be located in a book. Information regarding more recent issues and topics will be found in periodicals, which are magazines and professional journals that are published on a regular basis, such as weekly, bi-weekly, or monthly. Periodical databases help researchers locate particular articles from magazines and journals and typically provide abstracts, or summaries, of each article. General databases, such as *Reader's Guide* and *Lexis/Nexis*, include popular magazines as well as major academic journals. For topics not covered in general periodicals, search special databases, such as *ERIC*. Libraries keep copies of current issues of local newspapers, and they keep back issues on microfilm. *Lexis/Nexis* and *ProQuest* are useful tools for locating articles from national and international newspapers. When information is needed about contemporary individuals, biographical aids, such as *Who's Who in America*, serve as useful resources. Atlases, which are books of maps, and gazetteers, which are geographical dictionaries, are resources for facts about places around the world.

In addition to the library, the Internet serves a significant role in modern research, although the accuracy of information is a concern. The wealth of information available on the Internet is extensive, but unlike libraries, the Internet lacks quality-control mechanisms. Search engines, such as Google and Yahoo, index Web pages during searches for information, but they do not evaluate Web sites. In response to the questionable nature of many Web sites, virtual libraries have been created. Virtual libraries combine Internet technology with information organized in the same format as a traditional library. Although virtual libraries lack the quantity of the Internet, the information is screened for accuracy and reliability.

Conducting Interviews

Research interviews are another useful tool for gathering information for speeches, depending on the topic. College professors, business professionals, physicians, psychologists, and engineers all offer their own expertise that may prove useful and interesting in a speech. In order for an interview to be successful, a few steps need to occur.

1. Determine the purpose of the interview.
2. Write out questions that are intelligent and meaningful.
3. Choose an individual to interview and arrange an appointment.

During an interview, it is important to remain flexible and attentive. Follow-up questions help gain additional information from primary questions, which are prepared in advance. Open questions are broad questions designed to discover the interviewee's values and perspectives. In contrast, closed questions seek brief answers. Being appropriately dressed, arriving on time, and maintaining the purpose of the interview show respect for the interviewee's time. Taking accurate notes or recording the interview ensures that the information gathered will not be lost.

Speech Content and Supporting Materials

Effective speeches require evidence to validate and explain opinions and issues. Supporting material is content that is incorporated into a speech that provides information, maintains listener interest, and asserts persuasive evidence. Supporting materials include examples, narratives, testimonies, statistics, and quotations.

Major Types of Supporting Materials

Narratives	Stories told to illustrate an abstract concept and to illustrate a point
Examples	Specific instances used to illustrate a larger group of people, ideas, or conditions
Testimonies	Opinions of experts or eye-witness accounts that support a speaker's claim
Statistics	Numerical data that clarify a speaker's point
Quotations	Explanations or opinions used verbatim in a speech

Narratives, which are stories incorporated into a speech, help maintain listener attention because most people find stories interesting. Narratives, which help illustrate abstract ideas, come in three basic types: explanatory, exemplary, and persuasive. As suggested by the name, explanatory narratives explain events, such as the burning of Atlanta during the Civil War. Exemplary narratives are examples of excellence, such as rags-to-riches stories about famous people. Persuasive narratives attempt to change attitudes, such as stories about financially struggling families who would benefit from donations to charitable organizations. Anecdotes are brief stories that are usually humorous.

Like narratives, examples are useful when an abstract concept needs clarification for the audience. Brief examples, which are also known as specific instances, are typically one or two sentences in length, while extended examples are at least three sentences. Actual examples are those that describe real events, while hypothetical examples are imaginary. It is important to clarify for an audience whether an example is real or hypothetical in order to uphold the ethical nature of a speech.

Testimonies add substance to a speech, with expert opinions that support the speaker's claims. Although personal testimonies can be incorporated into a speech, listeners are generally more persuaded by expert testimonies. When using expert testimonies, it is important to make the competence of the individual clear to the audience, especially if the person's name is unknown to most listeners. The testimony's unbiased nature should be emphasized so that the information will have a significant impact on the audience. Testimonies should also be recent to be the most effective.

Statistics, which are verifiable summary figures, illustrate points in informative speeches. In persuasive speeches, statistics serve to provide the basis of claims and arguments. When included in speeches, it is important to remember that statistics should be:

- from reliable and perhaps multiple sources.
- recent to avoid misleading listeners with invalid data.
- used comparatively to make them easier to understand.
- used in moderation because a few interesting numbers are far more effective than an overwhelming amount of data.

Quotations that explain or illustrate a point can be effective in speeches, as long as they are not too lengthy or are overused. As with any supporting materials, acknowledgment of the person who made the quote should be included in the speech to avoid plagiarism.

Evaluating Supporting Material

Effective research will most likely result in more information than necessary, so knowing how to evaluate supporting materials is essential. Evidence should have the following characteristics:

- Relevant and significant
- Easily understood
- Striking and unique
- Credible, ethical, and accurate

Public speakers also support their assertions with proofs, which Aristotle described as either extrinsic or intrinsic. Extrinsic proofs support claims with objective evidence, such as laws and confessions. Intrinsic proofs, also known as artistic proofs, are based on the speaker's character, the emotional nature of the issue, and the logic of the argument to persuade listeners. Aristotle referred to three kinds of persuasive appeals, or intrinsic proofs, used in public speaking.

Types of Persuasive Appeals

Logos	The appeal to reason or logic
Ethos	The persuasive appeal of a speaker's moral character and knowledge
Pathos	The appeal to emotion

Logical proof, or logos, takes place when a speaker attempts to persuade an audience with rational evidence and arguments. In order for logical proof to be effective, evidence and supporting materials closely connect to the arguments presented in a speech. In modern society, ethos is referred to as source or speaker credibility. Credible speakers are viewed as knowledgeable about the speech topic, trustworthy, friendly, poised, and energetic. Emotional proof, or pathos, involves the use of emotional appeals to persuade an audience. Public speakers may evoke negative emotions from listeners, such as fear, guilt, shame, anger, and sadness. The goal of tapping into negative emotions is to convince listeners that the proposal presented in the speech will reduce such feelings. For example, a speech attempting to convince teenagers to stop smoking might include cancer and heart disease statistics in an attempt to arouse fear and ultimately the elimination of a harmful habit. Speeches may also arouse positive emotions, such as joy, pride, relief, hope, and compassion. For example, a speaker who is trying to encourage the audience to volunteer with the Red Cross would describe the feelings of pride associated with assisting hurricane and tornado victims.

In persuasive speeches, a speaker's goal is to argue a point with reasons supported by evidence. Every argument consists of a claim, which is the conclusion a speaker wants listeners to accept, and evidence, which consists of supporting materials. There are four primary types of arguments used in persuasive speeches.

Common Types of Arguments

Type	Definition	Example
Argue from example	Draw a conclusion from one or more instances or examples	I like the paintings of Monet, Renoir, and Cassatt. I like Impressionist art.
Argue from analogy	Illustrate similarities between two things or events	David likes Bach, Beethoven, and Brahms. I know Kate likes Bach and Beethoven, so she will probably like Brahms.
Argue from causation	Draw a conclusion that an event that occurs first is responsible for a later event	Home sales will increase because interest rates have fallen.
Argue from sign	Use an observable symptom or indicator as proof of a claim	The Republican candidate will be elected. She has more campaign workers and yard signs in the community.

Effective speeches incorporate multiple types of arguments and avoid common reasoning fallacies or errors. The most common types of fallacies that occur in public speeches are hasty generalization, false cause, invalid analogy, and ad hominem.

- *Hasty generalizations* occur when a speaker jumps to a conclusion without sufficient evidence.

- *False-cause fallacies* occur when a speaker makes the invalid assumption that one event causes another event, when in fact the events may have been coincidental.

- *Invalid analogies* occur when a speaker compares two events or things that are not alike.

- *Ad hominen* refers to the fallacy of attacking or praising the character or integrity of the person making the argument rather than dealing with the issue in question.

Organizing Your Speech

The process of organizing a speech takes time, but it provides a speaker with the opportunity to see which points need additional development and which ones need trimming. Organized speeches, whether they are informative or persuasive, are easier for audiences to follow and to remember. Speaker credibility also increases with speech structure because audience members are more likely to view an organized individual as competent.

The body of the speech needs organization before an introduction or conclusion is written. As mentioned earlier, the thesis statement serves as the starting point for developing main points. Main points are the major points made by a speaker in the body of a speech. Most speeches include two to five main points—more points may make a speech too confusing for listeners. Main points should be relevant and interesting to the audience and worded in a parallel format. Parallel statements help listeners understand and follow a speech more easily than points constructed in different grammatical styles. Main points should also be distinct, which means there should be no overlap among them.

After the main points have been determined, information and supporting materials need to be structured in a strategic organizational pattern. Strategic organization refers to arranging a speech in a specific way in order to achieve a specific result with a specific audience.

Organizational Patterns

The best organizational pattern for a speech depends on the topic, purpose, and audience. There are six types of organizational patterns used most often in public speaking:

- Topical
- Temporal
- Spatial
- Problem-solution
- Causal
- Motivated

The topical pattern of speech organization is useful when a topic is easily subdivided, such as the five branches of the U.S. military. The main points of a topical speech are parts of a whole. Topical order works well with both informational and persuasive speeches, so it is a commonly used pattern.

The temporal pattern of organization is also known as chronological order, and the main points follow a time pattern. Temporal patterns are most often used with informative speeches. For example, a speech about the construction of Mount Rushmore would be appropriate for a temporal pattern. The main points would follow the creation of Mount Rushmore from the first carving until its completion. Temporal patterns are also useful when explaining a process, such as how to change a flat tire.

Spatial order is a type of speech structure in which main points are organized in a directional pattern—top to bottom, left to right, east to west, or inside to outside. Speeches about the layout of a university or the skeletal structure of the human body would be suitable for spatial order. Spatial order is another organizational pattern that is most appropriate for informative speeches.

The problem-solution pattern is common among persuasive speeches when a speaker wants to convey the existence of a problem and to provide a solution. In the problem-solution structure, the first main point focuses on the existence of the problem, and the second main point offers a solution to the problem.

Causal order, or the cause-effect pattern, organizes main points to illustrate a cause-effect relationship. The causal order calls for dividing a speech into two main points, similar to the problem-solution pattern. A speech about teenage drug use might be appropriate for a cause-effect organization. Effects of illicit drug use by adolescents would follow the potential causes. However, causal order lends itself to some flexibility—either the causes or the effects can be presented first, depending on which order is more appropriate for the topic. Causal order is used in both persuasive and informative speeches.

The motivated sequence is an organizational pattern developed in the 1930s by Alan H. Monroe, a communications professor. Monroe created the pattern for sales presentations, but it has since been found useful in all types of persuasive and informative speeches. Motivated sequence is useful when a speaker wants listeners to respond in a positive way, so it is often employed in political speeches and advertisements. Rather than structuring a speech in three parts—introduction, body, and conclusion—the motivated sequence divides a speech into five steps:

> Step 1: Gain attention from listeners.
>
> Step 2: Establish a need or a problem.
>
> Step 3: Satisfy the need by offering a solution.
>
> Step 4: Visualize the need of being satisfied in the future.
>
> Step 5: Ask for action from the audience to ensure the need is satisfied.

More Organizational Patterns

While the six previously described organizational patterns are the ones most commonly used in public speeches, other patterns are available. Some are appropriate for both informative and persuasive speeches, while others are more useful with one type or the other. These patterns include:

- Statement of reasons
- Structure-function
- Pro-and-con

The statement-of-reasons pattern is most appropriate for persuasive arguments. In this format, a speaker who has three reasons presents the strongest reason last and the second strongest reason first. The weakest reason is placed in the middle. In this structure, the speaker hopes to leave listeners thinking about the most persuasive argument.

The structure-function pattern is especially useful with informative speeches in which a speaker wants to illustrate the structural and functional qualities of something. For example, a speech about the different parts of a local government and the operations that occur in each part would fit the criteria for the structure-function organization.

The pro-and-con or advantages-disadvantages pattern is appropriate for both informative and persuasive speeches. Informative speeches in which the speaker needs to explain the benefits and drawbacks of a particular product or method are most appropriate for this pattern. Persuasive speeches that discuss the value of one plan or idea over another often use a pro-and-con pattern.

Introductions and Conclusions

After the body of a speech is complete, focus should turn to the introduction and conclusion. The introduction of a speech serves a number of critical functions:

- Gain the attention and interest of the audience
- Preview the topic of the speech
- Establish speaker credibility and a connection with listeners

Speech introductions are typically 10 percent of the entire speech, so a speech that is 500 words in length needs an introduction that is 40–60 words. Creativity is the key to a good introduction, and there are six primary types of introductions commonly used by public speakers.

Types of Introductions

Startling statement	A shocking statement that relates to the speech topic
Rhetorical question	A question relevant to the topic that listeners answer mentally rather than vocally
Story	An interesting story related to the main point of the speech
Personal reference	An illustration of how the speech topic is relevant to audience members
Quotation	An attention-getting or thought-provoking quotation
Suspense	Wording that leaves the audience uncertain about the topic and raises listener curiosity

Keep in mind that introductions are only valuable if they directly relate to the speech topic. Irrelevant stories, quotations, or statements may initially intrigue listeners, but if the introduction fails to connect to the subject of the speech, listeners may become annoyed or confused. Establishing credibility and goodwill with listeners is critical during the introduction. An audience needs to perceive that a speaker is qualified to discuss a topic and has the best interests of listeners in mind.

Effective Conclusions

Since a conclusion may be the most lasting impression of a speech for listeners, effective speakers take the time to construct memorable ones. Speech conclusions serve three primary functions:

- Alert the audience that the speech is ending
- Summarize the speech
- Clarify what listeners should think or do in response to the speech

Conclusions should forewarn audience members that a speech is about to end. An abrupt ending to a speech may leave listeners confused, so providing signals to the audience is essential. Phrases, such as *in conclusion* and *to summarize,* are obvious cues that a speaker is preparing to stop. Experienced speakers use their voices and bodies to indicate the conclusion of a speech. Dramatic gestures, stepping away from the podium, pausing, and changing vocal pitch signal the end of a speech. A speaker who utilizes a crescendo ending builds a speech to a powerful and intense conclusion. In contrast, a dissolve ending evokes emotions by fading gradually to one final dramatic statement.

The second function of a speech conclusion is to summarize the main points and reinforce the thesis or central idea. Some speakers restate the main points, while others summarize the main ideas of the speech into a single statement. Quotations, dramatic statements, and references to information presented in the introduction are appropriate ways to reinforce main ideas.

The third function of a speech conclusion involves clarifying what audience members should think or do after the speech. The response that a speaker seeks from listeners is the anticipated response. Anticipated responses are not limited to persuasive speeches but apply to informative speeches as well. With informative speeches, the anticipated response is what an audience should remember, and with persuasive speeches, it is what listeners should think or do.

Appropriate Language and Style

The introduction, body, and conclusion of a speech are only effective if they flow well together, so effective public speakers address issues of language and style. Linking various ideas within a speech occurs with words and phrases known as connectives. Connectives help listeners understand the relationship between one concept and another. A speech without connectives lacks flow and confuses listeners. The four types of connectives used in public speaking are:

- Transitions
- Signposts
- Internal previews
- Internal summaries

Transitions are words or phrases that indicate when a speaker is moving from one point to another. Transitions are most commonly included when a speaker is shifting from the introduction to the body, from the body to the conclusion, and between main points in the speech. In the following examples, the connectives are underlined.

> Now that we have looked at what nanotechnology is, let's see how it is used.

Signposts are a second type of connective used in speeches. Signposts consist of brief statements that indicate to listeners where the speaker is in the speech. Sometimes, signposts are numerical, as indicated in the following example.

> The second reason to protect your skin with sunscreen is to prevent the development of melanoma.

Many speakers also use questions as signposts because questions invite listeners to think about the answer and become more attentive.

> So, why do teenagers begin smoking when they are aware of the health risks?

In addition to alerting audiences as to the speaker's location in a speech, signposts are also useful in signaling that an important point is coming up.

> Foremost, you need to remember that...

> Make sure that you keep this in mind...

> This is a critical point...

Internal previews are another type of connective used in the body of public speeches. As suggested by the name, an internal preview is a statement that tells the audience what to expect next. Internal previews differ from transitions and signposts because they are more detailed.

> In discussing the effects of World War II on Japan, we'll first look at the economic consequences of the war and then at the cultural impact.

Although internal previews are not necessary for every main point, they are useful when an audience may need assistance grasping concepts presented in a speech.

The fourth connective is an internal summary, which reviews the points that a speaker has just made. Internal summaries are especially useful when a speaker has finished discussing a complicated or especially significant point. Before moving on to the next point, the speaker will provide a statement in the form of an internal summary to remind an audience of what has just been presented.

Effectively used connectives help speakers form coherent speeches that are easy for listeners to understand. Most speakers use a combination of different connectives to unify the main points presented in a speech.

Make the Most of Your Words

Not only are connectives important in joining ideas presented in a speech, but words are important as well. The language a speaker uses during a presentation has a significant impact on the informative and persuasive nature of a speech. Words convey different meanings, and choosing the best ones to use in a speech can increase clarity for an audience.

Words have two basic kinds of meaning. The denotative meaning of a word is its literal and objective meaning found in a dictionary. For example, the dictionary definition of the noun *government* means *a branch of the ruling authority of a state or nation*. The connotative meaning of a word is subjective and variable. Therefore, the connotative meaning of the word *government* includes the feelings and emotions that the word suggests, which will vary within an audience. Some audience members may think of democracy or beneficial services that the government provides. However, others may associate government with bureaucracy, politics, and overspending. Effective public speakers choose words that are less likely to set off intense reactions, and they are aware of and sensitive to a word's denotation and connotation.

Using language clearly and specifically is essential to an effective speech because listeners do not have the benefit of following along with a written copy. In comparison to written language, oral style includes the use of familiar words, connectives, and references to the speaker, such as *in my opinion*, or *it seems to me*. Public speakers are also likely to use concrete words rather than abstract words. Concrete words refer to tangible objects that are easy to visualize, such as *flat tire, beagle,* and *digital camera*. Abstract words, such as *science, entertainment,* and *technology,* refer to ideas or concepts that conjure up different images for different people. Abstract words are typically more ambiguous than concrete words. Although the use of abstract words cannot be completely avoided, speeches dominated by concrete words are typically clearer for the audience.

While concrete words serve to improve the clarity of a speech, they can also be used effectively with imagery. Imagery refers to vivid language included in a speech that creates mental images of experiences, objects, or concepts. Concrete words establish sights, sounds, and emotions that draw listeners into a speech, while similes and metaphors bring life and creativity to a speech.

Similes make direct comparisons between two unlike things using *like* or *as:*

> As the rainstorm approached, the clouds swirled in the sky like cotton candy being twisted onto a stick.

Metaphors compare two dissimilar things without the use of *like* or *as:*

> The air in the crowded stadium was thick with anticipation while everyone waited for the concert to begin.

Language used in a speech should not only be vivid and clear, but it should also be appropriate for the occasion, the audience, the topic, and the speaker. First, public speakers must adapt their language to the formality of the occasion. For example, a teacher's presentation to a small group of co-workers would be less formal than one given to the school board. Second, appropriate language avoids jargon, slang, or technical words unless the audience is familiar with such terms. Specialized vocabulary, such as medical or cyber terms, is only appropriate if the audience understands it; otherwise, specialized words should be replaced with terms that are more general. Third, the speech topic also determines the appropriateness of language. A speech about how to build a birdhouse calls for straightforward language, but a speech about the art of Renoir may require imagery to convey an appreciation of his paintings. Finally, language should be appropriate to the speaker. Effective speakers convey a particular style through the language they employ. Studying the styles of other speakers may help develop an awareness of language used in public speeches.

DELIVERING A SPEECH SO AN AUDIENCE WILL LISTEN

Speech delivery takes time and practice to become polished. Speakers vary in how they present a speech, and what works for one person may not work for another. There are four basic methods of speech delivery.

Methods of Speech Delivery

Speaking impromptu	Speech involves little to no specific or immediate preparation
Speaking from a manuscript	Entire speech is written out and read
Speaking from memory	Entire speech is written out and memorized
Speaking extemporaneously	Speech is prepared and presented from a basic set of notes or an outline

Impromptu speeches occur in classroom and business settings and during job interviews. Effective impromptu speeches require speakers to maintain eye contact, respond to feedback, and organize thoughts. The disadvantages are the inability to research information and focus on style and language.

A manuscript speech enables the speaker to control the time it takes to present a speech, which is useful for televised speeches. Manuscripts also eliminate the fear of forgetting ideas or words. However, manuscripts often prevent speakers from sounding natural, maintaining eye contact, and responding to audience feedback.

Like a manuscript speech, a memorized speech allows a speaker to control timing and wording. Unlike a speaker who reads a speech, a speaker who memorizes one can make eye contact with the audience. However, an obvious disadvantage is forgetting sections of a speech.

Extemporaneous is the most common method of speech delivery. An extemporaneous speech is researched and planned, but the precise wording of the speech is not written out. Instead, speakers refer to brief notes or an outline to remember the ideas they wish to present and the order to follow.

Physical Aspects of Speech Presentation

In addition to the method of delivery, speakers need to consider the physical aspects of a speech presentation, such as voice, articulation, and bodily movements. Since a speaker's voice conveys the words and ideas of a speech, it is important to understand its various elements—pitch, volume, rate, and quality.

- *Pitch* is the relative highness or lowness of a speaker's voice. Changing pitch and emphasizing certain words and phrases can help communicate ideas effectively.
- *Volume* refers to the loudness or intensity of a speaker's voice. Problems with volume include fading off at the end of sentences, speaking too loudly, and speaking too softly.
- *Rate* is the speed at which a person talks. Most people speak an average of 150 words per minute. Speaking too fast, too slowly, or without any variation are problems associated with speech rate.
- *Quality* refers to the tone or sound of a speaker's voice. Clear, pleasant tones are desirable in public speakers; however, some people's voices are breathy, harsh, raspy, or nasally.

Articulation and pronunciation are additional elements related to speech delivery. Articulation refers to the movement of the tongue, palate, teeth, lips, jaw, and vocal cords to produce sounds. Pronunciation refers to the production of syllables in a word based upon accepted standards. For example, in the word *dictionary*, articulation refers to how each of the ten letters and their sounds are shaped—d-i-c-t-i-o-n-a-r-y. Pronunciation of the word refers to how the sounds are grouped and accented—dik'-shuh-ner-ee.

Problems associated with articulation and pronunciation plague some speakers, but most are easily corrected with awareness and practice. One common problem is the error of omission. An error of omission means that a speaker leaves off a sound or a syllable in a word, such as saying *comp-ny* instead of *comp-a-ny*. Another problem is the error of substitution, which means that a speaker substitutes an incorrect sound for a correct sound. Errors of substitution most often involve substituting *d* for *t* or *th*, such as *beder* instead of *better*. Errors of addition occur when speakers add unnecessary sounds to words, such as *ath-a-lete* instead of *ath-lete*. Pronunciation errors typically involve accenting words incorrectly and pronouncing silent sounds.

Pauses are another tool utilized by public speakers. Filled pauses are those that speakers fill with utterances like *ah*, *well*, and *um*. Filled pauses should be avoided because they give the impression that a speaker is unprepared or tentative. On the other hand, unfilled pauses of one or two seconds can be used to a speaker's advantage in many cases. Unfilled pauses are appropriate at the beginning of a speech as a speaker becomes settled or at transitional moments in a speech to indicate that one thought has ended and another is beginning.

Speakers not only communicate with their voices, they also communicate with their body language. Nonverbal bodily actions, such as eye contact, facial expressions, gestures, and movements, convey information to an audience. The most important nonverbal form of communication is appropriate eye contact with listeners. Speakers who do not make eye contact with an audience are often perceived as aloof, uncaring, and less credible than speakers who maintain eye contact. Facial expressions are understood universally, and they convey emotions such as anger, fear, boredom, and excitement. Gesturing with hands, arms, and fingers can help emphasize points. Movement refers to motion with the whole body, and during speeches, movement helps speakers and listeners remain attentive.

Effective Listening

Just as effective speaking requires practice and consideration, effective listening calls for work as well. Many people believe hearing and listening are the same activities, but that is not the case. Hearing is a physical function that involves the ear picking up sound waves and sending them to the brain. Listening is a selective activity that involves paying close attention to and interpreting what is heard. The listening process can be broken down into five steps:

1. *Receiving:* hearing transmitted sounds and selecting the ones to attend to or to ignore
2. *Understanding:* assigning meaning to what was said with regard to the thought and the emotion
3. *Remembering:* retaining and recalling information that has been heard
4. *Evaluating:* judging and criticizing the usefulness and truthfulness of a message
5. *Responding:* answering and giving verbal and nonverbal feedback

Listening can enhance critical thinking skills, and there are four types of listening.

Types of Listening

Appreciative listening	Listening for pleasure, such as to music or a comic's jokes
Empathic listening	Listening to give emotional support to the speaker, such as when friends listen to each other's problems
Comprehensive listening	Listening to understand a message, such as during a class lecture
Critical listening	Listening to evaluate a message and deciding to accept or reject the information, such as when a jury member listens to participants in a trial

Many people are poor listeners, but improving listening skills can be extremely beneficial in all areas of life. The primary reason for poor listening skills is people succumbing to physical and mental distractions rather than focusing on the message. Another cause of poor listening skills is focusing too hard on a message and trying to remember every detail rather than the overall theme. Poor listeners are also guilty of jumping to conclusions and making assumptions about what the speaker will say without actually listening closely. The final cause of poor listening occurs when the personal appearance and delivery style of the speaker earn more attention than the actual message—a case of judging a book by its cover.

Although poor listening skills are common, effective listening skills can be developed with practice. The first step to improving listening habits is realizing that listening is active rather than passive. Active listening is the structured process of listening and responding to a speaker. Active listening aids in both comprehension and retention and may involve any combination of the following activities:

- Sitting up straight
- Remaining quiet
- Silently paraphrasing
- Taking notes
- Organizing ideas
- Developing questions
- Assessing the speaker's organization
- Noticing the speaker's nonverbal behaviors

In addition to active listening, effective listening also involves listening with empathy, which means understanding the speaker's feelings and point of view. Effective listeners also listen with an open mind by recognizing personal biases and avoiding the prejudgment of a message. Listening for the total meaning of a message is another critical element of effective listening, especially when listening to speeches. Listening for the complete meaning of a speaker's message requires paying attention to verbal and nonverbal messages, connecting specific ideas to the thesis, and focusing on deep as well as literal ideas presented in a speech.

CRITICIZING AND EVALUATING SPEECHES

Effectively listening to a speech involves paying attention to what a speaker says and making every attempt to comprehend and retain the message. The final step of effective listening involves criticism. Criticism is the process of evaluating a message and deciding whether it is believable, thorough, and valuable based on specific standards. It is important that individuals understand how to criticize all types of communication for a number of reasons.

- Critical analysis aids in sorting through the bombardment of messages that people receive each day to determine which information is relevant and honest.
- Critical analysis encourages people to maintain evaluation standards and to appreciate the creativity of others.

The Latin origin of the term *criticism* means *able to judge or discern,* which is contrary to the negative connotation that many people associate with criticism. In fact, criticism may be both negative and positive, and it is an important aspect of improving public speaking skills. Giving constructive criticism requires active listening on the part of audience members.

Criticism of a speech should be based upon established standards and principles of public speaking. The following elements of a speech are often evaluated during classroom speech presentations, although they are applicable to any form of public speaking:

- Subject and purpose
- Audience, occasion, and context
- Research
- Thesis and main points
- Supporting materials
- Organization
- Style and language
- Introduction, conclusion, and connectives
- Delivery

When giving speech criticism, it is important to follow a few guidelines to make the process as valuable for the speaker as possible because the goal is to help individuals improve public speaking skills:

- Point out the positive more than the negative
- Provide specific comments rather than general ones
- Be objective instead of biased
- Give constructive comments
- Structure comments as I-messages
- Consider ethical responsibilities

First, stress positive elements of a speech presentation before mentioning the negative to show consideration for the speaker's feelings. Even the worst speech includes some positive characteristics, and it is important to find strengths before pointing out weaknesses.

Being as specific as possible when providing criticism is essential. Remember, the goal of speech criticism given in a classroom setting is to help improve public speaking skills. General or vague comments serve no useful purpose, while specific comments are very beneficial. For example, rather than telling a speaker that the supporting materials in a speech are good, a critic should explain that a particular example is good because of its interest or drama.

Third, speech criticism should be objective and devoid of bias. Bias is a prejudice that prevents impartial evaluation of a speech. Speeches about controversial topics, such as abortion, global warming, or same-sex marriage, may require a critic to set aside personal opinions or biases. Critics should focus only on the previously mentioned elements of speech evaluation, such as research, thesis, organization, and delivery. Similarly, speeches that assert a thesis with which a critic agrees should not be evaluated positively only because of the speaker's position on an issue.

In addition, criticism should be constructive, which means that a critic should explain how to improve a weak aspect of a speech. For example, instead of commenting that the conclusion was boring, it would be more constructive to tell the speaker that the conclusion would have been more effective if it had referred back to the quotation given in the introduction. In addition, criticism is more constructive when it is not overwhelming to the speaker. In other words, criticism should not be a lengthy list of problems but should focus upon a few aspects of the speech.

The phrasing of a comment is almost as important as the comment itself. Criticism of a speech is more effective when phrased as an *I-message* instead of a *you-message*. Rather than saying "you did not use enough examples in your speech," an effective critic might say "I would have been more persuaded by your arguments if your speech had included additional examples."

Finally, speech critics have ethical responsibilities to speakers. Ethical critics avoid mixing feelings towards a speaker with speech evaluation. Liking or disliking a speaker should have no bearing on the evaluation of a speech. As mentioned previously, bias towards the subject matter of a speech should not play a role in the ethical evaluation of a speech. Ethical critics are also sensitive to cultural issues. Ethnocentrism, which is the tendency to assess behaviors and values of your own culture as superior to those of another culture, does not affect the evaluations given by ethical critics. Ethical critics appreciate diversity and do not give positive or negative criticism based on gender, religion, or nationality.

POST-TEST ANSWER SHEET

1. Ⓐ Ⓑ Ⓒ Ⓓ   13. Ⓐ Ⓑ Ⓒ Ⓓ   25. Ⓐ Ⓑ Ⓒ Ⓓ   37. Ⓐ Ⓑ Ⓒ Ⓓ   49. Ⓐ Ⓑ Ⓒ Ⓓ

2. Ⓐ Ⓑ Ⓒ Ⓓ   14. Ⓐ Ⓑ Ⓒ Ⓓ   26. Ⓐ Ⓑ Ⓒ Ⓓ   38. Ⓐ Ⓑ Ⓒ Ⓓ   50. Ⓐ Ⓑ Ⓒ Ⓓ

3. Ⓐ Ⓑ Ⓒ Ⓓ   15. Ⓐ Ⓑ Ⓒ Ⓓ   27. Ⓐ Ⓑ Ⓒ Ⓓ   39. Ⓐ Ⓑ Ⓒ Ⓓ   51. Ⓐ Ⓑ Ⓒ Ⓓ

4. Ⓐ Ⓑ Ⓒ Ⓓ   16. Ⓐ Ⓑ Ⓒ Ⓓ   28. Ⓐ Ⓑ Ⓒ Ⓓ   40. Ⓐ Ⓑ Ⓒ Ⓓ   52. Ⓐ Ⓑ Ⓒ Ⓓ

5. Ⓐ Ⓑ Ⓒ Ⓓ   17. Ⓐ Ⓑ Ⓒ Ⓓ   29. Ⓐ Ⓑ Ⓒ Ⓓ   41. Ⓐ Ⓑ Ⓒ Ⓓ   53. Ⓐ Ⓑ Ⓒ Ⓓ

6. Ⓐ Ⓑ Ⓒ Ⓓ   18. Ⓐ Ⓑ Ⓒ Ⓓ   30. Ⓐ Ⓑ Ⓒ Ⓓ   42. Ⓐ Ⓑ Ⓒ Ⓓ   54. Ⓐ Ⓑ Ⓒ Ⓓ

7. Ⓐ Ⓑ Ⓒ Ⓓ   19. Ⓐ Ⓑ Ⓒ Ⓓ   31. Ⓐ Ⓑ Ⓒ Ⓓ   43. Ⓐ Ⓑ Ⓒ Ⓓ   55. Ⓐ Ⓑ Ⓒ Ⓓ

8. Ⓐ Ⓑ Ⓒ Ⓓ   20. Ⓐ Ⓑ Ⓒ Ⓓ   32. Ⓐ Ⓑ Ⓒ Ⓓ   44. Ⓐ Ⓑ Ⓒ Ⓓ   56. Ⓐ Ⓑ Ⓒ Ⓓ

9. Ⓐ Ⓑ Ⓒ Ⓓ   21. Ⓐ Ⓑ Ⓒ Ⓓ   33. Ⓐ Ⓑ Ⓒ Ⓓ   45. Ⓐ Ⓑ Ⓒ Ⓓ   57. Ⓐ Ⓑ Ⓒ Ⓓ

10. Ⓐ Ⓑ Ⓒ Ⓓ   22. Ⓐ Ⓑ Ⓒ Ⓓ   34. Ⓐ Ⓑ Ⓒ Ⓓ   46. Ⓐ Ⓑ Ⓒ Ⓓ   58. Ⓐ Ⓑ Ⓒ Ⓓ

11. Ⓐ Ⓑ Ⓒ Ⓓ   23. Ⓐ Ⓑ Ⓒ Ⓓ   35. Ⓐ Ⓑ Ⓒ Ⓓ   47. Ⓐ Ⓑ Ⓒ Ⓓ   59. Ⓐ Ⓑ Ⓒ Ⓓ

12. Ⓐ Ⓑ Ⓒ Ⓓ   24. Ⓐ Ⓑ Ⓒ Ⓓ   36. Ⓐ Ⓑ Ⓒ Ⓓ   48. Ⓐ Ⓑ Ⓒ Ⓓ   60. Ⓐ Ⓑ Ⓒ Ⓓ

answer sheet

POST-TEST

Directions: Carefully read each of the following 60 questions. Choose the best answer to each question, and darken its letter on your answer sheet. The Answer Key and Explanations can be found following this post-test.

1. Which of the following has the greatest impact on the consistency of an audience member's attitude?
   (A) Ethnicity
   (B) Religion
   (C) Gender
   (D) Age

2. An informative speech discussing the three branches of the federal government would most likely be arranged in which of the following patterns?
   (A) Temporal
   (B) Spatial
   (C) Topical
   (D) Causal

3. A speech given without any specific or advanced preparation is referred to by which of the following terms?
   (A) Impromptu
   (B) Manuscript
   (C) Spontaneous
   (D) Extemporaneous

4. Which of the following decreases a speaker's ability to respond to facial expressions?
   (A) Post-dinner speech
   (B) Large audience size
   (C) Homogeneous audience
   (D) Formal setting and occasion

5. Testimonies, narratives, statistics, and quotations are characterized as
   (A) types of arguments.
   (B) propositions of fact.
   (C) supporting materials.
   (D) emotional appeals.

6. *To inform* and *to persuade* are examples of which of the following elements of a speech?
   (A) General purpose
   (B) Specific purpose
   (C) Thesis statement
   (D) Topic sentence

7. Presenting another person's unique idea as one's own is an example of which of the following?
   (A) Self-fulfilling prophecy
   (B) Emotional appeal
   (C) Coercion
   (D) Plagiarism

8. Which of the following is the greatest benefit of using the Internet for researching a speech topic?
   (A) Sponsorship
   (B) Quantity
   (C) Credibility
   (D) Accuracy

9. A type of speech pattern that organizes main points in a directional pattern is known as
   (A) structure-function pattern.
   (B) spatial pattern.
   (C) causal pattern.
   (D) temporal pattern.

10. Which of the following is a characteristic of an ethical persuasive speech?
    (A) Name-calling
    (B) Nonparallel language
    (C) Incremental plagiarism
    (D) Representative evidence

11. A student interested in finding a speech topic related to trends and public opinions would most likely use
    (A) polls and surveys.
    (B) news magazines.
    (C) brainstorming.
    (D) personal inventory.

12. Which of the following refers to a short, humorous story included in a speech?
    (A) Brief example
    (B) Personal testimonial
    (C) Hypothetical example
    (D) Anecdote

13. Transitions and signposts are examples of which of the following?
    (A) References
    (B) Connectives
    (C) Internal summaries
    (D) Supporting materials

14. Which of the following is a primary benefit of a manuscript speech?
    (A) Time management
    (B) Maximum eye contact
    (C) Whole-body movement
    (D) Expository communication

15. Which of the following is characteristic of a statement-of-reasons pattern?
    (A) Strongest point presented first
    (B) Weakest point presented first
    (C) Strongest point presented last
    (D) Weakest point presented last

16. Which of the following best explains why most people have poor listening skills?
    (A) Ethnocentrism
    (B) Easily distracted
    (C) Taking notes
    (D) Focusing on nonverbal cues

17. Paraphrasing, sitting up straight, and formulating questions are characteristics of
    (A) appreciative listening.
    (B) empathic listening.
    (C) passive listening.
    (D) active listening.

18. Which of the following is a true statement about the use of testimonies in speeches?
    (A) Personal testimonies are more effective than expert opinions.
    (B) The time and place of a testimony is irrelevant.
    (C) The unbiased nature of the testimony should be established.
    (D) Expert testimonies should be included in all speeches.

19. The notion that the beliefs of your own culture are superior to the beliefs of other cultures is known as
    (A) multiculturalism.
    (B) ethnocentrism.
    (C) anthropology.
    (D) cultural identity.

20. Which of the following is a primary purpose of speech conclusions?
    (A) Apologize for errors
    (B) Answer questions
    (C) Repeat the introduction
    (D) Reinforce the thesis

21. Which of the following refers to the process of tailoring a speech for a specific audience and occasion?
    (A) Audience adaptation
    (B) Audience-centeredness
    (C) Situational audience analysis
    (D) Demographic audience analysis

22. Explaining how to improve a weak element of a speech is known as
    (A) contextual criticism.
    (B) unbiased criticism.
    (C) constructive criticism.
    (D) favorable criticism.

23. In a persuasive speech, the actions or thoughts expected of an audience are referred to as which of the following?
    (A) Performance orientation
    (B) Anticipated response
    (C) Confrontation reaction
    (D) Productive thinking

24. Which of the following is most important when including a quotation in a speech?
    (A) Uttered by a celebrity
    (B) Recently stated
    (C) Emotional quality
    (D) Relevant to topic

25. In which method of speech delivery does a speaker rely on brief notes?
    (A) Extemporaneous
    (B) Chronological
    (C) Impromptu
    (D) Manuscript

26. Which of the following alerts audiences to the subject of an upcoming main point?
    (A) Transition
    (B) Signpost
    (C) Leading question
    (D) Internal preview

27. Introductions are most effective if they have which of the following qualities?
    (A) Spatial organization
    (B) Topic relevancy
    (C) Parallel format
    (D) Distinct main points

28. Speech criticism should be based on
    (A) cultural norms.
    (B) popular opinions.
    (C) empathic listening.
    (D) established standards.

29. A speech body that includes statements beginning with *the first cause*, *the second cause*, and *the third cause* is using which of the following?
    (A) Supporting materials
    (B) Causal order
    (C) Signposts
    (D) Spatial order

30. A single word or a brief phrase included in a speech that indicates a speaker has completed one idea and is moving to a new one is known as
    (A) internal summary.
    (B) signpost.
    (C) internal preview.
    (D) transition.

31. The theme of a speech is expressed in which of the following?
    (A) General purpose statement
    (B) Thesis statement
    (C) Specific purpose statement
    (D) Speech title

32. Which of the following is a problem associated with speech rate?
    (A) Speaking too softly
    (B) Omitting sounds
    (C) Speaking too quickly
    (D) Fading at the end of sentences

post-test

33. Which of the following describes a speaker who exhibits competence, character, and composure?

    (A) Ethos

    (B) Mythic proof

    (C) Logos

    (D) Extrinsic proof

34. Which of the following will most likely establish speaker credibility?

    (A) Ask rhetorical questions

    (B) Choose a timely subject

    (C) Display a pleasant personality

    (D) Select culturally sensitive topics

35. Quotations used in speech introductions should have which of the following characteristics?

    (A) Familiarity with audience

    (B) Thought-provoking

    (C) Humorous

    (D) Suspenseful

36. Words that refer to tangible objects are known as

    (A) jargon.

    (B) concrete.

    (C) context.

    (D) abstract.

37. Pathos is another term for

    (A) emotional appeals.

    (B) speaker credibility.

    (C) logical appeals.

    (D) thesis statement.

38. In which of the following situations should the thesis statement be presented after the presentation of evidence?

    (A) Persuasive speech with a positive audience

    (B) Informative speech with a neutral audience

    (C) Persuasive speech with a hostile audience

    (D) Informative speech with an uneducated audience

39. A speaker who develops a speech to a powerful and intense conclusion is most likely using which of the following?

    (A) Motivated sequence

    (B) Crescendo ending

    (C) Dramatic gestures

    (D) Dissolve ending

40. Adding sounds to words where they do not belong is a problem associated with

    (A) articulation.

    (B) pronunciation.

    (C) pauses.

    (D) proxemics.

41. Which of the following compares dissimilar objects?

    (A) Alliteration

    (B) Transition

    (C) Connective

    (D) Simile

42. A story describing Mother Teresa's humanitarian ministry would be which type of supporting material?

    (A) Peer testimony

    (B) Expert testimony

    (C) Exemplary narrative

    (D) Hypothetical example

43. Hand and arm motions made by a speaker are known as
    (A) movement.
    (B) gestures.
    (C) posture.
    (D) poise.

44. Most speech introductions account for what percentage of the total speech?
    (A) 5 percent
    (B) 10 percent
    (C) 25 percent
    (D) 40 percent

45. Which of the following is most likely a benefit of using I-messages to give criticism?
    (A) Eliminates responsibility
    (B) Encourages listening
    (C) Reduces defensiveness
    (D) Stresses the positive

46. Which of the following is an advantage of an extemporaneous speech?
    (A) Prepare exact wording
    (B) Answer audience questions
    (C) Organize topics by strength
    (D) Respond to audience feedback

47. Which of the following forms the basis of extrinsic proofs?
    (A) Laws
    (B) Emotions
    (C) Credibility
    (D) Reasoning

48. Which of the following is most likely to change during the speechmaking process as research of the subject occurs?
    (A) Thesis
    (B) Residual message
    (C) Specific purpose
    (D) General purpose

49. Main points of a speech should be constructed as
    (A) compound sentences.
    (B) infinitive statements.
    (C) parallel statements.
    (D) rhetorical questions.

50. Whether language is appropriate for a speech is most dependent upon
    (A) feedback.
    (B) topic.
    (C) credibility.
    (D) length.

51. The emphasis of different words in a sentence is most dependent upon which of the following?
    (A) Pitch
    (B) Tone
    (C) Rate
    (D) Proxemics

52. A speaker at a fundraiser who describes the plight of starving families in Africa is using
    (A) exemplary narrative.
    (B) persuasive narrative.
    (C) testimony.
    (D) statistics.

53. How many main points are appropriate for most speeches?
    (A) One
    (B) Three
    (C) Six
    (D) Nine

54. A method of generating a speech topic that involves writing down many possible ideas in a brief amount of time is known as which of the following?
    (A) Tree diagram
    (B) Surveying
    (C) Brainstorming
    (D) Topoi

55. Which of the following is the most appropriate language to include in a speech?

    (A) Concrete and vivid

    (B) Visual and rhythmic

    (C) Abstract and technical

    (D) Connotative and multisyllabic

56. A speech topic that is appropriate for a particular occasion is characterized by

    (A) relevancy to the audience.

    (B) commonly known information.

    (C) wide-ranging subject matter.

    (D) numerous visual aids.

57. Which of the following is most useful when abstract ideas need clarification for an audience?

    (A) Quotations

    (B) Examples

    (C) Testimonies

    (D) Statistics

58. Questions that call for only brief answers from an interviewee are known as

    (A) open questions.

    (B) closed questions.

    (C) primary questions.

    (D) leading questions.

59. Which of the following is a primary benefit of organizing a speech?

    (A) Reduces the number of transitions

    (B) Incorporates parallel statements

    (C) Improves audience comprehension

    (D) Grabs the attention of listeners

60. An appropriate speech topic is characterized by which of the following?

    (A) Spatial organizational pattern

    (B) Positive ethical assertions

    (C) Extensive thesis support

    (D) Clearly illustrated examples

ANSWER KEY AND EXPLANATIONS

1. D	13. B	25. A	37. A	49. C
2. C	14. A	26. D	38. C	50. B
3. A	15. C	27. B	39. B	51. A
4. B	16. B	28. D	40. A	52. B
5. C	17. D	29. C	41. D	53. B
6. A	18. C	30. D	42. C	54. C
7. D	19. B	31. B	43. B	55. A
8. B	20. D	32. C	44. B	56. A
9. B	21. A	33. A	45. C	57. B
10. D	22. C	34. C	46. D	58. B
11. A	23. B	35. B	47. A	59. C
12. D	24. D	36. B	48. A	60. B

1. **The correct answer is (D).** Age has the greatest effect on the consistency or stability of a person's attitude. The opinions of younger people tend to change, while older people are more steadfast in their beliefs. Ethnicity, religion, and gender affect attitudes, but these factors are less relevant to the consistency of a belief.

2. **The correct answer is (C).** Topical would be most appropriate for a speech about the three branches of the government. Topical patterns are useful for speeches where the topic is easily subdivided, so in this case, each main point would address one branch of the government. Choices (A), (B), and (D) are less appropriate for a speech describing parts of a whole.

3. **The correct answer is (A).** An impromptu speech is one that is given without advanced preparation. Although impromptu speeches are often spontaneous, choice (C) is not the term used to describe such speeches. Manuscript and extemporaneous speeches are written in advance, so choices (B) and (D) are incorrect.

4. **The correct answer is (B).** A very large audience prevents a speaker from responding to facial expressions and body language. Distance from audience members and the sheer number of listeners makes it very difficult for a speaker to determine whether an audience is responding positively or negatively to a speech, so a speaker is less able to make adaptations. Choices (A), (C), and (D) are factors to consider when giving a speech, but they do not prevent a speaker from reading an audience.

5. **The correct answer is (C).** Testimonies, examples, narratives, statistics, and quotations are types of supporting materials used in public speeches. The main types of arguments used in speeches are those based on example, analogy, causation, and sign, so choice (A) is incorrect. Choice (B), propositions of fact, refers to a statement intended to convince an audience that something is true or false. Choice (D), emotional appeals, refers to the attempts made by speakers to arouse strong positive or negative emotions in listeners.

6. **The correct answer is (A).** The general purpose of a public speech is either to persuade, to inform, or to entertain. Choice (B) refers to the exact goal of a particular speech, such as *to persuade my audience to donate money to a local charity*. The thesis statement, choice (C), is the central idea of a speech, and it is what a speaker hopes listeners will remember. A topic sentence is the main idea of a paragraph, so choice (D) is incorrect.

7. **The correct answer is (D).** Plagiarism occurs when a person fails to credit a source for an idea and presents the idea as one's own. Using the words or ideas of another person without giving proper credit is plagiarism, even when words and phrases have been paraphrased. Coercion, choice (C), is the use of intimidation to gain compliance, which is unethical but not related to plagiarism. Choices (A) and (B) are not concepts related to plagiarism or ethics.

8. **The correct answer is (B).** Quantity of information is the greatest benefit of Internet research. Credibility and accuracy are often difficult to discern from Web-based information because anyone can establish a Web site, so choices (C) and (D) are incorrect. Businesses or public-interest groups often sponsor Web sites, but sponsorship, choice (A), does not necessarily guarantee the quality or objectivity of information.

9. **The correct answer is (B).** Speeches organized with a spatial pattern follow a direction. The structure of a place or an object is presented from top to bottom, inside to outside, or left to right, for example. Structure-function patterns, choice (A), divide a speech by the structure of an object and the function of the object. Choices (C) and (D) are not organizational patterns that follow a physical direction.

10. **The correct answer is (D).** An ethical persuasive speech is characterized by the use of representative evidence. Statistics, opinions, and examples are incorporated into speeches to support claims, but such information should represent the body of available evidence and not be one-sided. Name-calling and plagiarism are unethical, so choices (A) and (C) are incorrect. Parallel language improves listener comprehension but is irrelevant to ethics.

11. **The correct answer is (A).** Polls and surveys would provide a student with topic ideas related to trends and public opinions. Data such as the Gallup Poll is readily available on the Internet and provides useful information about consumer trends, technology, and productivity. The news found in magazines and newspapers is a good starting point for current events, but it is not the best source for trends and public opinions. Choices (C) and (D) are methods of generating ideas based on personal knowledge.

12. **The correct answer is (D).** Anecdotes are short, humorous stories that are often included in public speeches. Although brief examples, choice (A), are short, they are not by definition humorous. Hypothetical examples are examples that depict imaginary situations, so choice (C) is incorrect. Personal testimonies, choice (D), may be humorous at times, but not always.

13. **The correct answer is (B).** Connectives are words and phrases that link ideas in speeches. Transitions, internal summaries, and signposts are types of connectives, so choice (C) is incorrect. Supporting materials

support ideas but do not connect them, so choice (D) is incorrect.

14. **The correct answer is (A).** Manuscript speeches are fully written in advance, so managing time is their greatest strength. Speakers reading a manuscript have less eye contact with listeners than speakers who use other delivery methods. Moving around is not typically done when using a manuscript because the speaker is reading from one location. Expository communication informs or explains an idea, so choice (D) is incorrect.

15. **The correct answer is (C).** A speech that follows the statement-of-reasons pattern will present the strongest point last so that audiences will remember it. The second strongest argument is presented first, so choice (A) is incorrect. Choices (B) and (D) are incorrect because the weakest point is placed in the middle of the speech between the two stronger points.

16. **The correct answer is (B).** Being easily distracted by physical and mental activities and letting the mind wander best explain why most people are poor listeners. Taking notes and paying attention to verbal and nonverbal communication are activities of active listening. Ethnocentrism is the tendency of evaluating beliefs and behaviors based on one's own culture, so choice (A) is incorrect.

17. **The correct answer is (D).** Active listening involves paraphrasing, formulating questions, and focusing on nonverbal cues. Appreciative listening occurs when people are listening to music, so choice (A) is incorrect. Empathic listening occurs when a person provides emotional support to another, as when a psychologist listens to a patient. Choice (C) is a distractor.

18. **The correct answer is (C).** Speakers should emphasize the unbiased nature of a testimony so that the information presented in the testimony will have a significant impact on listeners. Choice (A) is incorrect because expert testimonies are more effective than personal testimonies. Choice (B) is incorrect because testimonies should be recent, which means time is important. Choice (D) is incorrect because not all persuasive speeches will warrant testimonial evidence.

19. **The correct answer is (B).** Ethnocentrism is the tendency to think that one's own culture has superior values and beliefs compared to other cultures. Choice (A) refers to accepting a variety of cultures within a specified location, such as a city, school, or neighborhood. Choice (C) is the study of human kind. Choice (D) refers to the culture with which a person associates.

20. **The correct answer is (D).** Reinforcing the thesis and reminding the audience of the main points of the speech is one of the primary purposes of speech conclusions. Referring back to an idea, story, or quotation used in the introduction is appropriate, but repeating the introduction is not. Apologies are generally not appropriate and serve only to weaken a speech, so choice (A) is incorrect. Questions would be answered after the speech conclusion in most cases, not during the conclusion.

21. **The correct answer is (A).** Audience adaptation refers to customizing a speech to a specific audience by considering the way ideas are presented. Vocabulary, visual aids, and presentation style are factors in adapting a speech to meet the needs of a particular audience. Choices (C) and (D) provide speakers with information useful in adapting a speech.

Audience-centeredness, choice (B), refers to focusing on the audience while preparing and presenting a speech.

22. **The correct answer is (C).** Constructive criticism occurs when a critic explains how to improve a speech weakness. Effective speech criticism is constructive and specific because the purpose of criticism is to help individuals improve their public speaking skills. Criticism should be free of bias, so choice (B) is incorrect. Choices (A) and (D) are distractors.

23. **The correct answer is (B).** Anticipated response refers to the response that a speaker seeks from listeners. In a persuasive speech, the anticipated response is what the speaker wants listeners to think or do. Choices (A) and (C) are terms referring to communication apprehension, and choice (D) is a term related to informative speaking.

24. **The correct answer is (D).** Quotations included in speeches should be relevant to the main point of an argument. Quotations do not have to be those of famous people, but if the person is unknown to most listeners, then the person's credentials should be indicated so that the quote has meaning. Choice (C) is incorrect because quotations do not need to be emotional to be effective.

25. **The correct answer is (A).** Extemporaneous speakers rely upon brief notes or an outline to remember key points and the order of presentation. Choice (B) is a speech organization pattern, not a delivery method. Manuscripts are fully written speeches. Impromptu speeches are not researched or prepared in advance, so choice (C) is incorrect.

26. **The correct answer is (D).** Internal previews alert audiences to the subject of the next main point to be presented. Transitional words or phrases, choice (A), are connectives that help a speaker move from one point to another, but they do not indicate the subject of the next point. Signposts tell listeners where a speaker is in a speech and do not indicate the next point, so choice (B) is incorrect. Choice (C) is a question during an interview that suggests a desired response.

27. **The correct answer is (B).** Topic relevancy is the key to an effective speech introduction. An interesting and catchy introduction that fails to connect to the rest of the speech only confuses listeners. Choices (C) and (D) are characteristics needed for effective main points in a speech. Choice (A) refers to a pattern of organization for the body of a speech, not the introduction.

28. **The correct answer is (D).** Established standards of public speeches serve as the basis for speech criticism. While some cultures accept criticism more easily than others do, cultural norms are not the basis of evaluating a speech. Similarly, popular opinion should not be a factor in the ethical evaluation of a speech. Empathic listening occurs when one person listens to the problems of another person, so choice (C) is incorrect.

29. **The correct answer is (C).** Signposts are connectives that help audiences keep track of points in a speech, such as *the first cause*, *the second cause*, and *the third cause*. Choices (B) and (D) refer to organizational patterns used in speeches. Supporting materials are the examples, narratives, and statistics included in a speech.

30. **The correct answer is (D).** A single word or a brief phrase indicating a speaker has completed one idea and

is moving to the next one is known as a transition. Signposts are brief statements that tell listeners where a speaker is in a speech, so choice (B) is incorrect. Choices (A) and (C) are complete statements rather than single words.

31. **The correct answer is (B).** The thesis statement of a speech indicates the theme or central idea of the presentation. The thesis should be what the audience remembers from a speech. Choices (A) and (C) are the goals of a speech, and they serve to guide the direction of a speech.

32. **The correct answer is (C).** Speaking too quickly is a common speech rate problem. Choices (A) and (D) are problems associated with volume. Choice (B), omitting sounds, is one of the major articulation problems that some speakers must overcome.

33. **The correct answer is (A).** Ethos, which is an intrinsic proof, refers to source credibility. The credibility of a source is based on competence, character, composure, sociability, and extroversion. Logos, or logical proof, refers to the appeals or arguments used by a speaker, so choice (C) is incorrect. Extrinsic proof, choice (D), is objective evidence, such as laws. Mythic proof, or mythos, choice (B), refers to the attitudes of a group or a society.

34. **The correct answer is (C).** A speaker who is personable, knowledgeable, and trustworthy establishes credibility with audience members. Asking rhetorical questions helps a speaker establish common ground with an audience. Speaking about a timely subject helps the audience realize the relevance of the speech, but it does not necessarily develop credibility. Before choosing a subject, a speaker should

consider the culture of the audience to avoid being offensive.

35. **The correct answer is (B).** A quotation used in an introduction should be thought-provoking and gain the attention of the audience. Quotations do not need to be ones that most people have heard, nor do they need to be ones made by famous people. Quotations may be humorous, but they do not have to be. The wording of suspenseful introductions makes the audience curious about the topic.

36. **The correct answer is (B).** Concrete words are those that refer to tangible objects such as *lettuce, motorcycle,* and *piano*. Words that are abstract, choice (D), refer to ideas such as *psychology, romance,* and *patriotism*. Jargon is technical terminology, so choice (A) is incorrect. Context refers to a word's relationship with other words, so choice (C) is incorrect.

37. **The correct answer is (A).** Pathos is the term coined by Aristotle that refers to emotional appeals. Public speakers who try to evoke sadness, guilt, pride, or compassion from listeners are using emotional appeals. Logos is the term for logical appeals, so choice (C) is incorrect. Ethos refers to speaker credibility, so choice (B) is incorrect. A thesis statement, choice (D), is the central idea or theme of the speech.

38. **The correct answer is (C).** A thesis statement should be presented to a hostile audience after evidence and arguments are provided in order to allow the speaker time to gradually shift audience attitudes into a positive state. Choices (A), (B), and (D) are situations in which a thesis statement should be clearly stated early in a speech to provide focus and clarity for the audience.

39. The correct answer is (B). A crescendo ending is characterized by the building towards a powerful and intense conclusion. A dissolve ending is emotional, but it fades gradually to a dramatic statement. Choice (A) is a type of persuasive pattern, and some speakers use choice (C) to signal conclusions.

40. The correct answer is (A). Adding sounds where they do not belong is an articulation problem. Common pronunciation problems include accent errors and the pronunciation of silent sounds, so choice (B) is incorrect. Filled and unfilled pauses are typical of many speeches but do not involve adding sounds to words. Proxemics refers to how space during a presentation is used by a speaker, so choice (D) is incorrect.

41. The correct answer is (D). Similes are used in speeches to compare dissimilar objects and enhance audience understanding. Alliteration refers to the repetition of initial consonant sounds in closely spaced words, and some speakers use it to add rhythm to a speech. Connectives, which include transitions and signposts, are used in speeches to join the main points of a presentation.

42. The correct answer is (C). Exemplary narratives are stories about excellence, such as Mother Teresa's humanitarian efforts for the sick and the poor throughout most of her life. Choices (A) and (B) are incorrect because testimonies are opinions supporting the speaker's claims rather than stories. Choice (D) is incorrect because Mother Teresa was a real person, and hypothetical examples are fictitious.

43. The correct answer is (B). Speakers emphasize points by gesturing with hands and arms. Movement involves moving the entire body rather than just the arms and hands, so choice (A) is incorrect. Posture refers to a speaker's position, such as upright or hunched. Poise is a speaker's confidence and manner during a presentation, so choice (D) is incorrect.

44. The correct answer is (B). Most speech introductions are 10 percent of the total speech length, so a 750-word speech would have an introduction of approximately 75 words. Choice (A) is too short to provide a solid introduction. Choices (C) and (D) are too lengthy; long introductions take away from valuable time addressing main points.

45. The correct answer is (C). I-messages are beneficial ways to relay criticism because they reduce defensiveness and resentment felt by the speaker. You-messages make the critic seem superior, whereas I-messages indicate an opinion that the speaker can either accept or reject. I-messages also show that a critic is willing to take full responsibility for criticism, so choice (A) is incorrect. I-messages may relay positive or negative information, so choice (D) is incorrect.

46. The correct answer is (D). Responding to audience feedback is the main advantage of extemporaneous speeches. Since the exact wording of the speech is not prepared, a speaker can elaborate when it is apparent that listeners are confused. Choice (C) refers to a speech organizational pattern rather than a method of delivery. Choice (B) can occur at the end of any type of speech and is not unique to extemporaneous speeches.

47. The correct answer is (A). Extrinsic proofs are based upon objective evidence, such as laws. Intrinsic proofs are based upon speaker credibility, emotional issues related to a subject, and logical arguments used to persuade listeners.

48. **The correct answer is (A).** The thesis statement is most likely to change and develop as research and analysis of the subject occurs. The general purpose, choice (D), and specific purpose, choice (C), of a speech are developed early in the speechmaking process and guide the eventual creation of a thesis. The residual message, choice (B), relates to the thesis because it is what a speaker hopes an audience will retain from the ideas presented in the speech.

49. **The correct answer is (C).** Main points of a speech should be written in a parallel grammatical structure, which means that each statement should be phrased in a similar way. Infinitive statements, choice (B), are appropriate for specific purpose statements. Rhetorical questions, choice (D), are often used in introductions to encourage listeners to consider a concept or an idea. Although writing a main point as a compound sentence, choice (A), is acceptable, the most important quality is the parallel structure of the main points.

50. **The correct answer is (B).** Topics, occasions, audiences, and speakers determine what language is appropriate for a speech. The language used in a presentation may determine speaker credibility; however, the appropriateness of language is not determined by speaker credibility. Speech length has little to do with language appropriateness, so choice (D) is incorrect.

51. **The correct answer is (A).** Pitch, which is the highness or lowness of a person's voice, can be used to emphasize words in a sentence. The difference between a statement and a question depends upon what word is emphasized. Tone, choice (B), refers to the quality of a speaker's voice, and rate, choice (C), refers to the speed of speech. Proxemics, choice (D), is the distance between a speaker and a listener.

52. **The correct answer is (B).** A persuasive narrative is a story told to change beliefs. In this case, the speaker is trying to raise funds, and a story about the plight of starving Africans may persuade the audience to donate money. Choice (A) is a story told about an excellent or admirable individual, such as a saint. Testimonies are expert opinions, so choice (C) is incorrect. The speaker does not provide numerical data, so choice (D) is incorrect.

53. **The correct answer is (B).** Most speeches have two to five main points that are developed within the body of a speech. Fewer than two points indicates that the speech topic needs to be expanded or that further research needs to occur. More than five points in a speech is confusing for listeners.

54. **The correct answer is (C).** Brainstorming, which can be done individually or in a group, involves writing down as many topics as possible in a short amount of time. Surveys involve studying polls and other data sources to find trends and societal opinions, so choice (B) is incorrect. A tree diagram, choice (A), is a method of limiting a speech topic by repeatedly dividing a topic into smaller and smaller parts. Topoi, choice (D), is based on ancient rhetoric techniques and involves asking and answering questions to generate topic ideas.

55. **The correct answer is (A).** Concrete, vivid words are the best choice for speeches because they provide clear images for listeners. Speech rhythm refers to the sound patterns created by the specific arrangement of words in a speech, so choice (B) is incorrect. Abstract or technical words, choice (C), may be confusing for some audiences, so words that are concrete and vivid are better choices. Although multisyllabic words, choice (D), may sound fancy, they are typically too confusing for audiences—straightforward, familiar language is a better choice.

56. **The correct answer is (A).** An appropriate speech topic is one that is relevant to the audience, which means that the topic should be current and interesting to listeners. Commonly known information would be boring for an audience, so choice (B) is incorrect. Choice (C) is incorrect because a speech topic should be narrow—a speaker would not be able to cover a broad topic with effectiveness in a specified amount of time. Choice (D) is irrelevant to the appropriateness of a topic.

57. **The correct answer is (B).** Examples and narratives are the most useful types of supporting materials when abstract concepts require clarification. Statistics illustrate points and provide the basis for claims, but numerical data is not likely to be used for clarifying abstract ideas. Quotations and testimonies support a speaker's claims, but they rarely serve as tools for clarification.

58. **The correct answer is (B).** Closed questions are narrow and call for brief responses. On the other hand, open questions, choice (A), are broad and require in-depth answers about values, goals, and opinions. Primary questions, choice (C), are those that are written in advance and typically cover the main points of an interview. The phrasing of leading questions, choice (D), suggests a desired response from the interviewee.

59. **The correct answer is (C).** An organized speech improves audience comprehension because information presented in a structured format is easier for listeners to follow and remember. Transitions and parallel statements, choices (A) and (B), are important to the flow of a speech, but they are not beneficial to speech organization. The introduction should grab audience attention, so choice (D) is incorrect.

60. **The correct answer is (B).** An appropriate speech topic is one that upholds positive ethical standards and assertions that aim toward improving rather than harming society. The spatial organizational pattern of a speech, choice (A), improves audience understanding, but is not relevant to the appropriateness of a speech topic. Choices (C) and (D) assist in making a speech effective, but neither relates to the appropriate nature of a topic.

SUMMING IT UP

- Ethics is the area of philosophy that concerns issues of morality, fairness, and justice. Public speakers face ethical dilemmas at every stage of the speechmaking process—from selecting a topic to presenting the final message. One of the most unethical public speaking actions taken is plagiarism—when a writer or a speaker presents the ideas or words of another person as their own.

- Audience-centeredness is making the audience the primary consideration during the speechmaking process and the speech presentation. Audience identification is the process of forming a bond with listeners by pointing out common beliefs, experiences, and goals. Audience analysis is the process of acquiring information about an audience in order to adapt a speech. Speakers learn about listeners through conventional wisdom, direct observation, questionnaires, demographic audience analysis, and situational audience analysis.

- Informing, persuading, and entertaining are the three general purposes for making a speech. An informative speech increases audience awareness and knowledge about a specific subject. A persuasive speech is designed to change the attitudes, behaviors, feelings, and beliefs of listeners. The purpose of an entertaining speech is to amuse the audience with humor and cleverness.

- Generating ideas for potential speech topics can be done by brainstorming as well as checking surveys, newspapers, and magazines. A tree diagram limits a speech topic by repeatedly dividing a topic into smaller parts. The Topoi method involves asking and answering questions to generate topic ideas.

- In addition to the library, the Internet serves a significant role in modern research, although the accuracy of information can be a concern. The wealth of information available on the Internet is extensive, but unlike libraries, the Internet lacks quality-control mechanisms.

- Research interviews are useful for gathering information for speeches. Follow-up questions help gain additional information from primary questions, which are prepared in advance. Open questions are broad questions designed to discover an interviewee's values and perspectives. Closed questions seek brief answers.

- In a speech, supporting material is content that provides information, maintains listener interest, and asserts persuasive evidence. Supporting materials include examples, narratives, testimonies, and statistics.

- Extrinsic proofs support claims with objective evidence, such as laws and confessions. Intrinsic or artistic proofs are based on the speaker's character, the emotional nature of the issue, and the logic of the argument to persuade listeners. Aristotle referred to three kinds of persuasive appeals, or intrinsic proofs, used in public speaking: logos, ethos, and pathos.

- Arguing from example, from analogy, from causation, and from sign are the common types of arguments. The most common types of fallacies in public speeches are hasty generalization, false cause, invalid analogy, and ad hominem.

- The thesis statement is the starting point for developing the main (major) points of the body of a speech. Most speeches include two to five main points. Main points should be relevant and interesting to the audience and worded in a parallel format. Main points should also be distinct—no overlap among them.

- The six types of organizational patterns used most often in public speaking are topical, temporal, spatial, problem-solution, causal, and motivated. Other organizational patterns include statement-of-reasons pattern, structure-function pattern, and the pro-and-con or advantages-disadvantages pattern.

- A speech's introduction serves to gain the audience's interest, preview the topic, and establish speaker credibility and a connection with listeners. Types of introductions include startling, rhetorical, story, personal reference, quotation, and suspense.

- Speech conclusions alert the audience that the speech is ending, summarize the speech, and clarify what listeners should think or do in response to the speech.

- Connectives help listeners understand the relationship between one concept and another. The four types of connectives are transitions, signposts, internal previews, and internal summaries.

- Words have two basic kinds of meaning. The *denotative* meaning of a word is its literal and objective meaning. The *connotative* meaning of a word is subjective and variable.

- The four basic methods of speech delivery are impromptu, from a manuscript, from memory, and extemporaneously.

- The physical aspects of speech presentation include voice, articulation, and bodily movements. Public speakers need to be aware of voice pitch, volume, rate, quality, articulation, and pronunciation. Common speaking errors include errors of omission, errors of substitution, errors of addition, and pronunciation errors.

- Nonverbal bodily actions, such as eye contact, facial expressions, gestures, and movements, convey information to an audience. The most important nonverbal form of communication is appropriate eye contact with listeners.

- The five steps in the listening process are receiving, understanding, remembering, evaluating, and responding. Types of listening include appreciative, empathic, comprehensive, and critical listening. Reasons for poor listening include giving in to physical and mental distractions, trying to remember every detail instead of the overall theme, jumping to conclusions and making assumptions, and judging the speaker's personal appearance and delivery style rather than the actual message.

- Criticism is the process of evaluating a message and deciding whether it is believable, thorough, and valuable based on specific standards. The Latin origin of *criticism* means *able to judge or discern*. Public speaking criticism should point out the positive more than the negative, provide specific rather than general comments, be objective instead of biased, be constructive, be structured as I-messages and not You-messages, and consider ethical responsibilities.

Fundamentals of College Algebra

OVERVIEW

DIAGNOSTIC TEST

Directions: Carefully read each of the following 20 questions. Choose the best answer to each question and circle your answer choice. The Answer Key and Explanations can be found following this Diagnostic Test.

1. Which of the following is the sum of the polynomials $2x^3 + 3x^2 + 4x + 7$ and $4x^3 - x^2 + 12$?

   (A) $6x^3 + 2x^2 + 4x + 19$

   (B) $2x^3 + 7x^2 + 3x + 19$

   (C) $6x^6 + 2x^4 + 4x + 19$

   (D) $8x^5 + 19$

2. Given $f(x) = 4x + 5$ and $g(x) = x^2 + 1$, which of the following is $[f(x)][g(x)]$?

   (A) $x^2 + 4x + 6$

   (B) $4x^3 + 5x^2 + 4x + 5$

   (C) $\dfrac{4x + 5}{x^2 + 1}$

   (D) $4x^2 + 9$

chapter 7

3. Which answer simplifies the expression $2\sqrt{12} - \sqrt{27} + 5\sqrt{48}$?
   (A) $5\sqrt{6}$
   (B) $21\sqrt{3}$
   (C) $21 + \sqrt{3}$
   (D) $27\sqrt{3}$

4. Simplify the rational expression $3x^3 - 27x$.
   (A) $3x^2(x - 9)$
   (B) $3x(x^2 - 6x + 9)$
   (C) $3x(x + 3)(x - 3)$
   (D) $3x^3(x - 27)$

5. Which of the following is the solution to the system shown below?

   $$\begin{cases} 3x + y = 11 \\ 2x + 3y = -2 \end{cases}$$

   (A) $(6, -7)$
   (B) $(2, -1)$
   (C) $(4, -2)$
   (D) $(5, -4)$

6. Which value is the solution for $|2x + 7| < 5$?
   (A) $-1 < x < 1$
   (B) $-6 < x < -1$
   (C) $1 < x < 6$
   (D) $x > -1$

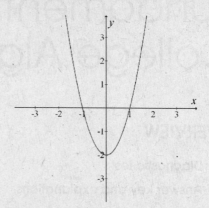

7. Which of the following quadratic equations represents the graph above?
   (A) $y = x^2 - 2$
   (B) $y = 2x^2 - 2$
   (C) $y = x + 2$
   (D) $y = -x^2 + 2$

8. Which answer solves the radical equation $\sqrt{4x + 1} = 5$?
   (A) 3
   (B) 4
   (C) 6
   (D) None of the above

9. Which of the following is the domain in interval notation of the function f defined by $f(x) = \sqrt{3x - 6}$?
   (A) $[-\infty, \infty]$
   (B) $[-\infty, 2)$
   (C) $[2, \infty)$
   (D) $[-\infty, 2)$

10. Which of the following is the inverse f^{-1} of the function $f(x) = x^2 - 5$?
    (A) $\dfrac{1}{x^2 - 5}$
    (B) $\sqrt{x + 5}$
    (C) $\sqrt{y^2 + 5}$
    (D) $\dfrac{1}{\sqrt{x + 5}}$

11. Which of the following is a simplification of the equation $\dfrac{\sqrt[4]{8}}{\sqrt{2}}$?

    (A) $\sqrt[4]{2}$

    (B) $\sqrt[4]{6}$

    (C) $\dfrac{4}{\sqrt{2}}$

    (D) $2\sqrt{2}$

12. Which of the following is the solution for q, given $\log(\log q) = 2$?

    (A) 10^{12}

    (B) 100^{10}

    (C) 10^{20}

    (D) 10^{100}

13. Which of the following is $i(5 - 2i)^2$ in the form $a + bi$?

    (A) $10 + 20i$

    (B) $21 - 20i$

    (C) $29 - 20i$

    (D) $20 + 21i$

14. Which of the following is an ordered pair for the function $f(x) = x^2 - x + 2$?

    (A) $(-3,8)$

    (B) $(5,-3)$

    (C) $(1,-1)$

    (D) $(3,8)$

15. Which of the following solves the equation $2x^2 - 5x + 3 = 0$?

    (A) $\dfrac{-5 \pm \sqrt{1}}{4}$

    (B) $\dfrac{2 \pm \sqrt{3}}{5}$

    (C) $\dfrac{\sqrt{3} + 1}{4}$

    (D) $\dfrac{5 \pm \sqrt{1}}{4}$

16. What is the factor of the equation $x^4 - y^4$?

    (A) $(x^2 + y^2)(x + y)(x - y)$

    (B) $(x^2 + y^2)(x + y)^2$

    (C) $(x + y)^2(x + y)(x - y)$

    (D) $2(x + y)\ (x - y)$

17. Which of the following shows the rational expression in its lowest terms?

    $$\dfrac{2x^2 + 4x + 2}{(x + 1)^2}$$

    (A) 2

    (B) $\dfrac{2x}{(x + 1)}$

    (C) $\dfrac{(x + 2)}{(x + 1)}$

    (D) 4

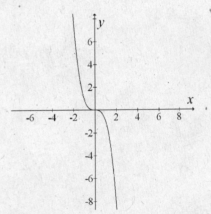

18. The graph above can best be described by which function?

    (A) $f(x) = -3x - 1$

    (B) $f(x) = -\log(x)$

    (C) $f(x) = x^3 - 3x + 3$

    (D) $f(x) = -x^3$

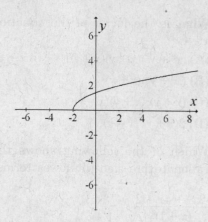

19. The graph above can best be described by which function?

(A) $f(x) = |x - 2|$

(B) $f(x) = \sqrt{x^2 - 2}$

(C) $f(x) = \log(x + 2) - 2$

(D) $f(x) = \sqrt{x + 2}$

20. What is the echelon form of the following linear set of equations?

$$\begin{cases} x - y + z = 2 \\ 2x + y - z = 1 \\ -x + 2y + 2z = 9 \end{cases}$$

(A) $\begin{bmatrix} 3 & 5 & 2 & 1 \\ 0 & 4 & 4 & 1 \\ 0 & 0 & 2 & 1 \end{bmatrix}$

(B) $\begin{bmatrix} 1 & -1 & 1 & 2 \\ 0 & 1 & -1 & -1 \\ 0 & 0 & 1 & 3 \end{bmatrix}$

(C) $\begin{bmatrix} 1 & 1 & 2 & 1 \\ 0 & 4 & 3 & 1 \\ 0 & 0 & 1 & 3 \end{bmatrix}$

(D) $\begin{bmatrix} 1 & -1 & 1 & 2 \\ 2 & 1 & -1 & 1 \\ -1 & 2 & 2 & 9 \end{bmatrix}$

ANSWER KEY AND EXPLANATIONS

1. A	5. D	9. C	13. D	17. A
2. B	6. B	10. B	14. D	18. D
3. B	7. B	11. A	15. D	19. D
4. C	8. C	12. D	16. A	20. B

1. **The correct answer is (A).** Add the two equations together. Rearrange terms and add coefficients of like powers of x:

$$(2x^3 + 3x^2 + 4x + 7) + (4x^3 - x^2 + 12) = 2x^3 + 3x^2 + 4x + 7 + 4x^3 - x^2 + 12$$
$$= 2x^3 + 4x^3 + 3x^2 - x^2 + 4x + 7 + 12$$
$$= (2 + 4)x^3 + (3 - 1)x^2 + 4x + (7 + 12)$$
$$= 6x^3 + 2x^2 + 4x + 19$$

2. **The correct answer is (B).** The correct method to solve this problem is to understand that $[f(x)][g(x)]$ asks us to multiply the two functions together. We can use the FOIL method to achieve the correct result:

$$(4x + 5)(x^2 + 1) = (4x)(x^2) + (5)(x^2) + (1)(4x) + (5)(1)$$
$$= 4x^3 + 5x^2 + 4x + 5$$

The correct solution is choice (B). Choice (A) is incorrect as it is the addition of the two functions. Choice (C) is also incorrect as the division of the two functions.

3. **The correct answer is (B).** Use the law of radicals to find the common radicand (i.e., the number under the radical symbol $\sqrt{\ }$). Look for factors of each number to determine if there is a common radicand. There's no need to consider the factors 1 and the number (i.e., $12 = 1 \times 12$) as this won't really help to simplify the radical.

Factors:

$12 = 2, 3, 4, 6$

$27 = 3, 9$

$48 = 2, 3, 4, 6, 8, 12, 16, 24$

You'll notice that 3 is a common factor of all three numbers. Next, factor out 3 from each of the numbers, simplify the radicals, and add the coefficients:

$$2\sqrt{12} - \sqrt{27} + 5\sqrt{48} = 2\sqrt{(4)(3)} - \sqrt{(9)(3)} - \sqrt{(16)(3)}$$
$$= 2\sqrt{4}\sqrt{3} - \sqrt{9}\sqrt{3} + 5\sqrt{16}\sqrt{3}$$
$$= (2)(2)\sqrt{3} - 3\sqrt{3} + 5(4)\sqrt{3}$$
$$= 4\sqrt{3} - 3\sqrt{3} + 20\sqrt{3}$$
$$= (4 - 3 + 20)\sqrt{3}$$
$$= 21\sqrt{3}$$

4. **The correct answer is (C).** Use the distributive property to break the equation into parts:

$$3x^3 - 9x = 3x(x^2 - 9)$$

Next factor $x^2 - 9$:

$$= 3x(x + 3)(x - 3)$$

Choice (C) is correct.

5. **The correct answer is (D).** Begin by solving the first equation for y. First, subtract $3x$ from both sides of the equation and simplify:

$$3x + y = 11$$
$$3x + y - 3x = 11 - 3x$$
$$y = 11 - 3x$$

Note: Instead of adding $-3x$ to both sides of the equation, there is a simple rule that saves steps. When you need to move a constant or variable to the other side of the equation, just change the sign and make the move. In this case, move $-3x$ to the other side of the equation.

$$\underset{\text{move}\rightarrow}{\underline{3x}} + y = 11$$

$$y = 11 \;\; \overset{\text{change sign}}{\overbrace{-3x}}$$

Now substitute the above value of y into the second equation and solve:

$$2x + 3y = -2$$
$$2x + 3(11 - 3x) = -2$$
$$2x + 33 - 9x = -2$$
$$33 - 7x = -2$$
$$-7x = -2 - 33$$
$$-7x = -35$$

The standard way to simply $-7x = -35$ is to multiply both sides by $-\dfrac{1}{7}$:

$$-7x = -35$$
$$-7\left(\frac{-1}{7}\right)x = -35\left(\frac{-1}{7}\right)$$
$$\left(\frac{-7}{7}\right)x = \frac{(-35)(-1)}{7}$$
$$x = \frac{35}{7}$$
$$x = 5$$

Like with addition and subtraction, there is a time-saving rule for multiplying or dividing both sides of an equation. The time-saving rule is to invert the value you wish to move and multiply the other side by this value. In this case, to get rid of the 7, we can just multiply the other side by $-\frac{1}{7}$ or put a -7 in the denominator.

$$\underset{\text{move}\rightarrow}{\underline{-7}}\ x = -35$$

$$x = \underset{\text{place in denominator}}{\frac{35}{-7}}$$

$$x = 5$$

Using $x = 5$ in the first equation, solve for y:

$$3(5) + y = 11$$
$$15 + y = 11$$
$$y = -4$$

Thus, the correct answer is $(5,-4)$, choice (D).

6. **The correct answer is (B).** The equation is in the form $|a| < b$, which is solved by removing the absolute value using the absolute value rule $-b < a < b$. Or, you can break the inequality into two equations $a > -b$ and $a < b$.

Doing this gives us:

$$2x + 7 > -5 \qquad\qquad 2x + 7 < 5$$
$$2x > -5 - 7 \qquad\qquad 2x < 5 - 7$$
$$2x > -12 \qquad\qquad 2x < -2$$
$$x > -6 \qquad\qquad x < -1$$

This gives us $-6 < x < -1$.

Thus, the correct answer is choice (B).

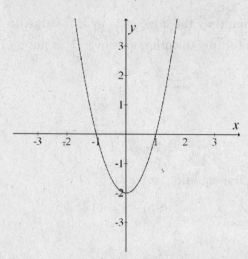

7. **The correct answer is (B).** We know from the graph above that the equation must meet the following criteria:

   a.   The graph crosses the x-axis twice, so the equation is second order, or contains x^2. Therefore, choice (C) cannot be a solution because it only contains a first-order x.

   b.   The graph crosses the y-axis at -2, so choice (D) cannot be a solution. Choice (D) crosses at 2 and because $-x^2$ is negative, it curves down, not up.

   c.   The graph crosses the x-axis at 1 and -1, and as a result, choice (A) cannot be a solution if we test for $(1,0)$.

$$y = x^2 - 2$$
$$0 = (1)^2 - 2$$
$$0 \neq -1$$

   d.   We know by process of elimination that choice (B) is the solution, which we can test with $(1,0)$.

$$y = 2x^2 - 2$$
$$0 = 2(1)^2 - 2$$
$$0 = 2 - 2$$
$$0 = 0$$

8. **The correct answer is (C).** The first step to solving the problem is to eliminate the square root by squaring both sides of the equation and solving:

$$\sqrt{4x + 1} = 5$$
$$\left(\sqrt{4x + 1}\right)^2 = 5^2$$
$$4x + 1 = 25$$
$$4x = 25 - 1$$
$$4x = 24$$
$$x = \frac{24}{4}$$
$$x = 6$$

So, the solution is choice (C).

9. **The correct answer is (C).** For the answer to be real, the value under the square root must not be negative. Knowing this, we set up an inequality where the answer must be greater than or equal to 0:

$$\sqrt{3x - 6} \geq 0$$
$$\left(\sqrt{3x - 6}\right)^2 \geq 0^2$$
$$3x - 6 \geq 0$$
$$3x \geq 6$$
$$x \geq \frac{6}{3}$$
$$x \geq 2$$

The domain in interval notation is given by $[2, \infty)$, making choice (C) the correct answer.

10. **The correct answer is (B).** The inverse notation is solved by first assigning y to $f(x)$ and switching y with x and solving for y, which gives the following:

$$y = x^2 - 5 \xrightarrow{\text{inverse}} x = y^2 - 5$$

Now solve for y:

$$x = y^2 - 5$$
$$y^2 = x + 5$$
$$y = \sqrt{x + 5}$$

Choice (B) is correct. A common mistake is choice (A), which is $\frac{1}{f(x)}$.

11. **The correct answer is (A).** Using $\sqrt[n]{b} = b^{\frac{1}{n}}$, we can simplify the equation:

$$\frac{\sqrt[4]{8}}{\sqrt{2}} = \frac{8^{\frac{1}{4}}}{2^{\frac{1}{2}}}$$

If we can make the radical in the numerator and the denominator the same, we can simplify using the rule $\left(\frac{a}{b}\right)^n = \frac{a^n}{b^n}$. To get to this point, we first need to make $2^{\frac{1}{2}} = 2^{\frac{2}{4}}$ and use the rule $(a^m)^n = a^{mn}$.

$$= \frac{8^{\frac{1}{4}}}{2^{\frac{2}{4}}}$$

$$= \frac{8^{\frac{1}{4}}}{2^{(2)\left(\frac{1}{4}\right)}}$$

$$= \frac{8^{\frac{1}{4}}}{\left(2^2\right)^{\frac{1}{4}}}$$

$$= \frac{8^{\frac{1}{4}}}{(4)^{\frac{1}{4}}}$$

$$= \left(\frac{8}{4}\right)^{\frac{1}{4}}$$

We can then simplify:

$$= \left(\frac{8}{4}\right)^{\frac{1}{4}}$$

$$= 2^{\frac{1}{4}}$$

$$= \sqrt[4]{2}$$

Choice (A) is correct.

12. **The correct answer is (D).** Log is understood to be base 10, so we can solve by using the transformation rule $y = \log_a x \longleftrightarrow a^y = x$, where $a = 10$, $y = 2$, and $x = \log q$:

$$\log(\log q) = 2$$
$$\log q = 10^2$$
$$\log q = 100$$

Next, we use the law again, where $a = 10$, $y = 100$, and $x = q$:

$$\log q = 100$$
$$q = 10^{(100)}$$
$$q = 10^{100}$$

13. **The correct answer is (D).** Using the rule $i^2 = 1$, we can solve the problem:

$$
\begin{aligned}
i(5 - 2i)^2 &= i(5 - 2i)(5 - 2i) \\
&= i[(5)(5) + (-2i)(5) + (-2i)(5) + (-2i)(-2i)] \\
&= i(25 - 10i - 10i + 4i^2) \\
&= i(25 - 20i + 4i^2) \\
&= i(25 - 20i + 4(-1)) \\
&= i(25 - 20i - 4) \\
&= i(21 - 20i) \\
&= 21i - 20i^2 \\
&= 21i - 20(-1) \\
&= 20 + 21i
\end{aligned}
$$

Choice (D) is correct.

14. **The correct answer is (D).** Each ordered pair should be substituted into the function to test for equality. Choices (B) and (C) offer incorrect solutions. Likewise, if we substitute $f(x) = -3$ and $x = 8$, we find that the solution is false:

$$
\begin{aligned}
f(x) &= x^2 - x + 2 \\
8 &= (-3)^2 - (-3) + 2 \\
8 &= 9 + 3 + 2 \\
8 &\neq 14
\end{aligned}
$$

If we substitute $f(x) = 3$ and $x = 8$, we find that the equation is true:

$$
\begin{aligned}
f(x) &= x^2 - x + 2 \\
8 &= (3)^2 - (3) + 2 \\
8 &= 9 - 3 + 2 \\
8 &= 8
\end{aligned}
$$

15. **The correct answer is (D).** Use the quadratic equation to solve, letting $a = 2$, $b = -5$, and $c = 3$:

$$
\begin{aligned}
x &= \frac{-b \pm \sqrt{b^2 - 4ac}}{2a} \\
&= \frac{5 \pm \sqrt{(-5)^2 - 4(2)(3)}}{2(2)} \\
&= \frac{5 \pm \sqrt{25 - 24}}{4} \\
&= \frac{5 \pm \sqrt{1}}{4}
\end{aligned}
$$

Thus, choice (D) is correct.

16. The correct answer is (A). The equation uses the formula $a^2 - b^2 = (a + b)(a - b)$ twice to solve. Use the rules of exponentials to convert $x^4 = (x^2)^2$:

$$(x^4 + y^4) = (x^2)^2 - (y^2)^2$$
$$= (x^2 + y^2)(x^2 - y^2)$$

Now use the formula again with $x^2 - y^2$:

$$= (x^2 + y^2)(x^2 - y^2)$$
$$= (x^2 + y^2)(x + y)(x - y)$$

Thus, choice (A) is correct.

17. The correct answer is (A). Use the distributive property to pull 2 out of the numerator. Factor the denominator and cancel out common factors. Remember $(x + 1)^2$ is $(x + 1)(x + 1)$. All of the $(x + 1)$ polynomials cancel themselves out in this problem.

$$\frac{2x^2 + 4x + 2}{(x + 1)^2} = \frac{2(x^2 + 2x + 1)}{(x + 1)(x + 1)}$$
$$= \frac{2(x + 1)(x + 1)}{(x + 1)(x + 1)}$$
$$= 2$$

Choice (A) is correct.

18. The correct answer is (D). If you have the basic graph shape memorized for various types of functions, you will quickly see that only choice (D) could look like the plot below. If you don't have these functions' graphs memorized, you can test to see which choices are correct. From the graph (shown here), it's obvious the solution passes through the origin, or (0,0). We can test to see if this ordered pair is a solution to each of the choices.

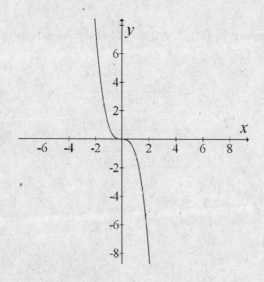

$A:$	$B:$	$C:$	$D:$
$f(x) = -3x - 1$	$f(x) = \log(x)$	$f(x) = x^3 - 3x + 3$	$f(x) = -x^3$
$0 = -(0)^3 - 1$	$0 = \log 0$	$0 = -(0)^3 - 3(0) + 3$	$0 = -(0)^3$
$0 \neq -1$	$0 \neq 1$	$0 \neq 3$	$0 = 0$

When $x = 0$ and $y = 0$, choices (A), (B), and (C) are not true, leaving only choice (D) as the correct answer.

19. **The correct answer is (D).** The plot shows no solution that is real for $x < -2$. This fact rules out choices (A) and (B), because they both have values for y when x is less than -2.

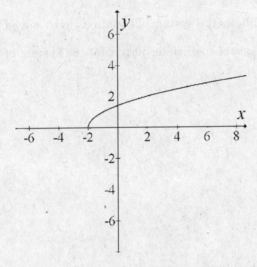

Choice (C), when plotted, is very similar to the graph. This solution might work; however, a $\log x$ always gives very large negative y-values as x approaches 0. In this case, choice (C) would have very large negative y-values as x approaches -2. Therefore, choice (D) is the correct answer.

20. **The correct answer is (B).** A coefficient matrix can be formed from the system of equations. Elementary row transformations are used to form the echelon matrix.

Step 1: Create the coefficient matrix from the equations:

$$\begin{bmatrix} 1 & -1 & 1 & 2 \\ 0 & 3 & -3 & -3 \\ -1 & 2 & 2 & 9 \end{bmatrix}$$

Step 2: Multiply the first row by -2 and add to the second row. Then divide the second row by 3:

$$\begin{bmatrix} 1 & -1 & 1 & 2 \\ 0 & 1 & -1 & -1 \\ -1 & 2 & 2 & 9 \end{bmatrix}$$

Step 3: Add the first row to the third row:

$$\begin{bmatrix} 1 & -1 & 1 & 2 \\ 0 & 1 & -1 & -1 \\ 0 & 1 & 3 & 11 \end{bmatrix}$$

Step 4: Subtract the second row from the third row. Then divide the third row by -4:

$$\begin{bmatrix} 1 & -1 & 1 & 2 \\ 0 & 1 & -1 & -1 \\ 0 & 0 & 1 & 3 \end{bmatrix}$$

The echelon form allows the system of equations to be solved. Choice (B) is correct.

Choice (D) is the correct coefficient matrix for the system of equations, but not in the echelon form.

FUNDAMENTAL ALGEBRAIC OPERATIONS

Learning algebra can seem like a difficult journey into the unknown, but the goal can be reached by taking one step at a time. All you need to be successful at anything is a good idea of what you want to accomplish, a map to show you the way, and the willingness to work toward your goal. This review is the map to help you reach your goal of understanding algebra. All you need to supply is the will and the work!

This review will walk you through various algebra topics. By following four steps while studying each section, you will be well on your way to your destination of learning algebra.

Steps to learning algebra:

1. *Know the language:* understand what words and symbols mean.
2. *Memorize the rules:* memorize the formulas in the tables.
3. *Follow the steps:* know the steps to solving the problems.
4. *Do the work:* practice, practice, practice!

Properties of Real Numbers

Algebra generally deals with real numbers. Real numbers include just about any number you might think of, including numbers like 0, −1/3, π, or $\sqrt{2}$. The only reason this matters is that there is another important type of number called a complex number. Complex numbers are more easily understood than their name might suggest, and we will discuss them in another section.

Table 1: Properties of Real Numbers

Commutative Properties	$a + b = b + a$, $ab = ba$
Associative Properties	$a + (b + c) = (a + b) + c$, $a(bc) = (ab)c$
Identities	$a + 0 = a$ or $a \cdot 1 = a$
Inverses	For every real number a, there is a negative number $-a$, such that $a + (-a) = 0$ For every real number except $a = 0$, there is a real number $1/a$ such that $a\left(\dfrac{1}{a}\right) = 1$
Distributive Properties	$a(b + c) = ab + ac$

Operations with Polynomials

Polynomials are any math expressions that use variables such as x, y, m, q, raised to a whole number called a power, with constants multiplied and added. Examples include:

$$\frac{1}{3}n + 3x^2 + 2,\ n^3 - 4n^2 + 2n - 3,\ -3xy^2,\ (x + 2)^2$$

It's important to know the names used to describe polynomials:

$$ax^n + b$$

a = constant, coefficient,

x = base, variable,

b = constant (note: b is really bx^0 where $x^0 = 1$, so the x isn't written)

n = exponent, power. The highest n in a polynomial is its order.

When working with polynomials it is important to understand the rules of exponentials. An exponential represents how many times a constant or variable is multiplied by itself.

$$a^n = \underbrace{a \cdot a \cdot a}_{n} \text{ or, for example, } a^2 = a \cdot a \text{ and } a^4 = a \cdot a \cdot a \cdot a$$

Polynomials can be added, subtracted, multiplied, or divided. For now, when working with polynomials you only need to remember that exponentials are added and coefficients are multiplied. Other rules for exponents will be discussed in a later section.

Addition and subtraction steps:

1. Rearrange the terms, and put the variable with "like powers" next to each other.

2. Combine the coefficients of like powers using the distributive property.

3. Add or subtract the coefficients.

Example 1: Find the sums of the polynomials $x^4 + 2x^3 - x^2 - 3$ and $2x^4 + 4x^2 - 5x + 4$.

Solution:

Step 1: Form the addition and put like powers together:

$$(x^4 + 2x^3 - x^2 - 3) + (2x^4 + 4x^2 - 5x + 3) = x^4 + 2x^4 + 2x^3 - x^2 + 4x^2 - 5x - 3 + 4$$

Steps 2 and 3: Combine the coefficients and add or subtract:

$$= (1 + 2)x^4 + 2x^3 + (-1 + 4)x^2 + (-5)x + (-3 + 4)$$
$$= 3x^4 + 2x^3 + 3x^2 - 5x + 1$$

FOIL Method to Find the Product of Polynomials

An important tool for multiplying polynomials is the FOIL rule. You will use it repeatedly to multiply first-order polynomials, meaning the highest power is x.

For example, if we wish to find the product of $(2x + 3)(3x - 4)$, we would multiply the polynomials in four steps: **F**irst, **O**utside, **I**nside, **L**ast.

Solution:

Step1: $\underset{\text{first}}{(2\underset{\smile}{x}} + 3)(3\underset{\smile}{x} - 4) = (2x)(3x) = 6x^2$
${\text{first}}{\text{first}}$

Step 2: $(\underset{\text{outside}}{\underline{2x}} + 3)(3x \underset{\text{outside}}{\underline{-4}}) = (2x)(-4) = -8x$

Step 3: $(2x + \underset{\text{inside}}{\underline{3}})(\underset{\text{inside}}{\underline{3x}} - 4) = (3)(3x) = 9x$

Step 4: $(2x + \underset{\text{last}}{\underline{3}})(3x \underset{\text{last}}{\underline{-4}}) = (3)(-4) = -12$

Add the four steps together:

$= 6x^2 - 8x + 9x - 12$

$= 6x^2 + (-8 + 9)x - 12$

$= 6x^2 + x - 12$

Multiplying Other Polynomials

Larger polynomials of higher orders can be multiplied as well.

Steps to multiply:

1. *Arrange:* Place the terms of one polynomial against the other entire polynomial.

2. *Multiply:* Use the distributive property of each group.

3. *Add:* Find the sum of the resulting terms using addition/subtraction steps.

Example 2: Find the product of $x^3 + 5x^2 - x$ and $x^2 - 2y + 1$.

Solution:

Step 1: Set up the multiplication:

$$\underset{\text{first}}{(x^3} + \underset{\text{second}}{5x^2} \underset{\text{third}}{-x)}\underset{\text{full equation}}{(x^2 - 2y + 1)} =$$

$$= \underset{\text{first}}{x^3} \underset{\text{full equation}}{(x^2 - 2y + 1)} + \underset{\text{second}}{5x^2} \underset{\text{full equation}}{(x^2 - 2y + 1)} \underset{\text{third}}{-x} \underset{\text{full equation}}{(x^2 - 2y + 1)}$$

Step 2: Multiply each grouping using the distributive property. If you look closely at the next step, it should become clear how to do this:

$= (x^3)(x^2) + (x^3)(-2y) + (x^3)(1) + (5x^2)(x^2) + (5x^2)(-2y) + (5x^2)(1) + (-x)(x^2) + (-x)(-2y) + (-x)(1)$

Step 3: Multiply the exponentials and combine as with addition. Remember that you multiply together the variables that are not alike:

$= x^{3+2} + (-2)x^3y + x^3 + 5x^{2+2} + (5)(-2)x^2y + 5x^2 - x^{1+2} + (-1)(-2)xy + (-x)$

$= x^5 - 2x^3y + x^3 + 5x^4 - 10x^2y + 5x^2 - x^3 + 2xy - x$

$= x^5 - 2x^3y + 5x^4 + (1 - 1)x^3 - 10x^2y + 5x^2 + 2xy - x$

$= x^5 - 2x^3y + 5x^4 - 10x^2y + 5x^2 + 2xy - x$

Factoring Polynomials Over Real Numbers

Many polynomials are the result of polynomials having been multiplied together. Factoring is the opposite of multiplying. Factoring is simply finding what polynomials were originally multiplied together. Table 2 below shows basic rules for factoring common polynomials. It's a good idea to memorize these rules.

Table 2: Factoring Rules for Polynomials

$$x^2 - y^2 = (x + y)(x - y)$$
$$x^2 + 2xy + y^2 = (x + y)^2$$
$$x^2 - 2xy + y^2 = (x - y)^2$$
$$x^3 + 3x^2y + 3xy^2 + y^3 = (x + y)^3$$
$$x^3 - 3x^2y + 3xy^2 - y^3 = (x - y)^3$$

Example 3: Factor the polynomial $6x^2 - 7x - 3$.

Solution: Unfortunately, some polynomials don't fit the rules above. Factoring these polynomials will often require the use of some trial and error—which means you need lots of practice to become skilled with these types of problems.

Think FOIL backwards to solve these problems. What values of $(ax + b)(cx + d)$ would arrive at the answer $6x^2 - 7x - 3$? For this solution to be true we know $ac = 6$ and $bd = -3$. Also we know that $bc + ad = -7$.

We know that 6 has factors 1, 6, 3, and 2. Also 3 has factors 1 and 3. We first should try -3 and 1 for b and d, and we can try 2 and 3 for a and b. With some trial and error, we can arrive at the solution.

$$6x^2 - 7x - 3 = (ax - 3)(bx + 1)$$
$$= (2x - 3)(3x + 1)$$

Remember to check your solution by multiplying the factors out to make sure your answer is correct.

RATIONAL EXPRESSIONS

The quotient or division of two polynomials forms a rational expression. Examples of rational expressions are:

$$\frac{5}{x-1}, \quad \frac{3x^2 + 2x + 7}{7x}, \quad \frac{5q + 1}{q + 1}$$

Multiplication and Division of Rational Expressions

To multiply and divide rational expressions you only need to know a few simple rules shown in Table 3 below. In this table, P and Q represent polynomials.

Table 3: Algebraic Rules for Rational Expressions

Cancellation property	$\dfrac{PS}{QS} = \dfrac{P}{Q}$
Multiplication	$\dfrac{P}{Q} \cdot \dfrac{R}{S} = \dfrac{PR}{QS}$
Division (multiply by the inverse of the denominator)	$\dfrac{\left(\dfrac{P}{Q}\right)}{\left(\dfrac{R}{S}\right)} = \dfrac{P}{Q} \cdot \dfrac{S}{R}$
Addition	$\dfrac{P}{Q} + \dfrac{R}{Q} = \dfrac{P+R}{Q}$
Subtraction	$\dfrac{P}{Q} - \dfrac{R}{Q} = \dfrac{P-R}{Q}$

Example 4: Multiply $\left(\dfrac{4y}{5}\right)$ and $\left(\dfrac{x+1}{2}\right)$.

Solution: Use the multiplication rule and solve:

$$\left(\frac{4y}{5}\right)\left(\frac{x+1}{2}\right) = \frac{(4y)(x+1)}{(5)(2)}$$

$$= \frac{(4y)(x) + (1)(4y)}{10}$$

$$= \frac{4xy + 4y}{10}$$

We can simplify further by extracting $4y$ out of the numerator:

$$= \frac{4xy + 4y}{10}$$

$$= \frac{4y(x+1)}{10}$$

$$= \frac{4y(x+1)}{10}$$

$$= \frac{2y(x+1)}{5}$$

Example 5: Divide $\left(\dfrac{4y}{5}\right)$ by $\left(\dfrac{x+1}{2}\right)$.

Solution: Use the division rule and solve:

$$\frac{\left(\dfrac{4y}{5}\right)}{\left(\dfrac{x+1}{2}\right)} = \left(\frac{4y}{5}\right)\left(\frac{2}{x+1}\right)$$

$$= \frac{4y(2)}{5(x+1)}$$

$$= \frac{8y}{5(x+1)}$$

Simplifying Rational Expressions

It is often helpful to simplify the polynomial, which means you want to get rid of common factors in the numerator and denominator. Simplification is best accomplished by factoring. Factoring pulls out more simple polynomials that often will cancel out.

Example 6: Simplify the rational expression $\dfrac{8x+12}{4}$.

Solution: Factor 4 out of the numerator and cancel this value because it's also in the denominator:

$$\frac{8x+12}{4} = \frac{4(2x+3)}{4}$$

$$= \frac{4(2x+3)}{4}$$

$$= 2x + 3$$

Example 7: Write the expression $\dfrac{x^2+2x+1}{x^2-1}$ in the lowest terms.

Solution: Factor the numerator. Fortunately, $x - 1$ is in both the numerator and denominator and can be canceled out:

$$\frac{x^2+2x+1}{x^2-1} = \frac{(x+1)(x+1)}{(x+1)(x-1)}$$

$$= \frac{x+1}{x-1}$$

EXPONENTIAL AND RADICAL EXPRESSIONS

Exponentials

Exponentials are very important. They only require a few rules, as shown in Table 4 below. Becoming skilled with exponentials is critical to your success with algebra, so solve many of these types of problems until you are comfortable with the rules.

Table 4: Rules for Exponentials

Product	$a^m a^n = a^{m+n}$
Product of a power	$(a^m)^n = a^{mn}$
Quotient to a power	$\left(\dfrac{a}{b}\right)^n = \dfrac{a^n}{b^n}$
Quotient	$\dfrac{a^m}{a^n} = a^{m-n}$
Zero exponent	$a^0 = 1$
Negative exponent	$a^{-n} = \dfrac{1}{a^n}$
Inversion	$\left(\dfrac{a}{b}\right)^{-n} = \left(\dfrac{b}{a}\right)^n$

Radicals

Radical expressions are those that use the symbol $\sqrt{}$ to represent roots of a variable. Radicals are really no different from exponentials. For example, the nth root of a would be expressed $\sqrt[n]{a}$, or $a^{\frac{1}{n}}$. Don't forget that for square roots where $n = 2$, the 2 is understood and that $\sqrt[2]{x}$ is simply written $\sqrt{x}$.

We can combine the exponential rules in Table 4 with the radical rules in Table 5 to solve numerous algebraic problems.

Table 5: Radical Expression Laws

$$\sqrt[n]{a} = a^{\frac{1}{n}}$$

$$a^{\frac{m}{n}} = \sqrt[n]{a^m}$$

$$\sqrt[n]{a} \cdot \sqrt[n]{b} = \sqrt[n]{ab}$$

$$\sqrt[n]{\frac{a}{b}} = \frac{\sqrt[n]{a}}{\sqrt[n]{b}}$$

$$\sqrt[mn]{a} = \sqrt[m]{\sqrt[n]{a}}$$

$$\sqrt[n]{a^n} = a \text{ , if } n \text{ is odd}$$

$$\sqrt[n]{a^n} = |a| \text{ , if } n \text{ is even}$$

Simplification of radicals is a popular test question. Radical simplification is also a part of many other types of questions.

Remember the following regarding simplified radicals:

- For $\sqrt[n]{x^m}$, m should be less or equal to n (i.e., no factors with an exponent greater than or equal to the index of the radical).

- No fractions should appear under the final radical sign.

- The index n should be as low as possible.

Example 8: Simplify the radical $\sqrt[4]{x^6 y^4}$.

Simplify by using the rules above to move values from under the radicals. One of the forms to use is $\sqrt[n]{a^n} = a$. By factoring out x^2 and rearranging, we can pull out xy:

$$\sqrt[4]{x^6 y^4} = \sqrt[4]{(x^4 y^4)(x^2)}$$
$$= \sqrt[4]{(xy)^4 (x^2)}$$
$$= \sqrt[4]{(xy)^4} \sqrt[4]{x^2}$$
$$= (xy)(x^{\frac{1}{2}})$$
$$= xy\sqrt{x}$$

As with exponentials, practice will help you to quickly learn these rules and become comfortable with how to use them.

LINEAR EQUATIONS

Linear equations are polynomials of the first order, i.e., x^1 or just x. Linear equations can have one or more variables. These polynomials are called "linear" because if you plot them on a graph they form a line.

Solving Single Variable Equations

When solving linear equations, you are trying to find the value of the variable that makes the equation true. What this means is that you want to use the simple rules in Table 1 to move values to the other side of the variable.

Example 9: Solve the equation $4x + 6 = -2$.

Solution: To solve this problem, we need to find the value of x that makes the equality true. We do this by first subtracting 6 from both sides and then multiplying each side by $\frac{1}{4}$:

$$4x + 6 = -2$$
$$4x + 6 - 6 = -2 - 6$$
$$4x = -8$$
$$\frac{1}{4}(4x) = \frac{1}{4}(-8)$$
$$\left(\frac{4}{4}\right)x = \frac{-8}{4}$$
$$x = -2$$

Methods of Solving Multiple Variable Problems

Mathematical problems that deal with more than one equation and contain more than one variable are called simultaneous equations. You can determine if these equations have common solutions. A common solution can be found by calculating where the equations are equal or where they intersect. For example, consider the following equations:

$$\begin{cases} x + 3y = -1 \\ 2x - y = 5 \end{cases}$$

You can graph these equations on a coordinate plane in order to find where they intersect. The following table shows values for y using the values of $x = (-2, -1, 0, 1, 2)$ for $x + 3y = -1$:

x	-2	-1	0	1	2
y	$\frac{1}{3}$	0	$-\frac{1}{3}$	$-\frac{2}{3}$	-1

The following table shows some of the solutions for $2x - y = 5$, using the values of $x = (-2, -1, 0, 1, 2)$ to find values for y.

x	-2	-1	0	1	2
y	-9	-7	-5	-3	-1

If we graph these values, we can see that these equations intersect at $(2,-1)$:

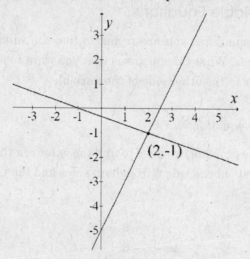

$$\text{Figure 1: } \begin{cases} x + 3y = -1 \\ 2x - y = 5 \end{cases}$$

Note that the value of $x = 2$ and $y = -1$ represented by the pair $(2,-1)$ is a solution to both equations. Therefore, it is a solution to the simultaneous equations.

Graphical analysis to find intercepts is not always the most practical method for solving these equations. Problems that involve solutions that are rational numbers such as $\frac{17}{32}$, or other complex solutions require a more structured approach. Fortunately, three other methods—the substitution method, the elimination method, and the matrix method—can be used to find solutions to these problems.

Substitution Method

The substitution method involves solving for one variable in one equation and substituting this solution into another equation. The substitution method uses the following procedure:

Step 1: Solve one equation for one of the variables in terms of the other variables.

Step 2: Substitute the equation from step 1 into the other equation resulting in an equation that contains only one variable.

Step 3: Find the solution to the equation obtained in step 2.

Step 4: Use the solution from step 3 with the expression from step 1 to find the solution to the system.

Example 10: Find the solutions to the simultaneous equations using the substitution method.

$$\begin{cases} x + 3y = -1 \\ 2x - y = 5 \end{cases}$$

Solution:

Step 1: We solve the first equation for x:

$$x + 3y = -1$$
$$x = -1 - 3y$$

Step 2: We substitute for x in the second equation. We obtain:

$$2x - y = 5$$
$$2(-1 - 3y) - y = 5$$

Step 3: We solve the equation from step 2:

$$2(-1 - 3y) - y = 5$$
$$-2 - 6y - y = 5$$
$$-2 - 7y = 5$$
$$-7y = 7$$
$$y = -1$$

Step 4: We can now substitute this value of y into the first equation:

$$x + 3y = -1$$
$$x + 3(-1) = -1$$
$$x - 3 = -1$$
$$x = 2$$

This gives us the solution $x = 2$, $y = -1$, which can be expressed as the ordered pair $(2, -1)$.

Elimination Method

Elimination is based upon the principle that an equation is equivalent if a value is multiplied, divided, added, or subtracted to both sides of an equation. Note that for multiplication and division, the number must be non-zero.

Using this method, simultaneous equations can be transformed so that when the equations are added or subtracted, variables are eliminated, thus allowing the equations to be solved. This method can take fewer steps than the substitution method, but it requires that the proper transformations be used.

Example 11: Using the elimination method find the solutions of the system:

$$\begin{cases} x + 3y = -1 \\ 2x - y = 5 \end{cases}$$

Solution: First, we can multiply equation 1 by –2. The value –2 is selected to allow us to eliminate the $2x$ by addition. Now, add equation 2 to equation 1:

$$\begin{array}{r} -2x - 6y = 2 \\ +\quad 2x - \ y = 5 \\ \hline -7y = 7 \end{array}$$

Now, we can easily solve, and we find $y = -1$. We can then substitute this value into either equation as we did in the substitution method and obtain the value of $x = 2$.

Matrix Method

The matrix method is basically the substitution method using the matrix form. This form is of greatest help when equations are complex or contain multiple variables. We can form what is called the coefficient matrix by taking the coefficients of each equation and placing them in the matrix. As an example, let's look at the set of equations we have been using:

$$\begin{cases} x + 3y = -1 \\ 2x - y = 5 \end{cases}$$

These equations can be written in matrix form called the coefficient matrix. This matrix represents the set of equations:

$$\begin{bmatrix} 1 & 3 & -1 \\ 2 & -1 & 5 \end{bmatrix}$$

The matrix method is very similar to the elimination method as we operate on each line of the matrix using elementary row transformations, which are:

1. Interchange any two rows.

2. Multiply all values of a row by any non-zero real number.

3. Multiply any row by any real value and add this row to another row.

The goal of solving using the matrix method is to put the matrix in the echelon form. The echelon form has a zero as the first member of the second row, zeros in the first and second member of third row, etc. Said another way, the echelon form has zeros everywhere below the main diagonal.

An example of the echelon form is the following matrix:

$$\begin{bmatrix} a & b & c & d \\ 1 & e & f & g \\ 0 & 1 & h & i \\ 0 & 0 & 1 & j \end{bmatrix}$$

Once a matrix is in the echelon form, we can then use this form to solve the equations.

Example 12: Solve the matrix $\begin{bmatrix} 1 & 3 & -1 \\ 2 & -1 & 5 \end{bmatrix}$

Solution: The first step is to multiply the first row by –2 and add this to the second row:

$$\begin{bmatrix} 1 & 3 & -1 \\ 2+(-2) & -1+(-6) & 5+(2) \end{bmatrix}$$

$$\begin{bmatrix} 1 & 3 & -1 \\ 0 & -7 & 7 \end{bmatrix}$$

This gives us the echelon matrix form, which we can easily put back into equation form:

$$\begin{cases} x + 3y = -1 \\ \quad -7y = 7 \end{cases}$$

Now the equations can easily be solved using the substitution method, which gives us $y = -1$ and $x = 2$.

$$-7y = y$$
$$y = -1$$

$$x + 3(-1) = -1$$
$$x - 3 = -1$$
$$x = 2$$

Don't feel bad if you find this method overly complicated or confusing because it is. However, for very large equations where you use a computer program, the matrix method is the ideal choice for solving simultaneous equations.

ABSOLUTE VALUE EQUATIONS AND INEQUALITIES

Inequalities

An inequality is a math statement where instead of two equations being equal, one equation is greater than the other (>), less than the other (<), greater than or equal to the other (≥), or less than or equal to (≤) the other. Solving inequalities is very similar to solving linear equalities except for one simple rule:

Inequality Rule: The inequality sign should be flipped whenever you multiply or divide by a negative number.

Intervals describe the solutions to inequalities. Brackets "[ ]"are used when a solution includes a number, and parentheses "( )" are used when a number is not included in a solution as shown in Table 6. The ∪ symbol means the union of two sets or "and."

Table 6: Typical Intervals

$a \leq x \leq b$	$[a, b]$	both a and b are included	![number line with closed bracket at a and closed bracket at b]
$a \leq x < b$	$[a, b)$	a is included but b is not	![number line with closed bracket at a and open paren at b]
$a < x \leq b$	$(a, b]$	b is included but a is not	![number line with open paren at a and closed bracket at b]
$a < x < b$	(a, b)	neither a nor b are included	![number line with open paren at a and open paren at b]
$x < a$	$[-\infty, a)$	a is not included	![number line ray left with open paren at a]
$x \leq a$	$[-\infty, a]$	a is included	![number line ray left with closed bracket at a]
$x < a$ and $x > b$	$(-\infty, a) \cup (b, \infty)$	neither a nor b are included*	![number line ray left with open paren at a and ray right with open paren at b]

*If a or b were included, then the "[" symbol would be used in place of the "(".

Example 13: Solve $-2 - 5x < 8$.

Solution:

$$-2 - 5x < 8$$
$$-2 - 5x + 2 < 8 + 2$$
$$-5x < 10$$
$$x > -2$$

Notice that the inequality sign was reversed in the last step because we divided by −5 to isolate x. Our solution is $x > -2$ or $(-2, \infty)$, which is represented with the following number line:

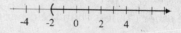

Absolute Values and Inequalities

The distance of any number from zero is the absolute value. Pipes "| |" are used around an equation for an absolute value. For example $|4| = 4$ and $|-4| = 4$.

Example 14: Solve the equation $x = |2 - 7|$.

Solution:

$$x = |2 - 7|$$
$$x = |-5|$$
$$x = 5$$

Inequalities can also use the absolute value sign. Table 7 below shows the rules that apply when using absolute values. When solving inequalities using absolute values, it is important to solve all possible solutions that can occur.

Table 7: Rules for Absolute Values

$|a|$	a
$|a| < b$	$-b < a < b$
$|a| > b$	$a < -b$ or $a > b$
$|a| = b$	$a = -b$ or $a = b$

Example 15: Solve $|-2x - 2| \leq 6$.

Solution: Using the rule in Table 7, first solve for $-2x - 4 \leq 6$, and then solve for $-2x - 4 \geq -6$:

$$-2x - 2 \leq 6 \qquad -2x - 2 \geq -6$$
$$-2x \leq 8 \qquad\quad -2x \leq -4$$
$$x \geq -4 \qquad\quad\; x \geq 2$$

Thus, $x \geq -4$ and $x \geq 2$, or simply $x \geq -4$, as shown in the number line:

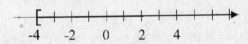

QUADRATIC EQUATIONS AND INEQUALITIES

Standard Factoring

A quadratic equation is an equation of the form $ax^2 + bx + c = 0$, where $a \neq 0$. Quadratic equations can be solved using the standard method of factoring. This method requires you to think about the FOIL method in reverse as was discussed in the factoring polynomial section.

Example 16: Solve the equation $2x^2 + 11x + 5 = 0$.

Solution: We know 5 is the product of 1 and 5. We know 2 is the product of 1 and 2. We should try the values and see if they work:

$$2x^2 + 11x + 5 = 0$$
$$(2x + 1)(x + 5) = 0$$

Sure enough, 1 and 5 work. We next solve for $2x + 1 = 0$ or $x + 5 = 0$. When we solve both of these equations, we find that $x = -\frac{1}{2}$ and $x = -5$.

Example 17: Solve the equation $x^2 = 7$.

Solution: We can solve this problem by using a factoring rule:

$$x^2 = 7$$
$$x^2 - 7 = 0$$
$$(x - \sqrt{7})(x + \sqrt{7}) = 0$$

Next, solve the equations $(x - \sqrt{7}) = 0$ and $(x + \sqrt{7}) = 0$. We find that $x = +\sqrt{7}$ and $x = -\sqrt{7}$. We express these solutions as $x = \pm\sqrt{7}$.

Completing the Square

Often, quadratic equations just don't seem to work out easily using the standard method. Completing the square allows you to change the quadratic so that it will easily factor. This involves adding a constant to both sides of the equation to make it factorable.

Steps for completing the square $ax^2 + bx + c = 0$:

1. Divide by a. The goal is that the coefficient of x^2 is 1.

2. Isolate the constant c by moving it to the right side of the equation.

3. Divide b by 2 and then square it.

4. Add the new number to both sides.

5. Factor to get a solution of the form $(x + a)^2$ or $(x - a)^2$.

6. Use the square root property and solve.

Example 18: Complete the square of $2x^2 + 8x - 10 = 0$.

Solution: Follow the steps for completing the square:

Step 1: Divide by a:

$$2x^2 + 8x - 10 = 0$$
$$\frac{2}{2}x^2 + \frac{8}{2}x - \frac{10}{2} = 0$$
$$x^2 + 4x - 5 = 0$$

Step 2: Isolate the constant c:

$$x^2 + 4x - 5 = 0$$
$$x^2 + 4x = 5$$

Note: Completing the square is just trying to find what value can be added to $x^2 + 4x + \underline{\quad} = 5$ in place of the $\underline{\quad}$ that makes the quadratic factorable.

Step 3: Divide b by 2 and square:

$$\left(4 \cdot \frac{1}{2}\right)^2 = \left(\frac{4}{2}\right)^2$$
$$(2)^2 = 4$$

Step 4: Add the new number to both sides of the equation:

$$x^2 + 4x - 3 = 0$$
$$x^2 + 4x + 4 = 5 + 4$$
$$x^2 + 4x + 4 = 9$$

Step 5: Factor:

$$x^2 + 4x + 4 = 9$$
$$(x + 2)^2 = 9$$

Step 6: Use square root rule and solve:

$$\sqrt{(x + 2)^2} = \sqrt{9}$$
$$(x + 2) = \pm 3$$

$$x + 2 = 3 \qquad x + 2 = -3$$
$$x = 3 - 2 \qquad x = -3 - 2$$
$$x = 1 \qquad x = -5$$

We arrive at the solution $x = 1$ and $x = -5$.

Quadratic Equations

For the most difficult quadratic equations, the best method to find the factors is using the quadratic equation. The good news here is that, in a pinch, you can solve any quadratic equations using this method.

If $ax^2 + bx + c = 0$, where $a \neq 0$, then the roots of the equation are given by:

$$x = \frac{-b \pm \sqrt{b^2 - 4ac}}{2a}$$

Example 19: Solve $x^2 + 2x - 6 = 0$.

Solution: Let $a = 1$, $b = 2$, and $c = -6$ and solve:

$$x = \frac{-(2) \pm \sqrt{(2)^2 - 4(1)(-6)}}{2(1)}$$

$$x = \frac{-(2) \pm \sqrt{4 + 24}}{2}$$

$$x = \frac{-(2) \pm \sqrt{28}}{2}$$

$$x = \frac{-2 \pm \sqrt{(4)(7)}}{2}$$

$$x = \frac{-2 \pm 2\sqrt{7}}{2}$$

$$x = -1 \pm \sqrt{7}$$

Polynomial Inequalities

Inequalities can be solved for higher-order polynomials.

Follow these steps to solve polynomial inequalities:

    Step 1: Rewrite the equation so that one side equals zero.

    Step 2: Solve the equality. Change the inequality sign to an equal sign.

    Step 3: Test each possible solution "region" using a value from that region in the polynomial.

The following example helps explain these steps.

Example 20: Find the solution to $x^2 + 2x > 3$.

Solution: Use the steps for solving polynomial inequalities.

Step 1: Rewrite the equation so that one side equals zero:

$$x^2 + 2x > 3$$
$$x^2 + 2x - 3 > 0$$
$$(x + 3)(x - 1) = 0$$

Step 2: Solve the equality of the problem (i.e., find x-intercepts for $y = x^2 + 2x - 3$):

$$x^2 + 2x - 3 = 0$$
$$(x + 3)(x - 1) = 0$$

Thus $x = -3$ and $x = 1$.

Step 3: Test each region with a value from that region and determine if the original equation is true or false.

Plot the values for x on a number line:

Region A   Region B   Region C
$x < -3$ $-3 < x < 1$ $x > 1$

Pick any value from each region and test this value in the original equation $x^2 + 2x - 3$ and determine if the solution is positive or negative.

Region A: Test value $x = -4$:

$$(-4)^2 + 2(-4) - 3 = 16 - 8 - 3$$
$$= 5 \text{ positive}$$

Region B: Test value $x = 0$ or $(0)^2 + 2(0) - 3 = -3$ negative

Region C: Test value $x = 2$ or $(2)^2 + 2(2) - 3 = 5$ positive

So, we find that the solution is positive for region A and C, where $x < -3$ and $x > 1$ or $(-\infty, -3) \cup (1, \infty)$.

EQUATIONS INVOLVING RADICALS

Solving equations with radicals involves a few simple steps:

1. Move one radical to one side of the equation and everything else to the other side.
2. Eliminate the radical by raising both sides by a power that is the reciprocal of the exponent.
3. Still have radicals? Repeat steps 1 and 2.
4. Solve the remaining equation.
5. Check for extraneous solutions.

Example 21: Solve the radical equation $\sqrt{10x - 4} - 4 = 0$.

Solution:

Step 1: Isolate the radical by putting it on one side:

$$\sqrt{10x - 4} = 4$$

Step 2: Get rid of the radical by squaring both sides of the equation:

$$\left(\sqrt{10x - 4}\right)^2 = 4^2$$
$$10x - 4 = 16$$

Step 3: All radicals are eliminated, so proceed to step 4.

Step 4: Solve the remaining equation:

$$10x - 4 = 16$$
$$10x = 20$$
$$x = 2$$

Step 5: Check the solution:

$$\sqrt{10(2) - 4} - 4 = 0$$
$$\sqrt{16} - 4 = 0$$
$$0 = 0$$

The solution is correct. $x = 2$ is the solution to the problem.

Rational exponents, which are of the form $a^{\frac{m}{n}} = b$, are solved using the same steps as above.

Example 22: Solve the rational equation $(x^2 + x - 5)^{\frac{2}{3}} - 1 = 0$.

Solution:

Step 1: Isolate the rational exponent by putting it on one side:

$$(x^2 + x - 5)^{\frac{2}{3}} = 1$$

Step 2: Get rid of the rational exponent by raising to the inverse of the exponent, or $\frac{3}{2}$:

$$\left((x^2 + x - 5)^{\frac{2}{3}}\right)^{\frac{3}{2}} = (1)^{\frac{3}{2}}$$
$$x^2 + x - 5 = 1$$

Note: $(1)^{\frac{3}{2}} = \sqrt[2]{(1)^3} = \sqrt[2]{1} = 1$

Step 3: All radicals are eliminated, so proceed to step 4.

Step 4: Solve the remaining equation:

$$x^2 + x - 5 = 1$$
$$x^2 + x - 6 = 0$$
$$(x + 3)(x - 2) = 0$$

Thus, $x = -3$ and $x = 2$ are two possible solutions.

Step 5: Check the solution for -3:

$$\left((-3)^2 + (-3) - 5\right)^{\frac{2}{3}} - 1 = 0$$
$$(9 - 3 - 5)^{\frac{2}{3}} - 1 = 0$$
$$1^{\frac{2}{3}} - 1 = 0$$
$$0 = 0$$

We have shown that -3 is a valid solution. Now check $x = 2$.

$$\left((2)^2 + 2 - 5\right)^{\frac{2}{3}} - 1 = 0$$
$$(4 + 2 - 5)^{\frac{2}{3}} - 1 = 0$$
$$(1)^{\frac{2}{3}} - 1 = 0$$
$$1 - 1 = 0$$

So, both 2 and -3 are roots to $(x^2 + x - 5)^{\frac{2}{3}} - 1 = 0$.

COMPLEX NUMBERS

Complex numbers help solve polynomials such as $x^2 = -b$. There are no real solutions to this problem, which means we need a new type of number. This number is the complex number.

The basic unit of a complex number is i, where $i = \sqrt{-1}$ or $i^2 = -1$. Complex conjugate numbers are of the form $a + bi$ where a represents the real unit and bi is the imaginary unit.

Basic math functions can be performed on complex numbers. It might be helpful to think of i as just another variable, the only difference being $i^2 = -1$.

Multiplication can be performed using the FOIL method. Addition of complex numbers follows the form $(a + bi) + (c + di) = (a + c) + (b + d)i$.

Example 23: What is the sum of $5 + 2i$ and $10 - 5i$?

Solution:

$$(5 + 2i) + (10 - 5i) = (5 + 10) + (2 - 5)i$$
$$= 15 - 3i$$

Example 24: What is the product of $(2 + 3i)$ and $(4 - 5i)$?

Solution:

$$(2 + 3i)(4 - 5i) = (2)(4) + (2)(-5i) + (3i)(4) + (3i)(-5i)$$
$$= 8 - 10i + 12i - 15i^2$$
$$= 8 + (-10 + 12)i = 15i^2$$
$$= 8 + 2i - 15(-1)$$
$$= 8 + 2i + 15$$
$$= 23 + 2i$$

Division of complex numbers involves multiplying the numerator and denominator by the complex conjugate of the denominator. The complex conjugate is basically just the complex number with the complex sign changed. When a complex number is multiplied by its conjugate, the i goes away.

Example 25: Solve $\dfrac{2}{3 + 4i}$.

Solution: To divide 2 by $3 + 4i$, first multiply both the numerator and the denominator by the conjugate of the denominator or $3 - 4i$:

$$\frac{2}{3+4i} = \frac{2}{(3+4i)} \cdot \frac{(3-4i)}{(3-4i)}$$

$$= \frac{(2)(3) + (2)(-4)i}{(3+4i)(3-4i)}$$

$$= \frac{6-8i}{(3)(3) - (4i)(3) + (4i)(3) + (4i)(-4i)}$$

$$= \frac{6-8i}{9 - 12i + 12i - 16i^2}$$

$$= \frac{6-8i}{9 - 16(-1)}$$

$$= \frac{6-8i}{25}$$

$$= \frac{6}{25} - \frac{8}{25}i$$

FUNCTIONS

Functions are easy to work with if you think of them as an equation where for a value of x we get exactly one value for y. For solving problems, it's helpful to think of functions as just special equations where y is written as $f(x)$. The equation $y = mx + b$ could be written as a function as $f(x) = mx + b$.

We can find where a function crosses the x-axis or the x-intercept by setting $y = 0$ and solve for x. The exact opposite is true to find the y-intercept where you set $x = 0$ and solve for y.

Domain and Range

A rational function is any function where the numerator and denominator are polynomials. An example of a rational function is:

$$f(x) = \frac{x^2 + 2x - 5}{x^2 - 2x - 8}$$

The domain of the function is all the allowable values for x. Be careful not to include any values of x where you would be dividing by zero. The range of the function is all values the function can take on for the given values of x.

Example 26: Find the domain of the function $f(x) = \frac{x-4}{x^2 + x - 2}$.

Solution: The only values where x causes the function to be divided by zero is where the denominator is equal to zero. Set the denominator equal to zero and solve:

$$x^2 + x - 2 = 0$$
$$(x-1)(x+2) = 0$$

Thus, $x = 1$ and $x = -2$ are not in the domain. The domain is all x not equal to 1 or -2. The function is plotted in the coordinate system. You can see that the function does indeed "bow up" or have a slope of ∞ when $x = 1$ or $x = -2$ in Figure 2.

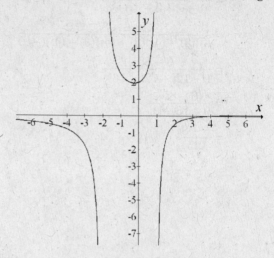

Figure 2: $f(x) = \dfrac{x - 4}{x^2 + x - 2}$

Inverse Functions

The inverse function, which is written f^{-1}, is the set of all ordered pairs of the form (y,x) where (x,y) belongs to f. The inverse is formed by interchanging x and y.

Example 27: If $f(x) = 4x - 6$ for all real numbers x, find the inverse function of f.

Solution: First exchange x and y and then solve for x. To confirm that the solution is indeed the inverse $f^{-1}(x)$, substitute the answer into the original function for x. The result should equal x:

$$x = 4y - 6$$

$$y = \frac{x + 6}{4}$$

$$f^{-1}(x) = \frac{x + 6}{4}$$

Note: $f^{-1}(x)$ is not the same as $f(x)^{-1}$. $f(x)^{-1} = \dfrac{1}{f(x)}$.

Operations and Functions

Functions can be operated on by addition, subtraction, multiplication, and division, just as you would do with numbers or polynomials.

Table 8: Function Operations

Sum of $f + g$	$(f + g)(x) = f(x) + g(x)$
Difference of $f - g$	$(f - g)(x) = f(x) - g(x)$
Product of f and g	$(f \times g)(x) = f(x) \times g(x)$
Quotient of $\dfrac{f}{g}$	$\left(\dfrac{f}{g}\right)(x) = \dfrac{f(x)}{g(x)}$
Composite function	$(f \circ g) = f\big(g(x)\big)$

Example 28: Given $f(x) = 3x - 4$ and $g(x) = 2x + 1$, find $f(x)g(x)$.

Solution: Use FOIL and solve:

$$
\begin{aligned}
[f(x)][g(x)] &= (3x - 4)(2x + 1) \\
&= (3x)(2x) + (-4)(2x) + (1)(3x) + (-4)(1) \\
&= 6x^2 - 8x + 3x - 4 \\
&= 6x^2 + (-8 + 3)x - 4 \\
&= 6x^2 - 5x - 4
\end{aligned}
$$

The composite function $(f \circ g) = f\big(g(x)\big)$ means that you replace the variable in $f(x)$ with the function $g(x)$.

Example 29: Given $f(x) = 3x - 4$ and $g(x) = 2x + 1$, find $f(g(x))$.

Solution: Replace the x in $f(x)$ with $2x + 1$:

$$
\begin{aligned}
(f \circ g)x &= 3(2x + 1) - 4 \\
&= (3)(2x) + 3 - 4 \\
&= 6x - 1
\end{aligned}
$$

Exponential Function

Exponential functions are of the form $f(x) = a^x + b$.

Example 30: Graph $f(x) = 2^x - 1$.

Solution: Pick values of x, such as $(-3, -1, 0, 1, 3)$, to find values of y.

x	-3	-1	0	1	3
y	$-\dfrac{7}{8}$	-0.5	0	1	7

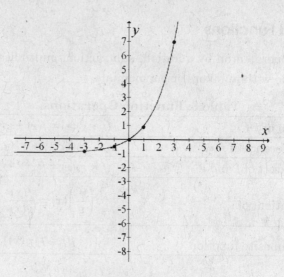

Figure 3: $f(x) = 2^x - 1$

Logarithmic Functions

A logarithmic function is the inverse of an exponential function. It is important when solving these functions to know how to convert from the exponential and logarithmic forms as shown in Table 9 below.

Logarithms written without a base are understood to be base 10. The natural log is written "ln" and uses the symbol e and follows the same rules as Log.

Table 9: Logarithm Laws

Law	Natural Log	Log
Transformation	$y = \ln x \longleftrightarrow e^y = x$	$y = \log_a x \longleftrightarrow a^y = x$
Log of 1	$\ln 1 = 0$	$\log_a 1 = 0$
Law of multiplication	$\ln (xy) = \ln x + \ln y$	$\log_a (xy) = \log_a x + \log_a y$
Law of division	$\ln \left(\dfrac{x}{y}\right) = \ln x - \ln y$	$\log_a \left(\dfrac{x}{y}\right) = \log_a x - \log_a y$
Exponent	$\ln (x^c) = c \ln x$	$\log_a (x^c) = c \log_a xq$
Change of Base	Not available	$\log_a x = \dfrac{\log_b x}{\log_b a}$ or $\log_a x = \dfrac{1}{\log_x a}$

Example 31: Solve the equation $\log_3(x - 4) = 2$.

Solution: Use the logarithm laws and solve:

$$\log_3(x - 4) = 2$$
$$x - 4 = 3^2$$
$$x - 4 = 9$$
$$x = 13$$

TWO-DIMENSIONAL GRAPHING

The basic parts of a two-dimensional coordinate plane are shown in Figure 4.

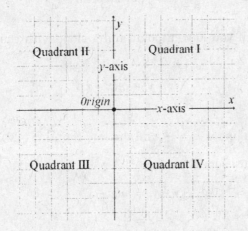

Figure 4: Rectangular Coordinate System

The steps for plotting an equation(s) are as follows:

1. Find ordered pairs that satisfy the equation. Pick values for x and solve for y. Generally, good picks for x can depend on the equation. For example, use values of x that result in $y = 0$, and notice the order of the equation as this determines the shape. A good rule of thumb is to pick one small negative value, −1, 0, 1, and a larger value (e.g., −5, −1, 0, 1, 5). Every plot will be different. The idea is to pick values that are easy to solve and really help show what the plot will look like.

2. Plot the values on the coordinate plane.

3. Connect the dots using extrapolation and interpolation. If you don't have enough points to clearly graph the equation, create more pairs.

4. Repeat steps 1 to 4 for the next equation.

Slope of a Line

The slope of a line is a measure of its steepness. You can find the slope of a set of points (x_1, y_1) and (x_2, y_2) by finding the change in y divided by the change in x.

$$m = \frac{\text{change in } y}{\text{change in } x} = \frac{y_2 - y_1}{x_2 - x_1}$$

Example 32: Find the slope of (4,3) and (8,6).

Solution: Use the point-slope equation:

$$\frac{6-3}{8-4} = \frac{3}{4}, \text{ or slope } m = \frac{3}{4}$$

You can find the line if you have a point and a slope with the following point-slope formula:

$$y - y_1 = m(x - x_1)$$

Example 33: Find the line if $m = \frac{3}{4}$ and the line contains (4,2):

Solution: Use the point-slope formula:

$$y - y_1 = m(x - x_1)$$
$$y - 2 = \frac{3}{4}(x - 4)$$
$$y - 2 = \frac{3}{4}x - \frac{3}{4}(4)$$
$$y - 2 = \frac{3}{4}x - 3$$
$$y = \frac{3}{4}x - 1$$

You can find the slope of a linear equation by putting it into the form $y = mx + b$, where m is the slope.

Table 10: General Slope Rules

$x_1 = x_2$ or $m = \infty$	Vertical line	$\vert$
$m = 0$	Horizontal line	—
m is positive	Line leans to the right	/
m is negative	Line leans to the left	\
$m_1 = -\dfrac{1}{m_2}$	Perpendicular lines	$\perp$
$m_1 = m_2$	Parallel lines	=

Graphing Forms

It's important to review the basic forms of lines and other polynomials. For example, a line is always of the form $y = mx + b$, and a parabola will contain a square. If you memorize the basic graphical forms, you'll be well on the way to easily solving algebraic equations.

Line: A line is always of the form $f(x) = mx + b$, where m is the slope and b represents the y-coordinate of the point where the line crosses the y-axis.

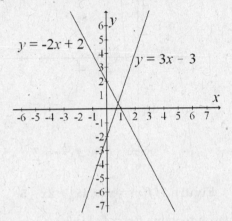

Figure 5: Example of Two Different Lines, $f(x) = -2x + 2$ and $f(x) = 3x - 3$

Quadratic: Any equation of the form $f(x) = ax^2 + bx^2 + c$. A quadratic with a positive a will bow up, a negative a will bow down. A larger value of a narrows the bow, while a smaller value of a makes the bow wider.

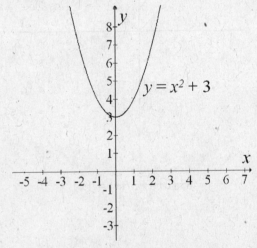

Figure 6: Example of a Quadratic, $f(x) = -x^2 + 3$

Cubic: A cubic is in the form $f(x) = ax^3 + bx^2 + cx + d$. A cubic will have two "humps." You will notice that as the order of the polynomial goes up, the number of "humps" on the graph is equal to the order minus one.

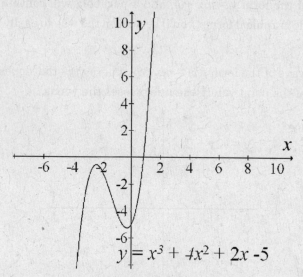

Figure 7: $f(x) = x^3 + 4x^2 + 2x - 5$

Absolute value: An absolute value $f(x) = |a|$, where a is any polynomial.

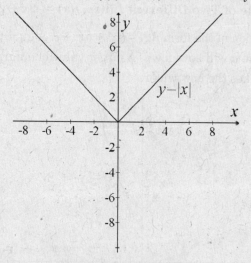

Figure 8: $f(x) = |x|$

Logarithm: A function with a log $f(x) = \log x$ will graph similarly to the following example.

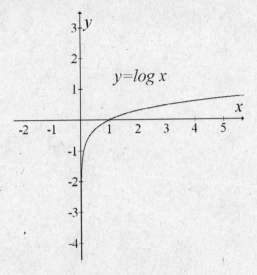

Figure 9: $f(x) = \log x$

As you can see, every type of function has a different shape. Knowing the way in which various functions plot can be beneficial in solving algebraic problems.

POST-TEST ANSWER SHEET

1. Ⓐ Ⓑ Ⓒ Ⓓ
2. Ⓐ Ⓑ Ⓒ Ⓓ
3. Ⓐ Ⓑ Ⓒ Ⓓ
4. Ⓐ Ⓑ Ⓒ Ⓓ
5. Ⓐ Ⓑ Ⓒ Ⓓ
6. Ⓐ Ⓑ Ⓒ Ⓓ
7. Ⓐ Ⓑ Ⓒ Ⓓ
8. Ⓐ Ⓑ Ⓒ Ⓓ
9. Ⓐ Ⓑ Ⓒ Ⓓ
10. Ⓐ Ⓑ Ⓒ Ⓓ
11. Ⓐ Ⓑ Ⓒ Ⓓ
12. Ⓐ Ⓑ Ⓒ Ⓓ

13. Ⓐ Ⓑ Ⓒ Ⓓ
14. Ⓐ Ⓑ Ⓒ Ⓓ
15. Ⓐ Ⓑ Ⓒ Ⓓ
16. Ⓐ Ⓑ Ⓒ Ⓓ
17. Ⓐ Ⓑ Ⓒ Ⓓ
18. Ⓐ Ⓑ Ⓒ Ⓓ
19. Ⓐ Ⓑ Ⓒ Ⓓ
20. Ⓐ Ⓑ Ⓒ Ⓓ
21. Ⓐ Ⓑ Ⓒ Ⓓ
22. Ⓐ Ⓑ Ⓒ Ⓓ
23. Ⓐ Ⓑ Ⓒ Ⓓ
24. Ⓐ Ⓑ Ⓒ Ⓓ

25. Ⓐ Ⓑ Ⓒ Ⓓ
26. Ⓐ Ⓑ Ⓒ Ⓓ
27. Ⓐ Ⓑ Ⓒ Ⓓ
28. Ⓐ Ⓑ Ⓒ Ⓓ
29. Ⓐ Ⓑ Ⓒ Ⓓ
30. Ⓐ Ⓑ Ⓒ Ⓓ
31. Ⓐ Ⓑ Ⓒ Ⓓ
32. Ⓐ Ⓑ Ⓒ Ⓓ
33. Ⓐ Ⓑ Ⓒ Ⓓ
34. Ⓐ Ⓑ Ⓒ Ⓓ
35. Ⓐ Ⓑ Ⓒ Ⓓ
36. Ⓐ Ⓑ Ⓒ Ⓓ

37. Ⓐ Ⓑ Ⓒ Ⓓ
38. Ⓐ Ⓑ Ⓒ Ⓓ
39. Ⓐ Ⓑ Ⓒ Ⓓ
40. Ⓐ Ⓑ Ⓒ Ⓓ
41. Ⓐ Ⓑ Ⓒ Ⓓ
42. Ⓐ Ⓑ Ⓒ Ⓓ
43. Ⓐ Ⓑ Ⓒ Ⓓ
44. Ⓐ Ⓑ Ⓒ Ⓓ
45. Ⓐ Ⓑ Ⓒ Ⓓ
46. Ⓐ Ⓑ Ⓒ Ⓓ
47. Ⓐ Ⓑ Ⓒ Ⓓ
48. Ⓐ Ⓑ Ⓒ Ⓓ

49. Ⓐ Ⓑ Ⓒ Ⓓ
50. Ⓐ Ⓑ Ⓒ Ⓓ
51. Ⓐ Ⓑ Ⓒ Ⓓ
52. Ⓐ Ⓑ Ⓒ Ⓓ
53. Ⓐ Ⓑ Ⓒ Ⓓ
54. Ⓐ Ⓑ Ⓒ Ⓓ
55. Ⓐ Ⓑ Ⓒ Ⓓ
56. Ⓐ Ⓑ Ⓒ Ⓓ
57. Ⓐ Ⓑ Ⓒ Ⓓ
58. Ⓐ Ⓑ Ⓒ Ⓓ
59. Ⓐ Ⓑ Ⓒ Ⓓ
60. Ⓐ Ⓑ Ⓒ Ⓓ

answer sheet

POST-TEST

Directions: Carefully read each of the following 60 questions. Choose the best answer to each question, and darken its letter on your answer sheet. The Answer Key and Explanations can be found following this post-test.

1. Find the function of the line that goes through the origin with a slope of 3.
   (A) $f(x) = 0$
   (B) $f(x) = 3x$
   (C) $f(x) = 3x + 1$
   (D) $f(x) = 3x - 1$

2. The relationship between Fahrenheit F and Celsius C temperature scales is given by $C = \frac{5}{9}(F - 32)$. If $0 \leq C \leq 100$, what are the corresponding values for F?
   (A) $-40 \leq F \leq 32$
   (B) $\frac{169}{5} \leq F \leq 230$
   (C) $32 \leq F \leq 230$
   (D) $32 \leq F \leq 212$

3. If $f(x) = x^2$ and $g(x) = x - 2$ and $h(x) = x^2$, find $f(g(h(x)))$.
   (A) $2x^2 + x - 2$
   (B) $x^4 - 4x^2 + 4$
   (C) $x^4(x - 2)$
   (D) $x^4 - 4$

4. Factor the polynomial $4qr + 2sr - 2qt - st$.
   (A) $(2q - t)(2r + s)$
   (B) $(4rq + s)(2qt + s)$
   (C) $(2q + s)(2r - t)$
   (D) $2(2qr + sr - qt) - st$

5. A piggy bank contains dimes and quarters totaling $7.00. If there are 7 more dimes than quarters, find the number of quarters.
   (A) 9
   (B) 12
   (C) 18
   (D) 25

6. Find the solution to $x^2 + x > 20$.
   (A) $(-\infty, 4)$
   (B) $(-5, \infty)$
   (C) $(-\infty, -5) \cup (4, \infty)$
   (D) $-5 \leq x \leq 4$

7. Which of the following is the factor of the polynomial $21q^2 - 13q - 20$?
   (A) $(7q - 5)(3q + 4)$
   (B) $(3q + 2)(7q - 10)$
   (C) $(3q + 5)(7q - 4)$
   (D) $(7q + 5)(3q - 4)$

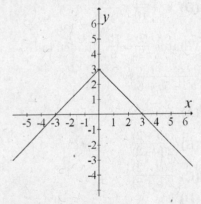

8. Which of the following best describes the graph above?
   (A) $f(x) = -|x| + 3$
   (B) $f(x) = x^2 + 3$
   (C) $f(x) = |-x + 3|$
   (D) $f(x) = -x^2 - 3$

9. Find the equation of a line that goes through the point (–2,3) and is perpendicular to the line that contains the points (4,2) and (3,5).

   (A) $y = -\dfrac{3}{2}x$

   (B) $y = -3x - 3$

   (C) $y = 3x + 9$

   (D) $y = \dfrac{1}{3}x + \dfrac{11}{3}$

10. What is the product of the rational expressions $\dfrac{x^2 + x - 2}{x - 1}$ and $\dfrac{3x + 7}{x + 2}$?

    (A) $\dfrac{3x^3 + 10x^2 + x + 14}{(x^2 + x - 2)}$

    (B) $3x + 7$

    (C) $\dfrac{3x + 7}{x - 1}$

    (D) $\dfrac{3x^3 - 14}{x^2 + x - 2}$

11. What is the product of $\left(x - \dfrac{1}{2}\right)$ and $\left(x + \dfrac{3}{5}\right)$?

    (A) $x^2 + \dfrac{11}{10}x + \dfrac{3}{10}$

    (B) $x^2 + \dfrac{3}{10}x - \dfrac{11}{10}$

    (C) $x^2 + \dfrac{1}{10}x - \dfrac{3}{10}$

    (D) $x^2 + \dfrac{11}{10}x - \dfrac{3}{10}$

12. What is $\dfrac{5b + 10}{2b - 6}$ divided by $\dfrac{b^2 - 4}{b^2 - 5b + 6}$?

    (A) $\dfrac{5}{2}$

    (B) $\dfrac{5(b + 2)}{2(b - 2)}$

    (C) $\dfrac{5(b - 2)}{2(b + 2)}$

    (D) 3

13. What values of x are not in the domain of the function $f(x) = \dfrac{x^2 + 2x + 2}{x^2 + 2x - 24}$?

    (A) 2

    (B) 4, –6

    (C) 2, 4, –6

    (D) 3, –8

14. Which of the following rational expressions when multiplied by $\dfrac{x^2 + 5x + 4}{x^2 - 16}$ equals 1?

    (A) $\dfrac{x - 1}{x + 4}$

    (B) $\dfrac{x - 4}{x + 1}$

    (C) 1

    (D) $\dfrac{-x^2 - 5x - 4}{x^2 - 16}$

15. Solve the quadratic expression $2x^2 - 4x - 20 = -14$.

    (A) 3

    (B) –1

    (C) (–3,1)

    (D) (3,–1)

16. $(5 + 3i)(5 - 3i) =$

    (A) 4

    (B) 16

    (C) $34 - 30i$

    (D) 34

17. Divide $3x^3y^3 + 6x^4y - 9xy$ by $3xy$ and choose the solution below.

    (A) $x^2y^2 + 2x^2y - 3xy$

    (B) $x^2y^2 + 2x^3 - 3$

    (C) $9x^4y^4 + 18x^5y^2 - 27x^2y^2$

    (D) $3x^3y^3 + 6x^4y - 6xy$

18. $\sqrt{5}\sqrt{45} =$

    (A) $3\sqrt{5}$

    (B) $9\sqrt{5}$

    (C) 15

    (D) 45

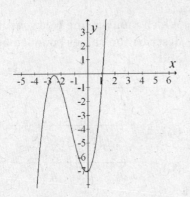

19. The graph above is best represented by which function?
(A) $f(x) = x^3 - 4x - x + 7$
(B) $f(x) = -x^3 + 4x + x - 7$
(C) $f(x) = x^3 + 4x^2 + x - 7$
(D) $f(x) = 4x^2 + x - 7$

20. What is the product of $\left(\sqrt{2} + 4\right)$ and $\left(\sqrt{8} - 4\right)$?
(A) $-12 + 4\sqrt{2}$
(B) $-12 + 12\sqrt{2}$
(C) $12 - 4\sqrt{2}$
(D) $12 + 8\sqrt{2}$

21. Find the ordered pair that represents the intercept of $2x + y = 11$ and $3x - y = 4$.
(A) $(5,3)$
(B) $(4,6)$
(C) $(1,3)$
(D) $(3,5)$

22. George just bought a brand-new truck for $19,500. He figures the truck will depreciate based on the function $f(a) = \dfrac{19,500 - 1000a}{a}$, where a is the age of the truck in years. How much will the truck be worth when it is 15 years old?
(A) $100
(B) $150
(C) $300
(D) $4500

23. $5y^{\frac{3}{4}} \cdot 2y^{-\left(\frac{2}{3}\right)} =$
(A) $7y$
(B) $7y^{-\left(\frac{1}{2}\right)}$
(C) $10y^{\frac{1}{12}}$
(D) $7y^{\frac{1}{12}}$

24. A woman buys 8 loaves of bread with a $10 bill. She receives 40 cents in change. How much does each loaf cost?
(A) $0.80
(B) $1.00
(C) $1.20
(D) $1.25

25. Find the echelon form of the system of equations:
$$\begin{cases} x + y + z = 4 \\ 2x + y - z = 3 \\ x + 3y + 2z = 4 \end{cases}$$

(A) $\begin{bmatrix} 1 & 1 & 1 & 4 \\ 0 & 0 & 3 & 5 \\ 0 & 0 & 0 & -2 \end{bmatrix}$

(B) $\begin{bmatrix} 1 & 1 & 1 & 4 \\ 0 & 1 & 3 & 5 \\ 0 & 0 & 1 & -2 \end{bmatrix}$

(C) $\begin{bmatrix} 1 & 1 & 1 & 4 \\ 0 & 1 & 3 & 9 \\ 0 & 0 & 1 & -2 \end{bmatrix}$

(D) $\begin{bmatrix} 1 & 1 & 1 & 4 \\ 1 & 1 & 3 & 5 \\ 1 & 1 & 1 & -2 \end{bmatrix}$

26. Find the inverse f^{-1} of the function $f(x) = \dfrac{1}{x - 1}$ for every real x.
(A) $x - 1$
(B) $\dfrac{1}{x}$
(C) $\dfrac{1}{x} - 1$
(D) $\dfrac{1}{x} + 1$

post-test

27. Find the equation of the line with a slope of –4 and the y-intercept = 8.

(A) $y = -4x + 40$

(B) $y = -4x + 8$

(C) $y = -4x + 32$

(D) $y = 4x - 8$

28. Use the method of substitution to find the solution(s) to the simultaneous equations shown below.

$$\begin{cases} x + 3y = 5 \\ x^2 + y^2 = 25 \end{cases}$$

(A) $(5,0), (-4,3)$

(B) $(58,21), (5,0)$

(C) $(3,-4), (0,-5)$

(D) $(-4,3), (5,5)$

29. Express the complex number $\dfrac{4}{(1+i)^3}$ in the form $a + bi$.

(A) $-1 - i$

(B) $-1 + i$

(C) $1 + i$

(D) $1 - i$

30. With electrical circuits, Ohm's law states that $V = IR$, where V = potential difference in volts, I is current in amps, and R is resistance in ohms. If $V = 120$ volts, what values of I correspond to $R \le 20$?

(A) $I \le 6$

(B) $I \ge 6$

(C) $I \le 8$

(D) $I \ge 10$

31. Which number line below would best describe the values bounded by $a > 5$ and $b < 12$?

(A)
$\qquad a \qquad\qquad b$

(B)
$\qquad a \qquad\qquad b$

(C)
$\qquad a \qquad\qquad b$

(D)
$\qquad a \qquad\qquad b$

32. Solve the quadratic $x^2 - 2x - 24 = 0$.

(A) 6

(B) $(-4,6)$

(C) $(4,-6)$

(D) 4

33. Solve $|x| > 5$.

(A) $(-\infty,-5) \cup (5,\infty)$

(B) $[-\infty,5] \cup [5,\infty]$

(C) $(5,\infty)$

(D) $(-\infty,5)$

34. Solve the equation $4v^2 + 20v - 25$.

(A) -25

(B) $\dfrac{-5}{2}$

(C) $\dfrac{-5}{2} \pm \dfrac{5\sqrt{2}}{2}$

(D) $\dfrac{5}{4} \pm \dfrac{5\sqrt{2}}{4}$

35. Solve the radical expression $\sqrt{9q - 3} - 7 = 0$.

(A) $\dfrac{40}{27}$

(B) $\dfrac{46}{9}$

(C) $\dfrac{52}{9}$

(D) 6

36. Find the solution(s) to the following simultaneous equations.

$$\begin{cases} x + 2y = -1 \\ 2x - 3y = 12 \end{cases}$$

(A) $(-2,3)$

(B) $(3,-2)$, $(3,0)$

(C) $(-2,5)$

(D) $(3,-2)$

37. Solve $|2x - 4| > 8$.

(A) $(-2,\infty)$

(B) $(-\infty,-2) \cup (6,\infty)$

(C) $[6,\infty)$

(D) $(-\infty,2) \cup (6,\infty)$

38. Given the equation $r = 3\sqrt{\dfrac{nv}{2pg}}$, solve the equation for g.

(A) $\dfrac{9pr^2}{2nv}$

(B) $\dfrac{2nv}{9pr^2}$

(C) $\dfrac{3nv}{2pr^2}$

(D) $\dfrac{9nv}{2pr^2}$

39. A baseball is hit into the air. The distance in feet h of the ball from the ground in t seconds is $h = -16t^2 + 120t$. How long will it take for the ball to rise to 200 feet high?

(A) 2½ seconds

(B) 5 seconds

(C) 2½ and 5 seconds

(D) None of the above

40. Solve the rational expression

$$2(x^2 + 7x + 20)^{-\frac{1}{3}} - 1 = 0.$$

(A) -3

(B) -4

(C) $(-3,-4)$

(D) No solution

41. Which of the following does NOT have a solution?

(A) $\sqrt{v - 3} = 5$

(B) $x^{\frac{1}{2}} = \sqrt{2x - 8}$

(C) $(8n)^{\frac{1}{3}} - 1 = 0$

(D) $\sqrt{w} + 4 = 0$

42. The sum of $(\sqrt{3} + 2i)$ and $(\sqrt{3} - 2i)$ is

(A) $\sqrt{3}$

(B) $2\sqrt{3}$

(C) $4 - \sqrt{3}$

(D) 7

43. What is the slope for the line that contains points $A(-3,2)$ and $B(5,0)$?

(A) $-\dfrac{1}{8}$

(B) $-\dfrac{1}{4}$

(C) $\dfrac{1}{8}$

(D) 4

44. What is the range of the function $f(x) = |x|$?

(A) $[0,\infty)$

(B) $(-\infty,0]$

(C) $(-\infty,\infty)$

(D) None of the above

45. The point represented by the ordered pair $(-3,-1)$ would be found in which quadrant of the rectangular coordinate system graph?

(A) Quadrant I

(B) Quadrant II

(C) Quadrant III

(D) Quadrant IV

46. Given $f(x) = 3x^2 - x - 4$ and $g(x) = 2x + 1$, find $f(x)g(x)$.
    (A) $6x^3 + x^2 - 9x - 4$
    (B) $2x(6x + 5)$
    (C) $3x^2 + x - 3$
    (D) None of the above

47. Which of the following is a simplification of $\dfrac{6x^4 y^{-3}}{3x^{-2} y^2}$?
    (A) $\dfrac{2x^6}{y^5}$
    (B) $\dfrac{2x^2}{y}$
    (C) $2x^2 y$
    (D) $\dfrac{3x^2}{y}$

48. If $f(x) = \dfrac{\sqrt{x+1}}{x}$ and $g(x) = \dfrac{1}{x}$, find $\dfrac{f(x)}{g(x)}$.
    (A) x
    (B) $\dfrac{\sqrt{x+1}}{x^2}$
    (C) $\sqrt{x+1}$
    (D) $\dfrac{1}{\sqrt{x+1}}$

49. If $f(x) = x^2 - 2x - 1$ and $g(x) = \dfrac{1}{x}$, find $f(g(x))$.
    (A) $\dfrac{1}{x^2 - 2x - 1}$
    (B) $x - 3$
    (C) $x - 2 - \dfrac{1}{x}$
    (D) $\dfrac{-x^2 - 2x + 1}{x^2}$

50. If $f(w) = \dfrac{2w + 1}{w - 3}$ and $g(w) = \dfrac{w - 1}{w - 3}$, find $\left(\dfrac{f}{g} \right)(x)$.
    (A) $2w^2 - 5w - 3$
    (B) $\dfrac{2w + 1}{w - 1}$
    (C) $\dfrac{w + 1}{2w - 1}$
    (D) None of the above

51. Find the zeros of the function $f(x) = 9x^2 - 12x + 4$.
    (A) $\dfrac{2}{3}$
    (B) $-\dfrac{2}{3}$
    (C) $\dfrac{2}{3} \pm \sqrt{3}$
    (D) $-\dfrac{2}{3} \pm \sqrt{3}$

52. Given that $f(x) = \log_4 (x + 2)$, find the solution where $f(x) = 2$.
    (A) 10
    (B) 14
    (C) 18
    (D) 22

53. $(x - y)^3$ is the factor of which cubic?
    (A) $x^3 - 3x^2 y - 3xy^2 - y^2$
    (B) $x^3 + 3x^2 y + 3xy^2 + y^2$
    (C) $x^3 - 3x^2 y + 3xy^2 - y^3$
    (D) $x^3 - 3x^2 y + 3xy^2 + y^2$

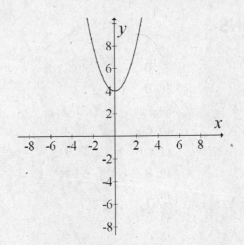

54. The graph above represents which function?

(A) $f(x) = x^2 + 4$

(B) $f(x) = x^2 + 3x - 7$

(C) $f(x) = x^3 + x + 4$

(D) $f(x) = -x^2 + 4$

55. Find the equation of the line that goes through the point $(5, -7)$ and is parallel to the line $8x + 4y - 6 = 0$.

(A) $y = -2x + 3$

(B) $y = 2x - 3$

(C) $y = -2x + \frac{3}{2}$

(D) $y = 2x - 19$

56. Solve $3x^2 + 1 = -5x$.

(A) $-\frac{5}{6} \pm \frac{\sqrt{13}}{6}$

(B) $\frac{5}{6} \pm \frac{\sqrt{13}}{6}$

(C) $-\frac{1}{6} \pm \frac{\sqrt{59}}{6}$

(D) $\frac{1}{6} \pm \frac{\sqrt{59}}{6}$

57. Solve the equation $x^2 = 11$.

(A) $\pm 3\sqrt{2}$

(B) $(11, -1)$

(C) $(5, 6)$

(D) $\pm\sqrt{11}$

58. Simplify the complex fraction $\dfrac{6 - \dfrac{3}{y}}{1 + \dfrac{3}{y}}$

and choose the correct answer.

(A) $2y - \dfrac{3}{y} + 5$

(B) $\dfrac{3(y - 1)}{y + 3}$

(C) $\dfrac{y - 6}{y + 3}$

(D) $\dfrac{3y - 1}{y + 3}$

59. Which of the following functions would be represented by the values below?

$x =$	0.5	1	2	3	5	10
$y =$	−0.3	0	0.3	0.5	0.7	1

(A) $f(x) = |x|$

(B) $f(x) = \log(x)$

(C) $f(x) = -\dfrac{1}{x}$

(D) $f(x) = x^2 - 1$

60. Which of the following proprieties describes $(2 \times 3) \times 2 = 2 \times (2 \times 3)$?

(A) Associative

(B) Commutative

(C) Identity

(D) Distributive

ANSWER KEY AND EXPLANATIONS

1. B	13. B	25. B	37. B	49. D
2. D	14. B	26. D	38. D	50. B
3. B	15. D	27. B	39. A	51. A
4. C	16. D	28. A	40. C	52. B
5. C	17. B	29. A	41. D	53. C
6. C	18. C	30. B	42. B	54. A
7. D	19. C	31. C	43. B	55. A
8. A	20. A	32. B	44. A	56. A
9. D	21. D	33. A	45. C	57. D
10. B	22. C	34. C	46. A	58. B
11. C	23. C	35. C	47. A	59. B
12. A	24. C	36. D	48. C	60. B

1. **The correct answer is (B).** We know the origin is (0,0) and using the point-slope formula we know:

$$y - y_1 = m(x - x_1)$$
$$y - 0 = 3(x - 0)$$
$$y = 3x$$

2. **The correct answer is (D).** First, set up the inequality for F and substitute the equation in for C.

$$0 \le C \le 100$$
$$0 \le \frac{5}{9}(F - 32) \le 100$$
$$0 \le \frac{5}{9}F - \left(\frac{5}{9}\right)32 \le 100$$
$$0 \le \frac{5F}{9} - \frac{(5)(32)}{9} \le 100$$
$$0 \le \frac{5F - 160}{9} \le 100$$
$$0(9) \le 5F - 160 \le 100(9)$$
$$0 \le 5F - 160 \le 900$$
$$160 \le 5F \le 900 + 160$$
$$\frac{160}{5} \le F \le \frac{1060}{5}$$
$$32 \le F \le 212$$

You can also solve this type of problem by breaking it into two inequalities and solving $0 \le \frac{5}{9}(F - 32)$ and $\frac{5}{9}(F - 32) \le 100$.

The solution is $32 \le F \le 212$. Choice (D) is correct.

3. **The correct answer is (B).** To solve a composite function, first insert $h(x)$ into the x of $g(x)$ and solve:

$$g(h(x)) = (x^2) - 2$$
$$= x^2 - 2$$

Now insert $g(h(x))$ into the x of $f(x)$:

$$g(h(x)) = (x^2 - 2)^2$$
$$= (x^2 - 2)(x^2 - 2)$$
$$= x^2 x^2 - 2x^2 - 2x^2 + 4$$
$$= x^4 - 4x^2 + 4$$

So, choice (B) is correct.

4. **The correct answer is (C).** If we group the first two terms and the last two terms, using the distributive properties, we can factor out $2r$ and t. $2q + s$ can then be factored out, leaving the solution.

$$4qr + 2sr - 2qt - st = (4qr + 2sr) - (2qt + st)$$
$$= 2r(2q + s) - t(2q + s)$$
$$= (2q + s)(2r - t)$$

5. **The correct answer is (C).** Let q = the number of quarters. Let d = the number of dimes. The following two equations can be created:

$$10d + 25q = 700$$
$$q + 7 = d$$

These equations can be reduced using elimination. Multiply the second equation by -25 and add the two equations together:

$$10d + 25q = 700$$
$$+ 25d - 25q = 175$$
$$\overline{35d = 875}$$

Solving for d, we can see that $d = 25$, which means there are 25 dimes. Substituting the number of dimes into either equation, we can find the number of quarters:

$$q + 7 = d$$
$$q + 7 = 25$$
$$q = 25 - 7$$
$$q = 18$$

We find that $q = 18$, so there are 18 quarters. Choice (C) is correct.

6. **The correct answer is (C).** A second-degree polynomial inequality requires testing all possible regions of the solution.

Step 1: Rewrite the equation so that one side equals zero:

$$x^2 + x > 20$$
$$x^2 + x - 20 > 0$$

Step 2: Solve the problem as if it were an equation:

$$x^2 + x - 20 = 0$$
$$(x + 5)(x - 4) = 0$$

Thus $x = -5$ and $x = 4$.

Step 3: Test each region with a value from that region and determine if the original equation is true or false:

Region A   Region B   Region C
$x < -5$ $-5 < x < 4$ $x > 1$

         -5 4

Pick a value from each region and test it in the original equation:

Region A $= -6$

$$x^2 + x - 20 = (-6)^2 + (-6) - 20$$
$$= 36 - 6 - 20$$
$$= 30 - 20$$
$$= 10$$
$$= \text{positive}$$

Region B $= 0$

$$x^2 + x - 20 = (0)^2 + (0) - 20$$
$$= 0 + 0 - 20$$
$$= -20$$
$$= \text{negative}$$

Region C $= 5$

$$x^2 + x = (5)^2 + (5) - 20$$
$$= 25 + 5 - 20$$
$$= 10$$
$$= \text{positive}$$

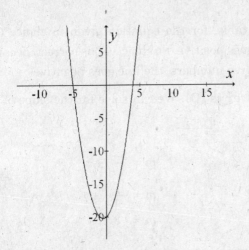

Thus, we can see that values from Regions A and C are greater than zero. So, our answer is $(-\infty, -5) \cup (4, \infty)$. Choice (C) is correct.

7. **The correct answer is (D).** The solution will be in the form $(aq + b)(cq + d)$, where $ac = 21$, $bd = -20$, and $bc + da = -13$. Trial-and-error testing of the factors of 21 and 20 along with these equations will lead to the solution.

   The value 21 has the factors 1, 21, 3, and 7. We can try 3 and 7, which would give us $(3q - b)(7q + d)$. We know 20 has the factors 1, 2, 4, 5, 10, and 20. Again, we can try 4 and 5 for b and d. We find that $(7q + 5)(3q - 4)$, choice (D), is a correct solution.

8. **The correct answer is (A).** It should be obvious that choices (B) and (D) can't be the solution because the line would be rounded, or parabolic in shape. The graph looks like an absolute-value plot, which points to either choice (A) or choice (C).

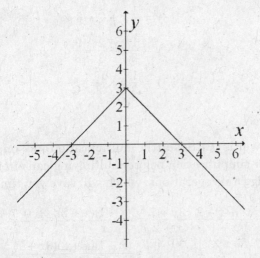

Let's plot a few points to see which is correct.

$x =$	0	3	5
A: $y = -\lvert x \rvert + 3$	3 ok	0 ok	−2 ok
C: $y = \lvert -x + 3 \rvert$	3 ok	0 ok	2 no

According to this table, for the equation given in choice (C), for great positive numbers the line goes positive. So choice (A) is correct, because the graphic shows that for great positive numbers, the line goes negative.

9. **The correct answer is (D).** We can solve for the slope of the second line using the slope formula, $m = \frac{y_2 - y_1}{x_2 - x_1}$:

$$m = \frac{5-2}{3-4}$$
$$m = \frac{3}{-1}$$
$$m = -3$$

The slope of our line is perpendicular, so it will be the negative reciprocal of -3, which is $-\left(\frac{1}{-3}\right)$, or $\frac{1}{3}$. The reciprocal of a number is simply 1 divided by the number. To find the reciprocal of a fraction, you need only to flip the fraction over or switch the numerator and denominator.

Now find the equation of the line using the point-slope formula:

$$y - y_1 = m(x - x_1)$$
$$y - 3 = \frac{1}{3}(x - (-2))$$
$$y - 3 = \frac{1}{3}(x + 2)$$
$$y - 3 = \frac{1}{3}x + \frac{2}{3}$$
$$y = \frac{1}{3}x + \frac{2}{3} + 3$$
$$y = \frac{1}{3}x + \frac{2}{3} + \frac{9}{3}$$
$$y = \frac{1}{3}x + \frac{11}{3}$$

Choice (D) is correct.

10. **The correct answer is (B).** Set up the multiplication and simplify the polynomials. Always remember simplification before multiplying can often lead to a reduction in the required algebraic operations, which will save you time.

$$\frac{x^2 + x - 2}{x - 1} \cdot \frac{3x + 7}{x + 2} = \frac{(x-1)(x+2)}{x-1} \cdot \frac{3x+7}{x+2}$$
$$= \frac{(x-1)(x+2)(3x+7)}{(x-1)(x+2)}$$

Using the cancellation property, we find that the solution is $3x + 7$. Choice (B) is correct.

11. The correct answer is (C). Use the FOIL method to multiply the two equations.

$$\left(x - \frac{1}{2}\right)\left(x + \frac{3}{5}\right) = \underbrace{(x)(x)}_{\text{First}} + \underbrace{\left(-\frac{1}{2}\right)(x)}_{\text{Outside}} + \underbrace{\left(\frac{3}{5}\right)(x)}_{\text{Inside}} - \underbrace{\left(\frac{1}{2}\right)\left(\frac{3}{5}\right)}_{\text{Last}}$$

$$= x^2 + \left(-\frac{1}{2} + \frac{3}{5}\right)x - \frac{3}{10}$$

$$= x^2 + \left(-\frac{1}{2} \cdot \frac{5}{5} + \frac{3}{5} \cdot \frac{2}{2}\right)x - \frac{3}{10}$$

$$= x^2 + \left(-\frac{5}{10} + \frac{6}{10}\right)x - \frac{3}{10}$$

$$= x^2 + \frac{1}{10}x - \frac{3}{10}$$

Choice (C) is correct.

12. The correct answer is (A). Set up the division using the division rule and simplify.

$$\frac{\dfrac{5b + 10}{2b - 6}}{\dfrac{b^2 - 4}{b^2 - 5b + 6}} = \frac{5b + 10}{2b - 6} \cdot \frac{b^2 - 5b + 6}{b^2 - 4}$$

$$= \frac{5(b + 2)}{2(b - 3)} \cdot \frac{(b - 2)(b - 3)}{(b - 2)(b + 2)}$$

$$= \frac{5(b + 2)(b - 2)(b - 3)}{2(b - 3)(b - 2)(b + 2)}$$

$$= \frac{5}{2}$$

Thus, choice (A) is correct.

13. The correct choice is (B). To find the domain we need to find what values of x are not solutions for the function. When the denominator $= 0$, there are no values for y. So, all we need to do is set the denominator $= 0$ and solve $x^2 + 2x - 24 = 0$.

To factor this equation, we're looking for the two numbers that when added together equal 2 and when multiplied equal -24. Let's try -4 and 6.

$$x^2 + 2x - 24 = 0$$
$$(x - 4)(x + 6) = 0$$

So,

$$x - 4 = 0 \qquad x + 6 = 0$$
$$x = 4 \qquad x = -6$$

So, for $x = 4$ and $x = -6$, the equation has no solution. You can see the equation approach ∞ and $-\infty$ at these values.

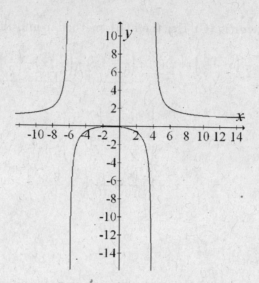

So, choice (B) is the correct answer.

14. The correct answer is (B). For two expressions to equal 1 means that dividing the two expressions by each other equals 1. Phrased another way, if the numerator and denominator are the same, the expression will equal 1. So, all that is needed is to find the inversion of $\dfrac{x^2 + 5x + 4}{x^2 - 16}$.

Invert the expression and use the division rule for rational expressions: $\dfrac{P}{Q} \cdot \dfrac{R}{S} = \dfrac{PR}{QS}$. Then simplify using the cancellation property $\dfrac{PS}{QS} = \dfrac{P}{Q}$:

$$\frac{1}{\dfrac{x^2 + 5x + 4}{x^2 - 16}} = 1 \cdot \frac{x^2 - 16}{x^2 + 5x + 4}$$

$$= \frac{x^2 - 16}{x^2 + 5x + 4}$$

$$= \frac{(x + 4)(x - 4)}{(x + 4)(x + 1)}$$

$$= \frac{x - 4}{x + 1}$$

Choice (B) is correct.

15. The correct answer is (D).

Solve this problem by completing the square.

Step 1:   Divide by a, which in this problem is 2:

$$2x^2 - 4x - 20 = -14$$
$$x^2 - 2x - 10 = -7$$

Step 2: Isolate the constant c:

$$x^2 - 2x - 10 = -7$$
$$x^2 - 2x = -7 + 10$$
$$x^2 - 2x = 3$$

Step 3: Divide b by 2 and square.

$$\left(-2 \cdot \frac{1}{2}\right)^2 = 1$$

Step 4: Add the new number to both sides of the equation:

$$x^2 - 2x + 1 = 3 + 1$$
$$x^2 - 2x + 1 = 4$$

Step 5: Factor:

$$x^2 - 2x + 1 = 4$$
$$(x - 1)^2 = 4$$

Step 6: Use square root rule and solve:

$$\sqrt{(x-1)^2} = \sqrt{4}$$
$$(x - 1) = \pm 2$$

$$x - 1 = 2 \qquad x - 1 = -2$$
$$x = 3 \qquad\quad x = -1$$

We arrive at the solution $x = 3$ and $x = -1$.

Choice (D) is correct.

16. **The correct answer is (D).** Solve the equation using the rules for i and the FOIL method. Remember $i^2 = 1$.

$$(5 + 3i)(5 - 3i) = (5)(5) + 15i - 15i - 9i^2$$
$$= 25 - 9i^2$$
$$= 25 - 9(-1)$$
$$= 25 + 9$$
$$= 34$$

17. **The correct answer is (B).** Solve this problem by setting up the division, using the addition/subtraction rule $\dfrac{P+R}{Q} = \dfrac{P}{Q} + \dfrac{R}{Q}$, and then simplifying using the cancellation property $\dfrac{PS}{QS} = \dfrac{P}{Q}$:

$$\frac{3x^3y^3 + 6x^4y - 9xy}{3xy} = \frac{3x^3y^3}{3xy} + \frac{6x^4y}{3xy} - \frac{9xy}{3xy}$$
$$= x^2y^2 + 2x^3 - 3$$

Choice (B) is correct.

18. **The correct answer is (C).** This problem can be solved by factoring $\sqrt{45}$ using the rule $\sqrt[n]{a} \cdot \sqrt[n]{b} = \sqrt[n]{ab}$:

$$\sqrt{5}\sqrt{45} = \sqrt{5}\sqrt{(9)(5)}$$
$$= \sqrt{5}\sqrt{9}\sqrt{5}$$
$$= 3\sqrt{5}\sqrt{5}$$
$$= 3\sqrt{25}$$
$$= 3(5)$$
$$= 15$$

Another approach is to multiply everything together and see if you can find the square root for the number. Fortunately, in this case, 15 is the square root of 225.

$$\sqrt{5}\sqrt{45} = \sqrt{225}$$
$$= 15$$

19. **The correct answer is (C).** We can immediately eliminate choice (D) because it's a quadratic function. The graph that is shown has one too many curves. We know the solution must be a cubic function due to the two changes in directions, or two "humps." The plot shows the function goes through the y-axis at $(0,-7)$. We can test the equations and eliminate choice (A) as it goes though $+7$ when $x = 0$.

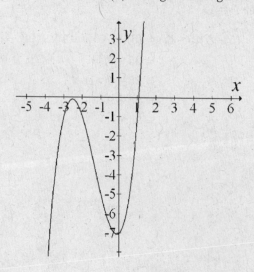

We can substitute a few points in the equations given by choices (B) and (C) to see which function might be our solution:

$x =$	0	1	5
B: $y = -x^3 + 4x + x - 7$	–7 ok	–3 ok	–102 no
C: $y = x^3 + 4x^2 + x - 7$	–7 ok	–1 ok	223 ok

From this test, we can see that choice (C) is the correct answer.

20. **The correct answer is (A).** Multiply the two equations together using FOIL. Simplify using the rule $\sqrt[n]{a} \cdot \sqrt[n]{b} = \sqrt[n]{ab}$:

$$\left(\sqrt{2} + 4\right)\left(\sqrt{8} - 4\right) = \sqrt{2}\sqrt{8} + 4\sqrt{8} - 4\sqrt{2} + (4)(-4)$$
$$= \sqrt{16} + 4\sqrt{8} - 4\sqrt{2} - 16$$
$$= 4 + 4\sqrt{(4)(2)} - 4\sqrt{2} - 16$$
$$= 4 + 4\sqrt{4}\sqrt{2} - 4\sqrt{2} - 16$$
$$= 4 + 4(2)\sqrt{2} - 4\sqrt{2} - 16$$
$$= 4 + 8\sqrt{2} - 4\sqrt{2} - 16$$
$$= (4 - 16) + (8 - 4)\sqrt{2}$$
$$= -12 + 4\sqrt{2}$$

Choice (A) is correct.

21. **The correct answer is (D).** First, solve for y using one of the two equations. The second equation will be used here:

$$3x - y = 4$$
$$-y = 4 - 3x$$
$$y = -4 + 3x$$

Substitute the value of $y = -4 + 3x$ into the other equation:

$$2x + y = 11$$
$$2x + (-4 + 3x) = 11$$
$$2x - 4 + 3x = 11$$
$$2x + 3x = 11 + 4$$
$$5x = 15$$
$$x = 3$$

Next, use the value of x to solve for y. Either equation will work for this step—pick the one where the math looks the easiest.

$$3x - y = 4$$
$$3(3) - y = 4$$
$$9 - y = 4$$
$$-y = 4 - 9$$
$$-y = -5$$
$$y = 5$$

Choice (D) is correct.

22. **The correct answer is (C).** Let $a = 15$ and solve:

$$f(a) = \frac{19{,}500 - 1000(a)}{a}$$
$$y = \frac{19{,}500 - 1000(15)}{15}$$
$$y = \frac{4500}{15}$$
$$y = 300$$

George's truck will be worth $300. So, choice (C) is correct.

23. **The correct answer is (C).** Use the rules for multiplying exponentials. Multiply the fractions in the exponent to find a common denominator and solve:

$$5y^{\frac{3}{4}} \cdot 2y^{-\left(\frac{2}{3}\right)} = (5)(2)y^{\frac{3}{4}-\left(\frac{2}{3}\right)}$$
$$= 10y^{\frac{3}{4}\left(\frac{3}{3}\right)-\frac{2}{3}\left(\frac{4}{4}\right)}$$
$$= 10y^{\frac{9}{12}-\frac{8}{12}}$$
$$= 10y^{\frac{1}{12}}$$

Choice (C) is correct.

24. **The correct answer is (C).** To solve this problem, we need to create the equation. Let b = the cost of each loaf of bread. We know the breads total cost is $8b$. If we add the 40 cents, or $0.40, to the total cost of the bread, we will get $10:

$$8b + 0.40 = 10$$
$$8b = 10 - 0.40$$
$$8b = 9.60$$
$$b = \frac{9.60}{8}$$
$$b = 1.20$$

Each loaf of bread costs $1.20. The correct answer is choice (C).

25. The correct answer is (B). The echelon form of the matrix will have zeros in the elements below the diagonal. The diagonal should be ones.

$$\begin{bmatrix} 1 & a & b & c \\ 0 & 1 & d & e \\ 0 & 0 & 1 & f \end{bmatrix}$$

Before we can find the echelon matrix, we need to form the coefficient matrix from the original equations:

$$\begin{bmatrix} 1 & 1 & 1 & 4 \\ 2 & 1 & -1 & 3 \\ 1 & 3 & 2 & 4 \end{bmatrix}$$

First, we can subtract row 1 from row 3:

$$\begin{bmatrix} 1 & 1 & 1 & 4 \\ 2 & 1 & -1 & 3 \\ 1-1 & 3-1 & 2-1 & 4-4 \end{bmatrix} = \begin{bmatrix} 1 & 1 & 1 & 4 \\ 2 & 1 & -1 & 3 \\ 0 & 2 & 1 & 0 \end{bmatrix}$$

This will give us a 0 in the first member on row 3. Next, multiply row 1 by –2 and add to row 2:

$$\begin{bmatrix} 1 & 1 & 1 & 4 \\ 2-2 & 1-2 & -1-2 & 3-8 \\ 0 & 2 & 1 & 0 \end{bmatrix} = \begin{bmatrix} 1 & 1 & 1 & 4 \\ 0 & -1 & -3 & -5 \\ 0 & 2 & 1 & 0 \end{bmatrix}$$

This gives us a 0 for the first member of row 2. Multiply row 2 by 2 and add to row 3:

$$\begin{bmatrix} 1 & 1 & 1 & 4 \\ 0 & -1 & -3 & -5 \\ 0-0 & 2-2 & 1-6 & 0-10 \end{bmatrix} = \begin{bmatrix} 1 & 1 & 1 & 4 \\ 0 & -1 & -3 & -5 \\ 0 & 0 & -5 & -10 \end{bmatrix}$$

Now we almost have the echelon matrix form. For the last step, simplify by multiplying row 2 by –1. Also, simplify by dividing row 3 by –5:

$$\begin{bmatrix} 1 & 1 & 1 & 4 \\ 0 & -1(-1) & -3(-1) & -5(-1) \\ 0 & 0 & \frac{-5}{-5} & \frac{-10}{-5} \end{bmatrix} = \begin{bmatrix} 1 & 1 & 1 & 4 \\ 0 & 1 & 3 & 5 \\ 0 & 0 & 1 & -2 \end{bmatrix}$$

This leaves the echelon form of the matrix. Choice (B) is correct.

26. **The correct answer is (D).** To find the inverse, exchange x with y and solve for y:

$$y = \frac{1}{x-1}$$

$$x = \frac{1}{y-1}$$

$$x(y-1) = \frac{1}{y-1}(y-1)$$

$$x(y-1) = 1$$

$$\frac{x(y-1)}{x} = 1\left(\frac{1}{x}\right)$$

$$y-1 = \frac{1}{x}$$

$$y = \frac{1}{x}+1$$

$$f^{-1}(x) = \frac{1}{x}+1$$

Choice (D) is correct.

27. **The correct answer is (B).** We know the line goes through the y-intercept at 8, which means $x = 0$ when $y = 8$, or (0,8) Knowing this point, we can use the point-slope formula $y - y_1 = m(x - x_1)$ to find the question of the line:

$$y - y_1 = m(x - x_1)$$
$$y - 8 = -4(x - 0)$$
$$y - 8 = -4x$$
$$y = -4x + 8$$

28. **The correct answer is (A).** The first equation can be solved for x so that $x = 5 - 3y$. Substituting $5 - 3y$ into the second equation for x gives:

$$(5 - 3y)^2 + y^2 = 25$$
$$25 - 30y + 9y^2 + y^2 = 25$$
$$10y^2 - 30y = 0$$

Thus, $y = 0$ is one solution to this equation. We continue to solve for y:

$$10y^2 - 30y = 0$$
$$10y = 30$$
$$y = 3$$

This give us the second solution $y = 3$. We next substitute $y = 0$ into the first equation and solve for x:

$$x + 3(0) = 5$$
$$x = 5$$

Lastly, we obtain the second solution for x by substituting $y = 3$ into the first equation and solving for x:

$$x + 3(3) = 5$$
$$x + 9 = 5$$
$$x = -4$$

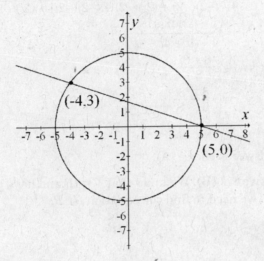

The solutions to this problem are (5,0) and (–4,3). Choice (A) is correct.

29. **The correct answer is (A).** To remove i from the denominator, you first need to multiply out $(1 + i)^3$. We know from Table 2 that $(x + y)^3 = x^3 + 3x^2y + 3xy^2 + y^3$:

$$\frac{4}{(1+i)^3} = \frac{4}{(1)^3 + 3(1)^2 i + 3(1)(i)^2 + i^3}$$

$$= \frac{4}{1 + 3i + 3(-1) + (i)^3}$$

$$= \frac{4}{1 + 3i - 3 - i}$$

$$= \frac{4}{-2 + 2i}$$

Next, we multiply the denominator by the complex conjugate:

$$\frac{4}{-2-2i} = \frac{4}{-2+2i} \cdot \frac{(-2-2i)}{(-2-2i)}$$

$$= \frac{(4)(-2)+(4)(-2i)}{(-2+2i)(-2-2i)}$$

$$= \frac{-8-8i}{(-2)(-2)+(2i)(-2)+(-2)(-2i)+(2i)(-2i)}$$

$$= \frac{-8-8i}{4+4i-4i-4i^2}$$

$$= \frac{-8+8i}{8}$$

$$= -\frac{8}{8} - \frac{8i}{8}$$

$$= -1-i$$

So, the correct answer is choice (A).

30. **The correct answer is (B).** We know that $V = IR$ and have the values of $V = 120$ and $R \le 20$. First, we need to find the equation for R.

$$V = IR$$

$$IR = V$$

$$IR\left(\frac{1}{I}\right) = V\left(\frac{1}{I}\right)$$

$$R = \frac{V}{I}$$

Now substitute this value of R into the inequality, plug in the value for V, and solve for I:

$$R \le 20$$

$$\frac{V}{I} \le 20$$

$$\frac{120}{I} \le 20$$

$$\frac{120}{20} \le I$$

$$6 \le I$$

So, when $I \ge 6$, we get $R \le 20$. Therefore, choice (B) is the correct answer.

31. **The correct answer is (C).** The number line represents what values are included in the solution. If "(" is used, then the value is not included, i.e., the value is > or <. If "[" is used, the value is included, i.e., the value is ≥ or ≤.

In this problem, we know 5 and 12 are not included. So at the points a and b on the number line, there should be a "(". This rules out choices (A) and (B).

We also know that the solution is less than b and greater than a, so we can rule out choice (D). Choice (C) is correct because it accurately describes our set of numbers.

32. The correct answer is (B). This problem can be solved by completing the square. Since $a = 1$, we can skip the first step, which is to "divide by a".

Step 2:   Isolate the constant c:

$$x^2 - 2x - 24 = 0$$
$$x^2 - 2x = 24$$

Step 3:   Divide b by 2 and square. $b = 2$ in this problem:

$$\left(2 \cdot \frac{1}{2}\right)^2 = 1$$

Step 4:   Add the new number to both sides of the equation:

$$x^2 - 2x + 1 = 24 + 1$$
$$x^2 - 2x + 1 = 25$$

Step 5:   Factor:

$$x^2 - 2x + 1 = 25$$
$$(x - 1)^2 = 25$$

Step 6:   Use square root rule and solve:

$$\sqrt{(x-1)^2} = \sqrt{25}$$
$$(x - 1) = \pm 5$$

$$x - 1 = 5 \qquad x - 1 = -5$$
$$x = 6 \qquad x = -4$$

We arrive at the solution $x = -4$ and 6.

Choice (B) is correct.

33. The correct answer is (A). Using the rules of absolute values, we know that $x < -5$ or $x > 5$, which is $(-\infty, -5) \cup (5, \infty)$. Choice (A) is correct.

34. The answer is (C). For complex polynomials like this one, it's probably best to use the quadratic equation. Let $a = 4$, $b = 20$, and $c = -25$.

$$x = \frac{-b \pm \sqrt{b^2 - 4ac}}{2a}$$

$$x = \frac{-(20) \pm \sqrt{(20)^2 - 4(4)(-25)}}{2(4)}$$

$$x = \frac{-20 \pm \sqrt{400 - (-400)}}{8}$$

$$x = \frac{-20 \pm \sqrt{800}}{8}$$

$$x = \frac{-20}{8} \pm \frac{\sqrt{16 \cdot 25 \cdot 2}}{8}$$

$$x = \frac{-5}{2} \pm \frac{\sqrt{16}\sqrt{25}\sqrt{2}}{8}$$

$$x = \frac{-5}{2} \pm \frac{(4)(5)\sqrt{2}}{8}$$

$$x = \frac{-5}{2} \pm \frac{5\sqrt{2}}{2}$$

Choice (C) is the correct answer.

35. The correct answer is (C). Use the steps for solving equations with radicals:

Step 1:   Isolate the radical by putting it on one side:

$$\sqrt{9q - 3} = 7$$

Step 2:   Get rid of the radical by squaring both sides of the equation:

$$\left(\sqrt{9q - 3}\right)^2 = 7^2$$
$$9x - 3 = 49$$

Step 3:   All radicals are eliminated, so proceed to step 4.

Step 4:   Solve the remaining equation:

$$9q - 3 = 49$$
$$9q = 49 + 3$$
$$q = 52$$
$$q = \frac{52}{9}$$

Step 5:   Check the solution:

$$\sqrt{9\left(\frac{52}{9}\right) - 3} = 7$$

$$\sqrt{52 - 3} = 7$$

$$\sqrt{49} = 7$$

$$7 = 7$$

The solution is correct, and $q = \frac{52}{9}$. Choice (C) is correct.

36. **The correct answer is (D).** We can solve the first equation for x and obtain $x = -2y - 1$. This value of x can be substituted into the second equation:

$$2(-2y - 1) - 3y = 12$$

$$-4y - 2 - 3y = 12$$

$$-7y = 14$$

$$y = -2$$

The value for y can be substituted into either equation to find the value of x:

$$x + 2(-2) = -1$$

$$x - 4 = -1$$

$$x = 3$$

Thus, the solution is $(3, -2)$. Choice (D) is correct.

37. **The correct answer is (B).** Use the rule for absolute values $a < -b$ and $a > b$ to eliminate the absolute value:

$$|2x - 4| > 8$$

$2x - 4 > 8$	$2x - 4 < -8$
$2x > 8 + 4$	$2x < -8 + 4$
$2x > 12$	$2x < -4$
$x > 6$	$x < -2$

The solution is $x > 6$ and $x < -2$, or $(-\infty, -2) \cup (6, \infty)$. Choice (B) is correct.

Note: For this type of solution, where the numbers go toward infinity, it is not correct to say $-2 > x > 6$. This notation should only be used for solutions like $x > -2$ and $x < 6$.

38. The correct answer is (D). This problem might look difficult, but it is not. To solve this problem we need to use the rules for equations involving radicals and solve.

Step 1:   Isolate the radical by putting it on one side:

$$r = 3\sqrt{\frac{nv}{2pg}}$$

$$\frac{r}{3} = \sqrt{\frac{nv}{2pg}}$$

Step 2:   Get rid of the radical by squaring both sides of the equation:

$$\left(\frac{r}{3}\right)^2 = \left(\sqrt{\frac{nv}{2pg}}\right)^2$$

$$\frac{r^2}{9} = \frac{nv}{2pg}$$

Step 3:   All radicals are eliminated, so proceed to step 4.

Step 4:   Solve the remaining equation for g:

$$\frac{r^2}{9} = \frac{nv}{2pg}$$

$$\frac{r^2}{9} = \frac{nv}{2pg}$$

$$\frac{r^2}{9}(2pg) = \frac{nv}{2pg}(2pg)$$

$$\frac{2pgr^2}{9} = nv$$

$$\frac{2pgr^2}{9}\left(\frac{9}{2pr^2}\right) = nv\left(\frac{9}{2pr^2}\right)$$

$$g = \frac{9nv}{2pr^2}$$

Choice (D) is correct.

39. The correct answer is (A). To solve this problem, we are looking to solve for t when $h = 200$. We can substitute these values into the following equations:

$$h = -16t^2 + 120t$$

$$200 = -16t^2 + 120t$$

$$0 = -16t^2 + 120t - 200$$

Now solve for t:

$$-16t^2 + 120t - 200 = 0$$

$$-8(2t^2 - 15t + 25) = 0$$

$$2t^2 - 15t + 25 = 0$$

We will use the quadratic equation where $a = 2$, $b = -15$, and $c = 25$:

$$x = \frac{-b \pm \sqrt{b^2 - 4ac}}{2a}$$

$$x = \frac{-(-15) \pm \sqrt{(-15)^2 - 4(2)(25)}}{2(2)}$$

$$x = \frac{15 \pm \sqrt{225 - 200}}{4}$$

$$x = \frac{15 \pm \sqrt{25}}{4}$$

$$x = \frac{15 \pm 5}{4}$$

$$x = \frac{20}{4}, \frac{10}{4}$$

$$x = 5, \frac{5}{2}$$

$$x = 2\frac{1}{2} \text{ seconds, and 5 seconds}$$

The solution is 5 seconds and 2½ seconds. How can you have two answers? When the ball is hit, the 2½ seconds is the time for the ball to rise to 200 feet. The 5 seconds is the time it takes to go back down below 200 feet. The question is asking how long it takes the ball to rise to 200 feet, so 2½ seconds, choice (A); is the correct answer.

40. **The correct answer is (C).** An exponential raised to a fraction is really just a radical. To solve this problem, we need to use the rules for equations involving radicals and solve.

Step 1:   Isolate the radical by putting it on one side:

$$2(x^2 + 7x + 20)^{-\frac{1}{3}} - 1 = 0$$

$$2(x^2 + 7x + 20)^{-\frac{1}{3}} = 1$$

$$(x^2 + 7x + 20)^{-\frac{1}{3}} = \frac{1}{2}$$

Step 2:   Get rid of the radical by raising both sides to −3. Use inversion $\left(\frac{a}{b}\right)^{-n} = \left(\frac{b}{a}\right)^{n}$ and the quotient to a power law $\left(\frac{a}{b}\right)^{n} = \frac{a^n}{b^n}$:

$$\left((x^2 + 7x + 20)^{-\frac{1}{3}}\right)^{-3} = \left(\frac{1}{2}\right)^{-3}$$

$$x^2 + 7x + 20 = \left(\frac{2}{1}\right)^{3}$$

$$x^2 + 7x + 20 = 8$$

Step 3:   All radicals are eliminated, so proceed to step 4.

Step 4:   Solve the remaining equation:

$$x^2 + 7x + 20 = 8$$
$$x^2 + 7x + 12 = 0$$
$$(x + 3)(x + 4) = 0$$

So, $x = -3$ and $x = -4$ are possible solutions.

Step 5:   Test the results. First test -3.

$$2((-3)^2 + 7(-3) + 20)^{-\frac{1}{3}} - 1 = 0$$
$$2(9 - 21 + 20)^{-\frac{1}{3}} - 1 = 0$$
$$2(8)^{-\frac{1}{3}} - 1 = 0$$
$$\frac{2}{8^{\frac{1}{3}}} - 1 = 0$$
$$\frac{2}{\sqrt[3]{8}} - 1 = 0$$
$$\frac{2}{2} - 1 = 0$$
$$0 = 0 \quad \text{Ok}$$

We see that -3 works out; let's test -4:

$$2((-4)^2 + 7(-4) + 20)^{-\frac{1}{3}} - 1 = 0$$
$$2(16 - 28 + 20)^{-\frac{1}{3}} - 1 = 0$$
$$2(8)^{-\frac{1}{3}} - 1 = 0$$
$$\frac{2}{8^{\frac{1}{3}}} - 1 = 0$$
$$\frac{2}{\sqrt[3]{8}} - 1 = 0$$
$$\frac{2}{2} - 1 = 0$$
$$1 - 1 = 0 \quad \text{Ok}$$

We see that -4 is also a solution.

Choice (C) is correct.

41. **The correct answer is (D).** We can solve each of the problems to determine if there is a solution. Generally, with this type of problem, it's best to start with the solution that looks the most obvious. All of the equations look like reasonable

problems except for choice (D). For choice (D) to have a solution, we would need to find a value for w that gives us a negative -4.

$$\sqrt{w} + 4 = 0$$
$$\sqrt{w} = -4$$

There is no solution, so choice (D) is the correct answer.

42. **The correct choice is (B).** To add the numbers, we simply group the real and complex and add:

$$(\sqrt{3} + 2i) + (\sqrt{3} - 2i) = (\sqrt{3} + \sqrt{3}) + (2 - 2)i$$
$$= 2\sqrt{3} + 0i$$
$$= 2\sqrt{3}$$

43. **The correct answer is (B).** We first need to determine the slope of the line that moves through the two points: $m = \dfrac{\text{change in } y}{\text{change in } x} = \dfrac{y_2 - y_1}{x_2 - x_1}$:

$$m = \frac{y_2 - y_1}{x_2 - x_1}$$
$$m = \frac{0 - 2}{5 - (-3)}$$
$$m = \frac{-2}{8}$$
$$m = -\frac{1}{4}$$

The slope is $-\dfrac{1}{4}$, so choice (B) is the correct answer.

44. **The correct answer is (A).** The range is the set of all values of the function for y. We can see from the plot below that y is never less than 0 and goes up to ∞.

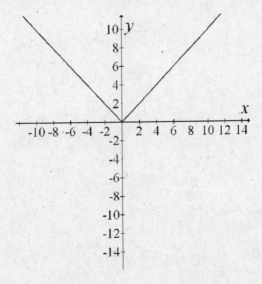

The answer is 0 to ∞ or $[0,\infty)$. Choice (A) is correct.

45. The correct answer is (C). The point (–3,–1) graphs as follows:

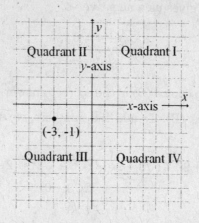

We can see the (–3,–1) falls in Quadrant III. Choice (C) is correct.

46. The correct answer is (A). Multiply the two functions:

$$f(x)g(x) = (3x^2 - x - 4)(2x + 1)$$
$$= (2x)(3x^2 - x - 4) + (1)(3x - x - 4)$$
$$= (2x)(3x^2) + (2x)(-x) + (2x)(-4) + 3x^2 - x - 4$$
$$= 6x^3 - 2x^2 - 8x + 3x^2 - x - 4$$
$$= 6x^3 + x^2 - 9x - 4$$

47. The correct answer is (A). Simplify this radical by multiplying by $\dfrac{x^2y^3}{x^2y^3}$. This helps eliminate the negative exponentials.

$$\frac{6x^4y^{-3}}{3x^{-2}y^2} = \frac{6x^4y^{-3}}{3x^{-2}y^2} \cdot \frac{x^2y^3}{x^2y^3}$$
$$= \frac{6x^4x^2}{3y^2y^3}$$
$$= \frac{6x^{4+2}}{3y^{2+3}}$$
$$= \frac{2x^6}{y^5}$$

There's another way to solve this problem. Solve by thinking about negative exponentials in a radical as just needing to move to the other side of the division line. While moving they change their sign:

$$\frac{6x^4 y^{-3}}{3x^{-2}y^2} = \frac{6x^4 \overbrace{y^{-3}}^{\text{move}}}{3\underbrace{x^{-2}}_{\text{move}}y^2}$$

$$= \frac{6x^4 \overbrace{x^2}^{\text{positive}}}{3y^2 \underbrace{y^3}_{\text{positive}}}$$

$$= \frac{6x^{4+2}}{3y^{2+3}}$$

$$= \frac{2x^6}{y^5}$$

48. The correct answer is (C). Divide the two functions and solve using the inversion law of rational expressions $\dfrac{\left(\dfrac{P}{Q}\right)}{\left(\dfrac{R}{S}\right)} = \dfrac{P}{Q} \cdot \dfrac{S}{R}$:

$$\frac{f(x)}{g(x)} = \frac{\dfrac{\sqrt{x+1}}{x}}{\dfrac{1}{x}}$$

$$= \frac{\sqrt{x+1}}{x} \cdot \frac{x}{1}$$

$$= \sqrt{x+1}$$

49. The correct answer is (D). To solve a composite function, insert $g(x)$ into the x of $f(x)$:

$$f(g(x)) = \left(\frac{1}{x}\right)^2 - 2\left(\frac{1}{x}\right) - 1$$

$$= \frac{1}{x^2} - \frac{2}{x} - 1$$

Find a common denominator to simplify:

$$= \frac{1}{x^2} - \frac{2}{x} - 1$$

$$= \frac{1}{x^2} - \frac{2}{x} \cdot \left(\frac{x}{x}\right) - 1\left(\frac{x^2}{x^2}\right)$$

$$= \frac{1}{x^2} - \frac{2x}{x^2} - \frac{x^2}{x^2}$$

$$= \frac{-x^2 - 2x + 1}{x^2}$$

Choice (D) is the correct answer.

50. The correct answer is (B). Find the quotient:

$$\left(\frac{f}{g}\right)(x) = \frac{\dfrac{2w+1}{w-3}}{\dfrac{w-1}{w-3}}$$

$$y = \frac{2w+1}{w-3} \cdot \frac{w-3}{w-1}$$

$$y = \frac{(2w+1)(w-3)}{(w-3)(w-1)}$$

$$y = \frac{2w+1}{w-1}$$

51. The correct answer is (A). Solve using the quadratic equation where $a = 9$, $b = -12$, and $c = 4$:

$$f(x) = \frac{-b \pm \sqrt{b^2 - 4ac}}{2a}$$

$$= \frac{-(-12) \pm \sqrt{(-12)^2 - 4(9)(4)}}{2(9)}$$

$$= \frac{12 \pm \sqrt{144 - 144}}{18}$$

$$= \frac{12 \pm 0}{18}$$

$$= \frac{12 \pm 0}{18}$$

$$= \frac{2}{3}$$

52. The correct answer is (B).

$$\log_4(x + 2) = 2$$

$$x + 2 = 4^2$$

$$x + 2 = 16$$

$$x = 14$$

53. The correct answer is (C). The solution can be found by multiplication:

$$(x - y)^3 = \underbrace{(x - y)(x - y)}_{\text{multiply}}(x - y)$$

$$= (xx - xy - xy + y^2)(x - y)$$

$$= (x^2 - 2xy + y^2)(x - y)$$

$$x(x^2 - 2xy + y^2) - y(x^2 - 2xy + y^2)$$

$$= x^3 - 2x^2y + xy^2 - x^2y + 2xy^2 - y^3$$

$$= x^3 - 3x^2y + 3xy^2 - y^3$$

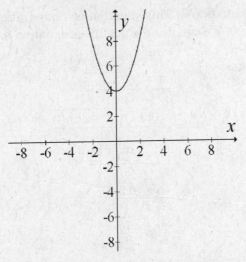

54. The correct answer is (A). First, we can rule out choice (C) because a cubic will have two "humps." We know choice (D) can't be correct because it is negative and would be a downward "U" shape. This leaves choices (A) and (B). We know that the function goes through the point $(0,4)$, so we can test to see if the function holds:

Equation A: $4 = (0)^2 + 4, 4 = 4$ Ok

Equation B: $4 = (0)^2 + (0) - 7, 4 \neq 7$ Not ok.

By the process of elimination and what we know about the plot of $f(x) = x^2 + 4$, we know choice (A) is the correct answer.

55. The correct answer is (A). First, we need to find the slope for the line represented by the equation $8x + 4y - 6 = 0$. We can do this by putting the equation in the line form $y = mx + b$, where m is the slope.

$$8x + 4y - 6 = 0$$
$$4y = -8x + 6$$
$$y = \frac{-8x + 6}{4}$$
$$y = -\frac{8x}{4} + \frac{6}{4}$$
$$y = -2x + \frac{3}{2}$$

Given this line equation, we now know that the slope is -2. The line we need to create needs to have a slope of -2 and go through $(5,-7)$. We can use the point-slope formula $y - y_1 = m (x - x_1)$:

$$y - y_1 = m(x - x_1)$$
$$y - (-7) = -2(x - 5)$$
$$y + 7 = -2x + 10$$
$$y = -2x + 10 - 7$$
$$y = -2x + 3$$

Choice (A) is correct.

56. The correct answer is (A). This equation is a quadratic and can be put in the form $3x^2 + 5x + 1 = 0$. We can use the quadratic equation to solve where $a = 3$, $b = 5$, and $c = 1$:

$$x = \frac{-b \pm \sqrt{b^2 - 4ac}}{2a}$$

$$= \frac{-(5) \pm \sqrt{(5)^2 - 4(3)(1)}}{2(3)}$$

$$= \frac{-5 \pm \sqrt{25 - 12}}{6}$$

$$= \frac{-5 \pm \sqrt{13}}{6}$$

$$= \frac{-5}{6} \pm \frac{\sqrt{13}}{6}$$

Choice (A) is correct.

57. The correct answer is (D). We can solve this problem by using the factoring rule:

$$x^2 = 11$$

$$x^2 - 11 = 0$$

$$(x - \sqrt{11})(x + \sqrt{11}) = 0$$

Next, solve each equation $(x - \sqrt{11}) = 0$ and $(x + \sqrt{11}) = 0$. We find that $x = \pm\sqrt{11}$. Choice (D) is correct.

58. The correct answer is (B). Use multiplication to find a common denominator, and then simplify using the addition/subtraction rule $\dfrac{P}{Q} + \dfrac{R}{Q} = \dfrac{P + R}{Q}$:

$$\frac{6 - \dfrac{3}{y}}{1 + \dfrac{3}{y}} = \frac{6\left(\dfrac{y}{y}\right) - \dfrac{3}{y}}{1\left(\dfrac{y}{y}\right) + \dfrac{3}{y}}$$

$$= \frac{\dfrac{6y}{y} - \dfrac{3}{y}}{\dfrac{y}{y} + \dfrac{3}{y}}$$

$$= \frac{\dfrac{6y - 3}{y}}{\dfrac{y + 3}{y}}$$

Now use the division rule $\dfrac{\left(\dfrac{P}{Q}\right)}{\left(\dfrac{R}{S}\right)} = \dfrac{P}{Q} \cdot \dfrac{S}{R}$ and then simplify by using the cancellation property:

$$= \frac{6y-3}{y} \cdot \frac{y}{y+3}$$

$$= \frac{3(y-1)}{y} \cdot \frac{y}{y+3}$$

$$= \frac{3(y-1)}{y+3}$$

Choice (B) is the correct answer.

59. The correct answer is (B). If we plot these points, we get a graph that looks a lot like a log. We can rule out answer choices (A) and (D), because a quadratic or absolute-value plot wouldn't look anything like the graph of the points given:

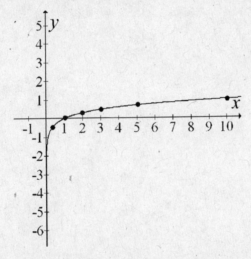

However, without a calculator it's difficult to compute values for $\log(x)$ other than perhaps 1 and 10. The values for 1 and 10 are correct for $\log(x)$. Let's test $f(x) = -\dfrac{1}{x}$, choice (C), to see if it could give us the values:

$$x = 0.5 \rightarrow -\frac{1}{0.5} = -2$$

$$x = 1 \rightarrow -\frac{1}{1} = -1$$

$$x = 2 \rightarrow -\frac{1}{2} = -0.5$$

$$x = 3 \rightarrow -\frac{1}{3} = -0.3333$$

$$x = 4 \rightarrow -\frac{1}{4} = -0.25$$

$$x = 10 \rightarrow -\frac{1}{10} = -0.1$$

We can put the values for choice (C) into the table to compare.

$x =$	0.5	1	2	3	5	10
$y =$	−0.3	0	0.3	0.5	0.7	1
C: $y =$	−2	−1	−0.5	−.333	−.25	−0.1

Looking at these values, it's obvious that choice (C) cannot be the correct answer. Log(x) is the only solution left, and it looks very close to the correct values. By the process of elimination, choice (B) is correct.

60. **The correct answer is (B).** The communicative property, $ab = ba$, describes the changing of the order of 2 and (2×3). Choice (B) is correct.

SUMMING IT UP

- Algebra generally deals with real numbers, which include just about any number such as 0, $-1/3$, π, or $\sqrt{2}$. Properties of real numbers include commutative, associative, identities, inverses, and distributive.

- Polynomials are any math expressions that use variables such as x, y, m, q, raised to a whole number called a power, with constants multiplied and added.

- An important tool for multiplying polynomials is the FOIL rule: **F**irst, **O**utside, **I**nside, **L**ast.

- Factoring is the opposite of multiplying. Factoring is simply finding what polynomials were originally multiplied together.

- The quotient or division of two polynomials forms a rational expression. Algebraic rules for rational expressions include the cancellation property, multiplication, division (multiply by the inverse of the denominator), addition, and subtraction.

- An exponential represents how many times a constant or variable is multiplied by itself. Exponential rules to master include product, product of a power, quotient to a power, quotient, zero exponent, negative exponent, and inversion.

- Radical expressions are those that use the symbol $\sqrt{}$ to represent roots of a variable.

- Linear equations are polynomials of the first order, i.e., x^1 or just x. Linear equations can have one or more variables. These polynomials are called "linear" because if you plot them on a graph they form a line.

- Problems that deal with more than one equation and contain more than one variable are called simultaneous equations. You can determine if these equations have common solutions by calculating where the equations are equal or where they intersect.

- The substitution method, the elimination method, and the matrix method can be used to find solutions to problems that involve rational numbers or other complex solutions.

- An inequality is a math statement where instead of two equations being equal, one equation is greater than ($>$), less than ($<$), greater than or equal to ($\geq$), or less than or equal to ($\leq$) the other. An important rule of solving inequalities is that the inequality sign must be flipped when multiplying or dividing by a negative number.

- The distance of any number from zero is the absolute value. Pipes "$|\ |$" are used around an equation for an absolute value. For example $|4| = 4$ and $|-4| = 4$.

- A quadratic equation is an equation of the form $ax^2 + bx + c = 0$, where $a \neq 0$. Quadratic equations can be solved using the standard method of factoring as well as by completing the square, which involves adding a constant to both sides of the equation so that it will easily factor.

- Complex numbers help solve polynomials such as $x^2 = -b$, which have no real solutions and require a new type, or complex number. The basic unit of a complex number is i, where $i = \sqrt{-1}$ or $i^2 = -1$. Complex conjugate numbers are of the form $a + bi$ where a represents the real unit and bi is the imaginary unit.

- When working with functions, think of them as an equation where for a value of x you get exactly one value for y. Consider functions as special equations where y is written as $f(x)$. The equation $y = mx + b$ is written as a function as $f(x) = mx + b$.

- A rational function is any function where the numerator and denominator are polynomials. The domain of the function is all the allowable values for x. The range of the function is all values the function can take on for the given values of x. The inverse function, which is written f^{-1}, is the set of all ordered pairs of the form (y,x) where (x,y) belongs to f. It is formed by interchanging x and y.

- Functions can be operated on by addition, subtraction, multiplication, and division, just as you would do with numbers or polynomials. Exponential functions are of the form $f(x) = a^x + b$. A logarithmic function is the inverse of an exponential function.

- Logarithms written without a base are understood to be base 10. The natural log is written "ln" and uses the symbol e and follows the same rules as Log.

- The slope of a line is a measure of its steepness. You can find the slope of a set of points (x_1,y_1) and (x_2,y_2) by finding the change in y divided by the change in x. You can find the slope of a linear equation by putting it into the form $y = mx + b$, where m is the slope.

- It's important to review the basic forms of lines and other polynomials:

  ○ A line is always of the form $f(x) = mx + b$, where m is the slope and b represents the y-coordinate of the point where the line crosses the y-axis.

  ○ A quadratic is any equation of the form $f(x) = ax^2 + bx^2 + c$. A quadratic with a positive a will bow up, a negative a will bow down. A larger value of a narrows the bow, while a smaller value of a makes the bow wider.

  ○ A cubic is in the form $f(x) = ax^3 + bx^2 + cx + d$. A cubic will have two "humps."

  ○ An absolute value $f(x) = |a|$, where a is any polynomial.

Technical Writing

OVERVIEW

- Diagnostic test
- Answer key and explanations
- What is technical writing?
- Reports: progress, feasibility, and laboratory
- Correspondence: memos, letters, and résumés
- Manuals, instructions and procedures, process descriptions, and proposals
- Organizing technical content
- How important is the document's appearance?
- Technical editing—a vital final step
- Post-test
- Answer key and explanations
- Summing it up

DIAGNOSTIC TEST

Directions: Carefully read each of the following 20 questions. Choose the best answer to each question and circle your answer choice. The Answer Key and Explanations can be found following this Diagnostic Test.

1. Which of the following summarizes only the scope and purpose of a document?
   - **(A)** Informative abstract
   - **(B)** Executive summary
   - **(C)** Descriptive abstract
   - **(D)** Closing summary

2. Which sequencing method would be most appropriate for the description of a new car model?
   - **(A)** Spatial
   - **(B)** Sequential
   - **(C)** Chronological
   - **(D)** Cause and effect

3. Which type of proposal would most likely be written by a university professor to request funding from a government agency for a scientific study?

   (A) Internal proposal

   (B) Sales proposal

   (C) Routine proposal

   (D) Grant proposal

4. The primary focus of most technical writing is

   (A) undocumented opinions.

   (B) global integration.

   (C) factual information.

   (D) supplemental data.

5. Which of the following is written specifically for repair technicians?

   (A) User manuals

   (B) Training manuals

   (C) Service manuals

   (D) Operator's manuals

6. An informal tone in a document is most appropriate when writing to

   (A) colleagues.

   (B) customers.

   (C) superiors.

   (D) academics.

7. It is most appropriate for a technical document conclusion to

   (A) interpret findings.

   (B) present a new idea.

   (C) cite useful references.

   (D) define technical terms.

8. The primary purpose of an inquiry letter is to

   (A) request an appointment.

   (B) ask about a service.

   (C) ask for a refund.

   (D) request a job.

9. The literal meaning of a word is its

   (A) connotation.

   (B) subordination.

   (C) denotation.

   (D) abstraction.

10. Which of the following would be most appropriate for describing how a rotary engine works?

    (A) Functional

    (B) Spatial

    (C) Chronological

    (D) Cause and effect

11. A brief definition of a technical term should be explained in a document's

    (A) appendix.

    (B) glossary.

    (C) bibliography.

    (D) table of contents.

12. Which of the following would most likely be written when a business is considering the development of a new service?

    (A) Feasibility report

    (B) Internal memo

    (C) Progress report

    (D) Solicited proposal

13. Which of the following involves the use of a synonym to explain the meaning of an unfamiliar word?

    (A) Sentence definition

    (B) Expanded definition

    (C) Parenthetical definition

    (D) Definition by components

14. The major difference between instructions and procedures is that procedures are intended for

    (A) unskilled users.

    (B) groups of people.

    (C) sales personnel.

    (D) new employees.

15. Learning as much as possible about the readers of a technical document is known as audience
    (A) purpose.
    (B) analysis.
    (C) planning.
    (D) adaptation.

16. A term with multiple meanings is best defined with a
    (A) negative definition.
    (B) parenthetical definition.
    (C) visual definition.
    (D) sentence definition.

17. Which of the following graphics is best for tracing steps in a process?
    (A) Table
    (B) Flowchart
    (C) Pie chart
    (D) Line graph

18. All of the following are elements of most laboratory reports EXCEPT
    (A) costs.
    (B) results.
    (C) equipment.
    (D) procedures.

19. Which of the following is appropriate for the placement of visuals in a technical document?
    I. In an appendix
    II. Near the text being clarified
    III. In the front matter of a document
    (A) I only
    (B) I and II only
    (C) II and III only
    (D) I, II, and III

20. Which of the following would be most appropriate for a nontechnical reader who needs to know the specific details of how a mechanism works?
    (A) Definition by cause
    (B) Sentence definition
    (C) Definition by components
    (D) Negative definition

diagnostic test

ANSWER KEY AND EXPLANATIONS

1. C	5. C	9. C	13. C	17. B
2. A	6. A	10. A	14. B	18. A
3. D	7. A	11. B	15. B	19. B
4. C	8. B	12. A	16. D	20. C

1. **The correct answer is (C).** A descriptive abstract summarizes in a few sentences the scope and purpose of a document. Choices (B) and (D) review the main points of a document. Choice (A) summarizes a report rather than just the scope and purpose.

2. **The correct answer is (A).** The spatial method of development is used to describe the physical appearance of something, such as a new car. The sequential method, choice (B), is for explaining systematic instructions. Chronological order, choice (C), explains a sequence of events, such as a car accident. The description of a car involves no cause-and-effect relationship, so choice (D) is incorrect.

3. **The correct answer is (D).** A professor requesting funding from the government for a study would submit a grant proposal. Internal and routine proposals are submitted within organizations, so choices (A) and (C) are incorrect. A sales proposal is used to gain business, so choice (B) is incorrect.

4. **The correct answer is (C).** Presenting facts is the main focus of technical documents. Technical documents may include expert opinions and supplemental data, such as statistics, but essential facts are the focal point. Technical writers need to consider whether a document will be read on a global level, but global integration is not a key consideration.

5. **The correct answer is (C).** Service manuals are written for repair technicians, and they contain troubleshooting charts to help diagnose equipment problems. User manuals, choice (A), are written for the people who use a product, not repair it. Training manuals, choice (B), are used as teaching tools with certain vocations, and operator's manuals, choice (D), are for trained equipment operators.

6. **The correct answer is (A).** An informal tone in technical writing is appropriate for colleagues and subordinates in most cases. Superiors and academics, such as professors, require a formal or semiformal tone. A semiformal or formal tone is also appropriate when communicating with customers.

7. **The correct answer is (A).** The conclusion of a technical document should interpret findings presented in the report. New ideas should not be introduced in a conclusion, so choice (B) is incorrect. References are cited in a bibliography, so choice (C) is incorrect. Technical terms should have been defined in the body of a document, so it would be too late to explain them in the conclusion.

8. **The correct answer is (B).** Inquiry letters are written to ask about a product, service, or procedure. Refunds are requested in claim letters, so choice (C) is incorrect. Job application cover letters are used to seek jobs, so choice (D) is incorrect.

9. **The correct answer is (C).** The denotation of a word is its literal meaning or dictionary definition. A word's connotation, choice (A), is the associations it brings to mind for different people, which may be positive or negative. Choices (B) and (D) are incorrect and have no relation to the meaning of words.

10. **The correct answer is (A).** Functional sequence is most appropriate for describing a mechanism, such as a rotary engine, while it is in action. Spatial sequence is used when a writer needs to describe what a device looks like and what it does while at rest. Chronological order would be used if the document focused on how to assemble a rotary engine.

11. **The correct answer is (B).** The glossary is where a writer defines technical and unfamiliar terms from a document. Expanded definitions may require an appendix, but terms defined briefly should be included in a glossary. Bibliographies cite references used for a document, and a table of contents lists where information can be located in a report or proposal.

12. **The correct answer is (A).** Feasibility reports are written when a business is considering a major change, such as developing a new service or moving a manufacturing facility. Memos are written to request information or announce policies within an organization, so choice (B) is incorrect. Progress reports, choice (C), describe the status of a large project, and solicited proposals, choice (D), are persuasive documents written to earn business.

13. **The correct answer is (C).** Parenthetical definition involves using a synonym or phrase to explain the meaning of an unfamiliar term in a document. Expanded definitions, choice (B), and sentence definitions, choice (A), are lengthier than a word or phrase. Choice (D) is a type of expanded definition.

14. **The correct answer is (B).** Procedures are used to clarify the rules and expectations that group members should follow in different situations. Instructions are the steps taken to complete a task. Procedures are for skilled individuals, so choice (A) is incorrect. Choices (C) and (D) are not the primary focus of procedures.

15. **The correct answer is (B).** Audience analysis refers to gathering information about the readers of a technical document in preparation for writing. Technical writers often adapt their messages after learning about the needs and knowledge of readers. The purpose of a technical document is an important aspect of writing preparation, but the terms used in choices (A) and (C) do not describe audience analysis.

16. **The correct answer is (D).** Sentence definitions are used for defining complex terms or terms that have multiple meanings. A parenthetical definition would not be sufficient for explaining the usage of a word with more than one meaning. Choices (A) and (C) are types of expanded definitions, which are only necessary when a term requires extensive details.

17. **The correct answer is (B).** Flowcharts are appropriate for tracing the steps or decisions in any type of procedure or process. A table, choice (A), helps organize explanations and numbers. Pie charts, choice (C), relate parts to the whole. Line graphs, choice (D), show changes over time.

18. **The correct answer is (A).** Results, equipment, and procedures are key

elements usually included in laboratory reports. In order for a test to be repeatable, an author must identify all equipment and procedures used. The costs associated with laboratory testing are not included in a laboratory report in most instances.

19. **The correct answer is (B).** A very large visual belongs in an appendix at the end of the document. Ideally, visuals are situated near the text they illustrate. The front matter of a document includes a list of figures or visuals but not the visuals themselves.

20. **The correct answer is (C).** Definition by components is a way to make a complex concept simpler by breaking it into parts, which would be useful for nontechnical readers. Defining a term by explaining its causes would not help clarify the way a device works, so Choice (A) is incorrect. A sentence definition, choice (B), would be too brief to explain the way a mechanism works. A negative definition, choice (D), would fail to explain the specifics of a mechanism's inner workings.

WHAT IS TECHNICAL WRITING?

Technical writing refers to any written communication pertaining to a job, such as memos, letters, instructions, reports, and proposals. Any document that contains industry-specific language is a type of technical writing. The purpose of most technical communication is helping readers understand a process, concept, or technology. Unlike essays written for class or poetry written for pleasure, technical writing focuses on facts rather than personal thoughts, feelings, and attitudes.

Almost every career involves an element of technical writing—science, engineering, business, health sciences, and technology. Doctors maintain patient records, scientists write lab reports, software engineers write manuals, and managers write personnel evaluations. Business owners and employees write progress reports, memos, letters, proposals, and manuals on a daily basis, and each document has its own purpose, style, and structure. Understanding the specific elements of technical communication is essential in the information-driven twenty-first century.

Purpose and Audience

Effective work-related writing clearly and efficiently conveys information to a specific audience. Before creating any type of workplace communication, whether it is a memo, report, or manual, writers should first consider the purpose of the document and the audience that will be reading it.

The purpose of any technical writing refers to what readers should know, believe, or do after having read a document. For most technical communication, the purpose involves defining, describing, or explaining. For example, a Realtor may write an e-mail to a first-time homebuyer defining terms such as "escrow" and "fixed-rate mortgage." An office manager may write a memo to her employees explaining how to enroll in a new insurance program. The purpose, or objective, of any technical document should be as specific as possible to simplify the writing task and to guarantee that the document achieves the writer's goal.

Another aspect of writing a technical document is the audience, which is the intended reader. For communication to be effective, the audience should be the chief consideration when planning and writing a technical document. Audience analysis refers to learning as much as possible about the individuals who will use a specific document. Understanding the knowledge, interests, and needs of readers enables a writer to adapt a message and tailor it to a specific audience. Adaptation of a message particularly relates to the level of technicality of a document.

Audience Technicality Level

Document User	Necessary Information	Example
Highly technical	Audience consists of experts in the subject matter; data does not require lengthy explanation	A physician giving a report to a surgeon about a patient's lab results and symptoms

Semi-technical	Audience consists of people with some technical knowledge but less than experts; data needs some explanation	A physician giving a report to first-year medical students regarding a patient's lab results and symptoms
Nontechnical	Audience consists of laypersons with no training in the subject matter; data needs to be translated into simple language that can be easily understood	A physician giving a report to a patient's spouse regarding lab results, symptoms, and treatment options

The technical background of the audience determines whether terms need to be explained. As shown in the table, colleagues with the same background need only straightforward data, but those unfamiliar with terminology expect interpretations and recommendations. In addition to technical knowledge, technical writers should consider other factors when analyzing the audience.

- What is the cultural background of the audience? Will a global audience read the document?
- What are most readers' experience and training in regards to the subject matter?
- What is the attitude of the audience about the subject matter?
- What are the needs and interests of the audience? What do readers expect from the document?
- Will multiple audiences that include experts, technicians, executives, and laypersons read the document?

Evaluating Data Validity

Before writing any technical document, a technical writer must evaluate the information that will be included. The sources and evidence used in a technical document should be both valid and reliable.

Collecting data is not difficult in the Internet age; however, not all sources are reliable. The source of information should be as current as possible, although some information changes very quickly. Information regarding technology is often outdated in a few months, so a document about diabetes treatments or data mining requires the most current research. Topics related to people, such as workplace ethics and flexible scheduling, benefit from both recent and historical research. A printed source published by a university or other respected organization is most likely reliable. Carefully scrutinize electronic sources and consider the following guidelines:

- What is the Web site's sponsor and domain type, i.e., .edu, .com, .gov, .net?
- What is the purpose of the Web page and message?
- When was the Web site most recently updated?
- What are the author's credentials and expertise?

For the most valid data, technical writers should avoid relying on a single source for information and should instead acquire a consensus from many different sources.

Evidence refers to any information used to support or refute a claim. Ethical technical writers strive for balanced evidence, which means avoiding exaggerations and including all pertinent facts. Factual statements, statistics, and expert opinions are examples of hard, verifiable evidence. Soft evidence refers to uninformed opinions and unverified data.

REPORTS: PROGRESS, FEASIBILITY, AND LABORATORY

Reports often provide the basis for decision making in the workplace, and they may be formal, informal, informational, or analytical. Informational reports focus on providing straightforward information—results of a customer survey, minutes of a department meeting, or profits and losses for the month. Analytical reports evaluate information, draw conclusions, and make recommendations. Formal reports are typically lengthy, require extensive research, and involve multiple writers. Informal reports lack extensive planning or research, and they often take the form of a memorandum. Executives and employees write numerous types of reports in the workplace, but progress reports, feasibility reports, and laboratory reports are the focus of this review.

Progress Reports

Progress reports, also known as status reports, keep the reader informed about activities, problems, and progress related to a large project. A project involving numerous steps may require the submission of regular progress reports—daily, weekly, or monthly. Progress reports are extremely useful with managerial decisions regarding work schedules, task assignments, funding, and supplies. Clients and managers expect progress reports to answer a number of questions:

- What has been accomplished since the last progress report?
- What tasks still need to be completed?
- Have there been any unanticipated problems?
- What is the expected timetable for completion?

The structure of a progress report often depends on the business, and many companies have specific forms they require for progress reports. However, every progress report pertaining to the same project should be organized in the same manner for the sake of consistency. In general, the first project report submitted for a project includes an introduction or overview that states the project, necessary materials, and anticipated completion date. Follow-up reports explain what work has been completed, what work remains to be done, scheduling information, budget updates, and recommendations.

Feasibility Reports

When a business considers the purchase of new equipment, development of a new product, or relocation of manufacturing facilities, executives initially attempt to assess the likelihood that the project or change will be successful. Feasibility reports help executives determine if an idea or a plan is both possible and practical. In some cases, a course of action may be possible but impractical because it would lower productivity or raise costs. Feasibility reports should address a variety of questions:

- Is this plan likely to be successful?
- What are the benefits and risks of the plan?
- What are other options?
- Is funding available?
- How would employees be affected?

Feasibility reports often begin with a purpose statement, such as *The purpose of this report is to determine the feasibility of moving our manufacturing facilities overseas.* The length of a feasibility report depends on the size of the project, but most follow a similar structure:

- *Introduction:* background information and purpose statement
- *Body:* review of options being considered based on criteria like costs and staff
- *Conclusion:* interpretation of findings
- *Recommendation:* author's opinion regarding the most feasible option based on the criteria discussed in the body of the report

Although the structure and length of feasibility reports varies, they should always review possible alternatives, provide specific recommendations, and include enough details to support the author's recommendations.

Laboratory Reports

Laboratory reports relay information gathered from an investigation or from laboratory testing. The format of a laboratory report varies by profession and organization, but basic elements exist in almost all laboratory reports:

- The reason for conducting the test or investigation
- Equipment and procedures used during the investigation
- Problems, results, and conclusions

The most critical aspect of laboratory reports is the equipment and procedures used during testing. Duplicating the test and assessing the accuracy of the investigation depend upon the equipment used and the procedures followed.

CORRESPONDENCE: MEMOS, LETTERS, AND RÉSUMÉS

Communicating with clients, colleagues, and potential employers occurs regularly, and it is an essential skill in the workplace. The style of any kind of correspondence depends on the intended audience. An informal or casual style is appropriate for correspondence with a well-known colleague, but a restrained or formal style is a better choice for correspondence with a new customer.

Memos

A memorandum is the primary method of communication for many organizations because of its ability to serve various purposes. Governments and businesses use memos for numerous reasons such as announcing policies, instructing employees, recommending action, and requesting information. Progress reports and meeting minutes are often structured in memo format as well. Keep in mind that memos are the chief method of in-house correspondence, so avoid hostile comments and unproductive complaints in order to maintain positive relationships with co-workers.

Memos, which may be sent on paper or as e-mail attachments, provide a record trail of decisions, responsibilities, progress, and actions, so they have legal implications. Although memo formats vary among different organizations and no one standard exists, most memos are structured similarly.

Information written in memos should be accurate, concise, and straightforward, and it should keep the reader in mind. Professionals do not read memos for pleasure, so using words efficiently is the key to writing reader-friendly memos. Topic headings are useful for memos that address many subtopics, and lists offer quick access to information.

Organize information in a memo either directly or indirectly. When using the direct pattern, present the main point of the memo first and follow it up with details. An indirect pattern is structured in an opposite manner. Present the details first before leading up to the main point of the memo. Most readers prefer the direct pattern because it addresses the main issue right away. However, the indirect approach may be appropriate when conveying bad news, such as employee layoffs.

Letters

Like memos, letters document information; however, memos and letters differ with regard to readers. Memos are a type of correspondence used among colleagues within an organization. Letters are a form of communication used to correspond with individuals outside of an organization, such as clients, customers, and contractors. Because of the difference in audience, letters are more formal in style and format than memos. Word choice is especially important in letter writing because readers outside of an organization will most likely be unfamiliar with the language and terminology common among those within an organization. In addition, letters typically require more background information than memos.

Business letters follow a specific format: heading, date, inside address, salutation, text, closing, signature, and title. The text of a business letter should include a brief introduction of no more than five lines that explains the purpose of the letter. The body paragraphs include the details of the message, and the conclusion summarizes the letter and encourages the reader to take some sort of action. Paragraphs in the body are typically kept to fewer than eight lines, and bulleted lists are included when necessary. An attention line may replace a salutation when a department or a position is the recipient of a letter instead of a single person. Although subject lines are common with memos, they may also be included in business letters to grab the attention of the reader.

Organization Name
MEMORANDUM

TO: Name/title of addressee
FROM: Name/title of sender with handwritten initials
DATE: For recordkeeping purposes
SUBJECT: Key words describing the purpose

Introductory Paragraph—Purpose of memo and brief background information

Body Paragraph(s)—Details, explanations, and arguments

Conclusion—Requests for specific action with dates and encouraging words to build positive relationships

Distribution and enclosure notations

People write business-related letters for numerous purposes, but three types stand out as the most common.

Types of Letters

Inquiry Letters	Written to ask about a product, service, or procedure; brief, direct, and clearly worded so reader understands what is needed
Claim Letters	Written to express disappointment with a product or service and to request a refund, replacement, or an apology
Job Application Letters	Written to accompany a résumé when seeking an internship or employment; explains how skills and experience match a specific job position

Résumés

During the job search process, a résumé serves as an important tool for illustrating qualifications to potential employers. Résumés should be limited to one or two pages and should be well organized, easy to read, and free of mistakes. It is especially important in résumé writing to use consistent punctuation, spacing, and formatting, as well as parallel grammatical structure. Action verbs and concisely stated descriptions of achievements and abilities are most appropriate. A résumé is the first impression that an employer has of a person, and it serves as the springboard for the next step in the hiring process. Employers disregard cluttered or confusing résumés.

Résumés vary in format, but most include the same basic categories of information:

- Name and contact information
- Job objective
- Qualifications summary
- Education and work experiences
- Awards, skills, and activities
- References

The job objective of a résumé assists the employer with understanding the goal of the applicant. *A full-time management position with a large department store* is an example of a job objective. Although qualifications summaries, also known as summary statements, are not included in all résumés, they are useful persuasive tools that highlight skills, experiences, and personal traits of a job applicant.

The placement of education and experience in a résumé depends on which credentials are more relevant to the job. Recent college graduates with limited work experience list education first, while individuals with years of work experience place education last. Present employment experience either in reverse chronological order—most recent to least recent—or by function or type of job experience. However, functional résumés are occasionally perceived by some employers as a way to hide employment gaps or excessive job changes.

MANUALS, INSTRUCTIONS AND PROCEDURES, PROCESS DESCRIPTIONS, AND PROPOSALS

Manuals

Manuals are documents that help people understand how to assemble, use, and repair products. Nearly every product sold to consumers—from waffle irons to automobiles—includes a manual. Different types of manuals serve a variety of purposes and audiences.

Types of Manuals

User Manuals	Written for both skilled and unskilled users of a product; include instructions regarding setup, operation, and maintenance as well as safety warnings and troubleshooting tips
Tutorials	Written as a self-study guide for the users of a product; intended to guide first-time users through the steps involved in operating a product
Training Manuals	Major teaching tool in vocational jobs; used to train people in a procedure or skill and often paired with audiovisual information

(continued)

Operator's Manuals	Written for trained operators of construction, computer, or manufacturing equipment for use on the job; includes instructions and safety information
Service Manuals	Written for repair technicians; contain troubleshooting charts for diagnosing problems

Before writing a manual, an author must consider whether the typical reader is a novice user, intermediate user, or expert user of the product or service. Audience determines the details to include and the terminology to use.

Instructions and Procedures

Instructions and procedures are two aspects of technical documentation that require clarification because they are frequently confused. Instructions are the steps required to complete a specific task safely and efficiently, such as installing a memory card into a laptop. People who have never performed a certain task are the typical audience for instructions. Printed manuals, online documentation, and brief reference cards are examples of common instructional documents. Instructional documents must be accurately written because consumers who are injured by a product due to faulty instructions may sue the technical writer. The misuse of power tools, medications, and cleaning products can lead to serious injuries, so all safety information and potential risks must be clearly explained to users in instructional documents.

Instructions that act as guidelines for people familiar with a task are called procedures. Procedures ensure safety within a group. For example, most businesses have written safety procedures that explain how to evacuate a building during a fire. Safety procedures include how to assist personnel with special needs, where to meet after evacuation, and who to contact for assistance. Written procedures also help maintain consistency. For example, police departments have specific procedures to follow when investigating a crime scene to ensure that officers gather, label, and store evidence correctly. Procedures help members of a group learn the expectations and rules related to a specific task.

Process Descriptions

A process description or a process explanation describes how something works and breaks down a process into steps or parts. The steps required to manufacture a DVD or the way a bank reviews loan applications are both typical subjects of process explanations. Well-written process descriptions include enough details so another person is able to follow the process through each step.

A process description begins with an introduction that provides an overview of the process or explains the importance of learning the process. Defining terminology and including visual aids helps make the process clear for readers. A technical writer clarifies each step of a process with transitional phrases and topic headings that indicate to readers that one stage is complete and another is beginning. A conclusion wraps up the process description by summarizing the major stages and describing a complete cycle of the process.

An item or process is best described in a specific order to enable the audience to understand. Technical writers use spatial sequence to describe a mechanism at rest and to explain what an object is, what it does, and what it looks like. Technical writers use functional sequence when describing a mechanism that is in action and discussing how a mechanism works. When describing the order of assembly and explaining how a mechanism is put together, technical writers use chronological sequence.

Proposals

Proposals are documents written to persuade readers to take some type of action. The intention of a proposal may be to persuade an audience to support a plan, authorize a project, or purchase a product. Reports and proposals have similar elements, but they differ in purpose. Although the recommendations section of a report may be somewhat persuasive, the majority of a report is informative. In contrast, a proposal is entirely persuasive in nature.

Numerous types of proposals are used in the workplace, and the organizational pattern, formality, and length of each kind varies. An internal proposal is submitted to personnel within an organization; an external or sales proposal is submitted to clients or potential customers. Short proposals include an introduction, body, and conclusion. In contrast, long proposals are divided into front matter, body, and back matter. The front matter includes the cover letter, title page, table of contents, and list of figures. The body includes the executive summary, introduction, problem description, rationale, cost analysis, personnel expertise, statement of responsibilities, organizational sales pitch, request for approval, and the conclusion. Back matter includes appendixes, bibliography, and glossary of terms.

Types of Proposals

Routine internal proposal	Written in short proposal format; used frequently in organizations for minor spending requests
Formal internal proposal	Used when requesting large amounts of money
Solicited proposal	External proposal written in response to a request for proposals (RFP) or an invitation for bids (IFB)
Unsolicited proposal	External proposal written and submitted without request
Sales proposal	External proposal that may be short or long depending on size of potential sale
Grant or research proposal	External proposal written to request funding for a project or study

ORGANIZING TECHNICAL CONTENT

Technical documents are often lengthy, so it is common for writers to include a summary of information, a conclusion, definitions, and report supplements to aid readers.

Summaries and Abstracts

Closing summaries, executive summaries, informative abstracts, and descriptive abstracts are four types of summarized information often included in technical documents.

Summaries and Abstracts

Closing summary	Included either at the beginning of the conclusion or at the end of the body; reviews main points and findings
Executive summary	Included before full report; combines main points of a report or proposal; often persuasive
Informative abstract	Included before full report; summarized version of report
Descriptive abstract	Included on the title page; summarizes in a few sentences the scope and purpose of the document

Informative abstracts and executive summaries are often confused because they are similar. An abstract is a summary of a written document that enables readers to determine whether to read an entire article. An executive summary combines the main points of a report or proposal, and it is often the only section of a longer document that is read. Executive summaries follow the same sequence as the full document with sub-headings to assist the reader. Most executive summaries are 10 percent of the length of the original document, while most abstracts are approximately 200 words long, regardless of the length of the original article.

Conclusions

The purpose of a conclusion in a technical document is to summarize information, interpret findings, and offer recommendations. Conclusions offer an author a final opportunity to emphasize a significant point that will remain with the reader. Throughout a document, writers explain evidence, but the conclusion sums up the analysis and leads to a recommendation, if the document requires the author's opinion. Depending on the type of document, a conclusion should have certain characteristics:

- *Summary:* represents the main points of the document
- *Interpretation:* coincides with findings presented in the document
- *Recommendations:* agree with purpose, evidence, and interpretations of the document

The purpose of the document and the reader's needs dictate the content of a conclusion. For example, a report may end with a recommendation, yet it might be more advantageous to conclude a sales proposal with a persuasive statement regarding the benefits of purchasing a product. Other methods of effectively concluding a document involve ending with a thought-provoking statement or quotation, asking readers to take action, making predictions, and presenting ideas to consider. Regardless of the approach used to conclude a document, writers should never introduce a new topic. Conclusions should always refer to the information and ideas presented in the document.

Definitions

Defining unfamiliar terms and concepts is critical for the clarity of a technical document. Definitions help readers understand the precise meaning of a word, concept, or process. Within various types of technical documents, definitions may have legal implications. For example, contracts and employee handbooks require clear definitions to ensure that all parties understand the legal terms and responsibilities. Technical writers employ a variety of methods when defining terms in documents.

Methods for Defining Terms

Parenthetical definition	Use a synonym or a clarifying phrase to explain the meaning of an unfamiliar word; easy to set up links in electronic documents
Sentence definition	Used for complex terms or when term has multiple meanings. Follows a fixed pattern: indicate the item to be defined, the class in which the item belongs, and the features that make the item unique from others in same class
Expanded definition	Used when extensive details are required about an item; may be a paragraph or numerous pages depending on the audience and purpose

Parenthetical and sentence definitions are appropriate when a reader only requires a general understanding of a term or a concept. However, expanded definitions may be necessary when a reader needs to know how something works or when a reader is semi-technical or nontechnical. Definitions can be expanded in a variety of ways:

- *Etymology:* describe the term's origin, such as Greek or Latin words

- *Background:* discuss history, development, and applications for the term, unless readers are only attempting to perform a task related to the term

- *Negation:* explain what the term does not mean

- *Operation:* explain how an item or process works

- *Analysis of parts:* explain how each element of a complex item works, which is especially beneficial to laypersons attempting to understand a technical subject

- *Visuals:* use to show the meaning of a process or concept

- *Comparison and contrast:* compare or contrast unfamiliar information with information the reader understands

- *Examples:* use those that match a reader's level of comprehension to describe how an item is used or how it works

Including definitions in a document is important to reader understanding, but determining where to place definitions can be tricky. If four or fewer terms need to be explained, then parenthetical definitions or hypertext links are appropriate because the flow of the text will not be disrupted. However, more than four terms requiring clarification calls for sentence definitions placed in the glossary of the document. Expanded definitions belong in the introduction if the term is essential to understanding the entire document. An expanded definition that explains a major point belongs in that specific section. An appendix is appropriate for an expanded definition that is merely a reference in a document and not essential to understanding a key point.

Report Supplements

Long documents need to be accessible to readers who may not have the time or interest to read the full text, and, as such, report supplements are beneficial tools. As mentioned previously, long documents have both front matter and back matter. The table of contents is part of the front matter, and the glossary and appendixes are part of the back matter.

Table of Contents

A formal document longer than ten pages usually includes a table of contents to simplify the process of locating information. Most writers place the table of contents after the title page and abstract but before the list of tables, the foreword, and the preface. A table of contents shows what is contained in a document and on what pages information can be located. In the table of contents, it is best to list the major headings of a document in the order in which they appear and include subheadings as well. Front matter is listed in Roman numerals, and page numbers begin with the first page of the report, most likely the introduction.

Glossary

The glossary of a document is an alphabetical listing of definitions. Technical terms or those that have a unique meaning in the document require definitions for reader comprehension. A glossary defines technical terms without breaking the flow of a document. Technical documents intended for laypersons may require a glossary, yet an audience of skilled readers may not need technical terms defined at all. In general, a document containing more than five technical terms calls for a glossary. Explain the meaning of five or fewer technical terms either within the text or in a footnote. Definitions should be concise and clear to enhance reader understanding. Insert a glossary after the appendixes and the bibliography in the back matter of a long document.

Appendix

An appendix is part of the back matter of a document, and it serves the purpose of clarifying or supplementing information presented in the text body. Documents may contain more than one appendix, but each appendix should address only one piece of information. Arrange multiple appendixes in a document in the order in which the information appears in the body. Each appendix begins on a new page and is identified with a letter beginning with *A* and an appropriate title. A document containing only one appendix does not require letters, only *Appendix* as the title. The following is a list of typical information that would be appropriate for an appendix:

- Experiment details
- Complicated formulas
- Interview questions and answers
- Quotations longer than one page
- Maps and photographs
- Sample questionnaires, tests, and surveys
- Large visual aids

Keep in mind that information is generally included in an appendix if it would interfere with the main body text or is too detailed or lengthy for the primary reader. However, writers should not include irrelevant information in appendixes or use too many of them.

HOW IMPORTANT IS THE DOCUMENT'S APPEARANCE?

It's often said that appearance is everything, and for technical documents—whether a report, memo, manual, proposal, or e-mail—this is definitely true. The proper use of titles and headings, page design, and visuals is extremely important when writing and composing technical documents.

Titles and Headings

Readers often base their decision to read a technical document upon the title. Well-written titles indicate a variety of information about a document—topic, tone, scope, purpose, and more. The most useful titles are concise yet specific. Avoid sentence form and redundancies in titles. The subject line acts as the title for memos and e-mails.

Within the body of a technical document, headings serve as titles of sections and subtopics. Headings have a number of purposes, especially in lengthy reports:

- Help readers find a particular section
- Divide information into logical pieces
- Highlight main points and topics
- Signal topic changes

Headings can be real time savers for readers and make a technical document more accessible. The way in which a heading is phrased depends on its function in the document. A topic heading is a brief phrase or word that is most appropriate when there are many subtopics in a document; however, they can be too vague for readers. Statement headings require a sentence or a detailed phrase and are useful when a specific detail about a topic needs to be addressed. Question headings draw readers into the topic, but they may be too informal for some documents.

Page Design

In addition to the facts and ideas presented in a technical document, the appearance of any written communication should be considered as well. Page design can emphasize certain aspects of a document and visually indicate the organization of information. Authors should keep readers in mind when designing pages and focus on using page design elements consistently throughout a document. The following elements of page design are effective tools for enhancing the appearance of a technical document.

Page Design Elements

Justification	Margins justified on the left are easier to read; fully justified appropriate for multiple columns.
Headings	Indicate organizational structure and help readers find information; type size or font should differ from main text.
Lists	Useful in presenting steps, materials, and recommendations.
Headers and footers	Often include section topic, date, page number, and title of document.
Columns	Single-column for larger typeface; double for smaller typeface. Avoid orphans and widows. Orphan is a word on a line by itself at the end of a column. Widow is a single line carried over to the top of a column.
Color	Useful in highlighting sections of a document to draw reader attention.
White space	Blank space between paragraphs and between sections visually helps readers know when one idea or section is beginning or ending.

Visuals

Visuals also improve a document's readability and appearance. A technical writer who needs to explain an idea more clearly than is possible with words will often turn to visuals. Drawings, photographs, and maps show readers what something looks like. Graphs and tables illustrate numbers and quantities. Flowcharts, diagrams, and organizational charts clarify relationships.

As with most elements of technical writing, audience and purpose determine what visuals should be utilized in a document. For example, numerical tables and schematics would be most appropriate for expert readers who are able to interpret information sufficiently. Basic graphs and diagrams are suitable for audiences with limited technical knowledge.

In general, use visuals when readers need to focus on a particular idea. Visuals serve to instruct or persuade the reader, and they draw the reader's attention to an important concept. Including visuals is also beneficial when an author anticipates that a document will be consulted by readers unfamiliar with the topic or by readers who only need to read specific sections of a document.

Types of Visuals

Tables	Data organized for easy comparison
Bar graphs	Translate numbers into shapes or colors; show comparisons
Line graphs	Show trends and changes over time, cost, size, rates, and other variables
Pie charts	Show parts of a whole
Gantt charts	Show how the phases of a project relate to each other
Pictograms	Use images or icons to represent quantities; useful for non-experts to grasp ideas
Flowcharts	Show steps in a process
Schematic diagrams	Show how components of a principle, process, or system function together
Drawings	Show real or imaginary objects; highlight specific parts; use exploded view to show how parts fit together

Visuals are especially effective when placed near the text they are clarifying. Especially large or lengthy visuals should be included in an appendix.

TECHNICAL EDITING: A VITAL FINAL STEP

If the appearance and content of a technical document are sound, but the writing is not readable, then the writer has not met the audience's needs. Editing is an important step in writing technical documents. Besides correcting grammar, punctuation, and spelling problems, an author needs to consider tone, unity, sequence, clarity, and conciseness.

Tone

The attitude expressed by a writer toward a subject is the tone of a document. For technical writing, tone depends on the purpose, audience, and method of communication. For example, an e-mail sent from one colleague to another may express a casual tone, while written communication to a superior or a client should have a professional tone. Tone indicates the distance between a writer and a reader; it also indicates the attitude of the author toward the topic and the audience. Although no rules exist for determining the most appropriate tone for a technical document, the following guidelines may be useful to writers:

- Use formal or semiformal tone when writing is intended for superiors or professionals.
- Use a semiformal or informal tone when writing is intended for colleagues and subordinates.
- Use an informal tone when a conversational style is desired, but avoid being too informal with profanity, slang, or poor grammar.

Unity and Sequence

The unity of a document refers to its single purpose and its presentation of information. A paragraph that exhibits unity pertains to one idea and does not deviate from it. When editing a technical document, an author needs to question whether each paragraph concentrates on a single topic, whether the entire document focuses on achieving one purpose, and whether all ideas flow logically together.

Information presented in a logical sequence creates a readable document. Certain sequence patterns, or methods of development, are useful when creating technical documents.

Sequence Patterns

Spatial	Describes the physical appearance of an object or area beginning at one point and ending at another; useful for product or mechanism descriptions
Chronological	Follows sequence of events; useful for explanations of how something is done or how an accident occurred
Sequential	Used for writing step-by-step instructions
Cause and Effect	Begins with either the cause or the effect; useful in reports discussing problems and solutions
Emphatic	Emphasizes important information; reasons or examples are arranged in decreasing or increasing order of importance; used when making recommendations or proposals
Comparison	Used when writing about one subject that is similar to another

Most writers blend various methods of development or use more than one in a single document. During the editing process, writers need to consider the unity of each paragraph and the way in which the paragraphs and sections link together.

Transitional phrases build unity and clarify the connection between different sections of a document. The smooth flow of ideas within a paragraph or between paragraphs is accomplished with the use of appropriate transitions. Readers are more easily able to make connections and understand the relationships between concepts when an author uses transitions in a document. Creating unity with transitions can be achieved in a number of ways:

1. Using transitional words and phrases (*therefore, nevertheless, meanwhile, in addition*)

2. Repeating major points or key words

3. Summarizing information presented in a previous paragraph

4. Using numbers to indicate steps in a process (*first, second, third*)

Logical sequencing and appropriate transitions unify concepts presented in technical documents.

Clarity and Conciseness

A logical presentation of information and clearly written sentences improve the overall clarity of a technical document. Editing for clarity requires focusing on sentence construction and word choice. Avoid ambiguity with clear phrasing, appropriate punctuation, and agreement between pronouns and antecedents. Proper word choice is important in avoiding ambiguity, which means being aware of the denotation and connotation of words. The denotation of a word is its literal meaning, or the definition found in a dictionary. The connotation of a word refers to the associations that a word has—both positive and negative. For example, the denotative meaning of *school* is a building where people receive an education, but the connotative meaning of *school* varies. For some people, *school* may generate negative memories of difficult classes, but other people may think about fun experiences with friends. Words used in technical documents should have precise denotations and appropriate connotations for both the audience and purpose.

Emphasis and subordination are necessary for clarity in writing. Stressing important ideas by positioning key words or ideas first or last in a sentence is known as emphasis. By organizing information in a paragraph from familiar to unfamiliar, a writer is also able to place emphasis on a key concept. Subordination in a sentence shows that a less important concept is dependent upon a more important concept. Subordinating conjunctions, such as *because, if, while, which,* and *since* indicate relationships in a sentence:

- A sedentary lifestyle is linked to obesity. A lack of exercise also puts people at risk for high blood pressure. *(The two ideas are equally important.)*

- A sedentary lifestyle, which is a risk factor for high blood pressure, is linked to obesity. *(The risk factor for high blood pressure is subordinated, and the link to obesity is emphasized.)*

- A sedentary lifestyle, which is linked to obesity, is a risk factor for high blood pressure. *(The risk factor for obesity is subordinated, and the link to high blood pressure is emphasized.)*

Failure to use emphasis and subordination will result in clauses and sentences that have equal importance in a document. Readers will be required to determine which concepts are most important, and their assumptions may not be what the author intended.

Writing with conciseness involves removing unnecessary words, phrases, and sentences from a document without impeding clarity. Concise does not necessarily mean brief, because lengthy reports may be concise. Two kinds of wordiness plague documents. One type of wordiness involves giving readers unnecessary information. Another kind involves using too many words to convey relevant information. Use the fewest words possible to express a concept, but do not omit information that is required for clarity.

Wordiness is a normal occurrence during draft writing, but editing should repair the problem. For example, eliminate phrases such as *basic and fundamental* or *each and every* because they bog down a document with redundancies. Excess qualification, such as *completely accurate,* adds to the wordiness of a document as well. Introductory phrases like *in order to, due to the fact that,* and *through the use of* can be easily replaced with single words—*to, because,* and *by*.

Another way to achieve conciseness and clarity is by using parallel sentence structure. Such a structure requires elements of a sentence to be similar in function and grammatical form. Parallelism enhances meaning, achieves emphasis, and eliminates wordiness as indicated in the following examples:

- Not parallel—*Our new SUV has other features such as a moon roof, a DVD player, and switching to four-wheel drive.*

- Parallel—*Our new SUV has other features such as a moon roof, a DVD player, and a four-wheel drive option.*

Parallel sentence structure is especially important when writing résumés, developing outlines, and creating tables of contents because it helps readers understand how the different parts of a document are related.

POST-TEST ANSWER SHEET

1. Ⓐ Ⓑ Ⓒ Ⓓ   13. Ⓐ Ⓑ Ⓒ Ⓓ   25. Ⓐ Ⓑ Ⓒ Ⓓ   37. Ⓐ Ⓑ Ⓒ Ⓓ   49. Ⓐ Ⓑ Ⓒ Ⓓ

2. Ⓐ Ⓑ Ⓒ Ⓓ   14. Ⓐ Ⓑ Ⓒ Ⓓ   26. Ⓐ Ⓑ Ⓒ Ⓓ   38. Ⓐ Ⓑ Ⓒ Ⓓ   50. Ⓐ Ⓑ Ⓒ Ⓓ

3. Ⓐ Ⓑ Ⓒ Ⓓ   15. Ⓐ Ⓑ Ⓒ Ⓓ   27. Ⓐ Ⓑ Ⓒ Ⓓ   39. Ⓐ Ⓑ Ⓒ Ⓓ   51. Ⓐ Ⓑ Ⓒ Ⓓ

4. Ⓐ Ⓑ Ⓒ Ⓓ   16. Ⓐ Ⓑ Ⓒ Ⓓ   28. Ⓐ Ⓑ Ⓒ Ⓓ   40. Ⓐ Ⓑ Ⓒ Ⓓ   52. Ⓐ Ⓑ Ⓒ Ⓓ

5. Ⓐ Ⓑ Ⓒ Ⓓ   17. Ⓐ Ⓑ Ⓒ Ⓓ   29. Ⓐ Ⓑ Ⓒ Ⓓ   41. Ⓐ Ⓑ Ⓒ Ⓓ   53. Ⓐ Ⓑ Ⓒ Ⓓ

6. Ⓐ Ⓑ Ⓒ Ⓓ   18. Ⓐ Ⓑ Ⓒ Ⓓ   30. Ⓐ Ⓑ Ⓒ Ⓓ   42. Ⓐ Ⓑ Ⓒ Ⓓ   54. Ⓐ Ⓑ Ⓒ Ⓓ

7. Ⓐ Ⓑ Ⓒ Ⓓ   19. Ⓐ Ⓑ Ⓒ Ⓓ   31. Ⓐ Ⓑ Ⓒ Ⓓ   43. Ⓐ Ⓑ Ⓒ Ⓓ   55. Ⓐ Ⓑ Ⓒ Ⓓ

8. Ⓐ Ⓑ Ⓒ Ⓓ   20. Ⓐ Ⓑ Ⓒ Ⓓ   32. Ⓐ Ⓑ Ⓒ Ⓓ   44. Ⓐ Ⓑ Ⓒ Ⓓ   56. Ⓐ Ⓑ Ⓒ Ⓓ

9. Ⓐ Ⓑ Ⓒ Ⓓ   21. Ⓐ Ⓑ Ⓒ Ⓓ   33. Ⓐ Ⓑ Ⓒ Ⓓ   45. Ⓐ Ⓑ Ⓒ Ⓓ   57. Ⓐ Ⓑ Ⓒ Ⓓ

10. Ⓐ Ⓑ Ⓒ Ⓓ   22. Ⓐ Ⓑ Ⓒ Ⓓ   34. Ⓐ Ⓑ Ⓒ Ⓓ   46. Ⓐ Ⓑ Ⓒ Ⓓ   58. Ⓐ Ⓑ Ⓒ Ⓓ

11. Ⓐ Ⓑ Ⓒ Ⓓ   23. Ⓐ Ⓑ Ⓒ Ⓓ   35. Ⓐ Ⓑ Ⓒ Ⓓ   47. Ⓐ Ⓑ Ⓒ Ⓓ   59. Ⓐ Ⓑ Ⓒ Ⓓ

12. Ⓐ Ⓑ Ⓒ Ⓓ   24. Ⓐ Ⓑ Ⓒ Ⓓ   36. Ⓐ Ⓑ Ⓒ Ⓓ   48. Ⓐ Ⓑ Ⓒ Ⓓ   60. Ⓐ Ⓑ Ⓒ Ⓓ

answer sheet

POST-TEST

Directions: Carefully read each of the following 60 questions. Choose the best answer to each question, and darken its letter on your answer sheet. The Answer Key and Explanations can be found following this post-test.

1. Which of the following transitions is most appropriate for indicating a logical relationship between two ideas?
   (A) Meanwhile
   (B) Therefore
   (C) Furthermore
   (D) Specifically

2. Which of the following provides information regarding which tasks of a large project need to be completed?
   (A) Investigative report
   (B) Feasibility report
   (C) Progress report
   (D) Test report

3. A technical document longer than ten pages almost always requires a(n)
   (A) glossary.
   (B) appendix.
   (C) list of tables.
   (D) table of contents.

4. Which of the following is the most frequently used form of communication within organizations?
   (A) Memos
   (B) Letters
   (C) Abstracts
   (D) Reports

5. The difference between a word's connotation and denotation is that the connotation of a word tends to
   (A) suggest an emotion.
   (B) require context clues.
   (C) describe tangible objects.
   (D) represent a literal meaning.

6. Which of the following may be too informal for a proposal?
   (A) Question headings
   (B) Statement headings
   (C) Minor topic headings
   (D) Major topic headings

7. Modifying the language used in a document to make it suitable for specific readers is an example of
   (A) abstracted information.
   (B) audience adaptation.
   (C) documented research.
   (D) audience analysis.

8. Which of the following is a common mistake in résumé writing?
   (A) Too many action verbs
   (B) Using reverse chronological order
   (C) Inclusion of a job objective
   (D) Unparallel grammatical structure

9. Which of the following does NOT need revision to correct an error in parallel structure?

(A) Although the exact cause of diabetes is uncertain, medical experts believe that both heredity and environment are significant factors.

(B) Achilles tendinitis is common among individuals who either play sports, such as basketball, or that suddenly increase the frequency of exercise.

(C) People diagnosed with epilepsy usually take medication to reduce the frequency, intensity, and a dangerous accident related to a seizure.

(D) Food and airborne allergies can cause symptoms that affect the skin, sinuses, digestive system, and breathing ability.

10. The glossary of a technical document is typically placed

(A) in an appendix.

(B) before the introduction.

(C) in the front matter.

(D) after the bibliography.

11. Feasibility reports are most often written to help determine whether an idea is

(A) successful and profitable.

(B) necessary and reliable.

(C) possible and practical.

(D) new and promising.

12. Which of the following is the most important consideration when determining the placement of definitions?

(A) Method of development

(B) Length of document

(C) Page design

(D) Text flow

13. Which of the following best indicates what an author wants a reader to know, believe, or do after reading a technical document?

(A) Executive summary

(B) Topic

(C) Purpose statement

(D) Outline

14. Equipment and procedures must be included in a laboratory report for the purpose of

(A) understanding results.

(B) duplicating the test.

(C) explaining the data.

(D) recalling information.

15. Which of the following is appropriate to include in an appendix?

I. Formulas
II. Sample tests
III. Photographs

(A) I only

(B) I and II only

(C) II and III only

(D) I, II, and III

In items 16–18, some part of the sentence or the entire sentence is underlined. Beneath each sentence, you will find four ways of phrasing the underlined part. Choice (A) repeats the original; the other three are different. If you think the original is better than any of the alternatives, choose answer (A). Otherwise, choose one of the others. In choosing answers, pay attention to grammatical correctness, appropriate word choice, and smoothness and effectiveness of sentence construction.

16. Natural gas is often found in coal beds where it was created by microorganisms, and it consists mostly of methane.

   (A) Natural gas is often found in coal beds where it was created by microorganisms, and it consists mostly of methane.

   (B) Natural gas, which consists mostly of methane, is often found in coal beds where it was created by microorganisms.

   (C) Natural gas is often found in coal beds, was created by microorganisms, and consists mostly of methane.

   (D) Natural gas is often found in coal beds and consists mostly of methane where it was created by microorganisms.

17. The new arena next to the highway is touted for its state-of-the-art design.

   (A) The new arena next to the highway is touted for its state-of-the-art design.

   (B) The new arena is next to the highway, and it is touted for its state-of-the-art design.

   (C) The new arena is touted for a state-of-the-art design, and it is located next to the highway.

   (D) The new arena, touted for its state-of-the-art design, is next to the highway.

18. The vice president was wrongly accused of mishandling the firm's largest marketing project by the stockholders.

   (A) of mishandling the firm's largest marketing project by the stockholders.

   (B) by the firm's largest marketing project of mishandling the stockholders.

   (C) of mishandling by the stockholders in the firm's largest marketing project.

   (D) by the stockholders of mishandling the firm's largest marketing project.

19. The main difference between laboratory reports and feasibility reports is that feasibility reports include

   (A) informal language.

   (B) instructions.

   (C) test results.

   (D) recommendations.

20. A document intended for an audience of subject matter experts would most likely be written in language that is

   (A) highly technical.

   (B) semi technical.

   (C) indefinite.

   (D) subjective.

21. Clarity in a technical document can best be achieved by

   (A) using abstract terms.

   (B) eliminating transitions.

   (C) including many appendices.

   (D) writing in parallel structure.

22. A word on a line by itself at the end of a column is known as a(n)
    (A) orphan.
    (B) header.
    (C) outlier.
    (D) widow.

23. A memo regarding salary cuts would most likely be organized
    (A) functionally.
    (B) indirectly.
    (C) spatially.
    (D) directly.

24. Which of the following visuals would be appropriate to use when showing steps in a process?
    I. Flowchart
    II. Schematic diagram
    III. Representational diagram
    (A) I only
    (B) III only
    (C) I and II only
    (D) I, II, and III

25. One significant difference between memos and letters is that letters tend to be more
    (A) informative.
    (B) formal.
    (C) technical.
    (D) brief.

26. A visual that shows how the phases of a project relate to one another is known as a
    (A) prose table.
    (B) pictogram.
    (C) bar graph.
    (D) Gantt chart.

27. What is the purpose of the conclusion in a feasibility report?
    (A) Express an opinion
    (B) Interpret the findings
    (C) Introduce alternatives
    (D) Review the costs

28. All of the following are methods for improving the unity of a document EXCEPT
    (A) using transitions.
    (B) repeating key points.
    (C) using enumeration.
    (D) explaining word origins.

29. A technical writer who wants to show what percentage of total monthly sales was generated by each department would most likely use a(n)
    (A) tree chart.
    (B) pie graph.
    (C) line graph.
    (D) organizational chart.

30. Which of the following visuals is most appropriate for nontechnical readers?
    (A) Multiline graph
    (B) Schematic diagram
    (C) Pictogram
    (D) PERT chart

31. All of the following are elements of the audience to consider when writing technical documents EXCEPT
    (A) methods.
    (B) attitude.
    (C) needs.
    (D) culture.

32. What is the customary place in a document to include a descriptive abstract?
    (A) At the end of the body
    (B) In the conclusion
    (C) On the title page
    (D) In the appendix

33. Which of the following is included in the back matter of a long proposal?
    (A) Bibliography
    (B) Cost analysis
    (C) Conclusion
    (D) Rationale

34. A line graph is most appropriate for showing
    (A) parts of a whole.
    (B) changes over time.
    (C) phases of a project.
    (D) sequence of events.

35. Unlike other types of technical documents, proposals are primarily written to
    (A) persuade readers.
    (B) describe products.
    (C) analyze audiences.
    (D) compare options.

36. Which of the following guidelines applies to preparing appendixes for a technical document?
    (A) Use numbers to identify each different appendix
    (B) Use a separate appendix for each major item
    (C) Limit each appendix to one page in length
    (D) Arrange appendices in order of importance

37. Which of the following is written in response to an RFP or an IFB?
    (A) Routine internal proposal
    (B) Sales proposal
    (C) Formal internal proposal
    (D) Solicited proposal

38. The conclusion of a sales proposal would most likely include
    (A) a discussion of a competitor's weaknesses.
    (B) persuasive statistics not presented in the body.
    (C) background information about procedures used.
    (D) a persuasive statement about a company's strengths.

39. Which of the following would be written to request approval for hiring an additional part-time employee?
    (A) Formal internal proposal
    (B) Progress report
    (C) Routine internal proposal
    (D) Feasibility report

40. Which of the following types of reports would be appropriate to organize in a chronological sequence?
    I. Trip report
    II. Feasibility report
    III. Laboratory report
    (A) I only
    (B) II only
    (C) I and III only
    (D) I, II, and III

41. Information in a technical document is best divided into logical pieces by
    (A) titles.
    (B) headings.
    (C) footers.
    (D) headers.

42. A status report provides information about accomplishments related to
    (A) multiple departments in an organization.
    (B) multiple projects in a given period.
    (C) one employee in an organization.
    (D) one project during a given period.

43. Which section of a long proposal is most often the only one read by an audience?
    (A) Costs
    (B) Methods
    (C) Executive Summary
    (D) Statement of Problem

44. Which of the following is the best way to determine the reliability of a printed source?
    (A) Publisher
    (B) Readability
    (C) Soft evidence
    (D) Publication date

45. Which of the following is the primary benefit of headings in a technical document?
    (A) Improve readability
    (B) Clarify style and tone
    (C) Enhance visual design
    (D) Summarize main points

46. Feasibility reports should include all of the following EXCEPT
    (A) review of all alternatives.
    (B) specific recommendations.
    (C) procedures and instructions.
    (D) interpretation of various options.

47. Which of the following would most likely be written by a construction supervisor after an employee is injured on the job?
    (A) Proposal
    (B) Trip report
    (C) Refusal letter
    (D) Trouble report

48. In which of the following situations would a drawing be most appropriate to include in a report?
    (A) To record the development of an event over time
    (B) To save space and add visual appeal for laypersons
    (C) To show cutaway views of internal mechanisms
    (D) To show distances and locations of specific sites

49. Which of the following elements of a résumé indicates the short-term and long-term goals of an applicant?
    (A) Qualifications summary
    (B) Purpose statement
    (C) Work experience
    (D) Job objective

50. Which of the following sentences does NOT need to be revised for clarity?
    (A) The CEO told human resources many times that the firm needed another sales agent.
    (B) Being so familiar with medical equipment, I would appreciate your assistance with the sales presentation for the pediatric clinic.
    (C) The office manager resents the vice president because he performed poorly during the first quarter of the year.
    (D) All active-duty police officers are not required to submit daily trip reports.

51. Terms included in a document's glossary are
    (A) limited to technological concepts.
    (B) listed in the order they appear.
    (C) arranged alphabetically.
    (D) explained in full detail.

52. Which of the following would a trained bulldozer driver use to review safety procedures?
    (A) Tutorials
    (B) Service manual
    (C) Training manual
    (D) Operator manual

53. Which of the following sentences needs to be revised because of a shift in voice?
    (A) The Web page was set up by the company's new intern, who is a computer science major at the local university.
    (B) The supervisor allows his crew to work overtime, but they are not permitted to work for other construction companies.
    (C) The laboratory tests indicate that the mice responded well to the new medication.
    (D) The maintenance crew reported water damage on the ground floor, and they spent most of the day attempting to repair the damage.

54. Which of the following elements of a long proposal would include the problem statement?
    (A) Product description
    (B) Cost analysis
    (C) Background
    (D) Site preparation

55. Which of the following would most likely be used by an engineer describing how a computer is assembled in a manufacturing facility?
    I. Spatial sequence
    II. Functional sequence
    III. Chronological sequence
    (A) I only
    (B) III only
    (C) I and II only
    (D) I, II, and III

56. The main difference between an informative abstract and an executive summary is that executive summaries are
    (A) presented orally.
    (B) slightly persuasive.
    (C) placed in the conclusion.
    (D) always 200–250 words.

57. Which of the following most improves the validity of information used in a technical document?
    (A) Statistical data
    (B) Web site graphics
    (C) Multiple sources
    (D) Web site sponsorship

58. The front matter of a long proposal includes all of the following EXCEPT
    (A) title page.
    (B) introduction.
    (C) cover letter.
    (D) list of figures.

59. The major difference between procedures and manuals is that manuals
    (A) assert opinions.
    (B) specify actions.
    (C) discuss results.
    (D) provide guidelines.

60. When writing an informative abstract, assume that the audience consists of
    (A) readers with different levels of knowledge.
    (B) academics from different subject areas.
    (C) highly technical subject-matter experts.
    (D) readers with no technical interests.

ANSWER KEY AND EXPLANATIONS

1. B	13. C	25. B	37. D	49. D
2. C	14. B	26. D	38. D	50. A
3. D	15. D	27. B	39. C	51. C
4. A	16. B	28. D	40. C	52. D
5. A	17. D	29. B	41. B	53. B
6. A	18. D	30. C	42. D	54. C
7. B	19. D	31. A	43. C	55. B
8. D	20. A	32. C	44. A	56. B
9. A	21. D	33. A	45. A	57. C
10. D	22. A	34. B	46. C	58. B
11. C	23. B	35. A	47. D	59. D
12. D	24. C	36. B	48. C	60. A

1. **The correct answer is (B).** Transitions like *therefore, consequently,* and *as a result* indicate logical relationships. Choice (A) is a transition used to show time. Choice (C) is used when an additional point is being made. Choice (D) is appropriate for introducing examples.

2. **The correct answer is (C).** Progress reports keep supervisors up to date on the status of a project. Choice (A) is a report written when information is requested about a particular subject. Choice (B) is a report that enables executives to determine whether an idea is possible and practical. A test report is similar to a laboratory report but smaller and less formal.

3. **The correct answer is (D).** A table of contents is usually included in documents longer than ten pages. Documents of any length that contain technical terms require a glossary, choice (A). An appendix, choice (B), is only needed if a report includes supplemental information. Only documents with many tables require a list, so choice (C) is incorrect.

4. **The correct answer is (A).** Memos are used very often within organizations to announce policies and convey instructions to employees. Memos may be printed or sent in e-mail attachments. Letters are a type of correspondence used to communicate with people outside of an organization. Choices (C) and (D) are less frequently used than memos.

5. **The correct answer is (A).** The connotation of a word refers to its emotional associations. The denotation of a word is its literal meaning, so choice (D) is incorrect. Concrete words usually describe tangible objects, so choice (C) is incorrect. Choice (B) is a distractor.

6. **The correct answer is (A).** Question headings are useful in drawing readers into reading about a specific topic, but they are too informal for some documents, such as proposals. Statement headings are more detailed than minor and major topic headings. However, choices (B), (C), and (D) are all appropriate for proposals.

7. **The correct answer is (B).** Audience adaptation refers to modifying the

information in a technical document to make it appropriate for a specific audience. Audience adaptation often occurs after a writer has analyzed the audience, so choice (D) is incorrect. Abstracts, choice (A), and documented research, choice (C), are elements of many technical documents, but neither refers to changing the language to suit the needs of readers.

8. **The correct answer is (D).** Inexperienced résumé writers often forget to write with a parallel structure, which means to use the same verb tense throughout for consistency. Action verbs and job objectives should be included in résumés, and many people present their experience in reverse chronological order.

9. **The correct answer is (A).** Choice (A) is written in parallel structure, which means that all elements in the sentence are alike in both form and function. Choice (B) is incorrect because *that suddenly* should be *who suddenly* to match *who either play*. Choice (C) is incorrect because *a dangerous accident* should be changed to *danger*. Choice (D) is incorrect because *breathing ability* should be changed to *airways*.

10. **The correct answer is (D).** A document's glossary is usually placed after the bibliography and appendices. Choice (A) is incorrect because a glossary is separate from the appendices. Choices (B) and (C) are incorrect because the glossary is part of a document's back matter.

11. **The correct answer is (C).** *Possible* and *practical* are the key ideas behind feasibility reports. An idea may be possible or promising, but whether it is practical determines if a company will go through with it. Choices (A), (B), and (D) are incorrect.

12. **The correct answer is (D).** Text flow determines the placement of definitions. Definitions are necessary for reader understanding, but they should not impede the flow of a document. Therefore, definitions are sometimes included in a glossary or an appendix. Choices (A), (B), and (C) are less important factors of definition placement.

13. **The correct answer is (C).** The purpose of any kind of technical communication is what readers should know, believe, or do after reading a document. Although an executive summary, choice (A), may include the purpose of a document, it serves to present a concise version of the full document. The topic is the subject matter of the document and does not necessarily indicate the author's purpose, so choice (B) is incorrect. Choice (D) is incorrect because the outline helps organize information and does not specify an author's objective.

14. **The correct answer is (B).** Duplicating the test requires clearly written information about the equipment used and the procedures followed. *Results* and *Conclusions* are two other sections of a lab report that would apply to choices (A) and (C).

15. **The correct answer is (D).** Complicated formulas, sample tests, and photographs are all appropriate for inclusion in an appendix. Other items that belong in appendices are large visual aids, maps, and interview questions and answers. Choices (A), (B), and (C) are incorrect.

16. **The correct answer is (B).** Choice (B) moves the information about methane closer to *natural gas* and places emphasis on the detail about coal beds. In choice (C), the verb tense changes from present to past.

The pronoun *it* in choice (D) is too far from *natural gas*, so the sentence is confusing.

17. **The correct answer is (D).** The pronoun *its* needs to be close to *arena* for the sake of clarity. Choices (A) and (B) have the pronoun too far from *arena*. Choice (C) is unnecessarily wordy.

18. **The correct answer is (D).** The stockholders did the accusing, so *by the stockholders* should be near *accused*. Choices (A) and (C) fail to place *by the stockholders* as close as possible to the word being modified—*accused*. Choice (B) falsely changes the entire meaning of the sentence.

19. **The correct answer is (D).** Feasibility reports include a recommendations section, but laboratory reports do not. Feasibility reports most likely include formal, rather than informal, language. Lab reports include procedures and test results, so choices (B) and (C) are incorrect.

20. **The correct answer is (A).** A document containing highly technical language is most appropriate for an audience that consists of subject matter experts, who would not require extensive explanations of data or terms. Semi-technical language is appropriate for an audience that consists of people with some technical knowledge who are not quite as knowledgeable as experts. Technical writing language is precise and objective, so choices (C) and (D) are incorrect.

21. **The correct answer is (D).** Writing in parallel structure, eliminating excess words, and sequencing information can enhance clarity in a document. Concrete terms are clearer than abstract ones, so choice (A) is incorrect. Transitions improve clarity, so choice (B) is incorrect. Appendixes do not necessarily improve clarity, and too many appendixes clutter a document with irrelevant information.

22. **The correct answer is (A).** When using columns in a document, orphans and widows should be avoided. An orphan is a word on a line by itself at the end of a column. A widow is a single line carried over to the top of a column. A header is information placed at the top of every page, such as the date and page number. An outlier is a statistical term.

23. **The correct answer is (B).** Indirect patterns are used in memos when presenting bad news to employees, such as layoffs and salary cuts. Direct patterns present the main point first, and indirect patterns present the main point last. Choices (A) and (C) are not terms used for the structure of memos.

24. **The correct answer is (C).** Flowcharts and schematic diagrams are appropriate for showing steps in a process or the relationships in a system. A representational diagram presents a realistic but simplified illustration of an item. Choices (A), (B), and (D) are incorrect.

25. **The correct answer is (B).** Letters tend to be more formal than memos. Memos are a form of in-house communication, while letters are sent to people outside of an organization, such as clients or customers. Both memos and letters provide information, so choice (A) is incorrect. Memos typically include technical language that would be understood by people in a specific workplace, and they are usually as brief as possible.

26. **The correct answer is (D).** Gantt charts show how the phases of a project interrelate. Prose tables, choice (A), organize verbal descriptions or instructions. Pictograms, choice

(B), are tables with representative symbols. Bar graphs show comparisons, so choice (C) is incorrect.

27. **The correct answer is (B).** The conclusion of a feasibility report interprets the findings of the study. The recommendation section is used to express the author's opinion, so choice (A) is incorrect. Options and costs are reviewed in the body of the report, so choices (C) and (D) are incorrect.

28. **The correct answer is (D).** Numbering steps in a process and using many transitions are both effective ways to enhance unity, so choices (A) and (C) are incorrect. Repeating key terms and major points, choice (B), helps the reader keep the purpose of a document in mind. Explaining word origins, choice (D), is appropriate for some documents, but it does not necessarily improve unity.

29. **The correct answer is (B).** A pie graph is used to relate parts to a whole, so it would be the best visual for showing what percentage of total sales each department generated. Tree charts, choice (A), show how different aspects of an idea relate to each other. Line graphs, choice (C), show how things change. An organizational chart, choice (D), would show how each department in a group is connected.

30. **The correct answer is (C).** A pictogram uses symbols instead of lines and bars to represent numerical amounts, so it is appropriate for nontechnical readers. A PERT chart, choice (D), is similar to a Gantt chart and is used to schedule activities on a project. Choices (A) and (B) are less appropriate for nontechnical readers.

31. **The correct answer is (A).** When performing an audience analysis, a technical writer should consider the attitude readers have toward the subject matter as well as the needs of the audience. Culture is a consideration when an international audience will read a document. Method is not an aspect of audience analysis, so choice (A) is the correct answer.

32. **The correct answer is (C).** Descriptive abstracts are included on the title page of documents. Choices (A) and (B) are where closing summaries are inserted. The appendix is not a typical location for summaries or abstracts, so choice (D) is incorrect.

33. **The correct answer is (A).** The back matter of a long proposal includes the appendixes, bibliography, and glossary. Among other information, the body of a long proposal includes the cost analysis, rationale, and conclusion. Choices (B), (C), and (D) are incorrect.

34. **The correct answer is (B).** Changes over time are best illustrated with a line graph. Choice (A) would be shown in a pie graph, and choice (C) would involve a Gantt chart. A sequence of events, choice (D), can be indicated in a flowchart.

35. **The correct answer is (A).** Proposals differ from other technical writing because their purpose is to persuade readers. Product description is an aspect of many different kinds of technical documents, so choice (B) is incorrect. Audience analysis occurs with most technical documents, so choice (C) is incorrect. Feasibility reports often compare options, so choice (D) is incorrect.

36. **The correct answer is (B).** Each appendix should relate to one major item. Letters are used to identify each appendix, so choice (A) is incorrect. Appendixes may be longer than one page, and they should be arranged in the order in which they are mentioned

in the text, so choices (C) and (D) are incorrect.

37. **The correct answer is (D).** Solicited proposals are written in response to a request for proposal (RFP) or an invitation for bids (IFB). Choices (A) and (C) are proposals submitted within an organization, typically for money. Research proposals are written to request project funding from government and private agencies.

38. **The correct answer is (D).** It is appropriate to include a persuasive pitch for a company, product, or service in the conclusion of a sales proposal. The conclusion should not be used to introduce new statistics or other information not presented in the body, so choice (B) is incorrect. A competitor's weaknesses and background information would not be appropriate in a sales proposal conclusion.

39. **The correct answer is (C).** Routine internal proposals are written for minor spending requests and permission to hire new employees. Choice (A) is used when requesting large amounts of capital. Progress reports describe how a project is going, and feasibility reports discuss the practicality of an idea.

40. **The correct answer is (C).** Trip reports and lab reports would both be appropriate to organize chronologically. Chronological order emphasizes time from one event to the next as would occur on a trip or during testing in a laboratory. Feasibility reports would most likely use the emphatic sequence or comparison-contrast sequence.

41. **The correct answer is (B).** Headings serve to divide information in a document into logical pieces easily recognized by readers. Headers, choice (D), and footers, choice (C), are at the top and bottom of pages and usually indicate the page number and date of a document. Titles, choice (A), provide readers with an indication of the subject of a document.

42. **The correct answer is (D).** A status report, which is also called a progress report, summarizes the accomplishments related to one project during a given period. A periodic activity report summarizes general activities in a given period, which may relate to one employee or multiple departments in an organization.

43. **The correct answer is (C).** The executive summary combines the main points of a proposal, and it is often the only section of a longer document ever read by an audience. Executive summaries follow the same sequence as the full document, but they are 10 percent of the length. Choices (A), (B), and (D) are proposal sections, but a concise version of each would be included in the executive summary.

44. **The correct answer is (A).** A printed source published by a university, professional organization, or museum is most likely reliable. Readability, choice (B), helps the audience understand information but does not increase reliability. Soft evidence is less reliable than hard evidence, so choice (C) is incorrect. The publication date, choice (D), is important in determining whether a source is current, but it is less important when determining reliability.

45. **The correct answer is (A).** Headings improve the readability of technical documents by helping readers easily locate information and recognize when topics have changed. Style and tone may be illustrated by document titles but less so with headings. Although headings break up the monotony

of paragraphs, they do not necessarily enhance the visual appeal of a document like graphs and charts do. Headings are not so specific that they summarize main points, but they do indicate the subject addressed in a section.

46. **The correct answer is (C).** A feasibility report should include a review of possible alternatives, specific recommendations, and an interpretation of options. Procedures and instructions are not elements of feasibility reports, so choices (A), (B), and (D) are incorrect.

47. **The correct answer is (D).** Trouble reports are written when an accident occurs, and they describe an incident in detail. Trip reports, choice (B), are written when an employee takes a business trip, and they provide information to managers about what occurred. A refusal letter, choice (C), is written to relay bad news, such as denial of a sales proposal.

48. **The correct answer is (C).** A drawing would be effective in a report when a cutaway view of an internal mechanism is needed. Choice (A) calls for a photograph rather than a drawing. Choice (B) describes why symbols and icons are included in some reports. Maps are useful when locations and distances need to be illustrated.

49. **The correct answer is (D).** The job objective of a résumé indicates a job applicant's long-term and short-term goals. The qualifications summary and work experience sections of a résumé describe an applicant's skills and work history. Choice (B) is not an element of résumés.

50. **The correct answer is (A).** Choice (A) is written clearly, while choices (B), (C), and (D) are not. Choice (B)

should be reworded to say *since you are so familiar*. It is unclear in choice (C) whether *he* refers to the *manager* or the *vice president*. *All* and *not* in choice (D) create a confusing sentence.

51. **The correct answer is (C).** Glossary terms are arranged alphabetically just like a dictionary. Terms are typically technical ones used in the field, which could be technology, medicine, business, or science, so choice (A) is incorrect. Appendixes are listed in the order they appear, but not glossary terms, so choice (B) is incorrect. Items in a glossary should be explained clearly and concisely, so choice (D) is incorrect.

52. **The correct answer is (D).** Trained operators of construction and manufacturing equipment turn to operator manuals for reviewing safety information. Tutorials, choice (A), and training manuals, choice (C), are for unskilled users of a product or a piece of equipment. Service manuals, choice (B), are used by repair technicians.

53. **The correct answer is (B).** Choice (B) needs to be revised because there is a shift from active voice (allows) to passive voice (are not permitted). *They are not permitted* should be changed to *he does not permit them*. Choices (A), (C), and (D) are correctly written.

54. **The correct answer is (C).** The background section of a long proposal describes the problem that a proposal attempts to address. A general description of the product or service offered by a company is included in choice (A). An itemization of cost estimates is provided in choice (B). Site preparation refers to any modifications that would be necessary to a customer's facilities.

55. **The correct answer is (B).** Chronological sequence is the best choice

for describing how a computer is assembled. Spatial sequence would be used to describe the appearance of a computer. Functional sequence would be appropriate for describing how a computer works.

56. **The correct answer is (B).** Executive summaries tend to be slightly persuasive because the writer is trying to convince readers of what to think or do. Abstracts and summaries are both typically read, so choice (A) is incorrect. Only a closing summary is placed in the conclusion, so choice (C) is incorrect. Informative abstracts are always 200–250 words, while executive summaries are 10 percent of the document's length.

57. **The correct answer is (C).** Multiple sources improve the validity of information presented in a technical document. Statistical data may be necessary in many documents, but if the data comes from only one source, it may not be reliable. The graphics and sponsorship of a Web site do not improve the validity of information on the site.

58. **The correct answer is (B).** The front matter of a long proposal includes the cover letter, title page, table of contents, and list of figures. The introduction is part of the body of a long proposal. However, short proposals are divided into introduction, body, and conclusion.

59. **The correct answer is (D).** Manuals provide guidelines and serve as a reference tool for users. Procedures specify what actions group members must take during certain situations, so choice (B) is incorrect. Manuals are not persuasive, so choice (A) is incorrect. Results are not discussed in manuals, so choice (C) is incorrect.

60. **The correct answer is (A).** Informative abstracts are written for general audiences that consist of readers with different levels of knowledge. Informative abstracts should not be written only for experts and academics, so choices (B) and (C) are incorrect. Many readers of abstracts do not have the time to read an entire report, but that does not mean they have no interest at all.

SUMMING IT UP

- Technical writing is any written communication pertaining to a job—memos, letters, instructions, reports, and proposals. Most technical communication helps readers understand a process, concept, or technology.

- Audience analysis means learning about the individuals who will use a specific document—their technical and cultural background, experience and training, attitude about subject matter, and needs and interests.

- The sources and evidence used in a technical document should be both valid and reliable. For the most valid data, avoid relying on a single source for information and instead acquire a consensus from many different sources. A printed source published by a university or other respected organization is most likely reliable.

- Progress or status reports keep readers informed about activities, problems, and steps forward related to a large project, whether on a daily, weekly, or monthly basis.

- Feasibility reports help executives determine if an idea or a plan is possible and practical. They should review possible alternatives, provide specific recommendations, and include details to support the author's recommendations.

- Laboratory reports, which relay information gathered from an investigation or laboratory testing, include the reason for conducting the investigation, equipment and procedures used, and problems, results, and conclusions.

- Memos are a type of correspondence used among colleagues in an organization. A direct memo presents the main point first, and details follow. An indirect memo begins with the details first, and the main point of the memo follows.

- Letters are used to correspond with individuals outside of an organization and are more formal in style and format than memos.

- A résumé is an employer's first impression of a person. Résumé writing should use consistent punctuation, spacing, and formatting; parallel grammatical structure; action verbs; and concisely stated descriptions of achievements and abilities.

- Manuals (user, tutorial, training, operator, and service) help people understand how to assemble, use, and repair products. An author must consider whether the reader is a novice, intermediate, or expert user of the product or service.

- Instructions are the steps required to complete a specific task safely and efficiently. People who have never performed a certain task are the typical audience for instructions, which must be accurately written to avoid causing injuries to consumers.

- Procedures are instructions that act as guidelines for people familiar with a task. Safety procedures include how to assist personnel with special needs, where to meet after evacuation, and who to contact for assistance.

- A process description or explanation describes how something works. Spatial sequence is used to describe a mechanism at rest. Functional sequence is used to describe a mechanism in action. Chronological sequence is used to describe the order of assembly.

- Proposals persuade readers to take some type of action. Long proposals are divided into front matter (cover letter, title page, table of contents, and list of figures), body (executive summary, introduction, problem description, rationale, cost analysis, personnel expertise, statement of responsibilities, organizational sales pitch, request for approval, and conclusion), and back matter (appendixes, bibliography, and glossary of terms).

- Closing summaries, executive summaries, informative abstracts, and descriptive abstracts are four types of summarized information often included in technical documents. An executive summary combines the main points of a report or proposal and is often the only section of a longer document that is read.

- The purpose of a conclusion in a technical document is to summarize information, interpret findings, and offer recommendations.

- Definitions help readers understand the meaning of a word, concept, or process. Use *parenthetical* definitions for four or fewer terms. Place *expanded* definitions in the introduction if the term is essential to understanding the entire document or in an appendix if not essential to understanding a key point. Use *sentence* definitions if more than four terms require clarification and place in the glossary.

- Headings serve as titles of sections and subtopics within the body of a technical document.

- Page design elements include justification, headings, lists, headers and footers, columns, color, and white space.

- Audience and purpose determine what visuals should be used in a document. Numerical tables and schematics are best for expert readers; basic graphs and diagrams are best for those with limited technical knowledge.

- For technical writing, tone (a writer's attitude toward a subject) depends on the purpose, audience, and method of communication. Use a formal or semiformal tone for superiors or professionals, a semiformal or informal tone for colleagues and subordinates, and an informal tone when a conversational style is desired.

- Information sequence methods include spatial, chronological, sequential, cause and effect, emphatic, and comparison. Transitional phrases build unity and clarify the connection between different sections of a document.

- A word's denotation is its literal meaning; connotation refers to the word's positive and negative associations.

- Concise writing involves removing unnecessary words, phrases, and sentences without impeding clarity. Check for parallel sentence structure so that elements of a sentence are similar in function and grammatical form.

NOTES

NOTES

Peterson's
Book Satisfaction Survey

Give Us Your Feedback

Thank you for choosing Peterson's as your source for personalized solutions for your education and career achievement. Please take a few minutes to answer the following questions. Your answers will go a long way in helping us to produce the most user-friendly and comprehensive resources to meet your individual needs.

When completed, please tear out this page and mail it to us at:

> Publishing Department
> Peterson's, a Nelnet company
> 2000 Lenox Drive
> Lawrenceville, NJ 08648

You can also complete this survey online at **www.petersons.com/booksurvey.**

---

1. **What is the ISBN of the book you have purchased? (The ISBN can be found on the book's back cover in the lower right-hand corner.)** _____

2. **Where did you purchase this book?**
   - ❏ Retailer, such as Barnes & Noble
   - ❏ Online reseller, such as Amazon.com
   - ❏ Petersons.com
   - ❏ Other (please specify) _____

3. **If you purchased this book on Petersons.com, please rate the following aspects of your online purchasing experience on a scale of 4 to 1 (4 = Excellent and 1 = Poor).**

	4	3	2	1
Comprehensiveness of Peterson's Online Bookstore page	❏	❏	❏	❏
Overall online customer experience	❏	❏	❏	❏

4. **Which category best describes you?**
   - ❏ High school student
   - ❏ Parent of high school student
   - ❏ College student
   - ❏ Graduate/professional student
   - ❏ Returning adult student
   - ❏ Teacher
   - ❏ Counselor
   - ❏ Working professional/military
   - ❏ Other (please specify) _____

5. **Rate your overall satisfaction with this book.**

Extremely Satisfied	Satisfied	Not Satisfied
❏	❏	❏

6. Rate each of the following aspects of this book on a scale of 4 to 1 (4 = Excellent and 1 = Poor).

	4	3	2	1
Comprehensiveness of the information	❑	❑	❑	❑
Accuracy of the information	❑	❑	❑	❑
Usability	❑	❑	❑	❑
Cover design	❑	❑	❑	❑
Book layout	❑	❑	❑	❑
Special features (e.g., CD, flashcards, charts, etc.)	❑	❑	❑	❑
Value for the money	❑	❑	❑	❑

7. This book was recommended by:
❑ Guidance counselor
❑ Parent/guardian
❑ Family member/relative
❑ Friend
❑ Teacher
❑ Not recommended by anyone—I found the book on my own
❑ Other (please specify) _____

8. Would you recommend this book to others?

Yes	Not Sure	No
❑	❑	❑

9. Please provide any additional comments.

_____

_____

_____

_____

_____

Remember, you can tear out this page and mail it to us at:

Publishing Department
Peterson's, a Nelnet company
2000 Lenox Drive
Lawrenceville, NJ 08648

or you can complete the survey online at **www.petersons.com/booksurvey.**

Your feedback is important to us at Peterson's, and we thank you for your time!

If you would like us to keep in touch with you about new products and services, please include your e-mail address here: _____